CW01011397

China and Africa

Chris Alden • Abiodun Alao • Zhang Chun • Laura Barber
Editors

China and Africa

Building Peace and Security Cooperation
on the Continent

Editors

Chris Alden
Department of International Relations
London School of Economics and
Political Science
London, United Kingdom

Abiodun Alao
African Leadership Centre
School of Global Affairs
King's College London
London, United Kingdom

Zhang Chun
Institute for Foreign Policy Studies
Shanghai Institutes for International
Studies
Shanghai, China

Laura Barber
Political and Security Analyst
London, United Kingdom

ISBN 978-3-319-52892-2
DOI 10.1007/978-3-319-52893-9

ISBN 978-3-319-52893-9 (eBook)

Library of Congress Control Number: 2017948293

Cover illustration: Tommy E Trenchard / Alamy Stock Photo

Printed on acid-free paper

This Palgrave Macmillan imprint is published by Springer Nature
The registered company is Springer International Publishing AG
The registered company address is: Gewerbestrasse 11, 6330 Cham, Switzerland

Acknowledgements

The editors would like to thank the following individuals and institutions for their unstinting support for this project: Elizabeth Sidiropolous, Neuma Grobbelaar, the South African Institute of International Affairs (SAIIA), the Shanghai Institutes for International Affairs (SIIS) and the Embassy of the People's Republic of China (Pretoria). We would also like to thank the Institute for Peace and Security Studies (IPSS) for its role in supporting the workshop in Addis Ababa in 2014. We wish to acknowledge the financial support of the FOCAC's China-Africa Joint Research and Exchange Programme for workshops in Johannesburg, Shanghai and Addis Ababa, and to SAIIA, SIIS and IPSS for providing institutional support for the researchers and the workshops.

CONTENTS

LIST OF FIGURES

List of Tables

Introduction: Seeking Security: China's Expanding Involvement in Security Cooperation in Africa

Chris Alden and Laura Barber

China's engagement in Africa, once characterised as decidedly non-interventionist in its pursuit of economic interests, is on course to becoming more deeply involved in the region's security landscape. While the conventions behind Chinese involvement remain bound to an economic core, the growing exposure of its interests to the vagaries of African politics and, concurrently, pressures to demonstrate greater global activism, are bringing about a reconsideration of Beijing's sanguine approach to the region. In particular, China faces threats on three fronts to its standing in Africa: reputational risks derived from its association with certain governments; risks to its business interests posed by mercurial leaders and weak regulatory regimes; and risks faced by its citizens operating in unstable African environments. Addressing these concerns poses particular challenges for Beijing

C. Alden (✉)
Department of International Relations, London School of Economics and Political Science, London, United Kingdom
e-mail: j.c.alden@lse.ac.uk

L. Barber
Political and Security Analyst, London, United Kingdom
e-mail: L.K.Barber@lse.ac.uk

C. Alden et al. (eds.), *China and Africa*,
DOI 10.1007/978-3-319-52893-9_1

whose desire to play a larger role in continental security jostles with the complexities of doing so while preserving Chinese abiding foreign policy principles and growing economic interests on the continent.

The result is increasing involvement in African security, be it through cooperation at the level of the UN Security Council and the African Union or in terms of deploying Chinese troops and providing greater financial assistance for peace support missions. This impulse has received further support with the announcement of a China-Africa Cooperative Partnership for Peace and Security in 2012, promising an integration of security into the FOCAC process. Linking this aspirational commitment to a more institutionalised form of involvement, however, remains problematic in part because of Chinese uncertainty as to the practical implications this holds for its established interests, as well as an underlying ambivalence towards some of the normative dimensions integrated into the African Peace and Security Architecture. These concerns in turn reflect wider debates within China as to the efficacy of expanding its role within the existing structures of regional and global governance.

This volume investigates the expanding involvement of China in security cooperation in Africa. It focuses on two dimensions in particular: (i) the sources of Chinese engagement in security – ranging from burgeoning exposure of Chinese economic interests to unstable conditions to the targeting of Chinese citizens by hostile and criminal groups – and how they have shaped Chinese policies in this sector; and (ii) case studies of China's involvement in country-specific Africa security contexts, including the content of Chinese contributions and responses of African governments and civil society to this expanding role. Finally, it provides a critical assessment of the challenges experienced by and facing the deepening of Chinese-African cooperation in security matters.

To understand China's gradualist engagement in African security affairs, one must understand the evolving context of China-Africa relations. China's contemporary phase of intensive engagement in African countries may have been instigated by a search for vital resources and market opportunities but its sustainability as a reliable source for China was always going to be predicated on building long-term stable relations. China's openness to economic engagement in all parts of Africa launched a period of rapid growth in bilateral economic ties, including multi-billion-dollar concessional loans to energy- and mineral-rich African countries linked to provisions for development of local infrastructure, followed by a range of smaller loans, grants, and investments by individual Chinese entrepreneurs. While traditional Western sources had shunned investment in some of the conflict-ridden, post-conflict, or fragile states like Sudan, or World Bank and donors sought to make loans conditional on domestic policy changes in countries like Angola, the opportunity that this presented to China to gain access to untapped resources in markets viewed in Beijing as closed was seized with alacrity.

But in countries operating under conditions of fragility where the very nature of regime legitimacy itself is contested as is its ability to enforce its rule over the population and territory, the security challenges are manifold as China was to discover. Under these difficult circumstances, Chinese officials were increasingly pulled into mediation efforts in places like Sudan and, through its permanent membership on the UN Security Council, involvement in peacekeeping operations and capacity building in post-conflict situations. Chinese migration, starting as a trickle in the late 1990s but growing steadily across the continent, introduced a new element of complexity as individual citizens became exposed to violence and crime.

While academic writings on the extensive role of China in Africa continue to increase, not much attention seems to have been placed on the rapidly growing security links between the country and the African continent. Due largely to the deep involvement of the country in Africa's natural resource politics and the controversial link it has developed with African leaders that have attained pariah status, attention has been placed on the politics of natural resource extraction and the alleged support China seems to be given to controversial African leaders like Presidents Bashir of Sudan and Robert Mugabe of Zimbabwe. Considerable interest has also been directed towards China's development policies and, to a lesser extent, Chinese migration. But while all these are important, the increasing role of security in the complex relationship between China and Africa is hardly examined.

In fact, China's growing role in African security has been quite profound to date, ranging from the extensive peacekeeping activities it has undertaken in a number of African states to ongoing mediation in conflicts like Sudan and even training of armed forces of some of countries. Security considerations have also come out in key controversial connections like resource-for development exchanges, and the expanding sale of armaments and the launching of satellite missions. All these apart, China's relationship with key regional organisations in the continent also has aspects of peace and security considerations. Indeed, it is widely assumed that the extensive military links China has established with a number of African countries have now shown other emerging powers operating in the continent, especially Russia, Brazil, and India, of the unwinnable nature of their rivalry with Beijing on the African continent.

Against the background of all the above considerations, there is a compelling need for a detailed study that looks at all the complex security links between China and Africa and how Africans have perceived the intricate military relationship their governments are establishing with China. It is also important to see how security considerations have intertwined with economic and domestic considerations issues to explain the diverse links between China and African countries. Thus the key aims and objectives of the proposed book are as follows: to provide a detailed study to focus on the intricacies of the military relationship between Africa and China, especially those aspects that have been neglected from current studies; to interrogate how security considerations come into the equation of other complex economic and social links China has developed with African states; to analyse how China's links with Africa's continental and regional organisations, especially the African Union, also connects with security links it has developed with key African countries; and finally, to assess how Africans, especially, civil society perceive the increasing involvement of China in the continent's security affairs.

In Chapter 2, 'Africa's Security Challenges and China's Evolving approach towards Africa's Peace and Security Architecture', Abiodun Alao and Chris Alden provide a comprehensive overview of the issues characterising the African security environment, the associated risks facing Chinese actors across the continent, and Beijing's emerging response to some of these challenges. This is with a view to assess whether China's role vis-à-vis Africa's peace and security architecture can be viewed as one of architect, builder, or sub-contractor.

In Chapter 3, 'China's Changing Role in Peace and Security in Africa', Chris Alden and Zheng Yixiao assess China's emerging role in Africa's security sector through contextualising Beijing's changing ambitions on the international stage and specific aspects of its policies as implemented on the continent. In particular, the authors frame the discussion within an overall picture of China's evolving approach towards maintaining its national interests, goals, and means in the arena of security and shed light on the country's multilateral cooperation against transnational security concerns in Africa, namely piracy and nuclear proliferation, and investigate two case studies of its military bilateral cooperation with African partners. They find that China's enhanced role in security exposes a set of inherent tensions within the lofty aims of a rising China and its actual operational role in Africa. For instance, while Beijing presents the need to cooperate with Western partners, those countries are the same ones that are in competition on a number of fronts with China.

In Chapter 4, 'Developmental Peace: Understanding China's Africa Policy in Peace and Security', Wang Xuejun argues that through China's expanding role in African and global security more generally, the country is increasingly becoming a norm-maker rather than norm-complier. In particular, Wang asserts that China's Africa policy regarding peace and security is guided by the uniquely Chinese concept of 'developmental peace', which differs from the liberal peace thesis underpinning Western approaches towards the continent. It is suggested that whereas the latter prioritises democratisation and institution-building in post-conflict environments, 'developmental peace' places emphasis on sovereign autonomy and embedding socioeconomic development strategies into the practices of conflict resolution and post-conflict reconstruction. As such, Beijing is introducing increasing flexibility into its 'non-interference' policy to ensure that it does not equate to non-involvement, yet respect for host state sovereignty and 'African ownership' remain the bedrock of the Chinese approach to addressing security challenges in Africa.

Meanwhile, China's physical involvement in conflict prevention and resolution is mainly manifested in its participation in UN peacekeeping operations in line with its role as a permanent member of the UN Security Council. In Chapter 5, 'China's Development-Oriented Peacekeeping Strategy in Africa', Xue Lei considers China's goals in African peace and security affairs from the particular perspective of its participation in UNPKOs. Xue maintains that Beijing upholds a preference for development-oriented and non-coercive approaches to humanitarian intervention. At the same time, however, it is found that through developing a deeper understanding of the complexity of conflict in the field, China has begun to develop a degree of flexibility and on a case-by-case basis is supportive of more robust approaches to international peacekeeping and peace interventions in the African context.

In addition to multilateral peacekeeping efforts, China's tangible security role can also be seen in the form of growing military ties with African states, including exchanges and assistance such as training loans for equipment. In Chapter 6, 'On China's Military Diplomacy in Africa', Shen Zhixiong deepens our understanding of Sino-African security cooperation by assessing the increasingly robust and diversified nature of military diplomacy conducted by the Chinese Government and the People's Liberation Army (PLA) since the end of the Cold War. In particular, Shen highlights the concurrent challenges that China faces amid such expanding military ties, for example, the suspicion and competition this has engendered among Western countries, particularly the United States, and the issue of managing the expectations of African governments. At the forefront of the challenges that PLA diplomacy must increasingly address, however, is the issue of protecting Chinese citizens from non-traditional security threats, such as attacks by non-state actors and state collapse, whilst at the same time adhering to China's guiding foreign policy principle of non-interference in other states' internal affairs.

In the seventh and final of the overview chapters, Zhang Chun argues that peace and security cooperation is and will increasingly become one of the core pillars of China-Africa relations. Indeed, at the 6th Ministerial Conference of the Forum on China-Africa Cooperation (FOCAC) in December 2015, both China and Africa promised to implement the 'Initiative on China-Africa Cooperative Partnership for Peace and Security', in which it is pledged to build a collective security mechanism in Africa and to jointly manage non-traditional security issues. However, Zhang assesses some of the key characteristics of such regional cooperation and challenges to its implementation in practice. In particular, such cooperation remains exclusively at the governmental level, China continues to view FOCAC primarily as a collective bilateral platform rather than a multilateral one, and policy differences between China and African states persist and emanate from opposing views on the principle of 'non-interference'. Zhang argues that promoting cooperation with African organisations will help China to overcome the dilemma posed by deepening engagement in African security on the one hand and Beijing's non-interference policy on the other, whilst also counterbalancing the pressures of the European Union, the United States, and other third-party cooperation with Africa.

The five chapters that comprise the second part of the book provide case studies of China's emerging role in African peace and security. The first three of them focus on Beijing's involvement in addressing conflict issues in Sudan and South Sudan, which has widely been viewed as a test case for China in the Africa peace and security space. In Chapter 8, 'China in international conflict management: Darfur issue as a case', Jian Junbo assesses Beijing's evolving conflict resolution role vis-à-vis Sudan's Darfur crisis that emerged in 2003, and how its policy of 'non-interference' became increasingly flexible in practice. Junbo details the characteristics of China's policy as it shifted over three stages: from indifference to tentatively persuading Khartoum to accept a peacekeeping force, to finally becoming actively involved in resolving the crisis, including by engaging with the Darfur rebel groups. Finally, the author highlights how certain characteristics of China's active approach in this case has since been replicated in other conflict zones outside of Africa, including Libya in 2011 and Syria in 2012–2013.

In Chapter 9, 'Sudan and South Sudan: A Testing Ground for Beijing's Peace and Security Engagement', Daniel Large offers a comprehensive survey of China's peace and security engagement with Sudan and South Sudan in terms of its North-South political axis and within South Sudan from 2011. In the case of South Sudan, Large argues that, besides offsetting accusations of a narrowly extractive role, or associations with arms supplies, what China has been attempting to do in the country could be regarded as representing an aspect of China's 'new type of big power relations' as enacted in Africa, seen in terms of its military projection, investment protection and efforts to support a political resolution of the conflict.

In Chapter 10, 'Lesson Learning in the Case of China-Sudan and South Sudan Relations (2005–2013)', Laura Barber argues that many of China's key perceptions and assumptions about the nature of conflict in Africa and its impact on its own interests have been challenged within the Sudanese conflict. She exemplifies this by drawing out the lessons that have been learnt by Chinese foreign policy actors along the trajectory of change to China's foreign policy within the Sudanese context, as detailed in the previous two chapters. This is with a view to assess what Chinese foreign policy actors are learning about the African context and how such lesson learning has gradually led Beijing's foreign policy institutions to reassess the nature of China's own role in fragile contexts, such as the Sudans, particularly regarding its contribution towards peace and security initiatives.

Turning to the Sahel and West Africa, in Chapter 11, 'China's New Intervention Policy: China's Peacekeeping Mission to Mali', Niall Duggan examines the nature of the conflict in Mali and Sino-Mali relations. This is with the view to assess whether the commitment of Chinese combat troops to the UN mission in Mali in July 2013 has marked the emergence of a new, more flexible interpretation of China's non-inference policy and the first step towards a more interventionist Chinese role in Africa. Duggan finds that in the Malian case, China's new intervention policy was bound by the principle of sovereignty and territorial integrity. Given that the conflict was driven by religious extremists and separatists who threatened the sovereignty and territorial integrity of Mali, China may increasingly seek to set an international precedent that governments should be protected by the international community against religious extremists and separatists.

In Chapter 12, 'China and Liberia: Engagement in a Post-Conflict County (2003-2013)', Guillaume Moumouni assesses China's evolving engagement in a post-conflict West African country, namely Liberia. The chapter focuses on the ten years of Chinese-Liberian cooperation between 2003 and 2013, following the resumption of diplomatic relations. It is a multi-dimensional study of Beijing's involvement in international efforts to stabilise the country, through not only security initiatives, such as UN peacekeeping, but also aid, infrastructure, trade, investment, and governance. Of note, Moumouni's analysis reveals how Beijing is increasingly aware that for Liberia's reconstruction efforts to succeed, they must be underpinned by effective governance of international reconstruction resources and the rule of law.

In the final case study chapter, 'Security Risks facing Chinese Actors in Sub-Saharan Africa: The Case of the Democratic Republic of Congo', Wang Duangyong and Zhao Pei draw on a case study from Central Africa, the Democratic Republic of Congo (DRC), to survey the threat sources and subsequent security risks facing Chinese actors operating in fragile African states. In particular, the study highlights how threats facing China's interests abroad can be generated by both local dynamics and the actions of Chinese actors themselves. Indeed, the authors highlight that it is a lack of sufficient understanding of local African contexts on the Chinese side that continue to limit the mitigation of the risks facing Chinese citizens operating in fragile African environments.

The third and final part of this book seeks to situate China's evolving peace and security role in Africa in the broader context of regional and global perspectives. In Chapter 14, 'China, Ethiopia and the West', Aaron Tesfaye highlights how deepening relations with Ethiopia has become increasingly central to both Chinese and Western efforts to support regional security efforts across the continent. Moreover, China's growing ties with Ethiopia has prompted increasing interaction between Beijing and Western on addressing security issues as a result of Addis Ababa's status as a political and diplomatic hub by hosting the headquarters of the African Union (AU), the United Nations Economic Commission to Africa (UNECA), and the African Standby Force (ASF).

One of the most visible symbols of China's growing commitment to supporting regional security efforts was perhaps Beijing's construction and handover of the towering Secretariat and modern Conference Centre to the African Union Commission (AUC) in Addis Ababa in January 2012. To contextualise this symbolic move, Charles Ukeje and Yonas Tariku in Chapter 15, 'Beyond Symbolism: China and the African Union in African Peace and Security', trace the genealogy of China's engagements with the Organization of African Unity (OAU) and its 2002 reincarnation, the AU, and how its current engagement is articulated and defined within the broader framework of the Forum on China-Africa Cooperation (FOCAC). Here, FOCAC, is viewed as an 'organisational' umbrella around which China's engagement with the AU is anchored. Finally, the chapter offers perspectives on the future of China vis-à-vis the AU in the area of peace and security; not only in terms of resourcing the Union and its activities, an area in which Beijing is playing a lead role only after the EU and the World Bank, but also on agenda setting where the potential for China to exercise stronger leverage is still limited.

In Chapter 16, 'Comparing China's Approach to Security in the Shanghai Cooperation Organization and in Africa: shifting approaches, practices and motivations', Rudolf du Plessis examines China's long-term security engagement with Central Asian states, specifically members of the Shanghai Cooperation Organization (SCO) in order to provide a comparison with China's peace and security engagements in Africa. Such a comparative study provides useful insights into the trajectory of China's future engagements in the African peace and security landscape. Indeed, whereas China is a relative newcomer on the African stage and is yet to consolidate its approach towards fragile African states and safeguarding its citizens and interests, Beijing has been actively involved in forging close security and diplomatic ties with its resource rich, yet politically unstable central Asian neighbours for more than two decades.

Many of the chapters in this volume reveal how China is playing an increasingly positive role in conflict-affected and fragile environments in Africa. However, one of the areas where China is sometimes perceived to play a more ambiguous role is with regard to arms transfers. This somewhat contentious element of Beijing's engagement in fragile states has also nonetheless become subject to evolution. In the final chapter of this section, 'China and the UN Arms Trade Treaty', Bernardo Mariani and Elizabeth Kirkham chart China's growing arms trade, especially with Africa, and the evolution of Beijing's arms export controls in tandem with its shifting position from initial suspicion to gradual acceptance of the international Arms Trade Treaty (ATT). They argue that greater Chinese compliance with such international standards in arms transfer control would begin to address the longer-term issue of Chinese arms transfers to conflict zones in Africa and beyond and the balance to strike between the profitability of arms sales against their potentially far-reaching negative consequences.

Finally, in the last chapter, Zhang Chun and Chris Alden reflect upon the challenges that greater engagement in African security environment, the institutional implications and the necessity of deepening substantive cooperation and understanding between Chinese and Africans at all levels.

Chris Alden holds a Professorship at the Department of International Relations, London School of Economics and Political Science (LSE), has published widely on China-Africa issues and is a research associate of the South African Institute for International Affairs (SAIIA) and Department of Political Sciences, University of Pretoria.

Laura Barber has a PhD from the Department of International Relations, London School of Economics and Political Science (LSE), on the topic of learning in Chinese foreign policy towards Africa with a particular focus on China-Sudan and South Sudan relations. She currently works as a political risk analyst based in London.

PART I

Africa's Peace and Security and China's Evolving Policy

Africa's Security Challenges and China's Evolving Approach to Africa's Peace and Security Architecture

Abiodun Alao and Chris Alden

Africa is a continent always in the news – most times for negative reasons. This is because the continent has always been on the receiving ends of global vicissitudes, having experienced issues like slave trade, colonialism, and neo-colonialism, among others. In the period immediately after the end of the Cold War (1990–2001), the continent accounted for 19 of the 57 total armed conflicts across the globe. Also, at about the same time, about 39% of the 48 countries in Sub-Saharan Africa enjoyed stable political conditions, while another 23% and 38% faced political turbulence and armed conflict, respectively. Against the background of its multiple experiences, there is the need for periodic stocktaking of the security situation in the continent. The need for this becomes all the more apparent because some of the security situations in the continent have, in the

A. Alao
African Leadership Centre, School of Global Affairs, King's College London, London, United Kingdom
e-mail: alao@dircon.co.uk

C. Alden
Department of International Relations, London School of Economics and Political Science, London, United Kingdom
e-mail: j.c.alden@lse.ac.uk

past, woken global consciousness, as were the cases during the Rwandan genocide, the civil wars in the DRC, Liberia, and Sierra Leone. Consequently, a report of the current security situation is required for any discussion on the continent's relationship with the outside world.

The objective of this chapter is to discuss the current issues currently occupying security attention in Africa and China's responses to some of these. While, of course, it is difficult to capture all the issues prevailing in the continent at any given time, a snapshot of the situation reveals at least five security issues currently dominating the continent's security outlook. These include: continued conflicts over natural resources; communal clashes and acrimonious inter-group relations within states; the problem emerging from religious radicalisation and violence; the challenges of the youth bulge; and unresolved issues surrounding democracy and democratic transitions. As a major power with an expanding global influence, all the developments taking place in Africa have impacted on China, and the country has subsequently responded to many of the security challenges identified above.

An Overview of the African Security Environment

The seemingly enduring nature of African security problems and the various attempts to resolve them have been constant feature of the post-colonial period, shaping relations between African states, their societies and the international community. At the heart of this situation is the condition of the African state and its weaknesses, variously diagnosed as rooted in structural legacies of colonialism and neo-colonial practices, a fundamental disjuncture between an elitist state and diverse societies, or suffering from deficiencies ranging from deep-set corruption to chronic policy mismanagement.[1] While the notion of constructing a sustainable state apparatus featured to a degree in the independence struggle and colonial rationalisations for maintaining suzerainty, this debate was largely abandoned in favour of a swift withdrawal of formal European control in most of Africa. The phenomenon of 'juridical sovereignty' and the rise of 'shadow states' and host of other pathologies affecting the African state diagnosed by Western academics in the wake of independence, exacerbated by clientalist practices, appropriate the state for personal gain and the devastating impact of structural adjustment policies aimed at resolving these dilemmas.

As a result, throughout much of this period, African security was conceived and addressed by independence leaders whose focus was on strategies aimed at dismantling colonial rule, engaging in post-colonial nation-building, primarily given expression through strengthening of authoritarian rule, and finding ways of accommodating foreign influence which was mostly framed within the terms of the exigencies of the Cold War. Bilateral defence agreements between African and selected foreign states were integral to post-colonial arrangements, with the French taking up the largest formalised role in Francophone states and engaging in military intervention invariably aimed at bolstering regime survival along with more selective support for particular African regimes by the United States, Britain, the Soviet Union, and Cuba. Localised African efforts at managing the problems of instability and state collapse during this period was limited, with a few notable exceptions, such as Tanzania's regime change in Amin's Uganda in 1979, OAU-sanctioned intervention into Chad in 1981, and Zimbabwe's extended military intervention into Mozambique's civil war from 1986 to 1992.

With the ending of the Cold War and the concurrent onset of a democratisation process across the continent, starting in Benin in 1991 and winding its way across much of Africa, a new security agenda for the continent began to take shape. It was one that was created primarily oriented towards managing these potentially volatile transitions away from authoritarianism and conflict and, as such, emphasised peacekeeping and the building of liberal institutions. This was formalised through the UN Security General's *Agenda for Peace* (1992; amended 1995) and reflected influential initiatives of the day such as the Commonwealth's Commission on Global Governance (1995).[2] African leaders, led by Salim Salim at the Organisation for African Unity (OAU), attempted to revitalise the regional approach to security on the continent in the early 1990s, laying the basis of many of the normative changes through the Conference on Security, Stability, Development and Cooperation in Africa.[3]

A turning point in the African security debate was finally reached with the massive failure of the international community and its African partners to stem the tide of instability, destruction and genocide in countries such as Somalia, Rwanda, Liberia, and the Democratic Republic of the Congo (DRC). These 'new wars' (to use the term applied at the time), said to be motivated by 'greed and grievance', exposed the severe deficiencies of some African states in managing complex claims to legitimacy and effective allocation of national resources variously rooted in ethnicity, chronic deprivation, and administrative corruption or failure.[4] The result was to spur on an expanded discourse, which diagnosed the sources of African instability as rooted in governance failures and aimed to address these through a range of policy prescriptions that included external intervention on humanitarian grounds and built on past precedences of comprehensive restructuring of the economic and governance institutions. Collectively characterised as 'liberal peace', and given expression through processes which led to the UN Summit on the Responsibility to Protect and the establishment of the Commission on Peacebuilding in 2005, these steps were realised in UN-sanctioned interventions in the DRC and Sudan.[5]

For Africa, these enhanced efforts at tackling security were integrated into the transformation of the OAU into the African Union (AU), a process that culminated in 2002 with the passage of the Constitutive Act. The African Peace and Security Architecture (APSA) that emerged from this process was a five-pronged organisation composed of the Peace and Security Council (PSC), the Early Warning System, the African Standby Force, the Panel of the Wise, the Peace Fund and the eight designated Regional Economic Communities (RECs – though only five presently lead in this area). The RECs, the building blocks of a continental union, have begun to develop regional forms of the AU's standby force and early warning system.[6] Notably, the AU provisions for intervention as described in Article 4 went well-beyond the OAU's defensive posture on sovereignty to one predicated on 'non-indifference', calling outright for intervention in cases of genocide, ethnic cleansing, and other forms of conflict, where the state had abrogated its responsibilities to its citizens.[7] Coupled to this was a more robust endorsement of peacebuilding, democratic governance, and institutional development, through the issuing of the Common African Defence and Security Policy in 2004 and the Declaration on Unconstitutional Changes of Government in 2009.[8]

The AU, unlike its predecessor, has demonstrated a willingness to be actively involved in continental security issues, having gone on to suspend nine member governments for constitutional violations, applied sanctions against six member governments, and authorised several peace support operations in the last decade.[9] Relations between the AU and the RECs, nonetheless, are widely seen to be 'imbalanced' and unclear, with some well-developed regional organisations like ECOWAS able to field strong peace support missions while others effectively dysfunctional in security matters.[10] Overall dependency on some key bilateral and multilateral partners, notably the EU and the UN, is evident: while African ownership of the APSA process is emphasised throughout, measured in financial terms, as it stands today, the position is mostly rhetorical as Western governments supply the bulk of the financial requirements (98%) of the operational components of the AU.[11]

Particular peacekeeping operations, such as UN-AU Mission in Darfur (UNAMID) have relied almost exclusively on funding support from EU sources.[12] Moreover, the promotion of formalised ties between the UN Security Council and the AU – the only such regional arrangements and one strongly driven by South Africa during its two-term tenure as a non-permanent member – ensures both that African security issues and AU involvement feature highly on the global agenda.[13] Finally, important security issues, such as the continuing spread of arms sales – dominated by the Western armaments industry and its Russian counterparts – remain largely outside of official processes of scrutiny.

Despite these changes to formal policy and greater international activism, improvements in African security still remain distressingly episodic, with regional leadership seen in peace support operations in West African conflicts and UN involvement limited to selective involvement in peacekeeping and monitoring operations in Somalia, DRC, and the Sudans. The security-development nexus, increasingly recognised by scholars as crucial to creating the requisite conditions for sustainable security, was rarely integrated into policy initiatives that would stem long-term security problems.

Indeed, given the continuing low levels of development in Africa, characterised by states saddled with spiralling debt burdens, incapable of providing domestic revenue and channelling into investment in public sector and a foreign investment community that rarely looked beyond the extractive sector, the dire conditions in Africa seemed fixed in a cycle of misery. It is a situation ripe for change and indeed, in the late 1990s a new robust actor entered the stage whose involvement was to set in motion conditions that would transform the continent's fortunes: China. But before looking at the involvement of the country, there is the need to provide a panoramic survey of the security challenges that China met at the time of its decisive entrance into the African security arena and afterwards.

Controversies Over the Ownership, Management, and Control of Natural Resource

In the last decade natural resources have been implicated in many conflicts that have brought Africa to the tribunal of international attention. From Liberia, Sierra Leone, and the Democratic Republic of Congo to Zimbabwe, Nigeria, and Angola, natural resources have been identified as a crucial factor in the 'cause' and 'prolongation' of conflicts. Put together, these conflicts could have accounted for up to a million deaths and the displacement of several millions. The attempt to subject the causes or effects have these conflicts have led to several catch phrases, including 'Greed and Grievance', 'Tragedy of Endowment', 'Paradox of Plenty', and many others. Broadly, the nexus between natural resources and conflict would seem to exist on three broad levels, with resource endowments being linked to conflict as a cause, as a means of prolongation, and as a factor in the resolutions.

As a cause of conflict, natural resource considerations have become easily identifiable in many communal conflicts, especially over the ownership and control of land. On a wider national level, however, it is ironic that rarely have natural resources been blatantly evident as the sole cause of conflict, in spite of recent econometric and quantitative analysis suggesting the contrary. More often than not, natural resource issues form core considerations in conflicts that are attributable to other causes. Issues such as ethnicity and religion (in cases of internal conflicts) or boundary and ideological disagreements (in cases of external conflicts) are some of the subterfuges often exploited to conceal the crucial aspects of natural resource considerations. Once open conflict commences, however, the importance of natural resource considerations becomes so obvious that even warring factions no longer make pretence about them.

As a reason for the prolongation of conflicts, however, natural resources' role has been quiet profound. Indeed, the notoriety that natural resources have had in their link to conflict has come because of the role the resources have played in prolonging conflicts on the continent. It was also because of the link with prolongation of conflicts that the natural resources got into the calculation of the United Nations, especially in the civil wars in Angola, the Democratic Republic of Congo (DRC), and Sierra Leone. Indeed, the organisation set up a number of commissions to investigate the link between natural resources and conflicts in these countries. The first of such commissions was the Fowler Commission, set up in 1998, to investigate the sanction bursting in Angola, while two commissions – the Ba-N'Daw and Kassim commissions – were set up to investigate the role of mineral resources in the DRC conflict.

While in recent times key natural resources like oil and diamonds have been associated with conflict, there were strings of other conflicts that have been associated with other natural resources like pastoralism, land, and water. Indeed, all the countries in the continent have recorded clashes, often communal, over the land and pastoral issues. Although the management of international river basins has not resulted in any major conflict among nations, it has remained an issue around which future concerns should be expressed.

Having provided a panoramic survey of the link between natural resources and conflict in Africa, it needs to be pointed out that the number of conflicts involving natural resources, while no longer attracting international attention, still remains high. There are several communal clashes over the ownership of land, a problem that is likely to become more profound because of the decision by many African countries to cede land to foreign countries and multinational corporations. Indeed, as I have argued elsewhere, land is Africa's most important natural resource, with its importance transcending economics into a breadth of social, spiritual, and political significance. Among other things, it is considered as the place of 'birth'; the place where the ancestors are laid to 'rest'; where the 'creator' has designated to be passed down to successive generations; and the final 'resting place' for every child born on its surface. Consequently, every society in Africa sees land as a natural resource that is held in trust for future generations, and the sacredness of this trust lies behind most of the conflicts over land in the continent. What further makes land vital to any discussion on conflict is that it is the 'abode' of most other natural resources – a characteristic that means that the controversies surrounding these resources often have to manifest through conflicts over the ownership, management, and control of land. It is thus likely that in the years ahead, issues surrounding land will continue to dominate attention in Africa, and the interest of Chinese in Africa's land must be viewed through this prism.

Two other natural resources whose management is crucial to understanding Africa's relationship with China are diamond and oil. As is well known the discovery of diamond in Zimbabwe, the country widely known as one of China's closest allies in the continent, has come with considerable controversies. Allegations of human rights violations have been rife, and the clash between the local claims of the diamond-producing communities and the desire of the central government to control the resource is almost certainly going to be at the centre of conflict in the country for quite some time to come. Consequently, any foreign country that has to navigate between the muddled waters of diamond politics in Zimbabwe will have to factor this into consideration. The other natural resource is oil, and the country that is most likely to be at the centre of attention here is

Nigeria. While there had historically been tension in the country's oil-producing region of Niger Delta, considerable peace was attained through some of the policies of the late President Umoru Yar'Adua. In recent times, however, there has been a resurgence of violence, and the government of President Mohammadu Buhari is facing a major security challenge that is likely to impact on all the countries with interest in Nigeria's oil endowment.

In concluding this discussion on the future of natural resources, it is important to point out that there is now a changing attitude to the management of these resources. While in the past Africa's natural resources were massively exploited without the people being able to question their leaders, today, these leaders are expected to be accountable. Again, while foreign multinational corporations have been able to milk the continent with impunity, there are now several court cases by African countries suing foreign multinational companies and even governments. For example, the government of Niger has sued French companies over the sharing formulae from uranium extraction. Nigeria's civil society groups in the oil-producing Niger Delta have successfully sued Shell as far as in American courts over pollution. Examples of this abound. Now many African countries have begun to say: 'So far, No further', to the disproportionate extraction of their natural resource endowment. Although as would be explained later there are still a number of challenges in the politics of resource extraction in the continent, remarkable progress has been made in giving voice to the people's concern about their natural resources. The African Union also came up with a Declaration on Illicit financial flow from Africa. But while there seems to be a reduction in the major conflicts surrounding natural resource management, the same cannot be said of the issues surrounding religious radicalisation and political violence.

Religious Radicalisation and Violence

One of the most disturbing features of the last decade is the extent to which religious radicalisation has created security challenges that have stunted development, destroyed advances made in the global search for democracy and good governance, and threatened harmonious relations within and among states. In the course of the decade, virtually all the continents of the world recorded one case or the other of extreme violence emanating from the expression of radical religious beliefs. What has made this category of violence particularly worrisome is the 'borderless' nature of its theatres, the indiscriminate extent of its victims, the spectacular forms of its targets, and the relative weakness of most of the affected countries to cope with the consequences of its aftermath. Against the background of the above, academic and policy responses to the phenomenon of radicalisation have dominated global discourses, with international organisations, especially the United Nations and its agencies, leading the way in the global search for a solution to a challenge that has become somewhat recalcitrant.

In a way, radicalisation is as much a 'cause' as it is a 'consequence' of insecurity. Key issues like youth vulnerability and exclusion, sharp disparities of wealth and aspiration, poor delivery of social services, governmental neglect, weak structures of governance, disenchantment with, and at times rejection of, the West, and quest for identity and greater authenticity are some of the causes and consequences that are relevant to radicalisation and violence. But inextricably tied with the phenomenon of violent radicalisation is its association with the stunting of development. Across the continent, consequences of radical religious views have reversed advances made in the area of political stability and economic development.

The manifestations of radicalisation in Sub-Saharan Africa are complex, as they often bring together different variables that may, on the surface, appear unconnected. For example, issues like ethnicity, political governance, and socioeconomic factors have come to underline the phenomenon in the region. Going briefly into specific, perhaps the first noticeable thing about radicalisation in Sub-Saharan Africa is that it is largely linked to the Islamic religion. Indeed, with the exception of the activities of the Lord Resistance Army in Uganda, there are no known cases of Christian radicalisation. Secondly, they are often targeted against the state, specifically determined to weaken internal stability within the state. The objective here is to give the population the impression that the state is 'incapable' of providing protection. The targeted outcome of this is to swerve the loyalty of the population from the government, thereby further weakening its structure and legitimacy.

Thirdly, more often than not they go for spectacular targets, especially those that would give them the publicity they so much crave for. Previous attacks of these groups have included major Malls, Embassies, United Nations Offices, Police Headquarters, Oil installations, and other similarly soft targets. It is also now being believed that the groups may want to make a template out of this pattern. For example, the Nairobi Mall bombing is fashioned against the Mumbai attack of November 2008.

This was later officially confirmed when Al-Shabaab tweeted saying: 'Remember Mumbai...it is going to be a long ordeal in Westgate'. Fourthly, they often have their bases in the rural areas, especially in those areas where impacts of governance are least felt, and only come to major cities to implement their terrorist activities. For example, the Al-Shabaab concentrates attention on the hinterland, where they appeal to nationalist sentiments of the local population against 'foreign occupation' and the Boko Haram operates in the Borno area of Nigeria. Fifth, apart from the widely known radical groups across the region, a string of new and smaller organisations seem to be emerging using the Islamic religion to address local political grievances. An example of this is the UAMSHO fighting for the autonomy of Zanzibar. Finally, most of them have financed their activities through illegal operations like smugglings, kidnapping, and through financial assistance coming from the Middle East and Asia-Pacific regions.

On the whole, in the last two decades, a number of violently radical Islamic groups have emerged to challenge central governments in the region. These include: Al-Qaeda in the Islamic Maghreb (AQIM), whose objective is largely the same of the international Al-Qaeda; Movement for Unity and Jihad in West Africa (MUJAO), which was a splinter group from AQIM, allegedly because it wants to create a voice for Black African members of AQIM. It looks up to Black figures like Usman Dan Fodio as sources of inspirations and wants to ensure the spread of radical Islam across West Africa; Ansar Dine, which wants to impose Islamic rule throughout Mali; Boko Haram, which officially repudiates Western education and desires to establish Islamic rule in Nigeria; and National Movement for the Liberation of Azawad (MNLA), which wants to protect the interest of the Malian Tuareg population.

The group was swelled with the return of Tuaregs from Libya; UAMSHO (meaning Uprising or Awakening in Swahili), created to contest the Union of Zanzibar with Tanganyika to form Tanzania in 1960 but now uses Islamic revivalism as a means of ensuring cohesion; Hizb Islam, which was linked with Al-Shabab until Fallout in 2012. Leader of Hizb, Shekh Hassan Dahir Aweys is considered as the father of militant Islam in Somalia and is currently in jail; Lord's resistance Army (LRA), Ansar al-Sharia, Battalion Sworn in Blood, which broke away from AQIM; and the Al-Shabaab, formed as a result of the collapse of the Somali State and it emerged from the Al-Ittihad Al-Islami, a militant Salafi extremist group. Officially declared allegiance with Al Qaeda in February 2012.

This leads to the crucial question as to the issues underlining radicalisation in Africa. The issues here are endless, but there are some key issues worth bringing out. Like most issues underlining radicalisation, geographical specificities do underline the issues surrounding radicalisation. However, there seems to be some key issues that seem to cut across most of the regions, and some of these are discussed in this section.

Economic Deprivation

The role economic depression plays in the process of radicalisation continues to be quite controversial. While there are those who believe that economic poverty and social issues like illiteracy are not factors in explaining radicalisation, there are also those who argue to the contrary. Indeed, across Africa, Asia, and the Middle East, economic and social deprivation are key issues in explaining radicalisation. Among others, three things are worth noting about the link between poverty and radicalisation: first, poverty and underdevelopment actually create grievances that radical groups have often exploited; second, poverty and under-development often coincide with limited or non-existence governance, which enables local and trans-national radicalisation to flourish; and finally, the lack of any future economic prospects for a huge and growing population of young people across most of these societies presents a huge challenge that radical groups might again exploit. In short, poverty of resources as well as poverty of prospects, choice, and respect has assisted in the thriving of violent radicalism.

Weakness of State Structures

Across most of the regions, structures of statehood continuously get weakened and religion seems to be filling gaps left by the near-collapse of local services, from road upkeep and education to the provision of medical facilities to recreation services. At a time of dreadful mismanagement, religious groups have stepped into the breach across many states. It was not unusual for these groups to provide facilities like hospitals, schools, and other social services. While the intention of most of these initiatives is to bring together members by establishing forms of unity that transcends religion, there is also the economic motive of making profit to further advance the course of the group. For example, in recent times, religious institutions in many West African countries have gone into provision of education. In a situation where government-run schools are badly managed and where private schools have taken over in the country, education has become a major area where private entrepreneurs have turned into and religious organisations have played an important role in this area. There are also efforts to bring youths together in Vocational trainings run by religious institutions.

Effects of (and Reactions to) Global Developments

A number of global developments also came to heighten the propensity for Islamic radicalisation and political violence in Africa. One of the earliest of these was the successful revolution of the Iranian people against their Shah, which led to an awakening of Islamist tendencies in some parts of West Africa, especially Northern Nigeria. The emergence of an Islamic government under the leadership of Ayatollah Khomeini and the subsequent humiliation it meted out to the United States provided inspiration to Muslims the world over and in particular, the youths who saw in Islam a viable alternative to the bipolar systems of capitalism or communism. The Islamist revival began in the 1980s, as young Muslims, radicalised by revolutions, began introducing variance of Islam that were of more radical dispositions. Two major global developments often evoke Islamic radicalisation in Africa. The first is the situation in the Middle East, especially between Arabs and the Israelis. Many African Muslims are united in their belief that Israel's attitude towards Arabs in the Middle East is unjust.

Effects of the Arab Spring

The Arab Spring has become one of the most important factors in explaining the question of Islamic radicalisation in Africa, especially the Sahel region. While the consequences of the phenomenon are many, two are particularly important in discussing the issue of Islamic radicalisation. First, the phenomenon further revealed the weakness of state structures in the continent, especially those not based on credible and sustainable democracy. Within few months, dictatorships that had existed in the continent for decades collapsed and went beyond collapsing state. The second and more profound emerged through the collapse of Libya. The sudden dispersal of thousands of Tuaregs that had fought in Ghadaffi's army resulted in their migration into northern Mali, where they reinforced an insurgency that was to engulf the whole of the Sahel region. As will be shown later, the collapse of the Ghadaffi regime in Libya created an upsurge of insurgency in the region. Indeed, many Tuaregs who were incorporated into the Ghadaffi force had to leave after the collapse of the regime, and their return to Mali ultimately led to a complex civil conflict in the country.

Consequences of State Collapse

State collapse has been known to be a crucial issue in understanding the ramifications of radicalisation, especially because of the link between the attendant absence of state structures and the emergence of competing forces aspiring to fill the gaps. An example of where state collapse has resulted in the emergence of radicalisation is in Somalia. In the country, the collapse of the state, to a large extent, was responsible for the emergence of the Al-Shabaab radical group, just as the collapse of Afghanistan ultimate led to the emergence of the Taliban and the provision of haven for many radical groups that ultimately emerged.

Youth Vulnerability and Exclusion

Africa's youth population (15–24 year olds) has been increasing faster than in any other part of the world. It is believed that there are about 200 million people in Africa that fall within this age-bracket. This makes this group to constitute 20% of the population, 40% of the workforce, and 60% of the unemployed on the continent. Increasingly, youth in the continent see themselves as the neglected majority in an unjust social setup. Indeed, across the continent, but especially in West Africa, young people have had to resort to crimes as a result of massive unemployment and limited informal economic opportunities. The background of civil conflicts across a number of countries in the region further increased the vulnerability of youths in the region to political violence as it also made available to them considerable amount of small arms and light weapons that came into circulation after the end of the Cold War.

It is thus not surprising that many youths were to become radicalised and we to participate in some of the most violent acts of Islamic radicalisation in the region. Attendant issues like urban migration, lack of critical family support, and absence of community-based youth projects have been known to further heighten vulnerability to radicalisation. In the same way, a World Bank Report points out that around two-thirds of Middle East and North African population is under the age of 30 and that 'lack of access, in combination with rising expectations brought about by education and the information revolution, creates frustration among youth and may even threaten the social fabric'. However, having identified that effects of youth neglect has been crucial to understanding Islamic radicalisation, notes of caution should be exercised, as it is not all the time that youths have taken on to violence to express their reaction to social neglect. Indeed, the percentage that has taken on to violence is significantly fewer than those who have made innovative ways of eking out a decent living.

But on the whole, it now seems certain that Africa's greatest asset is in its population, especially its youths. Presently, more than 60% of the continent's population is under 35 years. These youths are resilient and resourceful. While previously they had seen themselves as the neglected majority in an unjust social system, African youths are now coming out forcefully to be the voices of the continent. For example, from nothing youths in Nigeria developed the Nollywood film industry, making it the second largest in the world after India's Bollywood. Young musicians across the African continent are matching their European and American counterparts. In sports, African youths are making their mark even in foreign football leagues, with one of them winning African, European, and World Footballer of the Year awards all at once. In 2015, Nigeria's under-17 team won the FIFA World Cup for the 5th time – a feat unprecedented in the history of the competition.

Challenges of Political Governance: Third 'Termers', 'Sit-tighters', and other Political Issues

Although considerable success has attended the efforts to bring durable democracy to countries in the continent, there are still areas of concern in the democracy search. In some of the countries, as in the cases of the DRC, Burundi, South Sudan, and the Central African Republic (CAR), there are still considerable challenges. In the DRC, there are concerns that the incumbent President, Joseph Kabila, will ignore the mandated requirement to step down after the expiration of his second term in office. Indeed, indications are clear of his intention to do this. There are clampdowns on oppositions and insidious reworking of the justice and electoral system to enable him stay on in power. The cause of the opposition has not been helped by the various differences among them. However, there are attempts to put all these behind and for all the parties to come together and organise a coherent opposition against the President. Indeed, the situation in the DRC presents an interesting case. While in most cases Presidents reluctant to relinquish power have often gone for an unconstitutional third-term bid, What President Kabila seems to be doing is to prolong his stay in office as much as possible by prolonging election. A timetable allegedly prepared by the country's electoral body suggested in January 2015 that the election may be postponed by a minimum of more than a year. That same month, the government introduced an electoral law reform that required a national census to be carried out before the election. This has divided the country, with Pro and anti-Kabila groups campaigning for their respective causes. The situation in the DRC continues to be difficult. While the regime of President Kabila is no longer popular after 15 years in power, successive oppositions have not been effective enough to remove him from power. Many in opposition believe that this is the best opportunity that has ever presented itself to remove the President.

Burundi's situation is much more complex and there are clear indications that the country can most easily slide into a major civil conflict that may also involve neighbouring countries. The crisis in the country began after the President, Pierre Nkurunziza, who had assumed power in 2005, decided to go for a third term. Although his party nominated him for the position, it met with strong opposition from many of the population. There was a dispute as to whether the legal loophole being exploited was credible. Nkurunziza's transition desire triggered a failed coup attempt. This was followed by mass protests and a crackdown that later became a permanent state of violence. On average, it is believed that more than a hundred people a day have staggered across the Tanzanian border since the beginning of 2016. These people join the 250,000 or so who were already spread across Tanzania, Rwanda, Uganda, and the Democratic Republic of the Congo at the end of 2015. International efforts to halt the crisis are increasing but as yet, not much success has attended the efforts. The UN Secretary General, Ban Ki-Moon, has visited the country while the EU has halted aid payments to the country. The UK, European, and US governments have also imposed sanctions on several senior figures, and the African Union considers sending in peacekeeping troops.

After a referendum in January 2011, South Sudan became an independent country separate from Sudan in July 2011 even though at the time of independence there were still few contentious issues, including the division of oil revenues. Specifically, there was dispute about the region of Abyei, which necessitated a separate referendum to be held in Abyei on whether they want to join Sudan or South Sudan. In June 2011, there was a conflict between the Army of Sudan and the SPLA over the Nuba Mountains. Currently, South Sudan is at war with at least seven armed groups in nine of its ten states. The fighters accuse the government of plotting to stay in power indefinitely, not fairly representing and supporting all tribal groups while neglecting development in rural areas.

The situation changed in December 2013, when a political power struggle broke out between President Kiir and his ex-deputy Riek Machar. The president accused Mr Machar and ten others of attempting to overthrow his government. Civil war eventually broke out. A form of internationalisation of the war emerged when Ugandan troops joined South Sudanese government forces against the rebels. Up to 300,000 people are estimated to have been killed in the war. Although both men have supporters from across South Sudan's ethnic divides, subsequent fighting has been communal, with rebels targeting members of Mr Kiir's Dinka ethnic group and government soldiers attacking Nuers. More than 1,000,000 people have been displaced inside South Sudan and more than 400,000 people have fled to neighbouring countries, especially Kenya, Sudan, and Uganda, as a result of the conflict.

More than two decades after the genocide, the politics of political stability in Rwanda again came to public attention when there were attempts by President Kagame to embark on a third-term bid. In a referendum endorsed by 98% of the population, the President is now technically allowed by the constitution to stay in power until 2034. Already, he has accepted the mandate and has agreed to run in the next year Presidential election for a third term. Kagame's decision has evoked considerable controversies, especially as many think that the situation in neighbouring Burundi where a similar desires by an incumbent leader had caused problem should have dictated caution for the Rwandan President, there are also those who believe that Rwanda was no Burundi and that Kagame could not be compared with Nkunrunziza. The proponents of this position argue that during the past decade Rwanda's economic growth has averaged around 7% per year, and maternal and child mortality has fallen by more than 60%. Furthermore, they claim that the percentage of people living in poverty has dropped from 44.9% in 2011 to 39.1% in 2014. The decision to run for a third term has, however, been roundly criticised by the United States and Western European countries. Kageme, on his part remains adamant, pointing out in December 2015 that his desire to remain friends with some key external countries would not make him to compromise key issues that are fundamental for the future of his country.

The situation in Uganda continues to attract concern, especially President Museveni has only recently won another term of office, the fifth since he took power in 1986. There are now concerns that the president wants to remain perpetually in office. His major opponent in virtually all the elections, Kizza Besigye, has persistently complained of electoral fraud. What has further given grounds for concerns is the allegation of human rights abuse against the opposition leader, Kizza Besigye.

Of all these countries, however, the one with most concern for China is Zimbabwe. In recent times, the political situation in Zimbabwe has given considerable security concern. After the coalition government between the MDC and the ZANU PF ended and President Mugabe won an outright, even if extremely controversial election, the situation in the country continued to be unstable. Within the ruling party, there has been internal combustion that resulted in the former Vice President, Joyce Mujuru, being expelled from the party, while the opposition MDC continues challenging the dominance of the aging President Mugabe. Central to the political future of Zimbabwe and China's future relationship with the country is the succession dispute that has been going on about who replaces President Mugabe. With the president in his early 1990s, many believe that his days in office are numbered, and that the numbers are few. The country may thus have to wait until the succession issue is determined.

CHINA'S EMERGING AFRICAN SECURITY AGENDA

The difficulties increasingly experienced at all levels by China in the once inviting African terrain, from Chinese SOEs operating in the field encountering security threats to Chinese officials charged with addressing the fallout from the conduct of Chinese business practices and the accompanying diplomatic conundrums these circumstances produced, provided the context for a reconsideration of China's involvement in some forms of bilateral and multilateral intervention in Africa. The result has been a gradualist engagement in selective areas of African security, induced by problems confronting it on the ground in particular African countries but shaped by Beijing's privileged global position in multilateral security affairs. Reconciling this escalating involvement with the maintenance of its economic position and, concurrently, its established foreign policy principles formed the core challenge for Beijing.

Perhaps the most influential driver .of its gradualist shift away from a studied distance from African security issues has been China's standing as a permanent member of the UN Security Council. What this has meant in practical terms is that, with African issues representing over 60% of all issues going before the UN Security Council, Beijing is unable to maintain a position of studied abstention without incurring either Western or African criticism. This is exacerbated by the UN-AU institutional relationship involving an annual consultation between the UN Security Council and the AU's Peace and Security Council, reinforcing the focus on Beijing's position on issues that matter to African governments, and concurrently the number and size of UN peacekeeping operations on the continent.[14] One response seen since 1998 was a gradualist involvement in multilateral peacekeeping.[15] China's approach has evolved from disengagement to sponsorship of UN Security Council resolutions establishing peacekeeping missions, the founding of three Chinese peacekeeping training centres and direct participation in peacekeeping missions in Liberia, DRC, and Sudan[16] Chinese engagement in peacekeeping, which has involved an expansion of the number of troops as well as a standing as force commanders of two missions, has been limited to non-combatant roles. This changed with China's role in the UN peacekeeping operation in Mali authorised in mid-2013 involving 395 elite Chinese troops with as a mandate to protect for peacekeeping headquarters and ground forces, caused the UN's Special Representative for Mali to declare that 'China's important work has exceeded expectations.'[17]

All of this fits within the broader parameters of a more activist Chinese foreign policy, accentuated under the new presidency of Xi Jinping, and aiming to pursue an agenda for responsible change. The belief that China's rising great power status requires a revision of international institutions to reflect changing systemic dynamics and a commensurate commitment on the part of China for greater provisions of global public goods, has become an article of faith within the Chinese policy-making community. In this context, according to Breslin, a key Chinese goal is to 'empower the United Nations as the only legitimate decision making body when it comes to finding global solutions to either transnational problems or cases of domestic state failure'.[18] The elevation of the UN, where China's privileged status as a veto-wielding member of the Security Council acts as an ultimate guarantee of its interests, and increasingly framed within the principle of subsidiarity, which sees regional organisations as 'gatekeepers' of legitimate multilateral actions. These intellectual foundations for this evolving approach received further support from the Chinese research and academic community. Liberal internationalists like Wang Yizhou have argued for a movement towards a foreign policy of 'creative involvement', which introduces flexibility to Beijing's approach on security questions while Pang Zhongying offers a more cautionary interpretation of 'conditional intervention'.[19]

Other crucial influences on changes to Chinese foreign policy in Africa were experiences in Sudan and the anti-piracy campaign in the Gulf of Aden. The reputational damage that ties with Khartoum produced in the build-up to the 2008 Beijing Olympics was a harbinger of the challenges to come, as was the commensurate difficulties to 'ring fence' that experience as a once-off form of Chinese intervention. Nevertheless China's incremental approach to intervention in Africa has taken it from being absent from the seminal Comprehensive Peace Agreement of 2005 to one acting as the key mediator between Khartoum and Juba in 2013. Concurrently, China's involvement in the multinational naval task force off the coast of Somalia from 2009, itself the product of a shift in Chinese maritime strategy away from regional focus to one 'distance sea defence' and combatting non-traditional security issues, also won it praise abroad and at home.[20]

At the same time, even with these gradualist changes to foreign policy practices towards Africa security, promoting greater multilateral engagement in African security introduces troubling dilemmas for Beijing. According to Li Dongyan, the actual trajectory for peacekeeping and even more so peacebuilding into more substantive external involvement in domestic affairs is 'undermining the basic principles of the UN Charter and the fundamental rules of peacekeeping, and have already moved beyond those traditional peacekeeping agenda and tasks China is familiar with, i.e. peace and development'.[21] The problem for Beijing is that, even if liberal peace is itself coming under criticism in Western circles, as Li readily admits, they have already become institutionalised as 'prevailing norms across the United Nations'.[22] Efforts to address the matter of such liberal biases have inspired a Chinese formulation of R2P, articulated by Ruan Zhonghe with his notion of 'responsible protection', which may offer one way out of this dilemma over the longer term, but they are still subject to the reception and support of African and BRICS countries. Furthermore, as the overlapping claims of regional authority by the AU and the Arab League demonstrated in the case of Libya, as well as the slow and divisive response of the AU to the crisis in Cote d'Ivoire, seeking legitimacy for intervention from regional organisations poses its own set of problems.

FOCAC, the AU, and RECs

It was at the Forum for China Africa Cooperation (or FOCAC) process, a tri-annual meeting that serves as the diplomatic cornerstone of official ties between China and the continent and the site for joint declarations of intent, that China's new security policy towards Africa was officially unveiled in July 2012. Reflecting this 'new thinking' on security, Hu Jintao's declaration of at FOCAC V officially launched a China-Africa Cooperative Partnership for Peace and Security, a much expanded spectrum of peace and security-related engagement.[23] While he reiterated a commitment to building a 'harmonious world of durable peace and common prosperity', overall this new policy departure still remains vague and largely aspirational.[24]

China's ties with the AU is tied to the FOCAC process and the obstacles to a formal diplomatic relationship (which involved the Western Sahara issue) were only resolved in 2012.[25] While much publicity given over to the recent Chinese funding of a new AU headquarters and language training of AU employees, of greater significance is the direct and indirect support for African peace and security missions. Specifically, the Chinese government has provided the African Union Mission in Somalia (AMISOM) with a contribution of US $4.5 million worth of equipment and materials for use in combatting Al Shabaab. This builds on earlier support of US $1.8 million provided in 2007 to the African Mission in Sudan (AMIS), the predecessor of the hybrid UN-AU mission in Darfur (UNAMID). More recently, Chinese interest in cooperation with the AU has extended further to a call for greater involvement in its early warning system. According to Xia Liping, this would assist Beijing in providing a higher level of consular protection for its tourists and business people in Africa, who are said to be affected by 30% of all early warnings.[26]

As the AU accords importance to RECs, so too Chinese scholars like Wang Xuejun acknowledge their important position in the APSA. Nevertheless, to date, actual Chinese engagement in peace and security issues is limited to disaster management and trumpeting the development implications of their involvement as being their contribution to conflict prevention. In fact, Chinese relationships to the RECs is fundamentally commercial and developmental, rather than security-oriented. For example, Chinese diplomats operating in the respective sub-regions have been given official role as representatives to the Southern African Development Community (SADC) and the Economic Community of West African States (ECOWAS) in 2007 and established an ECOWAS-China Business Forum in 2008 and SADC-China Business Forum in 2011.[27] Similar arrangements have been put into place with IGAD, Comesa, and the East African Community. The latter in particular, though relatively new, has accelerated ties through a framework agreement signed in 2012 to promote greater trade, investment, and infrastructure development.

More generally, the financial support provided by China to APSA has been either channeled through UN sources or otherwise on a more ad hoc or even bilateral basis. For example, speaking to the AU in 2012 a senior Chinese official declared: 'As a permanent member of the UN Security Council, China will continue to actively participate in affairs concerning peace and security in Africa with a responsible attitude.'[28] In this context, Beijing announced that it would be providing RMB600 million 'free assistance' to AU over 3-year period for, among other things, peace and security. This ad hoc form of financial support is echoed at the REC level, where, for instance, the Chinese government signed an MOU with IGAD in November 2011, that included US $100,000 for operational costs.[29]

Contrast this with the German government's comprehensive financial and technical support for IGAD announced at the same time, involving long-term bilateral commitments of 3 and 20 million Euros, and further embossed through multilateralist cooperation by the European Union.[30] Humanitarian assistance features in China's multilateral and bilateral overseas engagement, including in post-conflict settings.[31] Chinese financial support for the work of UN entities such as the World Food Programme give meaning to its 'peace through development' approach, seen in a range of humanitarian and recovery projects implemented by Chinese companies in Darfur.[32] Even the UN Peacebuilding Fund, in spite of the internal Chinese debates on the underlying liberal norms, has received US $5 million from Beijing.[33]

And, at same time that there is a Chinese commitment to play a more active role in African security, the context and even the institutional architecture of the APSA is itself changing. South Africa's tenure as AU Chair, combined with its role on the Peace and Security Commission, may bring about a more robust form of engagement with Beijing. Resolving issues like the ambiguity of the AU's role as legitimating agent for multilateral and regional security operations, coupled to the lack of clarity over its coordinating function in specific interventions, complicates the operational requirements of peace support missions. This was evident in the confusion that accompanied the AU position on Libya while, by way of contrast, the contemporary intervention in Mali is an excellent example of the cooperation between the AU and the UN Security Council.[34] In addition, even within the AU bureaucracy itself there is lingering mistrust of Chinese intentions, which mitigates against the kind of cooperative relationship sought by Beijing.[35]

Conclusion: China and the African Peace and Security Architecture – Architects, Builders or Sub-Contractors?

China's gradualist approach to engagement in African security matters aims to address the complexities of an expansive role in international institutions and a significant economic presence on the continent. It remains, however, poised between what is at this stage a rhetorical commitment to deeper involvement in the APSA and the realities of actually engaging in these structures. In this context, three speculative scenarios of China's future involvement in African security are possible to discern; that is China as architect, as builder, or as sub-contractor.

The Chinese can be seen as potential architects of African security in the sense of introducing new norms of conduct or revising existing norms, aimed at diluting (if not replacing) the policy prescriptions of liberal peace which are seen to be at odds with Chinese global perceptions and narrower economic interests. The *sine qua non* of such a process will be of course an ability to tap into African concerns surrounding these norms, especially pronounced after decades of Western-led military missions and structural adjustment programmes under the rubric, respectively, of humanitarian intervention and economic development.

The Chinese can be seen as potential builders in the sense of co-ownership of a process, led by Africans and influenced by the seminal liberal ideas on intervention found in Article 4 of the AU's Constitutive Act. Here Chinese engagement will be decidedly multilateralist and capacity building in orientation, similar to other external powers in extending the ability of African governments and civil society to act on security, and the operating assumption will be that this be the most realistic way of ensuring the safety of its own economic interests in Africa.

Finally, the Chinese can be seen as potential sub-contractors in the sense of providing a technical solution to specific security problems facing its interests in Africa. Here, the involvement would be technical in content and selective in engagement in African security aimed at supporting and fulfilling the narrowest form of obligations without incurring the costs of deeper involvement. The focus will be fixed on securing Chinese economic interests and attendance to the diplomatic needs of its global reputation.

China is still in the formative stages of participation in global governance structures and, as such, needs to develop its capacity to provide the requisite international public goods expected of a major power. Though it has expressed a desire to play a deeper part in African security affairs, its interests are still largely defined by its economic concerns and the impact of African issues on its global reputation. That being said, one can expect Beijing to adjust its policy towards African security in innovative ways. This balance between adaptability and caution will continue to guide Chinese policy towards this topic in the future.

NOTES

1. For an overview of this topic see Paul Williams (2011), *War and Conflict in Africa* (Cambridge: Polity).
2. Commission on Global Governance (1995), *Our Global Neighbourhood* (Oxford: Oxford University), pp. 77–112.
3. Abou Jeng (2012), *Peacebuilding in the African Union: Law, Philosophy and Practice* (Cambridge: Cambridge University Press), p. 157.
4. See Mary Kaldor (2007), *New Wars* (Cambridge: Polity Press), p. 19.
5. Roland Paris (2004), *At War's End: Building Peace After Civil Conflict* (Cambridge: Cambridge University Press).
6. African Union (2010), *African Peace and Security Architecture (APSA): 2010 Assessment Study*, report commissioned by the AU Peace and Security Department, Zanzibar, Tanzania, November 2010, pp. 8, 12.
7. African Union (2000), *Constitutive Act of the African Union* (Addis Ababa: African Union).
8. Alex Vines (2013), 'A Decade of African Peace and Security Architecture', *International Affairs*, 89:1, pp. 90–91.
9. Ibid., pp. 91–93.

10. Judith Vorrath, 'Imbalances in the African Peace and Security Architecture', *SW Comments 29*, September 2012, p. 2; Also see African Union, *African Peace and Security Architecture (APSA)*.

11. Vorrath, 'Imbalances in the African Peace and Security Architecture', pp. 1–2.

12. Engel, Ulf and Joao Porto (2010), 'Africa's New Peace and Security Architecture: An Introduction', in Engel, Ulf and Joao Gomes Porto, eds., *Africa's New Peace and Security Architecture: Promoting Norms, Institutionalisating Solutions* (Farnham: Ashgate), p. 4.

13. Interview with South African diplomat, Pretoria, 19 July 2013.

14. According to one report, 75% of all UN peacekeepers are operating in Africa in 2013. Mark Paterson and Kudrat Virk (2013), 'Africa, South Africa and the United Nations Security Architecture', *Policy Brief 17*, Centre for Conflict Resolution, Cape Town, June.

15. This was cemented formally through the Chinese response to the Brahimi report and subsequent inclusion in the Chinese Defence White Paper in 2000. Pang Zhongying (2005), 'China's Changing Attitude to UN Peacekeeping', *International Peacekeeping* 12:1, pp. 88–89; Mark Lanteigne and Miwa Hirono (2013), *China's Evolving Approach to Peacekeeping* (London: Routledge), p. 48.

16. See Pang Zhongying (2005), 'China's Changing Attitude to UN Peacekeeping', *International Peacekeeping* 12:1. pp. 87–104.

17. 'China embraces peacekeeping operations', *The Diplomat*, thediplomat. com/china-power/china-embraces-peacekeeping-missions/, 9 August 2013, accessed 10 August 2013; People's Daily online', China to send peace forces to Mali', 15 July 2013, www.english.people.com.cn/09786/8325863.html, accessed 28 September 2013.

18. Shaun Breslin (2013), 'China and the Global Order: Signalling Threat or Friendship?' *International Affairs*, 89:9, p. 616.

19. Interview with Wang Yizhou (2012), Beijing 9 May 2013. Also see Wang Yizhou, 'Creative Involvement: A New Direction in Chinese Diplomacy', in Mark Leonard, ed., *China 3.0* (London: European Council on Foreign Relations); Pang Zhongying (2013), Presentation at London School of Economics and Political Science, January 2013.

20. Presentation by N Dehong (2013), Shanghai Institutes of International Studies, Shanghai, 5 May 2013; Gaye Christofferson (2009), 'China and Maritime Cooperation: Piracy in the Gulf of Aden', Institut fur Strategies-Politik-Sicherheits-und Wirtsschaftsberaturn, Berlin, pp. 3–4, 18, www.mercury.etherz.ch, accessed 30 September 2013.

21. Li Dongyan, 'China's Participation in UN Peacekeeping and Peacebuilding: prospects and ways forward,' *Foreign Affairs Review* 3:12, Beijing, Foreign Affairs University, 2012, translation David Cowhig, www.gaodawai.word

press.com/2015/11/06/cass-scholar-on-chinas-participation-in-un-peace keeping-and-peacebuilding-prospects-and-ways-forward.htm

22. Li Dongyan 'China's Participation in UN Peacekeeping and Peacebuilding: prospects and ways forward,' Foreign Affairs Review 3:12, Beijing, Foreign Affairs University, 2012, translation David Cowhig, www.gaodawai.word press.com/2015/11/06/cass-scholar-on-chinas-participation-in-un-peace keeping-and-peacebuilding-prospects-and-ways-forward.htm.

23. See the Fifth Ministerial Conference of the Forum on China-Africa Cooperation Beijing Action Plan (2013–2015), 23 July 2012, which states that China and Africa will 'strengthen cooperation in policy coordination, capacity building, preventive diplomacy, peace keeping operations and post-conflict reconstruction and rehabilitation on the basis of equality and mutual respect to jointly maintain peace and stability in Africa.' (at 2.6.1) On this initiative, '[t]o enhance cooperation with Africa on peace and security issues, the Chinese side will launch the "Initiative on China-Africa Cooperative Partnership for Peace and Security" will provide, within the realm of its capabilities, financial and technical support to the African Union for its peace-support operations, the development of the African Peace and Security Architecture, personnel exchanges and training in the field of peace and security and Africa's conflict prevention, management and resolution and post-conflict reconstruction and development.' (at 2.6.3)

24. FOCAC 5 Beijing Declaration, 23 July 2012.

25. Interview with a South African diplomat, Pretoria, July 2013.

26. Cited in Tadesse Debay (2012), 'Sino-African Cooperation in Peace and Security in Africa', *Seminar Report, Institute for Security Studies, Addis Ababa*, 22 May 2012.

27. Chris Alden and Gillian Chigumera, 'China and African Regional Organisations', SAIIA forthcoming.

28. Jia Qinglin (2012), Chairman of the National Committee of the Chinese Peoples Political Consultative Conference, speech presented at 18th summit of the African Union, *China Daily*, 30 January 2012, www.englishpeople daily.com.cn/90883/7714450/htm, accessed 12 September 2013.

29. Intergovernmental Authority on Development (2011), 'Cooperation with China', 21 November 2011, www.igad.int.

30. Intergovernmental Authority on Development (2011), 'IGAD and German Government Sign a New Phase of Development Cooperation Agreement', 22 November 2011, www.igad.int.

31. 'When African countries are hit by natural disasters or war, China always promptly offers humanitarian aid to them.' See *China-Africa Economic and Trade Cooperation* (Beijing: Information Office of the State Council, People's Republic of China, December 2010).

32. See Daniel Large (2012), 'Between the CPA and Southern Independence: China's Post-Conflict Engagement in Sudan', SAIIA Occasional Paper No. 115 (Johannesburg: SAIIA). In January 2011, for example, Beijing supported the G77 draft UNGA resolution on 'International Cooperation on Humanitarian Assistance in the Field of Natural Disasters, from Relief to Development', which stresses that 'Emergency assistance must be provided in ways supportive of recovery and long-term development.'
33. UN Peacebuilding Fund, unpbf.org/contributions/donors, accessed 3 October 2013.
34. Breslin, 'China and the Global Order, p. 631.
35. Interview with senior AU researcher, Addis Ababa, May 2013.

Abiodun Alao holds a Professorship at the African Leadership Centre, School of Global Affairs, King's College London, has published extensively on African studies. He is also a visiting professor at the Nigerian Defence Academy.

Chris Alden holds a Professorship at the Department of International Relations, London School of Economics and Political Science (LSE), has published widely on China-Africa issues and is a research associate of the South African Institute for International Affairs (SAIIA) and Department of Political Sciences, University of Pretoria.

CHAPTER 3

China's Changing Role in Peace and Security in Africa

Chris Alden and Zheng Yixiao

China has garnered increasing public attention as the visible presence of Chinese peacekeepers, diplomats, arms sales, and business interests is making a greater impact on the continental security landscape. China's expanding engagement in peace, security, and military affairs on the African continent – accelerating since the 2012 launching of the China-Africa Partnership for Peace and Security Cooperation – is poorly documented and understood by scholars and policy makers alike. The lauded performance of Chinese peacekeeping troops operating under the auspices of the United Nations (UN), the activist mediation efforts in war-torn South Sudan, and the supportive role played by the Chinese navy in the multilateral anti-piracy mission in the Gulf of Aden all point to a dramatic change in policy and posture in Africa. This contrasts with the assertive stance of the China's security policy and military in East and Southeast Asia, where a combination of the bold use of its maritime forces and construction of island military platforms are challenging the presumptions of US naval strategy and even unsettling neighbours in the region.

How does one make sense of Beijing's changing approach to security, which, on the one hand, largely aligns itself with multilateral approaches to fostering peace and security in Africa and, on the other hand, seems

C. Alden (✉) · Z. Yixiao
Department of International Relations, London School of Economics
and Political Science, London, United Kingdom
e-mail: j.c.alden@lse.ac.uk; y.zheng3@lse.ac.uk

© The Author(s) 2018
C. Alden et al. (eds.), *China and Africa*,
DOI 10.1007/978-3-319-52893-9_3

determined to challenge the prevailing military calculus in its 'near abroad' at the cost of peaceful diplomacy? The answer seems to reside in recognising that Beijing's leadership is defined by a determination to carve out a new global position for its military that is commensurate with and reflects its expanding economic status and interests on the international stage.

The aim of this chapter is to develop a better understanding of China's role in the security sector in Africa through both a contextualisation of its changing ambitions on the international stage and more specific focus on aspects of its policies as implemented on the continent. In particular, we will frame the discussion within an overall picture of China's evolving approach towards maintaining its national interests, goals, and means in the arena of security; assess the rationale and means of its participation in peacekeeping operations in Africa; shed light on China's multilateral cooperation against transnational security concerns, namely piracy and nuclear proliferation; and investigate two relevant case studies of its military bilateral cooperation with African partners.

CHINA-AFRICA RELATIONS IN HISTORICAL PERSPECTIVE

China's engagement in peace and security matters in Africa is the product of a range of evolving and gradually intertwining interests in ideological, diplomatic, economic, and demographic spheres. The pattern of uneven expansion characteristic of Chinese involvement in Africa, from relative obscurity as an external actor during the Cold War to a mercantilist power with a dominant trade and increasingly significant investment position on the continent, has defined the relationship up to the present day. This process has been largely driven by domestic developments in China itself in conjunction with the Communist Party of China's (CPC) perception of its strategic interests at the global level and manifested through a host of state actors and interests operating on the continent. For instance, during the Cold War, the degeneration of Sino-Soviet relations accelerated strategic competition in Africa, with Beijing backing alternative liberation movements in Southern Africa to those supported by the Soviet Union as well as selectively promoting regime change in favour of its candidates in West Africa.[1] Chinese staunch support for anti-colonialism did not preclude it from giving military and diplomatic support for liberation movements on the basis of their anti-Soviet credentials in Angola, South Africa, and Zimbabwe.[2] Furthermore, from the 1950s and up to the contemporary period, the competition with Taipei over formal diplomatic recognition – while muted today – exercised a defining influence to the structure of Beijing's foreign policy towards the continent.

The movement away from the ideological and internationalist politics of the Maoist era to Deng Xiaoping's inward-(and Westward) looking development strategy marked a shift – publically announced in Zhao Ziyang's tour of Africa in 1982 – in its Africa policy towards an explicitly commercial approach under its 'mutual benefit' use of Chinese aid. This latter approach was bolstered in 1998 with the 'going out' policy that used state resources to promote the expansion of state-owned enterprises into key sectors across the continent, coupled with the gradual movement of tens of thousands of migrants to Africa, and form the basis for China-Africa contemporary relations.

THE EROSION OF 'NON-INTERFERENCE' POLICY AND THE RISE OF CHINA'S CONTEMPORARY SECURITY CHALLENGES IN AFRICA

One of the nostrums of Chinese foreign policy is that it pursues an approach of 'non-interference' in domestic affairs of other states, one of the Five Principles of Peaceful Co-Existence trumpeted by Chinese officials since the 1950s. This tacit adoption of an unassuming posture in international peace and security was also consistent with China's overall foreign policy posture, which has largely eschewed international leadership and strategic boldness in favour of a low international profile and strategic restraint, as characterised by Deng Xiaoping's well-known maxim calling for a *taoguang yanghui* ('keep a low profile and high your strengths') international strategy. Until the arrival of the era of China's rise, Beijing's reliance on the 'non-interference' principle indeed illustrated a stark reality of China's international status: with little political or economic influence, Beijing had no option but to adopt a low-profile approach to peace and security issues in much of the so-called 'Third World'.[3]

Indeed, under such international circumstances, the best course of action was to avoid embroiling itself in international disputes and domestic conflicts of other states, as China had neither the capacity to influence the course of events nor substantial interests directly involved in the outcome of those events. Adherence to the non-interference principle allowed Beijing to remain uninvolved in many international and domestic conflicts by maintaining a somewhat disinterested and detached policy position and avoid taking sides on any specific policy question. Similarly, the almost ritualistic stress on peaceful resolution of conflict through political dialogue and negotiations, which is another characteristic Chinese policy stance on the question of peace and security, also serves as a politically convenient way of circumventing sensitive issues and difficult policy choice.

Proclaimed publically with great fanfare by Beijing in this period of economic expansion into Africa, the 'non-interference' principle caught the attention of African leaders weary of the decades-long implementation of intrusive policies through structural adjustment programmes and market dominance as well as the use of military intervention to prop up regimes friendly to Western interests. In fact, for some of China's most ardent advocates amongst African elites in Sudan and Zimbabwe, it was to be the possibility of securing Beijing's support as an alternative to reliance on the West that proved particularly appealing (as reflected in the launching of a plethora of 'Look East' policies by these aforementioned countries and other African states).[4] A corollary of this application of the 'non-interference' principle was an expectation on China's part that local host governments would be able to provide the requisite security for new-founded Chinese interests in their country.[5] Indeed, given the limited capacity of the Chinese military to project power beyond its region even in the early 2000s, there was little alternative to adopting this approach despite the fact that Chinese companies working in Africa – whether financed by Chinese loans or through international tender – along with their contracted employees were extremely vulnerable to targeted actions against them.

Though China's 'non-interference' principle may have guided its formal approach to Africa during the era of Deng Xiaoping and into Hu Jintao's rule, its ability to produce stable relationships that systematically guaranteed the security of its growing economic interests across the continent was increasingly shown to be suspect. In countries operating under conditions of fragility, where the very nature of regime legitimacy itself was contested as was the regime's ability to enforce its rule over the population and territory limited at best, Beijing could not escape the security challenges implied in greater involvement. Under these difficult circumstances, linking substantive investments and long-term loans to stability of resource supply was much more tenuous than Chinese officials had initially expected. The contracting of Chinese firms and their preference for Chinese labour in many of their projects has produced its own backlash amongst elements in the host country quick to point to the dire needs for local employment. Local criticism, once exclusively levelled at the cosy relationships between Western governments and firms with African elites, turned to the opaque package deals struck with Beijing. And most dramatically, Chinese migration, starting as a trickle in the late 1990s but growing steadily across the continent, introduced a new element of complexity into the local environment as individual citizens became exposed to crime. Three security challenges in particular confronted the Chinese government in the wake of this growing economic exposure to the African environment.

The first, *reputational security*, is the local and global image of the Chinese state and its implications. In the local context, the lack of transparency in deals and close ties with governing elites has meant that China was increasingly exposed to accusations of collusion with the sitting regime. In fact, as has been demonstrated in a number of African states, Chinese interests have been targeted explicitly by opposition forces for their role in bolstering regime interests or in more benign cases as a proxy for mobilising domestic support against the regime.[6] Linked to this was the potential damage to Beijing's carefully cultivated global image as an emerging power, whose intentions were attuned to African sensibilities and therefore should be viewed as benign. The uproar around Chinese support for Khartoum during the onset of the Darfur crisis in the 2000s in African capitals as well as the West underscored the negative impact that Chinese engagement in one African country could have on both its African foreign policy and global manoeuvrability.[7]

The second, *firm level security*, in this case the maintenance of China's economic interests in the local environment and, concurrently, its impact on broader perceptions of Chinese foreign policy intentions in Africa. While the government attention was squarely on the concerns of state-owned enterprises (SOEs) operating in strategic areas such as energy, the growing number of Chinese SMEs operating across the continent meant that Beijing found itself drawn into local disputes of limited economic consequence but inevitably holding wider ramifications. For SOEs, the reversal of their positions in local energy sector through the denial of licenses and effective nationalisation seen in cases as diverse as Angola, Nigeria, Chad, and Sudan conveyed a sobering message of uncertainty to their vested interests. Similarly, the widely publicised misconduct of some Chinese firms, symbolised by Chinese Non-Ferrous Metals Mining Corporation in Zambia, where an unremitting series of fatal accidents, egregious violations of local labour laws, and acts of violence against workers and management (all of which finally brought about its closure by the Zambian government in 2013) tarred China's business reputation in that country and beyond.[8] The conscious emphasis and rollout of corporate social responsibility practices by the State Council after 2006 reflected the state's continuing anxieties about this sector.

The third, *citizens' security*, is linked to the previous concern but manifested as hostage taking of Chinese nationals grew, crime against the rising number of Chinese businesses and tourists in Africa expanded, and, in its most dire form, threats to Chinese nationals in cases of the collapse of state authority as happened in Libya. As one Chinese scholar admitted, 'Chinese workers' safety faces high risk in Africa' and the accompanying firestorm of criticism that Beijing faced from its assertive 'netizens' whenever it failed to protect them in Africa was a growing source of anxiety for Chinese officials.[9]

Attacks on and kidnappings of Chinese workers in Sudan, or South Sudan's oil shutdown, and expulsion of a Chinese oil executive in early 2012, despite ongoing discussions with Beijing over large financial packages aimed at developing the oil and agricultural sectors, are recent examples of this phenomenon. Even a carefully crafted 'charm offensive' aimed at South Sudan did not spare Chinese interests there.[10] A spate of protests by local communities supplemented by unlawful police actions starting in 2012 and carrying into the next year targeted Chinese shopkeepers and miners in countries as disparate as Kenya, Senegal, and Ghana. The beating and ultimately expulsion of Chinese miners in Ghana provoked heated reaction by Chinese netizens, who declared: 'When will our government wake up and rescue our fellow countrymen from Ghana?'[11] Indeed, crime against Chinese citizens became an increasingly problematic phenomenon as the migrant community grew, replicating the apparent targeting of Chinese businesses in South Africa, home to the largest Chinese community. As a Chinese delegation to Tanzania declared during Xi Jinping's visit in April 2013, 'In the last three years, there have been a series of robbery incidents which targeted Chinese investors, including a woman who was killed last October. We think the government should consider this seriously to improve the business environment for Chinese and other investors in the country.'[12]

But above all, it was the impact of the so-called 'Arab Spring' in early 2011, which swept aside decades of authoritarian rule in Tunisia, Egypt, and Libya, that shook any remaining complacency that the Chinese government had about operating in a benign African environment. In particular, the loss and damages perpetuted by the Nato-led intervenion on Chinese interests in Libya imposed huge financial costs on the Chinese 50 projects there (with a total contract value of US $18.8 billion) and exposed the limited ability of China to protect either its economic interests, the firms, or even its 35,850 citizens living there.[13] These losses occurred despite the fact that, as the Minister of Commerce himself noted, China had no investments in Libya.[14] Worried officials mulled over the unexpected outbreak of unrest in other parts of the continent, including Angola, where a large Chinese presence (some Chinese estimates claim to be as high as 250,000 citizens) was coupled to the country's largest foreign source of oil.[15] Internally, the Chinese State Council set up a parallel body to its State-owned Assets and Supervision Commision (SASC) to regulate and monitor the assets and activities of SOEs operating overseas. Like US analysts, who sought to identify ways of safeguarding long-term US interests in the wake of the Arab Spring, Chinese officials also began a search for means of accomodating change while preserving their fundamental interests in the region.[16]

FITTING AFRICA INTO CHINA'S CONTEMPORARY APPROACH TO PEACE AND SECURITY

Against this background, the Chinese government produced its first ever publically released defence white paper outlining a new vision for China's role in international security affairs in May 2015.[17] Not only was the publication itself an extraordinary step, the message it conveys to the world is one of a newly assertive global power led by a Chinese president, Xi Jinping, who was no longer bound by the cautious strictures of the past. China's policy towards Africa needs to be fitted within this broader security posture whose centre piece is based on the country's geostrategic assessment of its expanding global interests and rising military capabilities. At the same time, it should be noted that the key features of this approach to defence were already in progress under the previous president, Hu Jintao, with his focus on 'new historic missions' for the Chinese military, which gave prominence to the PLA's role to 'safeguard China's expanding national interest' and to 'help maintain world peace', and called for the improvement of capabilities to match expanding economic interests.[18] Three aspects in particular are the focus of the comprehensive approach articulated by Xi Jinping's China: its global reach, its increasing ability to project power, and its search for military partnerships.

First, the ambit of China's defence strategy is decidedly global in scope, moving beyond the regional focus in East and Southeast Asia that has characterised most of its intensified interests historically and in the modern era, to one which embraces the extent of its widening engagement in the global economy. Trade dependency and China's vital resource reliance have created an open-ended requirement for access to regions far beyond its traditional strategic ambit and a concomitant need to secure sea-lanes and communication avenues on a global scale. This explicit acceptance of an enlarged role in international politics on the part of Beijing is effectively an abandonment of non-interference principle as a pillar of Chinese foreign policy. Indeed, as one observer suggests, there isn't even a mention of the 'Five Principles of Peaceful Co-Existence' in the new Defence White Paper.[19]

Second, Chinese desire to expand its ability to project power across the globe is calibrated alongside its current and projected capabilities and interests. This means, in part, fostering its own armament building and development programme to match the country's expanding economic and security interests. The emphasis on building a global navy is specified, a reflection of Xi Jinping administration's well-known admiration of late nineteenth-century American geo-strategist Alfred Mahan's work, is highlighted, with a promotion of 'near seas defence' (East China Sea, South China Sea, and Yellow Sea) and 'far seas protection' (notably the Indian Ocean and Asia-Pacific). Most interestingly, the Defence White Paper indicated that it would be shifting its approach over time as its capabilities and expected interests continued to expand globally, from 'far seas protection' to 'far seas defence' and even 'open oceans protection'.[20] Clearly there is an expectation over the medium term of a robust integration of Chinese interests with parts of Asia, Africa, and the Asia-Pacific of the type implied in the other Xi Jinping initiative, the 'One Belt, One Road' development strategy.

Third, there is a clear recognition that in order to accomplish this ambitious ratcheting up of its global security concerns, Beijing will need to work with like-minded partners with sufficient capabilities and shared interests. In this regard, the United States and European countries are named as prospective partners for China, as are other countries from regions like Africa within the expanding array of strategic partnership arrangements (now numbered at 60) that Beijing has designated. This is especially the case with military operations other than war (MOOTWs) – these include humanitarian assistance, peacekeeping, and disaster relief.

According to the US Department of Defence analysts, the restructuring of the Chinese military and its rapid build-up over the last few years has enabled Beijing to achieve the primary goal in the 'near seas' already but that it still needs more capabilities and platforms for the PLA navy and air force for 'far seas' force projection.[21] Notably, in the Defence White Paper, there is an explicit acknowledgement of necessity of accounting for varying Chinese interests in different global regions and the need to build capacity of an expeditionary force with naval and air force platforms for operation. In recognition of this, the Defence White Paper declares that the PLA would establish a joint operational command structure between the services.

The significance of China's White Paper on Defence for its relationship with Africa is that it sharpens our understanding of how it perceives its global and national interests in continental affairs and the consequent role it will assume in order to fulfil those requirements. It is clear that it delineates its involvement in security affairs along two axes, the *first* defined by its national interests and the *second* derived from its interpretation of its responsibilities as an emergent global power. National interests are principally understood to be economic in the African context, representing the country's dependency on energy and other resources, its firms' investments and operations on the continent, and the safety of their personnel as well as that of Chinese citizens more generally. Bilateral military relations provide an established platform for addressing longer generative security concerns while selective or opportunistic cooperation with other powers is envisaged as needs arise. In the multilateral sphere, China's interests are defined by its assumption of a role as a global power in international affairs. Given that approximately 70% of all issues put before the UN Security Council involve peace and security in Africa, there is a strong expectation that permanent members of the body will put resources towards addressing these concerns. Moreover, in this respect, the privileged institutional position that China holds within the international peace and security apparatus, that is to say its standing as a permanent veto-wielding member of the UN Security Council enables it to ensure (to the extent possible) that multilateralist outcomes do not jeopardise its national interests.[22] Of course, as events which followed on the Security Council's passage of UNSC Resolution 1973 demonstrated, playing a key role in the decision-making process still does not always guarantee a result commensurate to one's interests.

China's involvement in the anti-piracy campaign in the Gulf of Aden provides an early set of insights into how this global strategic calculus translates into defence policy in the African environment. Chinese naval forces were authorised by Beijing to participate in a multilateral naval task force in December 2008, which mandates, underwritten by a UN Security Council Resolution (where of course Beijing status as a permanent member helped to ensure that it would not stray beyond its vital interests), setting out the terms of the operation. China's special naval task force consisting of three ships acting as escorts for commercial carriers was dispatched to the Gulf of Aden. In operational terms, it initially coordinated directly with the Russian navy, a reflection of the fact that the actual Chinese naval fleet itself and accompanying training were all drawn from the Soviet era, but went on to organise anti-piracy training exercises with NATO and EU navies. Almost half of China's navy have rotated through on a series of over 22 deployments since 2008 – including its destroyers, frigates, and replenishment ships – thus giving them valuable 'far seas' experience while Chinese frigates and marines have been involved in the evacuation of Chinese nationals from Libya and Yemen.[23] Lacking an agreement with coastal states in the region, the Chinese navy did not dock for re-fuelling nor was it able to carry out normal rest and recreation afforded to the other navies. Despite these obstacles, according to one senior Dutch naval official, the Chinese conduct throughout the mission was 'exemplary'.[24]

UNDERSTANDING CHINA'S RATIONALE AND PARTICIPATION IN PEACEKEEPING OPERATIONS IN AFRICA

In response to the changing international circumstances in the era of China's rise, China has begun to enhance her engagement in international peace and security since the 2000s. This changing policy outlook essentially stemmed from the new policy requirements in relation to the demands on a 'responsible power' and the emerging need to protect the country's rapidly expanding economic and security interests in the world. On the one hand, Beijing's more active posture is a response to the growing international expectations within the international community, especially among many developing countries that have increasingly called for a greater Chinese role in supporting peace activities in Africa, the Middle East, and Asia. Meanwhile, Beijing has also come under increasing Western pressure to play a more constructive role with the United States encouraging China to act in a more responsible manner in international peace and security. In order to protect the nation's reputation, Beijing had no option but to meet the country's growing international responsibility by adjusting its non-involvement posture accordingly.

In fact, this policy adjustment is accompanied by the gradual weakening of the *taoguang yanghui* doctrine as China's overriding strategic imperative especially since the second half of the 2000s when China's overall national power and international status have been undergoing a dramatic transformation. As part of this emerging paradigm shift in Chinese foreign policy thinking (and as noted in the section above), the notion of non-interference has been subject to increasing doubt and scrutiny by Chinese scholars and policy analysts; and the topic is no longer deemed to be a strictly forbidden territory in the academic discourse, as various new thinking advocating greater involvement or intervention in global affairs (as well as in international peace and security) have emerged in China over the same period.[25]

This growing flexibility has been demonstrated by China's deepening involvement in international mediation efforts in many parts of the developing world. President Hu Jintao's call in 2004 for China to assume 'new historic missions' in international peacekeeping gave the official blessing to an incrementalist expansion in this area. The establishment of the offices of the special representatives (special envoy) of the Chinese government specifically designated for the Middle East issue, African affairs, and Korean Peninsular affairs over the course of the recent decade clearly represents an enhanced Chinese diplomatic effort in international mediation in some of the world hot spots.[26] What is most remarkable is the beginning of substantial Chinese diplomatic interest in international mediation in peace and security affairs outside its immediate periphery. The most illustrative example perhaps has been the case of Darfur, where Beijing is said to have managed to effectively use its good offices in 2007 to persuade Khartoum to accept hybrid United Nations-African Union peacekeeping force in Darfur.[27] Indeed, Africa has been the test case for China's evolving posture in international peace and security.

Although economic agenda continues to dominate the agenda of China-Africa cooperation under the FOCAC framework, security cooperation has gained increasing salience over the recent years to become one of the major arenas for the expansion of Sino-African cooperation beyond the traditional focus on economics and development.[28] In 2011, the Chinese government signed a memorandum of understanding with the Intergovernmental Authority on Development (IGAD), the regional organisation for the Horn of Africa, which included US $100,000 for operational costs, and a donation in 2012 of US $98 million (600 million yuan) for areas that included 'peace and security.'[29] This was followed in 2012 by the 'Initiative on China-Africa Cooperative Partnership for Peace and Security', an initiative designed to provide material and financial support to help strengthen Africa's indigenous capabilities for maintaining peace and security and had been incorporated into the existing FOCAC framework.

Another direct indicator of China's evolving attitude towards international peace and security has been the level of Chinese participation in UN peace operations. Over the course of the 2000s, China has taken steady steps to build up its peacekeeping capability and further integrate the Chinese armed and police forces into the UN peacekeeping system. In 2000, China's Ministry of Public Security established a peacekeeping civilian police training centre. In 2001, China's Ministry of National Defence set up the Office of Peacekeeping Affairs. In the following year, China formally joined the United Nations Level-1 Standby Arrangement System. Following Hu Jintao's 'historic missions' declaration in 2004, the Defence Ministry set up a Peacekeeping Centre as the PLA's first ever specialised facility for peacekeeping training and international exchange in 2009. In 2012, the Chinese military also introduced the 'PLA UN Peacekeeping Regulations'. As of September 2015, China has contributed a total of more than 30,000 peacekeepers in 29 peacekeeping missions since China's first participation in UN peacekeeping operations in 1990.[30] According to the 2013 Chinese defence white paper, China has become the biggest troop and police contributor among the five permanent members of the UN Security Council (since 2004); China also dispatches the most numbers of troops for engineering, transportation, and medical support among all the 115 contributing countries; and China pays and contributes the largest share of UN peacekeeping costs among all developing countries.[31]

Beijing is comfortable with an enlarged role in international peacekeeping on a multilateral platform under United Nations auspices.

Indeed, the official position on the condition of Chinese involvement in international peace and security has always emphasised the necessity of securing the support of the UN Security Council, the support of the relevant regional organisation, and the authorisation from the host government as the precondition for international intervention. However, it may be said that this 'conditional' approach is itself indicative of growing Chinese flexibility on the issue of intervention in international peace and security.

This growing Chinese involvement in international peace and security has reached a new level of activism since the advent of the new Chinese leadership at the end of 2013. What makes this round of activism distinctive is that it is not so much a passive response to international expectation (or pressure) as a proactive attempt to raise China's profile in this important domain of international policy. Arguably, this proactive posture has to be seen through the lens of China's overall foreign policy direction during the reign of President Xi Jinping, who is determined to push ahead with the so-called 'great power diplomacy with Chinese characteristics' (*zhongguo tese daguo waijiao*). What this entails is that the old foreign policy paradigm of Deng Xiaoping has virtually come to an end.

This growing Chinese ambition has been translated into concerted Chinese efforts to play a much more prominent role in global affairs, not only in the area of economic global governance but also in the management of international peace and security. An important tenet of the idea of 'great power diplomacy with Chinese characteristics' as applied to the global arena is the desire to boost China's global leadership status and great power influence by providing more international public goods. This is in keeping with the rationale behind the current leadership's unprecedented emphasis on the so-called 'Chinese solution' (*zhongguo fang'an*), which declares that China 'should develop a distinctive diplomatic approach befitting its role of a major country' and 'with a salient Chinese feature and a Chinese vision'.[32]

Accordingly, China has significantly stepped up its involvement in international peace and security since 2013. There has been a notable increase in Chinese activism in mediation efforts in the world's major trouble spots from sub-Saharan Africa to the Middle East and North Africa regions. Especially from 2014 onwards, Beijing has taken the initiative to actively use its good offices to promote political negotiations and peaceful settlement in the talks on a comprehensive agreement on the

Iranian nuclear issue, Afghanistan's military, political and economic transition and reconstruction efforts, South Sudan's domestic reconciliation process, the inter-ethnic reconciliation in Myanmar, and the political processes in Syria and between Palestine and Israel.[33]

Beijing's deepened engagement in those peace processes, especially in terms of the Chinese willingness to work with other major powers and to put forward Chinese initiatives and proposals, clearly reflects a new level of political activism in international peace and security and a proactive outlook on China's international responsibility, which is to some extent distinct from the country's previously more passive approach. This unprecedented global thrust in international security affairs does seem to indicate a rising Chinese-style internationalist tendency characteristic of the current Chinese leadership's diplomatic orientation. China's significant contribution to the international response to the Ebola crisis in Africa also demonstrates Beijing's commitment to supporting the international efforts to tackle non-traditional security threats facing the world.

Beijing has shown a new level of activism by seeking to play a leadership role in UN peace operations. In his address to the Leaders' Summit on Peacekeeping at the United Nations headquarters in September 2015, Xi Jinping announced a string of measures to back UN peacekeeping missions. Declaring that China is to join the new UN peacekeeping capability readiness system, Xi pledged that China would take the lead to set up a permanent peacekeeping police squad and would build a peacekeeping standby force of 8000 troops.[34] In view of the situation that the United Nations is chronically plagued by slow formation and deployment of its peacekeeping forces, the establishment of this standby force is said to be a 'robust contribution that has the potential to address critical gaps' in UN peacekeeping capabilities, and demonstrates 'China's leading role in supporting UN peacekeeping'.[35]

In this context, Africa has once again become the major theatre to demonstrate China's growing ambitions in international peace and security. In December 2015, Xi Jinping proposed that China and Africa lift their relationship to a comprehensive strategic cooperative partnership at the second FOCAC summit held in Johannesburg.[36] Cooperation in peace and security is said to be expanding steadily and have become one of the major agenda of China-Africa relations.[37] Security cooperation indeed featured prominently in the FOCAC Johannesburg Action Plan for 2016–2018 and China's second Africa policy paper issued in the same month, which reaffirmed the Chinese commitment to providing support to Africa for its development of collective security mechanism, made the pledge to provide the African Union with US $60 million of military assistance over the next 3 years in support of the operationalisation of the African Peace and Security Architecture, and promised to play a more active role in maintaining and promoting peace and security in Africa by seeking to 'exert a unique impact on and make greater contributions to African peace and security'.[38]

The other notable shift in China's role in the UN peace operations is Beijing's new willingness to contribute the so-called combat troops to peacekeeping missions, which marks a significant departure from the traditional Chinese practice that tended to focus Chinese participation on non-combat roles providing logistic support in engineering, transportation, and medical care.[39] In 2013, China sent its first ever security forces to join the UN peacekeeping mission in Mali.[40] Whilst this security unit was a protection and guard team mainly responsible for the security of the MINUSMA headquarters and the living areas of peacekeeping forces,[41] China further enhanced the country's security-force contribution by despatching a 700-member infantry contingent in South Sudan in 2015, which was the PLA's first infantry battalion (with a bigger security role than the protection and guard unit sent to Mali) to participate in a UN peacekeeping mission.[42] This new trend in Chinese participation in UN peace operations clearly demonstrates China's ambition to seek a much more prominent leadership position in UN peace operations.

Beyond these reasons, some foreign analysts have pointed out that Chinese participation in UN peacekeeping operations serves a variety of institutional purposes as well.[43] Given the lack of actual combat experience for the PLA, whose last military conflict occurred in 1979 during the border war with Vietnam, which ended in its defeat by Hanoi's forces, there is a genuine need for Chinese troops to gain real-life combat experience. In fact, China's White Paper on Defence takes up this concern directly, noting that these missions would contribute to efforts build up the PLA's combat capabilities, since they would allow the PLA troops to gain more real-work combat experience.[44]

MULTILATERAL COOPERATION ON TRANSNATIONAL SECURITY THREATS

China's involvement in the multilateral effort to patrol the Gulf of Aden to thwart a transnational security threat marked the first instance it had initiated military operations outside of periphery. Given the length of the mission, it was no surprise when the leasing of basing rights in Djibouti to China was announced in November 2015. Certainly, thinking with the Chinese military establishment, especially the navy, have indicated their interest in obtaining basing rights in the Gulf of Aden and Suez since at least 2009.[45] Admiral Yin Zhou rather audaciously let it be known in a public interview that the Chinese navy had endured considerable hardship in staying at sea during its anti-piracy operations without the same respite for rest and recreation that other navies were afforded and would welcome the establishment of a base in the region.[46]

The nature of the 10-year leasing agreement struck in Djibouti is one reminiscent of the decision to build naval basing facilities in Pakistan and Sri Lanka, that is, providing substantive investment towards the construction of harbour facilities in the town of Obock in exchange for basing rights for its navy aimed at improving its ability to operate in the region as well as linking it to a free trade zone and banking facilities for China.[47] Access to an airbase will allow Beijing to conduct surveillance missions in northern Africa and the Persia Gulf, as well as the eventual stationing of a contingent of Chinese marines to assist in evacuations of citizens and the rescue of hostages and other MOOTWs in the region. In the case of Djibouti, the existence of French, American, and Japanese ships operating out of the same small territory underscores the multi-national character of naval operations in the region. As Djibouti's Foreign Minister, Mahmoud Ali Youssofu, said:

> We don't want the Americans to leave but the Chinese invest billions of dollars in our infrastructure; that's what the Americans are not doing. So we are trying to keep the balance to see where our interest lies, as a small country with very limited resources.[48]

Looking to the future, the establishment of Chinese naval bases in other African ports is a necessity, especially given that sending a task force to the Gulf of Aden is over 4000 nautical miles away (a 10- to 2-week exercise in itself) and moving on to West Africa's Gulf of Guinea increases substantively the time at sea and attendant problems of re fuelling.[49] A search for a friendly country to build such a facility is already on, with rumours in circulation that Namibia has been approached by Beijing, though arguably a site closer to the Gulf of Guinea would be preferred. If so, alongside Djibouti and the prospective harbour at Bagamayo and presumed naval base there (see below), this would mark a major shift towards assuming an even stronger position in military affairs on the continent.

Another transnational security challenge on the African continent that is generally overlooked is that of nuclear security. China has constructed 'first generation'-type nuclear facilities in a number of African countries, including Nigeria and Ghana, where highly enriched uranium is produced as a by-product of the process. This is weapons-grade uranium and given the persistent instability and security threats in the northern arc of the Sahelian countries a matter of growing local and international concern. The increasing ability of radical Islamists to penetrate deep into the heart of these countries, where the Chinese reactors are found, opens up the possibility of actions aimed at stealing the fuel in order to make a 'dirty bomb'. Disclosures from computers discarded by the terrorists in Brussels indicated such actions are very much part of the terrorists' plans.[50]

In light of these concerns, a high-level summit on nuclear security convened in late March 2016 by Washington explicitly mentioned these Chinese nuclear facilities in West Africa as potential targets and Beijing has agreed working together with their American counterparts to convert such 'first-generation' reactors in China and abroad into producers of low-grade nuclear fuel.[51] For instance, Beijing had built a small Chinese nuclear facility at Ahmadu Bello University in 2004 in Kaduna state in northern Nigeria, 30 kW miniature neutron source reactor used for research in medical technology, petro-chemical analysis, and other scientific applications.[52] Along with an equivalent facility in Ghana, Chinese officials are currently working together US officials to convert the research reactor from producing highly enriched uranium fuel to low-enriched uranium fuel as part of a global effort to reduce the possibility nuclear theft.[53]

CHINESE BILATERAL COOPERATION IN MILITARY AFFAIRS WITH AFRICAN PARTNERS: POLICY ALIGNMENT OR CONTRADICTION?

The nature of China's bilateral cooperation in military affairs varies with different African countries, reflecting the status of diplomatic relations between them. Since the mid-2000s, the onset of the elaborated Chinese lexicon of 'strategic partnerships' and 'comprehensive strategic partnerships', which are signalling devices for a proximity of close ties with other states. Of particular significance is that 'comprehensive strategic partnerships' are supposed to allow for regular consultation at the ministerial level between China and the partner country, including defence and security portfolios, which will enable them to coordinate on topics of mutual concern and interest.[54] The concomitant efforts by China to increase bilateral partners' interests in its arms through exposure to military training programmes has had some successes as well, notably with the Chinese taking a dominant position in aircraft training in Tanzania, the Republic of Congo, and South Africa.[55]

In this context, a number of countries have developed close formal military cooperation with Beijing, amongst them Sudan, Angola, Tanzania, and Zimbabwe. The intermingling of Chinese military and security interests in a commercial sense with local African militaries and regimes is one characteristic of bilateral engagement. In this respect, though it is by no means the only country, Angola in particular has received attention in the Western press due to the role of a Chinese business figure, Sam Pa, with alleged links to security interests (and arrested in Beijing for corruption charges in October 2015), in funding infrastructure and mining projects there through a joint venture with Angolan military interests.[56] Tanzania and Zimbabwe will be examined in detail in this section as they represent in the first case an unbroken institutionalised form of military cooperation and in the second case a relatively recent expansion, promoting security and security-aligned commercial interests alongside more conventional military cooperation.

Tanzania's long-standing close diplomatic ties with China, stretching back to the earliest period of President Julius Nyerere's rule over the newly independent country, was accompanied by one of the world's few efforts to indigenise Mao Zedong's agricultural collectivisation programme and even draw in aspects of the cultural revolution into local policies.[57] This was all the more unusual given Beijing's direct interference in fostering a separatist Maoist movement on the island of Zanzibar from 1962, support which included the supplying of training and small arms, until the island's forcible incorporation into the Republic of Tanzania in 1965.[58] The closeness of the relationship was perhaps epitomised by Mao Zedong's personal decision to support the construction of the iconic Tazara railway – a build, operate, and transfer project on China's part aimed at providing alternatives to the routing of commerce via the minority regime in Rhodesia, colonial Portugal, or apartheid South Africa.[59] Alongside this initiative, Tanzanian-Chinese cooperation in military affairs grew over the decades to include joint training and military programmes, which involved the expansion of Tanzania's arms procurements and joint naval exercises off the Tanzanian coast in 2014.[60]

During President Xi Jinping's visit to Tanzania in March 2013, he announced the funding of $10 billion to build a modern harbour facility at Bagamayo, a site north of Dar es Salaam, with a capacity to handle 20 million containers (outstripping Port Said, Africa's leading port, which handles only 3 million containers).[61] The establishment of a special economic zone and loans for the expansion of rail and road infrastructure were negotiated alongside this announcement.[62] However, there were signs that not all is well with the proposed keystone Bagamayo harbour project. For instance, the Tanzanian government halted preliminary construction on a number of occasions there have been allegations in the parliament about corruption in the selection of contractors and sites, exacerbated by the initial rushing of legislation through parliament by the ruling party without debate.[63] By January 2016, after opposition candidates campaigned against the new port in the national elections the previous year, the entire project was suspended as the newly elected government sought to focus its resources on rehabilitating the port of Dar es Salaam.[64] The announcement in May 2016 that China had agreed to take over the rehabilitation and direct management of the Tazara railway, a long-standing request by Tanzanian officials, suggests that negotiations are moving to a more advanced stage.[65]

The case of Zimbabwe highlights the new characteristics of Chinese military involvement in Africa, its response to security interests, and commercial imperatives in line with localised regime interests.[66] Though ZANU-PF drew from Maoist guerrilla strategies to make gains in its liberation struggle against the Rhodesian regime in the 1970s, it was only with the suspension of Zimbabwe from the Commonwealth in 2002 and accompanying punitive measures by Western governments that Harare turned to China in earnest for economic assistance. Since the imposition of sanctions, the once solidly British oriented Zimbabwean military has shifted its focus towards China. The building of a 'listening post' in Mashona province managed by Chinese and Zimbabwean (along with Pakistani) intelligence and, with a US $98 million loan to support the construction of the National Defence College, was completed in October 2012, and it has gone on to serve as a training centre for the regional's militaries.[67] As Western sanctions targeted Zimbabwean military interests, the PLA stepped in to provide US $4.2 million in grants to support a range of undisclosed projects with its counterpart in 2014.[68] This was followed in December 2015 with an announcement that China would build a major airbase in the Marange area.

Close links between the Chinese military and the governing ZANU-PF party, which has appointed Zimbabwean military officers to manage key ministerial portfolios in recent years, were underscored by the privileged position of the Chinese military's commercial interests in exploiting mining licenses in the Marange diamond fields (through a joint venture between the Anhui group with the Zimbabwean military interests) as well as China's exemption from Zimbabwe's indigenisation laws (which require foreign investors to secede 51% ownership to indigenous Zimbabweans).[69] China is now the leading arms supplier to Zimbabwe – having replaced the British – and sold 139 military vehicles, 24 combat aircraft, ground-based military radar systems, aerial defence systems, small arms, ammunition, and police equipment to the country.[70] In the meantime, economic ties continued to strengthen with the Zimbabwean Finance Minister declaring that the country would officially begin using the Chinese yuan as part of a basket of foreign currencies.

At the same time, Mugabe's effort to raise US $27 billion for a recovery programme aimed at bringing the economy back on its feet after a decade of mismanagement, Western neglect, and targeted sanctions resulted in receiving a disappointing commitment of US $4 billion from Beijing in 2014 (that, as of 2016, were still to be implemented). Behind Beijing's reluctance to finance the recovery programme was the fear that China would lose money to local rampant corruption and the continued inability of Zimbabwe to pay back its outstanding US $60 million debt to China.[71] The result was that Beijing apparently insisted that any loans pro-offered to Harare would require the placement of Chinese officials directly into positions with the Zimbabwean government and parastatal offices to provide oversight and engineer reforms to management procedures, a position that stirred resentment within elements of ZANU-PF.[72] As the government newspaper editorial declared:

> (T)he thrust of Zimbabwe's cooperation with the East is to prioritise projects in which the cooperating country has expressed interest, and it is designed on empowerment value. But are these projects based on service provision? Looking around Zimbabwe, only projects relevant to military investment have been observed and a few hotels were constructed.[73]

The awarding of the Chinese version of the Nobel Peace Prize to Robert Mugabe in 2015 for his role in promoting world peace and its \$65,000 prize, perhaps an effort by interests based in Beijing to assuage him, was rejected by its recipient.[74] The subsequent cancellation of Anhui group's mining license in the Marange diamond fields in March 2016, coming in the wake of allegations that ZANU-PF presidential hopeful Ernest Mnangagwa was complicit in systematic corruption and the efforts by a faction led by Mugabe's wife to block him from succeeding the current president, suggests China is being drawn into the increasingly bitter succession struggle in Zimbabwe.[75]

Conclusion

China's role in peace and security in Africa has been dramatically enhanced over the last decade and a half. While a key driver for that expansion is framed within the larger global role that China seeks to play as a multi-lateral actor, a more consequential concern is found in the pursuit of Chinese national interest to preserve and secure its economic expansion in global markets and protect its citizens abroad that include Africa. Furthermore, through the implementation of this enhanced role in security, the Chinese have had to engage in closer bilateral military and diplomatic ties, which often overlap with commercial concerns in ways that deepen China's exposure to political risks.

At the same time, there is an inherent tension within the lofty aims of a rising China and its actual operational role in Africa that still needs further examination. For instance, while China presents the need to cooperate with Western partners, those countries are the same ones that are in competition on a number of fronts with China: either adept diplomacy or the abiding dependency will provide the enabling conditions for such collaborative action with China on peace and security matters in Africa. Moreover, the development imperatives, which drove Chinese policy makers to advocate a 'going out' strategy for its conventional industry, are being applied to its arms industry. Indeed, while not a key market for China, the continent nonetheless occupies an important position at this point in time.

Also, there seems to be a misalignment between Chinese diplomacy and the actions of its arms industry as seen in a number of cases in Africa, such as Zimbabwe in 2008 onwards and South Sudan in 2013, something that echoes uncomfortably with the conduct of Western governments and their own arms industry's actions on the continent.[76] Finding a balance between the different drivers that have been part of the transformation of China from inward-looking quietude to global activism in peace and security is a critical challenge to be facing in the coming decades.

NOTES

1. A revolt in Mali was supported by Beijing in 1962.
2. Chris Alden and Ana Cristina Alves (2008), 'History and Identity in the Construction of China's Africa Policy', *Review of African Political Economy* 115, pp. 43–58.
3. A term that was used during the Cold War and more recently was replaced by the 'South'.
4. See, for instance, Dan Large and Luke Patey, eds. (2011), *Sudan Looks East: China, India and the Politics of Asian Alternatives* (London: James Currey).
5. Interview with Chinese Consul-General, Juba, Sudan September 2010.
6. Botswana, South Africa, Ethiopia, Sudan and Nigeria are one of a number of examples.
7. Large and Patey, eds., *Sudan Looks East.*
8. See Ching Kwan Lee (2011), 'Raw Encounters: Chinese Managers, African Workers and the Politics of Casualization in Africa's Chinese Enclaves', in Alastair Fraser and Miles Larmer, eds., *Zambia, Mining and Neoliberalism* (Basingstoke: Palgrave).
9. Wang Xuejun (2010), 'China's Security Cooperation with Africa Under the Frame of FOCAC', in Papers for Conference on China, South Africa and Africa, SAIIA/ZNU, November, p. 124.
10. Dan Large (2012) 'Between the CPA and Southern Independence', *SAIIA Occasional Paper No. 115*, pp. 14–18.
11. Weibo post, cited in '124 suspected illegal gold miners arrested in Ghana: Chinese citizens' reactions split' *Offbeat China*, 6 June 2013, http://off beatchina.com/124-suspected-illegal-gold-miners-arrested-in-Ghana-Chinese citizens-reactions-split, accessed 10 June 2013.
12. *The Citizen* (Dar es Salaam), 'Chinese delegation's advice to Tanzania', 14 March 2012, www.chinaineastafrica.wordpress.com/2012/03/26/chi nese-delegations-advice-to-tanzania.
13. *Global Times* (2011), 'State Pays Libyan Compensation', 30 March 2011, www.globaltimes.cn/business/world/2011-03/639544.html, accessed 30 September 2013.
14. *China Wire* (2012), 'China Seeks Compensation in Libya', 7 March 2012.
15. Interview with Chinese officials in February and March 2011. The estimate is derived from Ji Dongye's report in 'Rule of Law Weekly', reposted in China Africa Project,www.chinaafricaproject.com/Chinese-people-in-

africa-an-inside-view-into-their-daily-lives-part-5-angola/, accessed 30 September 2013.

16. James Larocco and William Goodyear (2013), 'The Arab Spring: Safeguarding US Interests for the Long-Term', *Prism* 4:2, pp. 3–16.

17. See: *China's Military Strategy* (2015), The State Council Information Office of the People's Republic of China, May 2015, http://www.scio. gov.cn/zfbps/32832/Document/1435514/1435514.htm

18. Roy Kamphausen (2013), *China's Military Operations Other Than War: The Military Legacy of Hu Jintao*, SIPRI Conference, 18–19 April; Cortez Cooper (2009), 'The PLA Navy's "New Historic Missions": Expanding Capabilities for a Re-Emergent Maritime Power', Rand Corporation, CTT-32, Testimony Before the US-China Economic and Security Review Commission, 11 June 2009, pp. 2–3. The other focus was to consolidate the power of the CPC and ensure territorial integrity and national development.

19. Alexander Sullivan and Andrew Erickson (2015), 'The Big Story Behind China's New Military Strategy', *The Diplomat*, 5 June 2015.

20. *China's Military Strategy*, The State Council Information Office of the People's Republic of China.

21. Andrew Erickson and Capt Christopher Carlson (2016), 'Sustained Support: The PLAN Evolves Its Expeditionary Logistics Strategy', *Jane's Navy International*, 9 March 2016.

22. Shaun Breslin (2013), 'China and the Global Order: Signalling Threat or Friendship', *International Affairs*, 89:3, pp. 615–634.

23. Andrew Erickson and Austin Strange (2015), 'China's Global Maritime Presence: Hard and Soft Dimensions of PLAN Antipiracy Operations', *China Brief*, 15:9 (1 May), www.jamestown.org.

24. Discussions with Dutch Admiral, Ministry of Defence, Amsterdam, March 2015.

25. The most well-known proponent of a more interventionist posture is Wang Yizhou, who is associated with the idea of 'creative intervention'; see: Yizhou Wang (2011), *Creative Involvement: A New Direction in China's Diplomacy* (Beijing: Peking University Press); Yizhou Wang (2013), 'Creative Involvement: To Develop and Update a New Doctrine of Non-Interference Based on China-Africa Relations' (fazhan shiying xinshidai yaoqiu de buganshe neizheng xueshuo yi feizhou wei Beijing bing yi zhongfei guanxi wei anli de yizhong jieshuo), *Journal of International Security Studies*, 1.

26. 2002: Special Envoy of the Chinese Government on Middle East Issue; 2003: Ambassador for Korean Peninsular Affairs (Special Representative of the Chinese Government for Korean Peninsula Affairs since 2011); 2007: Special Representative of the Chinese government on African Affairs; 2013: Special Envoy of the Chinese Government on Asian Affairs; 2015: Special Representative of the Chinese Government on Latin American Affairs

27. China's diplomatic mediation in the Darfur crisis has been extensively discussed in the Chinese literature. See, for instance, Wenping He (贺文萍) (2010), 'The Darfur Issue: A New Test for China's Africa Policy' (达尔富尔问题: 中国非洲政策的新考验 daer fuer wenti zhongguo feizhou zhengce de xin zhengce), *Global Review* (国际展望 guoji zhanwang), No. 2.

28. This is reflected in the FOCAC's evolving agenda over the years. See: http://www.focac.org/eng/ltda/dsjbzjhy/hywj/t626387.htm; http://www.focac.org/eng/ltda/dwjbzjjhys/hywj/t954620.htm; http://www.focac.org/eng/ltda/dwjbzjjhys_1/hywj/t1327961.htm.

29. IGAD 2011.

30. Ruocheng Jin (2015), '外交部:中国坚定支持联合国维和行动,坚定维护世界和平', *Xinhuanet*, 29 September, http://news.xinhuanet.com/world/2015-09/29/c_1116715502.htm

31. See: *The Diversified Employment of China's Armed Forces* (2013), The State Council Information Office of the People's Republic of China, April 2013, http://www.scio.gov.cn/zfbps/gfbps/Document/1435337/1435337_6.htm

32. Xinhua (2014), '习近平出席中央外事工作会议并发表重要讲话', *Xinhuanet*, 29 November, http://news.xinhuanet.com/politics/2014-11/29/c_1113457723.htm; see also: http://www.fmprc.gov.cn/mfa_eng/zxxx_662805/t1215680.shtml

33. Chinese Foreign Minister Wang Yi has highlighted the notable increase in the intensity of China's international mediation efforts in a series of policy speeches and articles especially since 2014. See: http://www.fmprc.gov.cn/mfa_chn/ziliao_611306/zyjh_611308/t1222375.shtml; http://www.fmprc.gov.cn/web/wjbzhd/t1323795.shtml; http://www.qstheory.cn/dukan/qs/2015-12/31/c_1117609412.htm; http://www.fmprc.gov.cn/web/zyxw/t1343410.shtml

34. Xinhua (2015), 'Chinese President Pledges Support for UN Peacekeeping', *Xinhuanet*, 29 September, http://news.xinhuanet.com/english/2015-09/29/c_134671138.htm. At the same occasion, Xi also declared that China would actively consider the UN's request of sending more engineering, transportation and medical personnel to join peacekeeping missions, and would train 2000 foreign peacekeepers and carry out 10 mine-sweeping assistance programmes in the next five years.

35. Xinhua (2015), 'Interview: China's Pledge of Peacekeeping Force Helps Meet "critical" Gaps: UN Peacekeeping Chief', *Xinhuanet*, 5 October, http://news.xinhuanet.com/english/2015-10/05/c_134684960.htm; see also: http://www.mod.gov.cn/opinion/2015-10/06/content_4623213.htm

36. Xinhua (2015), 'Spotlight: Xi Charts Course for Upgrading China-Africa Ties at Landmark Summit', *Xinhuanet*, 5 December,

http://news.xinhuanet.com/english/2015-12/05/c_134886595.htm; see also: http://www.fmprc.gov.cn/mfa_eng/topics_665678/ xjpffgcxqhbhbldhdjbbwnfjxgsfwbfnfyhnsbzczfhzltfh/t1322278.shtml

37. See Chinese Foreign Minister Wang Yi's remarks on China-Africa relations at the press conference during the annual session of the National People's Congress in March 2015, http://topics.caixin.com/2015-03-08/ 100789163.html; see also Wang Yi's keynote speech on China-Africa relations, delivered at the 15th Lanting Forum in November 2015, http:// www.fmprc.gov.cn/mfa_eng/wjb_663304/wjbz_663308/2461_ 663310/t1319121.shtml

38. See: *China's Africa Policy Paper*, 4 December 2015, http://news.xinhuanet. com/english/2015-12/04/c_134886545.htm; *The Forum on China-Africa Cooperation Johannesburg Action Plan (2016–2018)*, December 2015, http:// www.focac.org/eng/ltda/dwjbzjjhys_1/hywj/t1327961.htm

39. Strictly speaking, the notion of 'combat troops' is not a formal United Nations term, see: Yun Li (2015), '中国首次派出真正的作战力量参与维和: 首支整建制维和步兵营开赴南苏丹，实现中国维和四大转变', *Xinhua Daily Telegraph*, 9 April, http://news.xinhuanet.com/mrdx/2015-04/ 09/c_134136845.htm. Nonetheless it is often used by the press to refer to security force; see: Kathrin Hille (2013), 'China Commits Combat Troops to Mali', *Financial Times*, 27 June, http://www.ft.com/cms/s/ 0/e46f3e42-defe-11e2-881f-00144feab7de.html#ixzz42gM1xkhc

40. Jing Chen(2013), '中国首次派出安全部队赴马里维和', *China Youth Daily*, 6 December, http://www.banyuetan.org/chcontent/sz/hqkd/2013125/ 87177.html; see also: http://mil.cnr.cn/jmhdd/gfsk/wgf/201307/ t20130704_512972523.html; http://news.xinhuanet.com/english/ china/2013-12/04/c_132940300.htm

41. Xinhua (2013) 'China to Send Security Force for Peacekeeping Mission in Mali', *Xinhuanet*, 28 June, http://news.xinhuanet.com/english/china/ 2013-06/28/c_132492919.htm

42. Li, '中国首次派出真正的作战力量参与维和: 首支整建制维和步兵营开赴 南苏丹，实现中国维和四大转变',; http://news.mod.gov.cn/headlines/ 2015-04/07/content_4578846.htm; http://news.mod.gov.cn/head lines/2015-04/07/content_4578796.htm;

43. Bates Gill and Chin-hao Huang (2009), 'China's Expanding Role in Peacekeeping: Prospects and Policy Implications', SIPRI Policy Paper no. 25, November 2009, p. 16.

44. According to the 2015 Defence White Paper, the PLA's participation in international peacekeeping is regarded as one of the military operations other than war (MOOTWs) that is said to be 'an important approach to enhancing their operational capabilities' and will be incorporated into 'mili-tary modernisation and PMS (preparation for military struggle)'. See:

China's Military Strategy (2015), The State Council Information Office of the People's Republic of China, May 2015, http://www.scio.gov.cn/zfbps/32832/Document/1435514/1435514.htm

45. Discussions with Chinese defence official.
46. 'China floats idea of first overseas naval base', 30 December 2009, http://news.bbc.co.uk/1/hi/world/asia-pacific/8435037.stm
47. 'With China's naval base, Djibouti could become 'Africa's Singapore', *International Business Times*, 2 April 2016, www.ibtimes.com/chinas-naval-base-djibout-could-become-africas-singapore.htm
48. Quoted in *China Africa News*, 4 April 2016, www.chinaafricaproject.com.
49. Andrew Erickson and Austin Strange (2015), 'China's Global Maritime Presence: Hard and Soft Dimensions of PLAN Antipiracy Operations', *China Brief*, 15:9, 1 May, www.jamestown.org.
50. 'Brussels Attacks: Nuclear Terrorism Is a Real Threat Says UN Watchdog', *The Telegraph*, 25 March 2016.
51. 'United States National Progress Report', Nuclear Security Summit 2016, White House Press Release, Office of the Press Secretary, 31 March 2016.
52. World Nuclear Association (2016), 'Emerging Nuclear Energy Countries', (updated February), www.worldnuclearassociation.org.
53. 'More effective steps in nuclear security are to be taken in China', CRI-English, 31 March 2016, www.english.cri.cn/12394/2016/03/31/3521s922602.htm.
54. For an example of how these comprehensive strategic partnerships operate in the South African context, see Chris Alden and Yu-Shan Wu (2016), 'South African Foreign Policy and China: Converging Visions, Competing Interests, Contested Identities', *Journal of Commonwealth and Comparative Politics*, 54:2, pp. 203–231.
55. 'Chinese arms companies are picking up pace in Africa and the Middle East', 21 October 2015.
56. 'Queensway tycoon Sam Pa is detained in Communist probe', *Financial Times* 14 October 2015, www.ft.com/cms/s/0/1a358d9c-725a-11e5-a129-3fcc4f641d98.htm#; Also see Lee Levkowiz, Marta McLeellan Ross and JR Warner (2009), 'The 88 Queensway Group – A Case Study in Chinese Investors Operations in Angola and Beyond', *US China-Economic and Security Review Commission*, 10 July 2009.
57. Gorden Hyden (1980), *Beyond Ujamaa in Tanzania: Underdeveloped and an Uncaptured Peasantry* (Berkeley: University of California).
58. Ng'Wanza Kamata (2013), 'Perspectives on Sino-Tanzanian Relations', in Seifudem Adem, ed., *China's Diplomacy in East and Southern Africa* (London: Ashgate).
59. See Jamie Monson (2011), *Africa's Freedom Railroad* (Bloomington: Indiana University Press).

60. This included the purchase of 24 Type 63A light amphibious tanks, 12 Type 07PA 120 mm self-propelled mortars, FB-6A mobile short-range air defence systems and A100 300 mm multiple rocket launchers 'China, Tanzania carrying out month long joint naval drills', *Defence Web*, 24 October 2014, www.defenceweb.co.za.

61. 'Kenya fights off port competition with $13 billion plan', Bloomberg News, 20 August 2013, www.bloomberg.com.

62. Chinese naval officials denied it was aimed towards a military function though rumors persist. 'Tanzania's $10bn China-funded port will start by 2015', African Capital Markets News, 30 October 2014, www.africancapitalmarketsnews.com

63. 'Don't build Bagamayo port', *The Citizen* (Dar es Salaam) 11 June 2015 www.thecitizen.co.tz/News-Dont-build-bagamayo-port.htm

64. 'Govt halts building of Bagamayo Port', *The Citizen* (Dar es Salaam) 8 January 2016, www.thecitizen.co.tz/News/govt-halts-building-of-Bagamoy-Port/htm

65. 'Tanzania: China takes over running of Tazara in plan to privatise the corporation', *The East African* 16 May 2016, www.allafrica.com/stories/201605170161.html

66. See Zhang Chun (2014), 'China-Zimbabwe Relations: A Model for China-Africa Relations?', *SAIIA Occasional Paper 205*, Braamfontein, November.

67. 'China's hand in Zimbabwe's military future', China Africa Reporting Project, Wits University, www.china-africa-reporting.co.za/2014/01/chinas-hand-in-zimbabwes-military-future/htm

68. 'Chinese army donates $4.2 million to Zimbabwe Defence Forces', *Defence Web* 8 May 2014 www.defenceweb.co.za/index.php?option=_content&view=article&id=345.

69. 'China tipping the trade balance in Zim', *Mail and Guardian* 8 February 2013, www.mg.co.za/2013-02-08-china-tipping-the-trade-balance-in-zim.htm

70. 'Chinese army donates $4.2 million to Zimbabwe Defence Forces', *Defence Web* 8 May 2014 www.defenceweb.co.za/index.php?option=_content&view=article&id=345; 'Zimbabwe Spending too Much on Defence and Military', *Defence Web* 15 October 2012, www.defenceweb.co.za/index.php?option=com_content&view=article&id=28C

71. 'China Puts Screws on Zim', *Mail and Guardian*, 23 January 2015, www.mg.co.za/article/2015-01-23-china-puts-screws-on-zim.htm

72. Ibid.

73. 'The Look East Policy Remains a Mirage', *The Standard* (Harare), 15 February 2015, www.thestandard.co.zw/2015/02/15/look-east-policy-remains.mirage.htm.

74. 'Mugabe rejects China Confucius peace award' 26 October 2015 www. thisisafrica.me/mugabe-rejects-china-confucius-peace-award,
75. 'Succession Rocks' *The Independent* (Harare), 18 March 2016 www.thein dependent.co.zw/2016/03/18/succession-rocks-diamond-mining.htm
76. Sharon Tiezzi (2015), 'UN Report: China sold $20 Million in Arms and Ammunition to South Sudan', *The Diplomat*, 27 August, www.thediplo matc.om/2015/08/un-report-china-sold-20-million-in-arms-and-ammuni tion-to-south-sudan/

Chris Alden holds a Professorship at the Department of International Relations, London School of Economics and Political Science (LSE), has published widely on China-Africa issues and is a research associate of the South African Institute for International Affairs (SAIIA) and Department of Political Sciences, University of Pretoria.

Zheng Yixiao has a PhD in International Relations from the London School of Economics and Political Science (LSE). His research interests include Chinese foreign policy and China-Australia relations.

CHAPTER 4

Developmental Peace: Understanding China's Africa Policy in Peace and Security

Wang Xuejun

In recent years, China's changing policy toward African peace and security and its implications has become an emerging topic in those academic and policy circles concerned with Sino-African relations.[1] A fundamental interest found in the current discussion is the emerging changes in China's policy toward Africa in peace and security. These changes are reflected in four dimensions. The first change is the sectoral expansion of security involvement, which ranges from peacekeeping to peace-building in Africa; secondly, as far as the actor identity is concerned, China is becoming a norm-maker rather than norm-complier; thirdly, actors that are involved in policy discussion are becoming more diversified from the national leaders to enterprises and other civil society organizations; fourthly, it is mainly through multilateralism that China participates in peace and security affairs in Africa. Moreover, Chinese bilateral diplomacy is increasingly aimed at African governments to influence their position toward international and regional peacekeeping.

At the same time, another important aspect of the current discussion is the influence of China's increasing presence in African peace and security affairs on the security situation of the African continent. In July 2012, the

W. Xuejun (✉)
Institute of African Studies, Zhejiang Normal University, Jinhua, Zhejiang, China
e-mail: 2003_wxj@163.com

C. Alden et al. (eds.), *China and Africa*,
DOI 10.1007/978-3-319-52893-9_4

Fifth Ministerial Meeting of the Forum of China Africa Cooperation was held in Beijing. At this meeting, China proposed a "China-Africa Peace and Security Cooperation Partnership Initiative" to further strengthen China's cooperation with Africa in the areas of peace and security. In China's second Africa policy published during the period of summit of the 6th FOCAC, China expressed its willingness "to explore means and ways with Chinese characteristics to constructively participate in resolving hot-button issues in Africa and exert a unique impact on and make greater contributions to African peace and security." The new initiative and activist attitude, raising high expectations from the international community of China's role in Africa's peace and security affairs, marked the formal expansion of Chinese policy interest in the African peace security environment.

There are two kinds of representative opinions among scholars responding to the topic. One is that China will maintain a conservative stance in African security affairs and will largely adapt to the unstable situation in Africa rather than try to reshape it.[2] The other is that China will construct a new paradigm of peace-building and play an increasingly active role in peace and security affairs in Africa.[3] In the view of the author, in order to make sense of China's changing policy toward African peace and security affairs, it is necessary to understand the structural logic of China's policy. The author proposes to adopt a domestic perspective of understanding foreign policy to understand and analyze China's Africa policy in peace and security. China's basic experience of maintaining internal stability is aimed at putting development the first priority, so China's idea for attaining peace can be summarized as "developmental peace," which is different from the liberal peace idea based on Western countries' experience. Influenced by this concept, China's policy toward Africa in peace and security assumes some distinctive features, which can be termed the "sovereignty plus development" model. In light of these developments, China's policy toward African peace and security is expanding and deepening the Sino-African cooperation under the structure of this model.

This chapter is divided into five sections. The next section discusses the international sources of developmental peace concept; the following section reviews and summarizes China's experiences in maintaining the internal order and stability of society, then puts forward the Chinese concept of developmental peace to summarize these experiences. The fourth section analyzes the nature and characteristics of China's Africa policy in peace and security guided by the "developmental peace" concept. The final section predicts the future trend of China's policy.

International Background and Sources of Developmental Peace Concept

Currently, the international practice of peace operations through which outsiders are involved in one country's internal conflict is an important component of global security governance. This kind of peace operations are usually led by the UN or regional organizations, taking on various forms including peace-enforcing, peacekeeping, peace-building, and post-conflict reconstruction. Because of Western countries' overwhelming position in the international peace and security architecture, the liberal peace model has long dominated the peace operations practice. One important feature of liberal peacekeeping is the emphasis placed on the use of military means. Early UN peace missions were essentially focused on military factors such as the inter-positioning of peacekeepers between warring factions. Gueli argues that, as a rule, this entailed separating warring factions from each other and assisting the withdrawal and assembly of opposing factions from cease-fire lines, without effectively addressing long-term development and peace-building activities.[4]

The post-Cold War history has proven that this traditional UN approach to peace interventions has generally attained only limited success and that conflict often breaks out as soon as peacekeeping forces withdraw. The chances of successful peace interventions have proven to be even lower when warring parties fight for the control over valuable natural resources. The UN conducted research in this regard, and the results indicated that 60% of African countries emerging from conflict stand to relapse into conflict. It has become evident that the traditional process of focusing on establishing security first, and then addressing developmental issues, is inadequate to effectively address modern complex emergencies.[5] In response to this, the UN introduced some changes in terms of approaches to peacekeeping operations with the aim of addressing some of the underlying causes of conflict during the early stages of a mission. These changes were introduced following the findings of the Report of the Panel on UN Peace Operations in 2000 – also known as the Brahimi Report.

The Brahimi Report encouraged the UN to update its peacekeeping doctrine and strategies to lay the foundations for peace-building. It also emphasized the need for a more integrated post-conflict peace-building strategy.[6] The report prescribed that the revised strategies for peacekeeping and peace-building need to combine in the field to produce more effective complex peace operations. By expanding the concept of peacekeeping beyond conventional military operations, the Brahimi Report gives some recognition to the underplayed role and untapped potential that initial development work can bring to address the causes of conflict and to prevent the recurrence of conflict. As part of the transformation that took place in the UN system, following the recommendations of the Brahimi Report, the UN made several structural changes to its organizational framework in order to play a more coordinating role in peace-building activities.

In December 2005, the UN established the Peace-building Commission (PBC) as an intergovernmental body. The establishment of the PBC was based on the fact that nearly 50% of the countries in which the UN intervened had slid back into conflict within 5 years of signing the peace agreement. This phenomenon has primarily been ascribed to the lack of effective coordination of activities, the lack of sustained commitment, poor financing and funding gaps, and poor coordination of peace-building activities.[7] Consequently, as part of the development of a new typology of UN peace missions, the so-called complex peace operations came up. The term is used by the UN to denote the inclusion of peace-building mandates into peacekeeping operations. Apart from monitoring ceasefire agreement and patrolled buffer zones, complex UN peace operations were expanded to include the organization of election, the disarmament and demobilization of combatants, and especially assisting in post-conflict reconstruction.

Complex peace operations highlight systematic thinking and integrated approach. In comparison with traditional peace operations, the critical change in the current complex peace mission model or the integrated missions model is increasingly focused on the development-security nexus. The international community has realized that social and economic developments are fundamental to internal order and stability. Recognizing the significance of the development in peace operations, some scholars try to put forward another important concept, developmental peace missions (DPMs). The concept of DPMs is defined as a post-conflict reconstruction intervention that aims to achieve sustainable levels of human security through a combination of interventions aimed at accelerating capacity-building and socioeconomic development, which would ultimately result in the dismantling of war economies and conflict systems, and replacing them with globally competitive peace economies.[8]

According to Gueli, the application of a systems approach to address conflict will enable decision-makers to effectively identify the most important activities and relationships in a manner that is useful for the development of policy to ensure sustainable development and peace on the African continent.[9] Essentially, the concept of DPMs is rooted in the following assumptions: speed and momentum do matter in peace missions; effective peace missions require integrated efforts; security and development are intimately linked (however, the one is not necessarily a precursor for the other); launching development and reconstruction work as soon as possible (even when conflict is continuing) can be a major incentive for peace; the window of opportunity to avert a return to conflict is very narrow; and effective targeting of this "window" or "reconstruction gap" requires that civilian reconstruction experts deploy alongside security forces.[10]

DPMs should therefore be defined not only as peace interventions, but also in effect, as "reconstruction interventions" that aim to achieve sustainable levels of human security through a combination of initiatives by the military and civilian components that are aimed at accelerating capacity-building and socioeconomic development.

Experiences of Achieving Internal Order and Stability in China

Through this short review of the history of the UN peace operations, we can easily see that international peace missions are shifting from putting most of attention and resources into military and political sectors to assisting host country emerging from the internal conflict with social and economic development. Developmental factors are becoming more and more significant features of the agenda of current peace operations. As the result of this trend, the theory of "developmental peace" is gaining adherents among western scholars. It is very interesting that this direction is coinciding with China's experience of maintaining internal order and stability in China. The following part will review and summarize China's experiences so as to understand China's policy toward Africa in peace and security.

The basic premise of understanding China's role in Africa's peace and security affairs from the domestic perspective is that a country's international peace intervention policy is a kind of projection of domestic peace experience onto foreign countries. Based on this assumption, not only can we explain and understand Chinese policy toward Africa in security and peace, but we can also better understand international peace intervention policy led by the West and the differences between China and the West in peace intervention policies. Obviously, according to this perspective plus other interactive factors in the Sino-African relationship, we can also make reasoned analysis and forecasts about recent trends of Chinese policy. This section discusses China's experiences in achieving social stability since the founding of the People's Republic of China, especially since the starting of political and economic reform and opening-up policy. There are at least four distinctive experiences.

The first one is promoting stability through development. In the era of Mao Zedong, although the new China established the independent national economic system, the national economic development suffered from political interference. The politicization of national development, from the "counter-insurgency" campaign *(sufan yundong)* to the anti-rightist movement *(fan you yundong)* initiated at the Mount Lu meeting as well as the decade-long "Cultural Revolution" *(wenhua sa geming)*, had seriously impeded China's national economy development process. Deng Xiaoping initiated the new era of China's reform and opening up, channelled the most of energies of the Communist Party of China (CPC) into promoting the economic development process. Consequently, China began gradually to step onto the track of fast development.

After that, China continued with this political legacy of the Deng Xiaoping era. In the Jiang Zemin era, development was regarded as the key to solve all problems in China, designated as the top priority of the Communist Party. In the Hu Jintao era, he invented the "scientific development" concept, which stressed that the development was still the most important task of China.[11] "The Chinese Dream" proposed by Xi Jinping is actually a rich, strong, and prosperous blueprint, which insists taking economic development as the core task. Therefore, from the founding of new China through the era of reform and opening up and on to the present day, China's experience underscores the fact that development is fundamental to bringing about peace and stability. Since the political reform such as the democratic process and so on made relatively little progress, the development has become the most basic means to maintain and consolidate the regime legitimacy of the Communist Party of China.

The second experience of China in achieving security and stability is subordinating the political democratic reform to national stability. China believes that hasty democratization, particularly radical Western-style democracy, is not suitable for China because it could produce a destructive effect on peace and stability in China. This experience is mainly drawn from the domestic and international experience in the early 1990s. China believes that the reason why it can largely maintain domestic political stability in the post-Cold War era is that it withstood the third democratization wave promoted by the West immediately after the Cold War. The Soviet Union and East European countries, on the other hand, embraced liberalism through "new thinking" and as a consequence their Communist regimes collapsed. Consequently, these countries fell into political turmoil and economic difficulties, which lasted more than 10 years. Based on these experiences, the Chinese government insists that democracy should be a kind of gradual process and avoided radical democratic reforms that are likely to lead China into unpredictable turmoil.

Based on the aforementioned perceptions, China adopted gradual and conservative political reform measures, including inner-party democracy, political decentralization, and the rule of law. Among them, the most important policy measure is absorbing the emerging economic and intellectual elites into government's decision-making system. Some scholars summarized political reform in China as "democracy of governance techniques" (*zhidao mingzhu*).[12] Some scholars summarized China's experiences of political development ever since the Deng Xiaoping era as "administrative arrangement instead of political reform" (*xingzheng xina zhengzhi*) or "administranization of politics," thinking that it is a set of deliberate system arrangement in which the increasing need of new elites is met while necessary consideration is pay to vulnerable groups.[13] So far, at least, China's gradual reform of authoritarian political system has achieved considerable success, having not only consolidated the state power, but also generally maintained peace and stability.

The third important experience is strengthening the power of the state while concurrently weakening social forces. Since the 1980s, the basic line of the Communist Party of China is usually summarized as "one center plus two basic points." Among them, one very important point is to uphold and strengthen the leadership of the Communist Party of China. The Chinese government under the leadership of the CPC controls vast political and economic resources and has strong capacity for action. Meanwhile, the strategy of the Chinese government is to keep social groups under rigid control. Under this kind of control, dependent non-government organizations are permitted to exist and develop, while all independent NGOs are not permitted to grow freely no matter whether they have assumed the tendency of rebellion against the government or whether they have committed the act of rebellion. In this environment, social forces absolutely independent of government do not exist.[14] This ruling strategy cast the state-society relationship in China into a kind of "strong state-weak society" model.

China's fourth experience in maintaining prosperity and stability is to uphold sovereignty and through the process of national development. This point is reflected in China's strong sense of sovereignty and the principle on safeguarding sovereignty and being self-reliant. In the early years of new China, China followed two basic principles, including "constructing a new kitchen" (*ling qi luzhao*) and "clean the room before treat the guest," to establish new diplomatic relations, which were intended to eliminate the legacy of imperialism and establish and develop new diplomatic relations with other countries on the basis of sovereignty principle. In the Mao Zedong era, Chinese diplomacy insisted on maintaining the autonomy and avoiding to be dominated by two external powers, including the United States and the Soviet Union, regardless of the cost of "striking two enemies with two fists" (*liangge quantou daren*). After the reform and opening up, China began to integrate into the international system through the process of modernization while still adhering to national autonomy.[15] In the process of reform and opening, state sovereignty and security are always put in the first place and become one important precondition of all other reform measures.

DEVELOPMENTAL PEACE THESIS AND CHINA'S POLICY: TOWARD AFRICA IN PEACE AND SECURITY

Based on the experiences in maintaining social order and domestic stability in the past 60 years, especially during the past 35 years in implementing the reform and opening policy, China constructed its own perception of domestic peace, which was different from the *liberal peace* thesis. It can be termed *developmental peace* or *peace through development*. As a kind of distinctive idea, the developmental peace thesis believes that social and economic development is the fundamental way to sustainable domestic peace. Meanwhile, it also places emphasis on gradual political and social reform and strengthening of national sovereignty in the process of advancing political and economic development.

China's developmental peace idea is different from the liberal peace thesis based on the Western experiences. Western countries' experiences in attaining internal peace and stability are generally summarized as the liberal model, which includes two central things, democratization plus marketization.[16] In international peace intervention operations, the West usually extends their experiences into those African countries emerging from internal conflict and war. As a consequence, the West's peace intervention policy always emphasizes immediate democratization and institution-building in post-conflict environment. However, directed by the developmental peace idea, China's policy toward Africa in peace and security is very different from the West's policy. It put special emphasis on the effect of autonomy and social economy development on conflict resolutions and post-conflict reconstruction, so it can be characterized as the *sovereignty plus development* model. This kind of policy model has some distinctive features.

First, it highlights African ownership and sovereignty in conflict management and post-conflict reconstructions on the continent. Not only is this point embodied in China's policy discourse in many international multilateral conferences and forums, but it is also reflected in China's practice of participating in peacekeeping and post-conflict reconstruction in Africa. On April 26, 2013, Amb. Li Baodong, then China's permanent representative to the UN, made remarks at a thematic debate of the UN General Assembly entitled "the peaceful resolution of conflicts in Africa" to urge active support for Africa's peace endeavor. He stated that:

> African people understand more deeply the issues existing on their own continent, African parties involved in local conflict are inclined to accept mediation and peace proposal conducted by the mediators from their own continent. The international community should have faith in the wisdom and experience of the African people, fully listen to their voices, respect Africa's will and comprehensively and actively support Africa's endeavor to resolve the African problems in the African way.[17]

In its actual participation in peacekeeping in Africa, China insists on sovereignty and nonintervention principle. However, this seemingly conservative position does not mean that China never engages with African countries or other actors in internal peace and conflict issues in Africa. On the contrary, China often participates in peace operations on the continent including peacekeeping and peace-building led by the African Union or the United Nations.

Furthermore, with the expanding interests in recent years, it is playing a larger role in African conflict management.[18] Admittedly, while taking part in peace operations in Africa, China pursues multiliteralism principle, which is reflected in the attitude of respecting AU's position. Sometimes, China also pursues bilateral approaches to exert influence on some African countries' domestic politics. China's role in Darfur's conflict resolution in the early 10 years of the new century is a case to the point. Either in the former situation or the latter, China always holds a consistent attitude of mutual equality and respect toward African countries or regional organizations.

Secondly, China highlights the concept of *peace through development*, while holding onto a prudent position on institution-building and hasty democratic elections in post-conflict countries in Africa. China's developmental peace thesis insists that social economic development is the most important precondition of sustainable internal peace, so it prefers helping African countries with national development rather than hasty democratization so as to build the basis of long and stable peace. The distinctiveness of the "peace through development" strategy is not only embodied in the fact that China places development cooperation at the heart of its strategy toward Africa, but it is also reflected in the fact that it focuses most of its resources on basic areas in the activities of peace-keeping and peace-building in Africa, which is termed the infrastructure-constructing model. This model invests most of political and economic resource in building roads, bridges, and hospitals while channeling few resources to superstructure area such as institution-building, urging hurried democratic election, etc.[19]

Thirdly, as far as conflict resolution approach is concerned, China insists on maintaining national unity and territorial integrity, highlights equal negotiation to resolve conflict peacefully, and opposes the use of coercive means and making prescription from outside to settle dispute and build peace in conflict-afflicted African countries. On the contrary, Western countries, dominated by the liberal peace thesis are inclined to use coercive and divisive means to contain violence and make peace. Those differences are reflected in many cases, including Eritrea issue, Kosovo issue, and South Sudan issue, as well as the recent policy toward the Democratic Republic of Congo.

Fourthly, China places emphasis on cooperation with host governments of African countries and the African Union while relatively neglecting interactions with civil society organizations. This point is a kind of projection onto Africa of China's traditional thinking model based on the reality of "strong state-weak society" in China. By doing so, China expects that this kind of cooperation between the Chinese government and African authority agents to bring peace to the continent. However, notably, the state-society relations in most of African countries are very different from the one in China. "Strong society–weak state" model features in most African countries. Many societal organizations, including nongovernmental organizations, trade unions, tribe groups, even antigovernment forces, are important actors as the government in shaping peace or conflict in relevant African countries. Therefore, China's government-to-government cooperation model is not well suited to the local environment in African countries.[20]

DEVELOPMENTAL PEACE AND FUTURE OF CHINA'S SECURITY POLICY TOWARD AFRICA

Obviously, there is a big difference between China's security policy toward Africa under the guidance of the developmental peace concept and the West's peace intervention policy in Africa under the guidance of the liberal peace concept. Currently, the liberal peace thesis based on Western countries' experience largely dominates international peace intervention practices, including preventive diplomacy, peacekeeping, and peace-building in Africa. Despite the dominative influence of the Western liberal peace thesis, China's increasing involvement in African peace and security affairs is beginning to have an impact. Some scholars even suggest that China is starting to construct a new paradigm for international peace intervention practices in Africa.[21] In fact, the two peace intervention paradigms have already begun to interact and exerted influence on each other.

More importantly, because of poor performance of international peace-building dominated by the liberal peace thesis in Africa, the international community and Africa begin to emphasize the autonomy of the continent, African indigenous tradition, and necessity of conflict management. The trend of China's policy toward Africa in peace and security in future is an important issue to be considered against the background of multiple interactions between the internal factor of the continent and the external factor, between the West and China. The West expects China to be more deeply involved in African conflict management, including conflict media-tion, peacekeeping, and peace-building, to play a greater role in African peace and security affairs on the premise of accepting Western norms.

Africa appreciates China's security policy for its respecting African autonomy and ownership in conflict resolution operations; meanwhile, they also hope China to participate more deeply in the internal affairs of African continent and provide more constructive assistance to promote peace, development, and good governance in Africa. Under the pressure of two kinds of expectation, what is the likeliest trend of China's peace and security policy toward Africa?

This chapter argues that the trend of greater engagement on the part of China's policy toward peace and security in Africa is primarily shaped by China's developmental peace concept, China's expanding and deepening interests in Africa, and the complicated interaction between the three sides, including the West, Africa, and China. First, in order to protect its expanding interests in Africa, China will become more involved in African continent in peace and security affairs. In addition, to participation in peacekeeping operations in Africa, China will become more frequently and more extensively engaged in conflict mediation, conflict resolution, and post-conflict reconstruction, for currently African countries' internal conflict, coups, or civil war has tied tightly up with Chinese economic security and personnel security. Just as Chen Jian, the former Chinese Ambassador to the UN, said, "In the past, unrest, civil war, military coups and so on, which took place far in the other side of the earth, have no direct association with Chinese interest, China can hold a detached attitude towards them. However, from now on, the situation has changed greatly".[22]

In the end of 2008, China actively pushed the Democratic Republic of Congo and Rwanda to resolve the conflict in eastern Democratic Republic of the Congo.[23] Two Chinese Special Representatives for African Affairs, Liu Guijin and Zhong Jianhua, respectively, conducted fruitful mediation in the former Darfur issue and current two Sudanese relations issue. Those actions reflect the fact that China has begun to play an active and constructive role in African conflict prevention and mediation. China's successful experience in those areas will encourage China to continue to play a more constructive role in African conflict prevention and mediation by the means of special envoy diplomacy or others alike. In the area of peace-building, China will expand the scope of participation, go beyond the previous "road construction, hospital and bridge building" mode, and participate in more extensive activities such as peace and security professionals training, youth profession training, helping repatriate combatants, providing opportunities of employment, etc. For China, these activities are feasible and within China's capabilities and resources. Moreover, these social works are in the domain of low politics so they will not risk breaking the principle of nonintervention to sovereignty of African countries. It should be noted that some Western scholars argue that China holds a completely detached attitude toward military coups and conflict in Africa, regards military coup as a normal phenomenon of African politics and try to accept and adapt to it rather than strive to create African political stability.[24] This opinion, if not completely wrong, is at least partly wrong. In fact, China has begun to reflect upon how to cope with African countries' internal political instability into consideration in recent years. The China's efforts to promote peace between two Sudan and internal peace in South Sudan from 2011 to now are the case in point.

As far as the peace concept is concerned, China's policy toward African peace and security affairs will still be subject to the developmental peace concept. On the contrary, since peacekeeping and peace-building operations on the African continent, which remain dominated by Western liberal peace concepts, have made only a limited contribution to conflict resolution in Africa, China will not simply and blindly engage in those kinds of international peace operations, which prioritize the liberal project, but continue to focus on the role of economic and social development projects in the peacekeeping and peace-building industry.

China will continue holding a cautious attitude to institution-building, legality construction, and democratic elections in emerging post-conflict countries. In other words, China will not abandon the philosophy of its own characteristics just to accept the Western concept of liberal peace. It means that the principle of nonintervention will be retained in China's policy toward Africa, meanwhile China's attitude toward African peace and security affairs will be more positive; its policy will be more flexible, assuming initiative, creativity, and constructiveness.[25] For instance, in the year of 2012, the Chinese government cooperated with Angolan police to jointly crack down on Chinese criminal gangs in Angola, which created a new mode of cooperation in domestic security affairs. However, it is nearly unimaginable that China would set up military bases in Africa or conduct unilateral military interference with African countries.

From the perspective of the interaction between China, Africa, and the West, China will be more respectful of African ownership and indigenous culture of conflict management, rather than simply accepting or rejecting the liberal peace concept of Western countries and international institutions. In this respect, China seems to be like a materialist or realist, the West seems to be like arrogant idealist, while Africa is more like a pragmatist. The future of peace in Africa will be a result of interaction of all the varieties of external forces. In the light of the strength of the Western hegemony, while it is difficult for China to replace the liberal peace concept with the developmental peace concept as a core framework for managing African conflict, at the same time, the need for better integration of development into African conflict management will only increase in the coming years.

Notes

1. Saferworld, *China's Growing Role in African Peace and Security*, Saferworld Report, London, November 2011; Saferworld, *Tackling Insecurity in the Horn of Africa: China's Role*, Saferworld Seminar Report, London, January 2012; Ivan Campbell et. al. (2012), *China and Conflict-Affected States: Between Principle and Pragmatism*, Saferworld Report, London, January 2012; 'Roundtable: China's Role in International Conflict Management: Sudan and South Sudan,' *Global Review*, Winter 2012; Daniel Large (2012), 'Between the CPA and Southern Independence: China's Post-Conflict Engagement in Sudan', *SAIIA Occasional Paper*, No. 115; Jonathan Holslag (2011), 'China and the Coups: Coping with Political Instability in Africa,' *African Affairs*, 110:440, pp. 367–386; Chris Alden and Dan Large (2013), 'China's Evolving Policy Towards Peace and Security in Africa: Constructing a New Paradigm for Peace Building?' in Mulugeta Gebrehiwot Berhe and Liu Hongwu eds., *China-Africa Relations: Governance, Peace and Security* (Addis Ababa: Institute for Peace and Security Studies); Wang Xuejun (2012), 'Review on China's Engagement in African Peace and Security,' *China International Studies*, 32, January/February 2012; Chris Alden, Zhang Chun, Bernardo Mariani, Daniel Large (2011), 'China's Growing Role in African Post-Conflict Reconstruction,' *Global Review*, 6.
2. Holslag, 'China and the Coups,' pp. 367–386.
3. Alden and Large, 'China's Evolving Policy Towards Peace and Security in Africa'.
4. R. Gueli and S. Liebenberg (2008), *Developmental Peace Missions: Synergising Peacekeeping and Peace-Building in Transition Periods* (Pretoria: CSIR), p. 15.
5. Laetitia Olivier (2008), *Pursuing Human Security in Africa Through Developmental Peace Missions: Ambitious Construct or Feasible Ideal?* Master Thesis, Stellenbosch University, p. 46.

6. UN Security Council, Report of the Panel on United Nations Peace Operations, 21 August 2000, http://www.un.org/en/ga/search/view_doc.asp?symbol=A/55/305

7. Olivier, *Pursuing Human Security in Africa Through Developmental Peace Missions*, p. 56.

8. N. Madlala-Routledge and S. Liebenberg (2004), 'Developmental Peacekeeping: What are the Advantages for Africa?', *African Security Review*, 13:2, p. 128.

9. R. Gueli, S. Liebenberg, and E. Van Huyssteen (2006), *Developmental Peace Missions: Policy Guidelines and Background Reports, CSIR Report*, p. 21.

10. Ibid., p. 22.

11. See CPC National Congress reports from 12th to 18th Congress.

12. Ren Jiantao (2008), 'Strategical Alternatives of Mode of Chinese Democratization,' *Academia Bimesteris*, 2.

13. Kang Xiaoguang (2002), 'Administrative Arrangement Instead of Political Reform Review: On Political Development and Political Stability in Mainland China in 1990s,' *Twenty-First Century*, 5, August 2002.

14. Ibid.

15. Yang Xuedong (2006), 'National Independence and China's Development Path,' *Social Science*, 3.

16. Roland Paris (2004), *At War's End: Building Peace After Civil Conflict* (Cambridge: Cambridge University Press).

17. 'Declaration Reaffirms Importance of UN-African Union Partnership, Capping Two-day Event amid Calls for Africans to Take Charge of Peace Efforts,' 67 General Assembly, Plenary and Thematic Debate, 74th Meeting, GA/11366, April 26, 2013.

18. International Crisis Group (2009), 'Growing Roles of China in UN Peacekeeping,' *Asia Report*, No. 166, April 2009; Saferworld, *China's Increasing Role in Peace and Security in Africa*.

19. Li Dongyan (2012), 'China's Approach and Prospect of Participation in UN Peacekeeping and Peacebuilding,' *Foreign Affairs Review*, 3.

20. Wang Xuejun, 'Review on China's Engagement in African Peace and Security'.

21. Alden and Large, 'China's Evolving Policy Towards Peace and Security in Africa'; Sara van Hoeymissen (2011), 'China, Sovereignty and the Protection of Civilians in Armed Conflict in Africa: The Emergence of a "Third Paradigm" of International Intervention?', in Jing Men and Benjamin Barton, eds., *China and the European Union in Africa: Partner or Competitor?* (Burlington: Ashgate Publishing Ltd.).

22. Chen Jian (2010), 'China's Multilateral Diplomacy Facing New Tasks,' *Jiefang Daily*, October 25.

23. Saferworld, 'China's Growing Role in African Peace and Security'.
24. Jonathan Holslag (2011), 'China and the Coups: Coping with Political Instability in Africa,' *African Affairs*, 110:440, pp. 367–386.
25. See Wang Yizhou (2011), *Creative Involvement: A New Direction in China's Diplomacy* (Beijing: Beijing University Press); Lu Shaye (2013), 'Some Thoughts on China-Africa New Type of Strategic Partnership,' *New Strategy Studies*, 1.

Wang Xuejun has a PhD in international relations, and is an associate researcher in the Institute of African Studies of Zhejiang Normal University. His research areas include African peace and security issues, China's relations with Africa, and the West powers' security strategy toward Africa.

CHAPTER 5

China's Development-Oriented Peacekeeping Strategy in Africa

Xue Lei

INTRODUCTION

China's growing involvement in African affairs is increasingly seen to be a key development in international relations. At the start of its increasing trade and investment since the new millennium, China predominantly acted as an equal trading partner, a source of foreign direct investment (FDI), and new aid-donor for African countries. As this relationship has continued to grow amid the rising prominence of African peace and security issues in global affairs, China finds itself increasingly entangled in security challenges and affected by instability in Africa. The coupling of Darfur crisis and 2008 Beijing Olympic Games by some NGOs from developed countries around 2006 and 2007 made it difficult for Beijing to ignore the critics. This has also coincided with China's rethinking of its national interests and foreign policy goals, with the protection of overseas interests now an integral part of China's overall security and development goals. The protection of Chinese overseas interests includes various policy concerns, such as the protection of Chinese citizens abroad, securing stable energy supplying sources, and ensuring the safety of maritime transportation lanes. Meanwhile, China's rising status as a global power

X. Lei (✉)
Center for Maritime and Polar Studies, Shanghai Institutes for International Studies, Shanghai, China
e-mail: frankxuelei@hotmail.com; xuelei@siis.org.cn

C. Alden et al. (eds.), *China and Africa*,
DOI 10.1007/978-3-319-52893-9_5

has redefined the country's approach to dealing with global security issues and other countries' internal conflicts.

To fulfill its promise as a responsible major power,[1] China is aware that it needs to take more of a proactive role in conflict prevention and resolution throughout the world. China has tried in its own way to engage and influence the stances of various African governments. During this process, China's physical involvement is mainly manifested in its participation in UN peace-keeping operations, which it regards as a suitable method considering its role as a permanent member of the UN Security Council as well as an approach causing least harm to its reputation and the principles of respect for sovereignty and noninterference long held in China. As such, it is important to consider both China's goals in African peace and security affairs and the particular perspective of Chinese participation in UNPKOs. In this regard, China's growing role has demonstrated an evident policy-learning process, with it gradually adapting its behaviors in response to pressure and feedback both at home and abroad.

China's Security Strategy in Africa: Pursuit of Balanced Goals

China's growing engagement in African peace and security affairs has generally displayed a preference for incrementalism and pragmatism, with a focus on encouraging stability and a gradual change of the status quo. Moreover, China's agenda in Africa is arguably characterized by a development-oriented approach. China views its main task as promoting development in Africa and maintaining positive trade and investment relations with African countries, with its security agenda deeply embedded within such an economic and social perspective.

Historically speaking, China had not left a giant footprint in Africa comparable to that of European colonialism or the two superpowers in Cold War era. So there are no strong geopolitical considerations underpinning China's involvement in African peace and security affairs. Most of the focus has been put on addressing nontraditional security threats, such as internal fragility and violent extremism. Such a security agenda has been implemented using noncoercive characteristics and predominantly through two major activities: political and diplomatic involvement in conflict prevention and resolution and participation in UN peacekeeping operations in Africa. China's role manifests itself particularly on multilateral platforms, with a focus on political and diplomatic measures and stressing the involvement and consent of all relevant parties. That said, China has been striving to maintain certain balance between various policy goals while becoming involved into African peace and security affairs, which has vividly demonstrated China's policy concern on sustaining its basic principles for foreign diplomacy and at the same time making appropriate adjustments to better address the real and complex security threats and challenges.

Noninterference and Persuasive Diplomacy

The noninterference principle has long been one of the fundamental values underpinning China's engagement and cooperation with the outside world, particularly Africa. In China's view, today's world is still mainly dominated by sovereign states, with sovereignty being the essential element in state-hood. The right to independence inherent to state sovereignty forms the basis of the noninterference principle. In China's understanding, the essence of such a principle lies in the respect for various approaches and roads adopted by countries around the world in advancing their domestic political, economic, and social development. It has been the guiding principle for China's involvement in African affairs. However, with global affairs becoming increasingly interconnected and the nature of conflicts undergoing great change,[2] the traditional noninterference principle based on absolutist doctrine has become outdated.

There needs to be fresh understanding and interpretation of noninterference and international intervention. In recent years, China has gradually adapted to the new reality and stepped away from a rigid position concerning intervention measures to a qualified consent in some cases. China has noticed and welcomed the increasing role of the UN in preventive diplomacy, including the Council's informal interaction with parties concerned and the mediation efforts made by UN Secretary-General or his special envoys. In comparison, persuasive diplomacy may be a better term deriving from preventive diplomacy in highlighting China's stress on behind-the-scenes consultation and voluntary compliance, with China's diplomatic work on Darfur region and relations between the two Sudans being cases in point.[3]

At the same time, when the issue of authorization from an international authority arises, China views the UN Security Council to be in a better position to assume the role as a legitimate international intervener based on the power conferred by the UN Charter. The primary elements considered include the protection of civilians in armed conflicts, the seriousness of humanitarian crises, spillover effect of civil conflicts, and the treaty or other legal obligations undertaken by relevant countries. There is also the need to fully consult and consider the positions of relevant regional organizations. Under many circumstances, regional organizations usually take proactive pioneering role in addressing related crises. China attaches more importance to the role of UN in enhancing capacity-building and institution-building for various regional organizations, in line with the perception that any measures of prevention should be first attempted at regional or subregional level.

In Africa, China's regional approach mainly rests on its cooperation with the African Union (AU), and Beijing usually respects and endorses the policies and stances of the AU. For instance, the AU has in several cases denied the recognition of African governments coming into power by means of military coup, while China usually holds the view that it won't question the legality or constitutionality of means used by foreign governments in grabbing power. Yet, in those cases, under the AU policy of nonrecognition, China will always show due respect to the collective will of AU member states. Thus, China's adherence to the noninterference principle has been based on a regional approach in Africa, which may be better suited for striking a balance between upholding of principles and the necessity for intervention.

Security and Development

Currently the discussion over governance and nation-building in relation to development has become increasingly linked to security. The World Bank's *2011 World Development Report* provides a systematic exploration on the close connection between maintaining security and pursuing development goals. Some statistics have shown that a civil conflict costs the average developing countries 15–30 years of GDP growth.[4] According to the *Peacebuilding and Statebuilding Goals* adopted by member countries of the G7+ Group of Fragile or Conflict-affected Countries, the rebuilding process for postconflict fragile states and those facing rising domestic tensions covers almost every aspect of governmental responsibility, including legitimate politics, security, justice, economic foundations, and revenues & services.[5] In this way, the development issue has become more politicized and securitized, with success hinging greatly on the smoothness peace processes. However, the "nexus" between development and security is anything but static or one-dimensional. There is consequently confusion and contestation over which values and actions should be pursued in their name.[6]

Jan Eliasson, former UN Special Envoy to Darfur (2006–2008), once referred to the Darfur case to exemplify such a connection: "in the Darfur mission, we were frustrated at the lack of recovery programs alongside humanitarian efforts. A water well, a school, a health clinic in a village could have demonstrated to the population and rebel leaders that peace was a better option than war. This could have increased the chances of bringing all factions to the negotiating table".[7]

In practice, China argues that peacekeeping operations should be implemented in such a way that is conducive to dealing with the root causes of conflicts and forging a solid base for subsequent large-scale rebuilding work.

Until recent years, China has mainly dispatched noncombating troops to join peacekeeping forces, with engineering corps and medical teams constituting the major components of Chinese peacekeepers. This demonstrates China's longstanding position that there needs to be a comprehensive approach in dealing with situations in conflict-affected societies. For China, the priority issue is to promote sustainable development so as to eliminate the vicious cycle of conflicts.

There are some new developments in relation to troop categories since 2013, with an infantry unit deployed in Mali and an infantry battalion in South Sudan. It signals China's new commitment to UN peace operations and the prospect of deeper involvement.

Peace and Justice

The pursuit for peace and justice has been eternal work of human kind. It is usually argued that there will never be permanent peace without justice. This view certainly manifests the truth in many cases. However, while postconflict societies remain in a condition of fragile peace, an overemphasis on realizing justice may undermine unstable peace processes. There is therefore perhaps a need for a subtle balance between the two policy goals while they are in conflict with each other. In recent years, China has paid great heed to the importance of overcoming impunity and promoting accountability in the cases of atrocity crimes. China supports the efforts of relevant countries in building national capacities and exercising jurisdiction in the case of grave international crimes.[8]

However, China takes a more cautious or even suspicious view of the jurisdiction of the International Criminal Court (ICC), since an independent international judicial body may override state sovereignty and ignore national administrative and judicial processes. China has consistently taken the view that the ICC should strictly observe the principle of complementarity as stipulated by the *Rome Statute*. China believes that international criminal justice cannot be pursued at the expense of the peace process, nor should it impede processes of national reconciliation. Due to concerns over the ICC's hearings on cases involving Kenyan leaders, the Extraordinary Session of the Assembly of the AU adopted a resolution on relations between African countries and the ICC on 12 October 2013. The decision requires that "no charges shall be commenced or continued before any international court or tribunal against any serving AU Head of State or Government or anybody acting or entitled to act in such capacity during their term of office".[9] Based on this decision, the AU presented a draft resolution to the Council for a deferral of the ICC cases against Kenya's President and Vice President.

China shares this concern and supported the motion of the African countries, recognizing that Kenya is currently in a critical situation in the fight against terrorism in East Africa, and that due respect needs to be paid to the dignity of democratically elected Kenyan leaders. The subsequent failure of the Council to pass a deferral resolution has compromised its power to oversee threats to international peace and security. The essence of the principle of the complementarity of the ICC in relation to national processes resides precisely in the idea that, in a society haunted by the memories of civil conflicts and mass atrocities, judicial processes should always be accompanied by processes of national reconciliation, where the latter can only be achieved not internationally but locally.

DEVELOPMENT OF UN MULTIDIMENSIONAL PEACEKEEPING OPERATIONS

Efforts by the UN in Enhancing Effectiveness of Peacekeeping Operations

In recent years, with the demands for deployment of UN peacekeeping missions arising from various places of the world, there has been increasing concern that the capabilities of the UNPKO are overstretched. Meanwhile, the increasingly complex nature of security challenges met by peacekeeping forces also presents a difficult job for personnel working in the field. In order to adapt to the new demands and challenges, the UN has advocated for a multidimensional peacekeeping mission with integrated strategies. The key theme of this approach is an emphasis on a coordinated strategy that includes various stakeholders and the need for comprehensive planning on issues of maintaining peace and advancing recovery and reconstruction.

In 2009, the Security Council identified several areas where further reflection is required to improve the preparation, planning, monitoring and evaluation, and completion of peacekeeping operations: (1) ensuring that mandates for peacekeeping operations are clear, credible, and achievable and are matched by appropriate resources; (2) better information sharing, particularly on military operational challenges; (3) increasing its interaction with the Secretariat in the early phase of mandate drafting and throughout mission deployment; (4) earlier and more meaningful engagement with troop and police contributing countries before the renewal or modification of the mandate of a peacekeeping operation; (5) greater awareness in the Security Council of the resource and field support implications of its decisions; (6) enhanced awareness in the Security Council of the strategic challenges faced across peacekeeping operations.[10] From China's perspective, a better formulated peacekeeping strategy also requires enhanced cooperation between the Council's various mechanisms, such as the Working Group on Peacekeeping Operations and troop-contributing countries (TCCs), with more attention given to communication between TCCs and the Secretariat.[11]

Some specific efforts have been made to address practical problems existing in past peacekeeping operations. First, under the guidance of integrated missions, the leadership structure in the field was further strengthened to make the multidimensional peacekeeping and peacebuilding missions better coordinated. It has been clearly defined that the Special Representative of the Secretary-General (SRSG) has overall authority over the activities of the UN in the field. The SRSG is aided by two Deputy SRSG (DSRSG) with one of them being the Residential Coordinator/Humanitarian Coordinator (RC/HC). This arrangement has enhanced the SRSG's capacity to influence all UN activities in their territory and ensure come degree of coherence.[12]

Second, in order to address the shortage of critical peacekeeping equipment and ensure rapid deployment of peacekeeping troops at the start-up period, some measures on storage of certain strategic reserves have been adopted. The Strategic Deployment Stock (SDS) established under General Assembly resolution 56/292 of 27 June 2002 has been one of the critical policies in addressing challenges to rapid deployment. The major goals pursued by the SDS were laid down by the "Brahimi Report", which demanded the deployment of a traditional mission within 30 days and a complex peacekeeping operation within 90 days. In the Secretary-General's report, it mentioned that "material readiness, including SDS, systems contracts, services contracts and inter-Mission transfers, has proved to be one of the key elements for developing such a rapid and effective deployment capability".[13] Since the establishment of SDS, US $165 million worth of equipment has been issued to various missions.[14]

Parallel with the focus on material readiness and reserve of critical equipment, the UN is now trying to introduce new technology in peace-keeping missions. The recent experimental deployment of Unmanned Aerial Vehicles (UAV) in the Democratic Republic of Congo has aroused great interest. It can save large amount of resources and also promote greatly the efficiency of peacekeeping missions in patrolling and surveillance. Yet there are still some political and military issues, such as its legal implications and operational management to be clarified before introducing into other missions.[15]

Third, due to the concern over long-term existence of some peace-keeping missions, the demand for a clear and coherent transition and exit strategy for peacekeeping operations has gained great momentum. Given the role of the Security Council in authorizing peace missions, the first consideration for exit strategies naturally rests with clearly defined mandates from the Council. This can both define clear scope of maneuver for peacekeeping missions and help the Council schedule a clear timetable for the exit of peacekeeping missions as well as transition to peacebuilding process. It also heavily depends on the national defense capacity of the host states, which requires the expeditious process of security sector reform as well as capacity-building and training programs for the military and police personnel in the relevant states.

Fourth, considering that African countries have been the major theaters of peacekeeping missions, there has also been discussion on the predictability, sustainability, and flexibility of financing for UN-mandated peace operations undertaken by the AU. One relevant panel report included several key recommendations: UN and AU to take concrete steps to strengthen their mutual relationship and develop a more effective partnership when addressing issues on the joint agenda; establish a voluntary-based multidonor trust fund to focus on comprehensive capacity-building for conflict prevention and resolution and institution building.[16]

Challenges to Current UNPKOs

In the view of Professor Adebayo, there are three key factors in influencing the successfulness of UN peacekeeping missions in Africa: "(1) the interests of key permanent members and their willingness to mobilize diplomatic and financial support for peace processes; (2) the willingness of belligerent parties to cooperate with the UN to implement peace accords or, in cases where such cooperation is not forthcoming, the development of an effective strategy to deal with potential 'spoilers'; (3) the cooperation of regional players in peace processes, as well as their provision of diplomatic and/or military support to UN peacekeeping efforts."[17] Despite the efforts made by the UN to promote the effectiveness, efficiency, and responsiveness of peacekeeping missions, some major challenges still remain and sometimes even become more prominent.

First, just as the above-mentioned elements have shown, the political willingness of major powers has always been crucial to the impact of peacekeeping missions. For instance, in recent cases, the France's increasingly robust role in African countries such as Mali and Central African Republic has proved to be vital for the deployment of peacekeeping troops and maintenance of order in the said countries. However, one obvious feature for the involvement of France is that the relevant countries have mainly been former French colonies, that is, the issue of political will of the major powers in playing a robust role still remains.

Second, the complexity of engagement with nonstate armed groups remain a challenge. Generally speaking, nonstate armed groups are defined as distinctive organizations that are willing and able to use violence for pursuing their objectives; not integrated into formalized state institutions; and possess a certain degree of autonomy with regard to politics, military operations, resources, and infrastructure.[18] Recent cases have demonstrated the increasing influence and damage caused by some non-traditional actors, including terrorists' organizations and organized criminal groups, such as Al-Shabaab in Somali, Boko Haram in Nigeria, and the Da'esh in Iraq and Syria. In contrast with the armed factions with a political goal in forming governments, these new actors are more unruly and even against any governance regime, and therefore commonly become spoilers in peace process. The challenge for peacekeeping missions is whether the current strategy is applicable to these new nonstate actors and also whether military strategy requires a more prominent role of law enforcement units in dealing with nonstate actors.

Third, due to the concern over lack of governance in certain conflict-ridden regions, one of the goals that the UN is pursuing is the extension of state authority. This means that the UN may provide assistance to the incumbent governments to extend the reach of their governance and authority so as to promote peace and order in the relevant countries. The intervention brigade deployed in the Democratic Republic of Congo in 2013 has been just such a case as it joined forces with government troops to neutralize the armed groups in eastern Congo. There are two problems related to such a new development. One is concerned with the impartial role of the UN and peacekeeping troops, and the other relates to the origins of instability and tensions inside such countries as sometimes the government actors may be a spoiler of peace processes or may also perpetrate of serious crimes against civilians. As such, there remains a need to improve such a policy stance so that it can more effectively help consolidate peace. The point lies in striking a delicate balance between stability and justice. The strengthening of state authority should always be coupled with an inclusive national dialogue and reconciliation process.

CHINESE INVOLVEMENT IN PEACEKEEPING MISSIONS IN AFRICA

An Overview of Chinese Participation in UN Peacekeeping Operations

In the past three decades, China has shown a great change in attitude toward UN peacekeeping operations. At the beginning, China viewed peacekeeping as another instrument used by hegemonic powers to legitimize and support their actions of expanding sphere of influence and interfering into domestic affairs of many small and medium-sized countries.[19] To some extent, this view had succinctly reflected the fierce competition for dominance and control between the two superpowers. Since the end of Cold War, China gradually recognized the contribution of peacekeeping toward the maintenance of global peace and stability. The

Hammarskjold Principles of consent-based neutrality and nonuse of force except for self-defense also fitted well with China's adherence to the noninterference principle. Since the late 1990s, China has taken an increasingly prominent role in UNPKOs by dispatching more military and civilian personnel to join various operations.[20] China also joined the UN peacekeeping standby mechanism in 1997. As Gill and Huang have observed, Chinese peacekeepers are consistently rated among the most professional, well-trained, effective, and disciplined contingents in UN peacekeeping operations.[21]

In practice, China always argues that peacekeeping operations should be conducted in a way conducive to dealing with the root causes of conflicts and forging solid base for a subsequent large-scale rebuilding work. Based on such consideration, Chinese peacekeepers have been mainly composed of engineering and medical units. The work of Chinese peacekeepers has made great contribution to early recovery of conflict-affected local community and laid solid foundation for subsequent comprehensive rebuilding process. At the same time, China is a major contributing coutnry to the policing component of peacekeeping operations. The riot police or civilian police dispatched constitute an indispensable part of the process of restoration of justice and order in the local community. The engagement of Chinese police staff with local police staff is also much helpful to capacity building in local police institution and personnel.

In its recent mission to Liberia, China dispatched the first Formed Police Unit (FPU) to African countries. In an interview with journalists, one official from the peacekeeping office of Ministry of Defense stated continued efforts to improve the performance of Chinese peacekeeping troops, which include: (1) continuing with the deployment of peacekeeping troops in Congo, Liberia, Lebanon, Sudan Darfur, South Sudan, and Mali through selection of high-quality soldiers for troop rotations; (2) enhancing training program for peacekeepers by further improving the existing three-tiered training system combined with primary-, medium-, and advanced-level training; (3) strengthening the capabilities of peacekeepers in compliance with guidelines, professional skills, communicating skills, contingency resolution, and self-protection; and (4) securing the logistical support for peacekeepers through the formation of a comprehensive support system.[22]

China's deeper involvement in UN peacekeeping operations will inevitably lead to comprehensive change in the UN conflict management system.

Indeed, the power configuration in decision-making and implementation processes of UN peacekeeping operations may experience great transformation over the coming years. With the involvement of Western countries in UN-led peacekeeping operations having become greatly weakened since the mid-1990s,[23] especially in the African continent which has long been one of the focal areas of UN peacekeeping operations, the need for emerging powers to increase their involvement has become more urgent for the effectiveness of peacekeeping operations.

The immediate consequence of this strategic shift of Western countries' policies is the aggravated problems of shortage of military personnel, resources, and equipment, in particular the shortage of some critical equipment, such as the transport helicopters, which has become a significant bottleneck restraining the implementation of peacekeeping operations. Against this backdrop, the growing involvement of emerging countries, including China, Brazil, South Africa, Nigeria, and Ethiopia, will be conducive to the mitigation of constraints the UN now faces. The growing contribution to UN peacekeeping operations by emerging countries will is also likely to prompt shifts in the power configuration of the international conflict management system.

China's Adherence to Basic Principles of UNPKO

With the rising complexity of both the international and domestic environment for peacekeeping operations, differences surrounding the UN's guiding peacekeeping principles also loom large. These principles of "consent-based, impartiality, non-use of force except for self-defense or enforcing mandates" have been the guiding principles and remain the corner stone of UN PKOs; however, Western countries have endeavored to expand the scope of conflict situations applicable for peacekeeping operations, with the intention of including confrontational conflict situation into the scope of peacekeeping operations so as to expand the power of peacekeeping forces in terms of using force. Meanwhile, emerging powers insist that peacekeeping operations should maintain a neutral stance to prevent escalation in interstate or intrastate conflicts. With the growing influence by China and other emerging powers in decision-making processes regarding peacekeeping operations, it is hoped that confusion regarding the norms and principles underpinning UN peacekeeping may be clarified or corrected.

Many TCCs have shown great concern over the potential impacts of expansionary mandate on their peacekeeping troops in the field. In practice, this may lead to confusion of guidelines for fieldwork. It may also pose potential threat or danger to peacekeepers that previously stand in a neutral or impartial position and are not a party to the civil conflicts. The *Status of Force Agreement* between the UN and Host States also made it clear that the peacekeepers should not be put under the jurisdiction of host states. However, with peacekeeping troops becoming directly involved in complex civil conflicts, their immunity from local jurisdiction may come into question.

In resonance with the views of other emerging powers, China has been arguing for a principle-driven approach to peacekeeping operations. The current expansive mandate for peacekeepers will likely cause great damage to the impartiality of peacekeeping missions, which has long been the unique advantage of peacekeeping operations. By maintaining the principle of impartiality, peacekeeping missions can establish conditions for further political and diplomatic measures to consolidate the peace process. In this vein, China also urges the Council to further clarify and make practical mandates for peacekeeping missions.[24]

China's Adaptation to Complex Security Challenges

While bearing in mind the basic principles of PKOs, China also has clear knowledge of the complex and fragile situation many peacekeeping missions have been encountering in the field. Current situations in many fragile postconflict societies have even been further aggravated by the involvement of more terrorist organizations and other organized-crime groups. Such a varied background demands more flexibility in designing the mandates of peacekeeping missions. With all the complexity and difficulties in mind, China now tries to experiment with a more pragmatic approach in accommodating stances and concerns of various stakeholders.

The Council's decisions in sending an "intervention brigade" to the Democratic Republic of Congo (DRC)[25] and establishing UN Multidimensional Integrated Stabilization Mission in Mali (MINUSMA)[26] have revealed a cautious and pragmatic approach on the Chinese side, as the country's decisions to support the two resolutions was based on a thorough consideration of political processes and specific situations in the two country-cases.

In the case of the DRC, China's decisions was made against the backdrop of the *Peace, Security and Cooperation Framework for the Democratic Republic of Congo and the region*, which had the approval and commitment of 11 stake-holding countries to work together to break the recurring cycle of violence. Indeed, the consent of legitimate governments in the two countries largely informed China's position. The use of robust force also falls well within the scope of being by invitation from legitimate governments in host countries under international law. Traditionally, it has been a usual practice of China to align more with stances of the incumbent governments in various conflict-ridden countries, and this shift therefore reveals China's growing preference for maintaining stability and continuity in respective countries or regions. That said, it should be noted that the DRC intervention brigade has been regarded as an exceptional case, which has no precedential effect.

In the case of Mali, China's peacekeepers included a subunit of garrison troops composed of 170 soldiers who are responsible for safeguarding the safety of MINUSMA headquarters and camps, marking the first time for China to deploy "combat" troops to peacekeeping operations.[27] China's Ministry of Defense spokesman made it clear that China doesn't recognize the existence of "combat" troops in UNPKOs since these peacekeeping missions, with their purposes for maintaining peace, are not a party to the civil conflicts.[28] Such a clarification in fact signals that China has overcome the conceptual difficulty in deploying troops to perform any function in peace-keeping missions, which may further enhance China's participation in UNPKOs. As the Ministry of Defense spokesman stated, the new type of Chinese personnel in the Mali mission "expands the composition of Chinese formed peacekeeping troops... and also promotes Chinese army's participation in UNPKOs to a new level".[29]

CONCLUSION

China has become an increasingly important actor in African security affairs. China's focus on a development-oriented approach, persuasive diplomacy, and noncoercive means may demonstrate an alternative to the robust approach of humanitarian intervention usually advocated by the Western countries, which put more stress on peacekeeping troops' coercive intervention despite the lack of consent of major relevant parties, while often causing the loss of neutrality and deep entanglement with the civil conflicts. In the meantime, with China's growing understanding of the complexity of the situations in the field, it is demonstrating a certain degree of flexibility and is trying to introduce new measures that will produce a more robust approach to its peacekeeping engagement. In the future, we are likely to see China still following a balanced path characterised by heeding to both the guidance of primary principles of noninterference and impartiality while at the same time engaging in practical means of dealing with threats and challenges in the field.

NOTES

1. In his speech made at the 51st Munich Security Conference, Chinese State Councilor Yang Jiechi reiterated that "as a responsible member of international community, China has been a strong force in maintaining world peace and promoting global development". See Yang Jiechi (2015), "Forge an Outlook of Common, Comprehensive, Cooperative, and Sustainable Security, Build Together a Better World of Perpetual Peace and Common Development", 7 February 2015, http://www.fmprc.gov.cn/web/ziliao_674904/zyjh_674906/t1235255.shtml, accessed on April 5, 2015.
2. Despite the steady decline of interstate conflicts, a large portion of world population has still been obsessed with the curse of conflicts. The rising influence of intrastate conflicts and various forms of violence have presented new security challenges to the national governments around the world as well as international institutions such as the United Nations. What has been accompanied with these changes was the growing complexity and difficulties of available solutions. Under the new security environment, conflicts have always been connected with collapse of state order, shift of governmental authority to some evil or criminal groups. Hence, there comes the urgency and necessity of peacebuilding or statebuilding missions. The international community needs to find new ways to address such new security challenges. See Bernard Wood (2001), "Development Dimensions of Conflict Prevention and Peace-Building: An Independent Study Prepared for the Emergency Response Division, UNDP", *Bureau for Crisis Prevention and Recovery, UNDP*, June 2001 (updated February 2003); Timothy D. Sisk (2013), "Enhancing International Cooperation: From Necessity to Urgency in Responding to Intrastate Conflict", *Global Governance* 19, pp. 503–506; "United Nations Security Council Open Debate on Maintenance of International Peace and Security: Conflict Prevention", S/PV.7247, 21 August 2014.
3. Jonathan Holslag (2007), "China's Diplomatic Victory in Darfur", *Brussles Institute of Contemporary China Studies (BICCS) Background Paper*, 1 August 2007. Also see "Partnerships for Peace and Development: South Sudan and China", *Saferworld Briefing*, 31 May 2013.

4. Jan Eliasson (2011), "Peace, Development and Human Rights: The Indispensable Connection", *The Dag Hammarskjöld Lecture 2011*, 18 September 2011, Uppsala, Sweden.
5. International Dialogue on Peacebuilding and Statebuilding (2011), *A New Deal for Engagement in Fragile States*, 30 November 2011.
6. Björn Hettne (2010), "Development and Security: Origins and Future", *Security Dialogue*, 41:1, February 2010.
7. Eliasson, "Peace, Development and Human Rights".
8. "Speech by Chinese Permanent Representative to the United Nations Li Baodong at the Security Council Open Debate on the Promotion and Strengthening of the Rule of Law in the Maintenance of International Peace and Security", 7 October 2012, S/PV.6849, p. 12.
9. Extraordinary Session of the Assembly of the African Union, Ext/Assembly/AU/Dec.1 (October 2013), 12 October 2013.
10. United Nations Security Council, S/PRST/2009/24, 5 August 2009.
11. "Statement by Ambassador Li Baodong at the Security Council Open Debate on the Working Methods of the Security Council", 26 November 2012, http://www.china-un.org/eng/chinaandun/securitycouncil/t993924.htm, visited on March 20, 2013.
12. Louise Fréchette (2012), "UN Peacekeeping: 20 Years of Reform", *CIGI Papers*, 2, April, p. 9.
13. "Report of the Secretary-General on Implementation of the strategic deployment stock, including the functioning of the existing mechanisms and the award of contracts for procurement", A/59/701, 14 February 2005.
14. See http://www.unlb.org/sds.asp, accessed on 31 March 2014.
15. "Statement by Ambassador Wang Min at the Security Council Open Debate on United Nations Peacekeeping Operations", 11 June 2014, http://www.china-un.org/eng/chinaandun/securitycouncil/thematicissues/peacekeeping/t1168830.htm, accessed on 10 October, 2014.
16. "Support for AU Peacekeeping", *Security Council Report Update Report*, 3, 22 October 2009.
17. Adekeye Adebayo (2011), *UN Peacekeeping in Africa: From the Suez Crisis to the Sudan Conflicts* (Lynne Rienner Publishers), p. 227.
18. Claudia Hofmann and Ulrich Schneckener (2011), "Engaging Non-State Armed Actors in State- and Peace-Building: Options and Strategies", *International Review of the Red Cross*, 93:883 (September), p. 604.
19. In the 1970s, China didn't vote in any Security Council resolutions authorizing the establishment of new peacekeeping missions and rejected sharing assessment to peacekeeping budget. See Zhao Lei (2007), *Constructing Peace: Evolution of China's Diplomatic Behavior Towards the United Nations* (Jiuzhou Publishing House), pp. 196–197.

20. China's awareness of the legitimacy embedded in UN authority and the prominent role of peacekeeping operations in the maintenance of international peace and security may have led to more active participation by China. See Zhou Qi (2010), "China's Changing Attitude Towards UN Peacekeeping Operations and Its Reasons", *Human Rights*, 2, p. 57.
21. Bates Gill and Chin-Hao Huang (2009), "China's Expanding Role in Peacekeeping: Prospects and Policy Implications", *SIPRI Policy Paper No. 25*, November 2009, p. 25.
22. "China Will Take More Active and Substantial Role in International Peacekeeping Operations", *Journal of Chinese Youth*, 5 December 2013, p. 4.
23. The US Presidential Decision Directive 25 issued in 1994 after the tragic event happened in Mogadishu set out restrictive criteria for subsequent US involvement in multilateral peace operations. See Paul D. Williams (2015), "Enhancing US Support for Peace Operations in Africa", *Council on Foreign Relations Special Report No. 73*, May 2015, p. 15.
24. See "Speech of Chinese Permanent Representative to the UN Ambassador Liu Jieyi at the Security Council's Annual Meeting with Commanders of Peacekeeping Operations", 9 October 2014, http://www.china-un.org/chn/zgylhg/jjalh/alhzh/whxd/t1199126.htm, accessed on 11 November 2014.
25. UN Security Council, S/RES/2098 (2013), adopted at 6943rd meeting, 28 March 2013.
26. UN Security Council, S/RES/2100 (2013), adopted at 6952nd meeting, 25 April 2013.
27. Based on the experiences in Mali, in 2014, China decided to dispatch its first formed unit of infantry battalion with 700 peacekeeping soldiers to United Nations Mission in South Sudan (UNMISS).
28. "Chinese Peacekeeping Troops Will Assume the Security and Guarding Task in Mali", 27 June 2013, http://www.mod.gov.cn/affair/2013-06/27/content_4458431.htm, accessed on 2 August 2013.
29. "China Will Take More Active and Substantial Role in International Peacekeeping Operations", p. 4.

Xue Lei is a research fellow of the Center for Maritime and Polar Studies, Shanghai Institutes for International Studies. He received a PhD degree for international law at the East China University of Political Science and Law in 2010. His main research fields include peacekeeping, peacebuilding, and UN Security Council.

CHAPTER 6

On China's Military Diplomacy in Africa

Shen Zhixiong

"Security cooperation has so far been one of the least eye-catching dimensions of the evolving Sino-African relationship",[1] although in recent years, rapid development of Sino-African relations and the ever increasing Chinese influence in Africa have aroused people's attention to issues such as China–Africa security cooperation and military relations. After the end of the Cold War and with the advent of the twenty-first century, activities of military diplomacy in Africa conducted by the Chinese government and the People's Liberation Army (PLA) have become more robust and diversified, providing a special perspective to review Sino-African security cooperation and China's African strategy and policy.

MILITARY DIPLOMACY IN CHINESE PERSPECTIVE: DEFINITION, FORMS, AND ROLES

Military diplomacy has gained more prominence in the international arena since the end of the Cold War. Armed forces and defense ministries have participated in a growing range of peacetime cooperative activities

S. Zhixiong
Political Science, College of International Relations, Renmin University,
Beijing, China
e-mail: szx-ndu@hotmail.com

worldwide. As noted by Cottey and Froster, military diplomacy has been experiencing a shift since the end of the Cold War and the key shift is that military diplomacy "is now being used not only in its longstanding *realpolitik* role of supporting the armed forces and security of allies, but also as a means of pursuing wider foreign and security policy goals."[2] However, just as states employ a spectrum of military diplomatic activities, the terms used by different governments to define these activities are equally colorful. As the leading and most active player of military diplomacy after the end of the Cold War, the United States adopted the terms "Peacetime Engagement" or "Military-to-Military Relations" rather than "Military Diplomacy". The United Kingdom began to formally use the term "defense diplomacy" in The *Strategic Defence Review White Paper 1998*.[3] In December 2000, a Policy Paper named *Defence Diplomacy*[4] was issued by the Ministry of Defence, UK.

It was in the early 1990s that military diplomacy began to attract the attention of the Chinese government. The People's Liberation Army has been more actively engaged in military diplomacy of various kinds. Military diplomacy as a term first appeared in the *China's National Defence in 1998*, which stated that "Chinese armed forces have been active in participating in multilateral military diplomatic activities...China has been active in developing an omni-directional and multi-level form of military diplomacy."[5] Since then, the term "Military Diplomacy" has appeared frequently in media reports. Although the significance, objectives, and principles of military diplomacy were stated in the defense white papers, a definition of military diplomacy has not been given. As a result, the definition and activities of military diplomacy are still under hot discussion in the academia in China. Different scholars define military diplomacy differently in light of their own understanding.[6]

With reference to various definitions and in light of the practice of China's military diplomacy, military diplomacy can be defined as follows: it is the exchanges, negotiation, and activities with relevant departments of other states, group of states or organizations, conducted by the defense ministries and armed forces of a sovereign state, and organizations or individuals authorized by the government, with the aim to promote and achieve national interests and national security. It is an important component of the overall diplomacy of a certain state, as well as embodiment of the national defense policy of this state in external relations.[7]

There are diversified forms of military diplomacy practiced by different countries. To facilitate research, it is reasonable to categorize them according to the objectives, as well as their timescales. The first category is Media Management. It refers to timely news and information release and reaction and clarification of inaccurate news and reports. The second category is Exchanges and Communication. It refers to communication and exchanges between countries with the objective of reducing suspicion, increasing transparency, and promoting mutual trust or economic gains. The third category is Relations Building. The most important characteristic of this category is that certain cooperative relations or preventive mechanisms are established. The last category is International Responsibility. A country intends to show its sense of international responsibility through these activities. (See Table 6.1)

As an important component of overall national diplomacy, the ultimate goal of military diplomacy is to safeguard and promote national interests, especially national security interests. At the same time, military diplomacy is the peaceful use of military strength. It combines both soft- and hard-powers and plays relevant roles of both military and diplomacy in practice.

Military diplomacy of various forms plays at least the following six roles: first, to shape a favorable international strategic environment through international exchanges and cooperation.[8] Second, military diplomacy seeks to avoid misunderstanding and misjudgment by enhancing trust and reducing suspicion so as to create conditions to prevent, manage, and defuse crisis. Third, it is utilized to express goodwill and project a favorable international image by participating in peacekeeping or humanitarian relief operations.

Table 6.1   Four categories of military diplomacy

Categories	Activities
Media Management	News and information release (through spokesperson, websites, white papers, military reports, etc.)
Exchanges and Communication	High-level military visits; Functional visits; Warship visits; International symposiums and workshops; Noninstitutionalized joint exercises; International training & education and Arms trade and transfer
Relations Building	Military Attachés; Confidence Building Measures; Defense industry cooperation; Institutionalized cooperation to counter nontraditional threats; Joint tactics development; Provision of military bases; Alliance
International Responsibility	Arms control and disarmament talks; Peacekeeping operations; Disaster relief operations; escort missions

Fourth, to promote the development of the army and national defense by learning the advanced military thought, military technology, and tactics through bilateral exchanges. Fifth, to expand influence by enhancing recipient's trust in and reliance on the national defense structure, military command system and weapons and equipment. Sixth, it is also a way of deterring the potential adversary by showing the strength of the armed forces in the course of bilateral military exchanges and joint military exercises.

HISTORICAL REVIEW OF CHINA'S MILITARY DIPLOMACY IN AFRICA

To have a better understanding of the current China's military diplomacy in Africa, a brief historical review is necessary. With the founding of the People's Republic of China (PRC), the PLA began to engage in foreign military relations in a more systematic way. In light of the evolution of China's overall foreign policy and the changes in the international situation, the history of PLA's military diplomacy in Africa can be divided into six periods as follows:

The first period (from 1949 to the end of the 1950s) witnessed the beginning of China's military diplomacy in Africa. After the founding of the PRC, the Chinese government adopted the "lean to one side" policy. The policy of "leaning to one side" declared that China would lean to the side of socialism. Therefore, military cooperation and communication with socialist countries became the main content of China's military diplomacy in this period. This period also witnessed the beginning of China's developing defense relations with and providing military assistance to Africa. Although faced with an extremely difficult situation, China provided some military assistance to several African countries, such as Algeria and Guinea.[9]

A main feature of the second period (from 1960 to the beginning of the 1970s) was the active provision of military assistance and support to newly independent countries and independent movements in Africa. Whereas the US hostility toward China did not change, China's relations with the USSR dramatically deteriorated at the end of the 1950s. At the same time, decolonization and independent movements in Africa and Asia were gathering momentum. In this period, the newly independent countries and independent movements in Africa were the main targets of China's military diplomacy in Africa. Active provision of military assistance was the main form. During the visit to Africa at the end of 1963 and beginning of 1964, Premier Zhou Enlai announced the "Eight Principles" for providing economic and technological assistance to foreign countries, which also served as the guiding principles for military assistance. In this period, Algeria and Tanzania were the major recipients of Chinese military assistance.

The third period (from the beginning of the 1970s to 1978) commenced with a thaw in Sino-US relations. Thereafter, China's relations with other Western countries improved. Anti-hegemonism, especially the hegemony of the Soviet Union, became the primary task in China's foreign policy. China continued to provide military assistance to some newly liberated and independent countries and liberation movements. China's policy of military assistance suffered setbacks in this period, which witnessed both the climax and disruption of China's assistance to Algeria. After the beginning of the construction of the Tanzania–Zambia Railway, China enhanced its military assistance to Tanzania.[10]

The fourth period (from 1979 to 1989) is a period of adjustment in terms of both Sino-African relations and China's military diplomacy in Africa. Based on the strategic assessment that peace and development are the themes of the world, China adopted the policy of "Reform and Opening up" to develop its economy. In order to serve this policy, China's foreign policy was gradually adjusted to be the Independent Foreign Policy of Peace. China adjusted the scope, objects, scale, and means of military assistance to Africa. With regard to the object, China had gradually reduced its support to some leftist parties and antigovernment forces. In terms of forms and means of military assistance, China replaced the purely free assistance with combination of free assistance and assistance with loans. In terms of the content of assistance, the proportion of financial assistance to weapons and equipment assistance has been adjusted. In addition, forms and ways of training African military students had experienced changes.[11] As a result, this period witnessed the rapid decline of military assistance to the liberation movements in Africa.

The fifth period (from 1990 to 1999) commenced with the end of the Cold War. During the first few years of this period, China's military diplomacy encountered setbacks. China's military diplomacy with Western countries was almost reduced to nil. However, the end of the Cold War opened up a new and broader space for China's military diplomacy. From 1993, China's military diplomacy began to develop in an all-dimensional and multilevel direction. A new pattern in China's military diplomacy had taken form. Beginning in 1996, China enhanced its efforts of military diplomacy in Africa, which resulted in much more high-level military visits to African countries.[12] In addition, "China's effort in peace-keeping operations in Africa from the 1990s is steadily and quickly transformed from unwilling participation to responsible contribution."[13]

The sixth period (from 2000 to now) witnesses further development of China's military diplomacy in Africa. "The establishment and continuous development of the Forum on China-Africa Cooperation and the Chinese government's sincere implementation of its commitment of assistance to Africa elevated the Sino-African relations to a new level."[14] China's military diplomacy also enjoyed rapid development with a closer cooperation in security affairs and more diversified exchanges with African countries. To cope with the threat of Somalian piracy, the Chinese government decided to send PLA naval fleets to the Gulf of Aden to carry out escort missions in December 2008.

CURRENT CHINA'S MILITARY DIPLOMACY IN AFRICA

Objectives of China's Military Diplomacy in Africa

China's military diplomacy is an important adjunct to overall diplomacy and a major means to achieve national defense objectives. Objectives and nature of China's military diplomacy in Africa are defined by its Africa policy and defense policy.

With the rapid development of Africa and the rise of China, Africa has become of higher strategic significance to China at least in the following three aspects: (1) it is the strategic pivot of China's diplomacy with valuable political and diplomatic meanings; (2) it is an important partner to achieve economic recovery and development; and (3) it is an arena for China to exhibit and build its national image.[15] Therefore, "enhancing solidarity and cooperation with African countries has always been an important component of China's independent foreign policy of peace. China will unswervingly carry forward the tradition of China-Africa friendship, and proceeding from the fundamental interests of both the Chinese and African peoples, establish and develop a new type of strategic partnership with Africa, featuring political equality and mutual trust, economic win-win cooperation and cultural exchange."[16]

The general principles and objectives of China's Africa policy are sincerity, friendship, and equality; mutual benefit, reciprocity, and common prosperity; mutual support and close coordination and learning from each other; and seeking common development.[17] With regard to security affairs, "China will strengthen efforts to participate constructively into African peace and security affairs on the basis of adherence to the principle of non-interference."[18]

China's armed forces unswervingly implement the military strategy of active defense. Besides safeguarding national sovereignty, security, and territorial integrity and supporting the country's peaceful development, another fundamental policy and principle of China's national defense is deepening security cooperation and fulfilling international obligations. According to the latest defense white paper, *The Diversified Employment of China's Armed Forces*, "China's armed forces are the initiator and facilitator of, and participant in international security cooperation. They uphold the Five Principles of Peaceful Coexistence, conduct all-round military exchanges with other countries, and develop cooperative military relations that are non-aligned, non-confrontational and not directed against any third party . . . China's armed forces work to promote dialogue and cooperation on maritime security; participate in UN peacekeeping missions, international counter-terrorism cooperation, international merchant shipping protection and disaster relief operations; conduct joint exercises and training with foreign counterparts; conscientiously assume their due international responsibilities; and play an active role in maintaining world peace, security and stability."[19]

Therefore, the objectives of China's military diplomacy in Africa can be generalized as follows: The first objective is to shape a favorable regional and international environment for peaceful development. The rapid rise of China, especially the steady efforts of modernization of the PLA, has aroused concerns in Western countries, as well as its neighboring countries. Under the influence of the so-called "China Threat", even some African countries began to worry about the uncertainty of China peaceful development. In addition, seeing the emergence of China, many African countries began to pin much higher expectations on China. Because military diplomacy can enhance transparency of China's capability and intention, reduce suspicion, and promote mutual trust, it can be employed as a useful means to enhance their understanding of and support for China's peaceful development. China's constructive participation into security affairs, including peacekeeping and antipiracy efforts, is conducive to safeguarding regional peace, which is certainly desirable for shaping a favorable environment for the peaceful development of China.

The second objective is to safeguard national interests in Africa by supplementing bilateral political and economic relations. On the one hand, military cooperation between states is a major index of the intimacy of bilateral relations. On the other hand, military assistance and cooperation undoubtedly supplements and cements economic and political relations. With the rise of China and the rapid development of Sino-African relations, China has more and more political, economic, and security interests in Africa. To safeguard these national interests, it is necessary for the military diplomacy to play a supplementary role by means of cementing bilateral relations. "To promote high-level military exchanges between the two sides and actively carry out military-related technological exchanges and cooperation"[20] is no doubt an important measure to strengthen bilateral relations. Moreover, non-traditional security threats such as terrorism and piracy are still rampant in Africa. China's enterprises, investment, citizens, and shipping are becoming increasingly exposed to various non-traditional security threats. In consideration of the relative weakness of military strength of some African countries, China takes it as an important responsibility to provide assistance to enhance the security and military capabilities of African countries and promise that "it will continue to help train African military personnel and support defense and army building of African countries for their own security".[21]

The third objective is to promote the building of a harmonious world by shouldering international security responsibility and duties. The promotion of China's peaceful development highlights that "China advocates the building of a harmonious world of durable peace and common prosperity and works with other countries in pursuing this goal. To China, it is both a long-term objective and a current task."[22] As a permanent member of the UN Security Council, China shoulders important responsibility for regional peace and harmony in Africa. China aims to make contributions to regional peace and building of a harmonious world through various activities of military diplomacy in Africa, including active participation in peacekeeping and escort missions and enhanced cooperation in the non-traditional security fields.

The last objective is to project an image of a responsible and peace-loving country to the world. China's national image has not caught up with the fast development of its economy in the international arena, which has become an increasingly important issue. One Western scholar noted that "China's greatest strategic threat today is its national image.... How China is perceived by other nations will determine the future of Chinese development and reform."[23] As a result of the continuous efforts of "demonizing China" by some Western countries, many misunderstanding and accusation of China's African strategy, such as "neo-colonialism", "resources plundering", and "indifference to human rights" appeared and gained ground, which brought about negative influence to China–Africa relations. The Chinese government recognizes this problem and is keen to project China as a main responsible and peace-loving nation to the world, which was reflected by the reiteration of "peaceful development" in the governmental reports as well as speeches of the leaders. Active participation in peacekeeping, disaster relief operations, arms control efforts, and some other activities in Africa are meant to project a positive image abroad for China and the PLA.

The Pattern of China's Military Diplomacy in Africa in the Twenty-First Century

In the twenty-first century, the PLA conducts active military exchanges and cooperation with militaries of other countries and "has created a military diplomacy that is all-directional, multi-tiered and wide-ranging."[24] Nevertheless, "its military diplomacy in Africa remains limited compared to defence exchanges in other regions".[25] Constrained by historical, practical, and strategic factors, China's military diplomacy in Africa is mainly focused on the following several areas:

Military exchanges and communication. It is the most common phenomenon of modern military diplomacy and includes many different forms. First, exchanges of military visits. It is an important and fundamental form of PRC's military exchanges with other countries. As highlighted in *China's African Policy*, the Chinese government attaches great importance to high-level military exchanges with African countries. Bilateral high-level military exchanges between China and African counries have been remained at a stable and relative high level. "The frequency of high-level military delegations visits between China and Africa increased at the end of the 1990s, but has largely remained constant over the past decade."[26] "Bilateral military exchanges between China and African counries have remained stable at an annual average of 26."[27]

Second, military attaches. "By August 2009 . . . China established military attaché offices in 109 countries, and 101 countries established military attaché offices in China."[28] It is estimated that China has nearly 20 military attaché offices in Africa,[29] whereas African countries increased their permanent defense attaché offices in Beijing from 13 in 1998 to 18 in 2007.[30]

Third, defense dialogue. In April 2003, China and South Africa established the China–South Africa Defence Committee to exchange views on international and regional security situation as well as cooperation between the armed forces of two sides. So far, five meetings of the Defence Committee have been held.

Fourth, exchanges of warship visits. In July 2000, a PLA naval fleet paid a visit to South Africa and Tanzania, which was PLA Navy's first visit to Africa. In October 2008, a frigate of South Africa Navy visited Shanghai, China, which was the first visit of a South African warship to China. In April 2011, a PLA naval fleet visited Durban, South Africa. In 2002 and 2010, after passing through the Suez Canal, PLA naval fleet called at Alexandria, Egypt.

Fifth, functional exchanges. Functional exchanges covering military education, training, communications, logistics, equipment, and technologies have been on the increase.[31] "It increases high-level visits and exchanges between junior and intermediate officers, and seeks to broaden cooperation fields with these countries. For the first time, China sent a hospital ship, the Peace Ark, to visit the Republic of Djibouti, the Republic of Kenya, the United Republic of Tanzania, the Republic of Seychelles and other African countries and provided humanitarian medical service. Also for the first time, China hosted workshops for heads of military academies from English-speaking African countries, for directors of military hospitals from French-speaking African countries, and for intermediate and senior officers from Portuguese-speaking African countries."[32]

A workshop for heads of military academies from French-speaking African countries was also held in May 2011.[33]

Military assistance. Some scholars believe that "China offers at least modest quantities of military assistance or training to nearly every African country with which it has diplomatic relations."[34] According to the statistics of a foreign scholar, the major African recipients of China's military assistance are Angola, Ghana, Mozambique, Zimbabwe, Sudan, and Tanzania, and most of the assistance was provided in the forms of loan or donation of materials or equipment. The loans were mainly used to improve the facilities of recipients, such as building or renovation of headquarters, Ministry of Defence, training centers, upgrading military communication, or construction of hospital. The equipment or materials were mainly uniforms, ambulances, counter-mine, military trucks, and other logistics materials.[35] And it is necessary to highlight that much of China's military assistance were out of humanitarian reasons rather than commercial purposes, which were mainly reflected in de-mining support provided by China. In recent years, China has provided free de-mining equipment to Angola, Mozambique, Chad, Burundi, Guinea-Bissau, Sudan, and Egypt and funded the mine-sweeping operation in Ethiopia.[36]

Military training. To African countries, military training is also an important means of military assistance and has been a major component of China's military diplomacy in Africa since the beginning of bilateral military relations. After the Reform and Opening up of China, especially after the 1990s, foreign military training of the PLA got rid of the bondage of ideology, and the objects of foreign training were broadened to the majority of developing countries and even some developed countries. At present, there are more than 20 military colleges and training organs being involved in foreign military training.[37] More and more foreign officers came to study in the PLA colleges. In 2007 and 2008, "some 4,000 military personnel from more than 130 countries have come to China to study at Chinese military educational institutions."[38] A large part of them are from African countries. Besides regular training, PLA provides some short-term training courses. For instance, it held de-mining training courses for Angola, Mozambique, Chad, Burundi, Guinea-Bissau, and both northern and southern Sudan.[39] In addition, "in 2009, for the first time, China sent a medical detachment to Africa to hold a joint operation with Gabon, to conduct medical training and rescue exercises, and to provide medical assistance for local residents".[40]

Peacekeeping in Africa. China earnestly fulfills its international responsibilities and obligations and supports and actively participates in UN peacekeeping missions. The Chinese peacekeeping troops and specialized peacekeeping personnel "are mainly tasked with monitoring ceasefires, disengaging conflicting parties, providing engineering, transportation and medical support, and participating in social reconstruction and humanitarian assistance". "To date, the PLA has dispatched 22,000 military personnel to 23 UN peacekeeping missions . . . So far, China is the biggest troop and police contributor among the five permanent members of the UN Security Council. It also dispatches the most numbers of troops for engineering, transportation and medical support among all the 115 contributing countries. China pays and contributes the largest share of UN peacekeeping costs among all developing countries."[41]

The majority of China's peacekeeping personnel and troops are now in Africa. By December 2012, 1,842 PLA officers and soldiers have implemented peacekeeping tasks in nine UN mission areas. Among them, about 80% carried out UN missions in Africa.[42] It is worth noting that "Chinese peacekeepers are consistently rated among the most professional, well-trained, effective and disciplined contingents in UN peacekeeping operations"[43]

Escort missions in the Gulf of Aden and waters off Somalia. In line with relevant UN resolutions, China dispatched naval ships to conduct escort operations in the Gulf of Aden and waters off Somalia on December 26, 2008. They are mainly charged with safeguarding the security of Chinese ships and personnel passing through the Gulf of Aden and Somali waters, and the security of ships delivering humanitarian supplies for the World Food Program and other international organizations, and shelter pass-by foreign vessels as much as possible. Until now, the escort mission in the Gulf of Aden and waters off Somalia has become regular mission of the PLA Navy. "As of December 2012, Chinese navy task groups have provided protection for four WFP ships and 2,455 foreign ships, accounting for 49% of the total of escorted ships. They helped four foreign ships, recovered four ships released from captivity and saved 20 foreign ships from pursuit by pirates."[44]

Contribution and Characteristics

In comparison with the military diplomacy of other countries, China's military diplomacy in Africa has the following characteristics: First, it is peaceful. "The underlying idea of China's military diplomacy is 'peace and harmony are the most precious'",[45] which was manifested in the basic principles and policy of China's diplomacy and ideas of "New Security Concept" and "Harmonious World". In line with both China's interest of peaceful development and common aspiration of African countries and peoples, peace is obviously both an objective and a characteristic of China's military diplomacy in Africa.

Second, it is cooperative. In practicing military diplomacy in Africa, the PLA has attached great importance to cooperation with not only African countries but also international and regional organizations, including the UN, AU, and other subregional organizations. In addition, as noted by a foreign scholar, "there is no evidence that China's military aid aims at counterbalancing other powers, such as the United States", "despite the strategic importance of Africa, China does not attempt to safeguard its stronghold by unilaterally projecting military power."[46]

Third, it is equal. Equality has long been a general principle of China in developing relations with African countries. "China adheres to the Five Principles of Peaceful Coexistence, respects African countries' independent choice of the road of development and supports African countries' efforts to grow stronger through unity."[47] Bilateral military relations were developed on an equal footing between China and African countries, and military assistance was provided with no political conditions attached.

Fourth, it is subordinate. Being subordinate has dual meanings here. On the one hand, as an important component and adjunct of China's overall diplomacy, military diplomacy should serve, and be subordinate to, the overall diplomacy. On the other hand, "China believes the solution of African hotspot issues need support and help from the international community, but the international community should sincerely respect AU and African countries' dominant role in solving African issues and should refrain from 'exceeding its duties and meddling in others' affairs".[48] That is to say, China's military diplomacy is not seeking to play a dominant role in resolving African security issues, which forms a striking contrast to the practice of some other major powers.

Fifth, it is modest. China neither has nor seeks to establish a large-scale military presence in Africa. "China has no bases in Africa like the United States or France, nor does it train African soldiers to deal with hostility perceived by China as a threat to its national interests."[49] In terms of the scale of military assistance and the amount of military training, China lags far behind that of the United States. "Hence, China's military diplomacy in Africa remains modest, and it certainly has not kept up with the impressive number of trade officials posted in African countries to strengthen economic ties in the last few years."[50]

It is fair to say that China's military diplomacy in Africa, peacekeeping missions in particular, makes an important contribution to regional peace, stability, and development. "China's higher profile in peacekeeping reinforces both the perceived legitimacy and the effectiveness of UN peace missions…AU and UN officials believe, the presence of Chinese peacekeepers sends a reassuring message and helps the mission to project an image of being inclusive, impartial and genuinely multilateral."[51] In addition, "Chinese peacekeepers are well accepted and have participated in improving local populations in Africa",[52] "over the past 22 years, Chinese peacekeepers have built and repaired over 10,000 km of roads and 284 bridges, cleared over 9,000 mines and various types of unexploded ordnance (UXO), transported over 1 million tons of cargo across a total distance of 11 million km and treated 120,000 patients",[53] among which most of them were accomplished in Africa.

Besides these contributions, China's efforts in strengthening military exchanges and providing military assistance and training have been helpful to strengthen the self-peacekeeping and security capabilities of AU and subregional organizations, as well as the technology and security capabilities of various African countries. For example, at the supreme foreign military training base of China, the College of Defense Studies at National Defense University has trained over 4000 senior military officers and government officials, among which more than 300 took the positions of military leaders, ministers of defense, chiefs of general staff, and commanders of different services in their respective countries.[54] Many of these outstanding graduates of the CDS, NDU are from African countries.

By making an important contribution to regional peace and development, China's military diplomacy in Africa has achieved its objectives. And China's diplomacy as a whole "has played an indispensible role in enhancing comprehensive development of state-to-state relations, safeguarding national sovereignty, security and development interests, promoting modernization construction of the army and national defense, and maintaining world peace."[55]

CHALLENGES AND PROSPECTS

Taking the current African situation into consideration, China's military diplomacy in Africa is facing with several major challenges.

The first and biggest challenge comes from suspicion and competition from Western countries. Although China's active participation in the African peace and security fields has won universal recognition from the international community, especially African countries, Western countries are still deeply suspicious and wary of China. The China's model of peacekeeping and peace construction (or 'peacebuilding') in Africa is different and adheres to two basic principles. The first is noninterference and respect for sovereignty of African countries; the second is attaching equal importance to peace and security and economic development and believing that economic development is the precondition of peace and security. However, Western countries put human rights above sovereignty and believe that freedom and democracy are the precondition of sustainable peace in Africa.[56]

What's more challenging is the large-scale expansion of military presence in Africa by some Western countries, especially the United States. To carry out the "global war on terrorism," America has greatly expanded its military presence in Africa. With the establishment of the AFRICOM, American military has conducted diversified activities of military diplomacy in Africa. At the same time, Americans have established an arch-shaped strategic axis stretching from Djibouti, South Sudan, and Uganda to the DRC.[57] The United States has greatly enhanced its military cooperation with these countries. In addition, at the end of 2012, the United States announced that it will send troops to 35 African countries. It is reported that the Americans have established a network of UAV bases in Djibouti, Burkina Faso, Ethiopia, Kenya, Uganda, Seychelles, and Niger. In a sense, America's expanding large military presence in Africa demonstrates militarization of its African policy and means ever more military intervention in African security affairs by the American troops. Obviously, it is also can serve as a means by which America can contain China's influence in Africa.[58] It is a grave challenge to China's military diplomacy in Africa, as well as China's Africa strategy.

The second challenge originates from misunderstanding and gaps of understanding. There are some kinds of misunderstanding about China's Africa strategy and gaps of understanding between China and African countries. As noticed by a former Chinese Special Representative of African Affairs, a great challenge is the gaps of understanding about the ideas of governance and ideology between China and African countries. "They (African countries) accepted a set of Western ideas, especially ideas of humanitarian intervention and responsibility of protection, on which China has reservations."[59] With the rapid rise of China, especially the rapid development of Sino-African relations, such misunderstanding and criticisms of China's Africa policy as "China Threat", "Neo-Colonialism", and "Resource Plundering" appeared in Western countries and spread to Africa, which will inevitably cause negative impact upon China. At the same time, "in recent years, with the rise of China's overall national strength and international influence, African countries pin much more expectations on China and hope China to have more participation into African peace and security affairs. However, since China is still a developing country, there is a gap between Chinese real capability and expectations of African countries. Moreover, it takes time to accumulate experience."[60]

The third challenge lies in the security situation in Africa. Although the political and security situation in Africa is generally stable, Africa is faced with both turbulence in some countries and serious diversified nontraditional security threats in others. The deeper China ventures into the resource-abundant African continent, the more it stumbles upon various security challenges. With more and more Chinese enterprises entering into Africa, there is a concurrent expansion of Chinese emigrants in Africa. There is little authoritative statistics about Chinese emigrants to Africa though one scholar estimated that the number of overseas Chinese in Africa exceeded 1 million at the end of 2012.[61]

Security of these overseas Chinese aroused unprecedented attention of the Chinese government. In February 2011, the turbulent situation in Libya posed grave security threats to Chinese institutions, enterprises, and nationals there. To protect the security of these overseas Chinese, "the Chinese government organized the largest overseas evacuation since the founding of the PRC, and 35,860 Chinese nationals were taken home. The PLA contributed ships and aircraft to the effort."[62] The large numbers of overseas Chinese in Africa put forward new requirement on the PLA military diplomacy in Africa. In addition, more and more Chinese nationals are becoming the major targets of armed robbery, murder, kidnapping, and even terrorist attacks, which also require the PLA to strengthen international cooperation in these fields. In one word, how to protect national interests and security of nationals while adhering to the traditional general principles became an important question that China's military diplomacy has to answer.

Looking forwad, nevertheless, China's military diplomacy in Africa has a huge potential and bright future, since it enjoys many strategic opportunities: First and foremost, it has been a commitment of the Chinese government that "China will continue to firmly support Africa in its endeavor to independently resolve regional issues and make greater contribution to peace and security in Africa."[63] "China will launch the 'Initiative on China-Africa Cooperative Partnership for Peace and Security', deepen cooperation with the AU and African countries in peace and security, provide financial support for the AU peace-keeping missions in Africa and the development of the African Standby Force, and train more officials in peace and security affairs and peace-keepers for the AU."[64]

Certainly, there are some other opportunities: in terms of the international and regional situation, peace and development remain the defining features of the times and the common aspiration of both Chinese and African peoples. The rapid development of China and African economies and ever closer relations provide foundation and incentive for both sides to have more security cooperation and military exchanges. Modernization of the PLA has created material conditions for it to play a more active role in the military exchanges in Africa and make much more constructive contribution to regional peace. The ever transparent and experienced PLA has become more and more confident in conducting military exchanges with other countries.

However, to ensure a bright future for China's military diplomacy in Africa, the Chinese government and the PLA should pay attention to the following points. First, more strategic coordination between security policy and development policy. Security and development are the two basic difficulties closely correlative to each other, which requires major countries' greater attention while dealing with African issues. However, as noticed by a scholar, "at present, China's development policy and security policy towards African to a larger degree are independent or in parallel with each other. There is neither coherence nor strategic coordination".[65] With the deepening of Sino-African relations, especially the ever more fierce competition from Western countries, it is necessary for China to combine development policy with security policy. Under the general framework of the FOCAC, more coordination and cooperation should be conducted among relevant departments, institutions, and enterprises.

Second, more support for the "African Peace and Security Architecture". The AU, subregional organizations and major regional countries in Africa have spent major efforts on safeguarding regional peace and stability, actively push forward the construction of African collective security mechanism by establishing the "African Peace and Security Architecture" and have been committed to "solve African issues in African way".[66] To support African countries and relevant organizations to play a dominant role in African security affairs, it is necessary for China to provide more support to the construction of the "African Peace and Security Architecture". And it is necessary for the PLA to strengthen functional dialogues with the Architecture.

Third, more communication and coordination with Western countries, especially the United States. Due to historical reasons, Western countries have played an important role in coping with security issues in Africa. To cope with some security threats and solve security issues, it is necessary for China to strengthen communication and coordination with them. Importance of coordination with them has been testified by the escort missions in the Gulf of Aden, in which a certain degree of coordination and cooperation has been proved to be effective. As noted by a scholar, China may take tentative steps to develop coordination and cooperation in African security affairs with the United States through the framework of the FOCAC.[67] On such a basis, it is beneficial for the PLA and the US Army to have communication and cooperation on African security affairs.

Fourth, more practical cooperation to cope with non-traditional security threats. African countries are still suffering from various non-traditional security threats. Since major countries and African countries share more common and overlapping interests in the nontraditional security threats in comparison with traditional ones, there are more opportunities and broader space for them to cooperate in this regard. As mentioned above, China's national interests and Chinese nationals have been increasingly exposed to these non-traditional security threats. Practical cooperation in this field is conducive to African security and stability, as well as protection of China's national interests and Chinese nationals in Africa. Therefore, it is reasonable for the PLA to provide more assistance and strengthen cooperation with African countries in the field of nontraditional security threats.

Fifth, more public diplomacy conducted by the PLA. To project a good image in Africa, the AFRICOM has attached great importance to public diplomacy. It is proven that public diplomacy conducted by American troops is accepted and welcomed by the ordinary African people. There are about 1,500 peacekeeping troops and dozens of military attachés in Africa. Some kinds of public diplomacy were practiced by them in Africa, which was highly appreciated by the local people. However, these activities dwarf before the tremendous public diplomacy efforts by the US AFRICOM troops. It is recommended that the PLA peacekeeping troops and military attachés in Africa expend more effort on activities which build closer relations with and will be readily accepted by the local people, providing a clearer picture of what China has done for the African people.

NOTES

1. Jonathan Holslag (2009), 'China's Vulnerability in Africa and Options for Security Cooperation with Europe,' *Clingendael Asia Forum*, 11 December 11, http://www.Clingendael.nl/asia/forum.
2. Andrew Cottey and Anthony Forster (2005), *Reshaping Defence Diplomacy: New Roles for Military Cooperation and Assistance* (Oxford: Oxford University Press), p. 7
3. *The Strategic Defence Review White Paper* 1998, Ministry of Defence, UK, p. 22, http://www.parliament.uk/Templates/BriefingPapers/Pages/BPPdfDownload.aspx?bp-id=RP98-91.

4. 'Defence Diplomacy,' *Policy Papers*, No. 1, Ministry of Defence, UK 2000b, http://www.mod.uk/issues/cooperation/diplomacy.htm/.
5. *China's National Defence* (1998), Information Office of the State Council, the People's Republic of China, July 1998, http://www.china.org.cn/e-white/5/index.htm.
6. See for example, Xiong Wuyi and Zhou Jiafa, eds. (2000), *Military Encyclopedia* (Beijing: Great Wall Publishing House), p. 1240; Qian Qichen, ed. (2005), *Dictionary on World's Diplomacy* (Beijing: World Affairs Press), p. 956; Zhu Meisheng, eds. (1999), *An Introduction of Military Thoughts* (Beijing: National Defence University Press), p. 1; etc.
7. Guo Xinning (2010), *On Military Diplomacy and China's Practice* (Beijing: National Defence University Press), p. 94.
8. Wang Qiaobao (2013), 'China's Military Diplomacy in the Last Decade—Retrospect and Prospect,' *Global Review*, 2, p. 21.
9. Xu Weizhong (2010), 'Chinese Participation in African Security Cooperation and Its Tendency,' *West Asia and Africa*, 11, p. 12.
10. Ibid.
11. Ibid., pp. 86–88.
12. Ibid., p. 95.
13. Kossi Ayenagbo et al (2012), 'China's Peacekeeping Operations in Africa: From Unwilling Participation to Responsible Contribution,' *African Journal of Political Science and International Relations*, 6:2, p. 22.
14. Xie Yixian, ed. (2009), *Contemporary History of China's Diplomacy, 1949–2009* (Beijing: Chinese Youth Press), p. 516.
15. Luo Jianbo (2013), 'Why Sino-African Relationship so Important?,' *Study Times*, 1 April 1.
16. Chinese MOFA (2006), *China's African Policy*, January, http://www.fmprc.gov.cn/eng/zxxx/t230615.htm.
17. Ibid.
18. Lu Shaye (2013), 'Seizing Opportunities and Overcoming Difficulties to Promote the Development of China-Africa Relations,' *China International Studies*, 2, p. 4.
19. *The Diversified Employment of China's Armed Forces*, Information Office of the State Council, the People's Republic of China, April 2013, http://eng.mod.gov.cn/Database/WhitePapers/.
20. *China's African Policy*.
21. Ibid.
22. *China's Peaceful Development*, Information Office of the State Council, the People's Republic of China, September 2011, http://english.gov.cn/official/2011-09/06/content_1941354.htm.
23. Joshua Cooper Ramo (2007), 'Brand China,' *Working Paper*, No. 827, The Foreign Policy Centre, February 2007.

24. Qian Lihua (2012), 'Proactively Forging Ahead and Innovating Military Diplomacy,' *Qiu Shi Theory*, 15, p. 48.
25. Jonathan Holslag (2008), 'China's Next Security Strategy for Africa,' *BICCS Asia Paper*, 3:6, p. 15.
26. Saferworld (2011), *China's Growing Role in African Peace and Security*, Saferworld Report, January, 2011. p. 38.
27. Holslag, 'China's Next Security Strategy for Africa,' p. 10.
28. Qian Lihua (2009), 'Review of China's Military Diplomacy in the Past 60 Years,' *Qiu Shi Theory*, 18, p. 28.
29. Weizhong, 'Chinese Participation in African Security Cooperation and Its Tendency,' p. 14.
30. David H. Shinn (2008), 'Military and Security Relations: China, Africa, and the Rest of the World', in Robert I. Rotberg, ed., *China into Africa: Trade, Aid and Influence* (Washington, DC: Brookings Institute Press), p. 163.
31. Wang Xuejun (2012), 'Review on China's Engagement in African Peace and Security,' *China International Studies*, 32, January/February 2012, p. 34.
32. *China's National Defense in 2010*, Information Office of the State Council, The People's Republic of China, March 2011, http://english.gov.cn/offi cial/2011-03/31/content_1835499_11.htm.
33. 'Wei Fenghe Meeting with All Participants of Seminar of Presidents of Francophonie-African Military Institutions,' *China MOD*, May 31, 2011, http://news.mod.gov.cn/diplomacy/2011-05/31/content_4244597.htm.
34. Shinn, *Military and Security Relations: China, Africa, and the Rest of the World*, p. 161.
35. Holslag, 'China's Next Security Strategy for Africa,' p. 11.
36. Xuejun, 'Review on China's Engagement in African Peace and Security,' p. 34.
37. Xiao Tianliang (n.d.), ed., *Military Diplomacy of PRC* (Beijing: National Defence University Press), p. 206.
38. *China's National Defense in 2008*, Information Office of the State Council, the People's Republic of China, January 2009, http://english.gov.cn/offi cial/2009-01/20/content_1210227.htm.
39. Ibid.
40. *China's National Defense in 2010*.
41. *The Diversified Employment of China's Armed Forces*.
42. Ibid.
43. Bates Gill and Chin-Hao Huang (2009), 'China's Expanding Role in Peacekeeping: Prospects and Policy Implications,' *SIPRI Policy Paper*, 25, November 2009, p. 26.
44. *The Diversified Employment of China's Armed Forces*.
45. Qiaobao, 'China's Military Diplomacy in the Last Decade,' p. 22.

46. Holslag, 'China's Next Security Strategy for Africa,' pp. 10, 15.
47. *China's African Policy.*
48. Shaye, 'Seizing Opportunities and Overcoming Difficulties to Promote the Development of China-Africa Relations,' p. 4.
49. Holslag, 'China's Next Security Strategy for Africa,' p. 12.
50. Ibid, p. 10.
51. Gill and Huang, 'China's Expanding Role in Peacekeeping,' p. 27.
52. Kossi Ayenagbo et al, 'China's Peacekeeping Operations in Africa,' p. 32.
53. *The Diversified Employment of China's Armed Forces.*
54. 'National Defence University Comprehensively Facilitate Training Foreign Military,' *Jiefanjun Bao*, March 15, 2009.
55. Lihua, 'Proactively Forging Ahead and Innovating Military Diplomacy,' p. 48.
56. Xuejun, 'Review on China's Engagement in African Peace and Security,' p. 41.
57. Li Anshan (2013), 'Obama's Africa Trip and Implications for China,' *The Contemporary World*, 10, p. 33.
58. Ibid.
59. Liu Guijin (2012), 'Foreign Assistance and Hijack: Problems and Dilemma of China-Africa Relations,' *World Affairs*, 4, p. 33.
60. Shaye, 'Seizing Opportunities and Overcoming Difficulties to Promote the Development of China-Africa Relations,' p. 6.
61. 'Turbulent Africa and Virginian for Chinese Migrants,' *Xinhua*, November 15, 2013, http://news.xinhuanet.com/edu/2013-11/15/c_125705827.htm.
62. *The Diversified Employment of China's Armed Forces.*
63. 'Xi Jinping Delivers a Speech at the Julius Nyerere International Convention Center in Tanzania, Stressing China and Africa Will Always Remain Reliable Friends and Faithful Partners,' Chinese MOFA, March 25, 2013, http://www.fmprc.gov.cn/eng/topics/xjpcf1/t1025803.shtml.
64. *Open Up New Prospects for A New Type of China-Africa Strategic Partnership*, Speech by H.E. Hu Jintao, President of the People's Republic of China, At the Opening Ceremony of the Fifth Ministerial Conference of The Forum on China-Africa Cooperation, Beijing, 19 July 2012, http://www.focac.org/eng/ltda/dwjbzjjhys/zyjh/t953172.htm.
65. Zhang Chun (2009), '"Development-Security Nexus": The African Policies of China, EU and USA,' *Chinese Journal of European Studies*, 3, p. 86.
66. Shaye, 'Seizing Opportunities and Overcoming Difficulties to Promote the Development of China-Africa Relations,' p. 2.
67. Wang Hongyi (2013), 'Finding the Way for Cooperation Between China and America in Africa,' *China International Studies*, 2.

Shen Zhixiong is an associate professor, Department for Strategic Studies, National Defence University, China. He holds a masters degree from Westminster University, UK and is currently a doctoral candidate at Remin University, China.

China-Africa Cooperative Partnership for Peace and Security

Zhang Chun

INTRODUCTION

With China's engagement in Africa's growth, the needs for China to play a proactive role in African peace and security affairs are definitely rising. As one of the most important pillars of the comprehensive strategic and cooperative partnership between China and Africa, peace and security cooperation now is and will be one of the most significant dimensions of China-Africa relations, thanks to the launch of the "Initiative on China-Africa Cooperative Partnership for Peace and Security" (ICACPPS) at the 5th Ministerial Conference of the Forum on China-Africa Cooperation (FOCAC) in July 2012.[1] At the FOCAC Johannesburg Summit in December 2015, both China and Africa promised to:

> Implement the "Initiative on China-Africa Cooperative Partnership for Peace and Security", support the building of the collective security mechanism in Africa, and jointly manage non-traditional security issues and global challenges.[2]

Z. Chun (✉)
Institute for Foreign Policy Studies, Shanghai Institutes for International Studies, Shanghai, China
e-mail: zhangchunster@163.com

However, why did China propose such an initiative at the 5th FOCAC meeting? What will be the main components of this initiative? How will China and Africa jointly make it materialize? What are the roles of China and Africa respectively? For sure, there are a lot of challenges ahead to be scrutinized. This chapter tries to answer above questions with an introduction of the state of the art of China-Africa peace and security cooperation and exploration of the reasons why China choose to upgrade its cooperative partnership with Africa in terms of peace and security cooperation, and suggest the key issues or tasks for building this cooperative partnership for peace and security.

State of the Art of China-Africa Peace and Security Cooperation

China always attaches great importance to China-Africa peace and security cooperation, referred by all and each FOCAC Ministerial Conferences. The 2006 *China's African Policy* white paper lists the four dimensions of China-Africa peace and security cooperation, including military cooperation, conflict settlement and peacekeeping operations, judicial and police cooperation, and nontraditional security cooperation.[3] In 2012, then Chinese President Hu Jintao proposed the ICACPPS for upgrading this cooperation further. The second Africa policy paper states that China will support Africa in realizing peace and security, deepen military cooperation, and support Africa in confronting nontraditional security threats.[4] Currently, China-Africa peace and security cooperation is proceeding on the bilateral, regional and continental, and international levels simultaneously.

Bilaterally, China has developed close cooperation with African countries that have diplomatic relations with China. China always promotes high-level military exchanges between two sides and actively carries out military-related technological exchanges and cooperation. To strengthen bilateral peace and security cooperation, China and African countries jointly established relatively strong institutions. Twenty-eight African countries have defense attachés in Beijing, while 18 Chinese defense attaché offices in Africa plus one delegation of Chinese People's Liberation Army (PLA) Chief Military Experts in Tanzania with more than 100 Chinese military officials there to help the country to build its military capacity. China is now training African military personnel mainly through receiving African military officials at Chinese National Defense University and sending military experts to

African military universities or institutions. China is also assisting several African countries to build their own National Defense Universities, including Zimbabwe and Tanzania. Furthermore, China has engaged in military technical and arms and ammunitions sales to African countries for supporting defense and army building of African countries for their own security. Though lacking in official data, some Western observers claim that China shares some 15% of Sub-Saharan African arms market.[5] Others claim that the proliferation of small arms and light weapons in Sub-Saharan Africa has experienced significant contributions from China, especially based upon disclosures of new weapons and ammunition.[6]

Besides military cooperation and exchange, China has close cooperation with African countries bilaterally in the fields of judicial and law enforcement. The two parties learn from each other in legal system building and judicial reform so as to better prevent, investigate, and crack down on crimes. Under the framework of FOCAC, there was a subforum named "Forum on China-Africa Cooperation- Legal Forum" (FOCAC Legal Forum) that intends to build a dialogue mechanism for strengthening China-Africa legal exchanges and to promote the all-round development of China-Africa cooperation in various fields. The key issues related to peace and security topics covered by this subforum include experience sharing of legal system building and implementation; combating transnational organized crimes and corruption; cooperating on matters concerning judicial assistance, extradition and repatriation of criminal suspects, and fighting against illegal migration, improving exchange of immigration control information, etc.[7]

Continentally and regionally, China has cooperated with the African Union (AU), East Africa Community (EAC), Economic Community of West African States (ECOWAS), Southern African Development Community (SADC), and so on. As mentioned by successive FOCAC ministerial conferences,

> The two sides expressed their appreciation of the leading role of African countries and regional organizations in resolving regional issues, and reiterated support for their efforts in independently resolving regional conflicts and strengthening democracy and good governance and oppose the interference in Africa's internal affairs by external forces in pursuit of their own interests.[8]

China always tries hard to deepen cooperation with the AU and African countries in peace and security in Africa, to provide financial support for the AU peacekeeping missions in Africa and development of the African

Standby Force, and to train more officials in peace and security affairs and peacekeepers for the AU. Meanwhile, China insists on the principle of African Solutions to African Problems (ASAP), respecting African ownership in terms of African peace and security affairs. In February 2013, when visiting China first time after her assumption of AU Commission Chairman, Nkosazana Dlamini-Zuma and Chinese Foreign Minister Yang Jiechi co-chaired the fifth strategic dialogue between China and AU, the first of which was held in 2008. Zuma thanked China for its enduring support for the peace and development in Africa, noting that Africa regards China as a trustworthy partner, and discussed with Yang Jiechi, then foreign minister how to deepen this partnership.[9]

China also plays a positive role in Africa's continental and regional peace and security architecture building, including the AU's Peace and Security Council (PSC) and the Africa Standby Force (ASF). Even though regional mechanisms for responding to conflict and insecurity have suffered from weak capacity, limited resources, and in some cases an absence of political will, their role and influence are slowly growing. China is increasingly engaging with them and has provided modest amounts of financial support for peacekeeping operations and capability-building efforts. For example, China has provided the AU with $1.8 million for its peacekeeping mission in Sudan and given smaller amounts of money to the AU mission in Somalia and West Africa's subregional peace fund. At the FOCAC Johannesburg Summit in December 2015, China strengthened its commitments through,

> Continuing to support the African Union, its Regional Economic Communities and other African sub-regional institutions that play a leading role in coordinating and solving issues of peace and security in Africa and further continues to support and advocate for African solutions to African challenges without interference from outside the continent.

> And providing the AU with US$60 million of free military assistance over the next three years, support the operationalization of the African Peace and Security Architecture, including the operationalization of the African Capacity for the Immediate Response to Crisis and the African Standby Force.[10]

Multilaterally, China participates in various international efforts for improving African peace and security situations. China realizes the significance of increased exchanges and cooperation between the United Nations and the African Union in the field of African peace and security, and will continue to support the United Nations in playing a constructive role in helping resolve the conflicts in Africa, take an active part in the peace keeping missions of the United Nations in Africa, and intensify communication and coordination with Africa in the UN Security Council. For example, Chinese President Xi Jinping has announced at the UN Peacekeeping Summit in September 2015 that,

> China will proactively consider sending at the request of the UN more personnel of engineering, transportation and medical treatment to participate in peacekeeping operations. In the next five years, China will train 2,000 peacekeepers for all countries and launch 10 mine-sweeping assistance programs. In the following five years, China will provide free military aid worthy of 100 million USD in total to the African Union, so as to support the establishment of the African Standby Force and the African Capacity for Immediate Response to Crisis.[11]

There are at least three examples that can prove China's significant contributions in this regard.

The first is China's contributions to UN peacekeeping operations in Africa. Chinese peacekeeper sending began from the end of the 1980s when China sent its first election observers to Namibia in 1989. Since 2000, China has increased its troop contributions to UN peacekeeping missions by twenty-fold.[12] The majority of these troops are deployed in Africa, where they contribute to efforts to help resolve some of the continent's most persistent peace and security challenges. China has sent personnel to peacekeeping operations in Mozambique, Sierra Leone, Liberia, the Democratic Republic of Congo, Cote d'Ivoire, Burundi, Sudan, Western Sahara, Ethiopia, and Eritrea. Under the framework of the comprehensive strategic and cooperative partnership between China and Africa, currently China has participated in six peacekeeping operations in Africa with more than 2,100 peacekeepers and is the biggest peacekeeping troop contributor in the five permanent members of UN Security Council (Table 7.1), with about three-fourths of total Chinese peacekeepers worldwide.

The second case is China's participation in the international anti-piracy efforts in Somalia coast. Since 2008, under the UN authorization, China joined the international fight against piracy for the first time. The goal is to protect the safety of Chinese ships and crews as well as ships carrying humanitarian relief materials for international organizations. As part of the

Table 7.1   Peacekeeping operations China participating (February 2017)

Mission	Troops	Police	Experts on Mission	Total
MINURSO			12	12
MINUSMA	398			398
MONUSCO	221		13	234
UNAMID	235			235
UNMIL	26	171		197
UNMISS	1050	9	4	1063
Total	1930	180	29	2139

Source: UN Peacekeeping Department, *UN Mission's Summary Detailed by Country*, 28 February 2017, accessed 25 March 2017, http://www.un.org/en/peacekeeping/contributors/2017/feb17_3.pdf

international efforts to check piracy, a contingent from the Chinese navy, operating as an independent unit, has been offering escort and rescue missions along the Gulf of Aden. Since December 2008, Chinese forces successfully conducted some 900 missions, escorting more than 6,000 vessels, half of them were foreign vessels, contributing a lot to the safety of the international waters.[13] It is important to point out that China also tries to strengthen cooperation with other countries to help establish secure sea lanes off Somalia's coast in the process.

And the third case is China's mediation efforts in easing the crisis over Darfur. China helped push forward the Sudanese government, the AU, and the UN reaching consensus on the deployment of the hybrid force to Darfur in 2007. From mid-2006, the Chinese government began to persuade President Al Bashir to moderate his position. In their two meetings — at the first China-Africa Summit in November 2006 and Chinese President Hu Jintao's Sudan visit in February 2007 — President Hu talked to President Al Bashir about Chinese concerns with the Darfur crisis and hoped Sudan government to accept the arrangement of a hybrid UN-AU forces.[14] Finally, the Sudanese government agreed to accept it in mid-2007, which did not come easily; and the international community has applauded China's efforts in this area.

MAIN CHARACTERISTICS OF CHINA-AFRICA COOPERATION

At the bilateral, regional and continental, and global levels, China's support for peace and security in Africa is an indication of the country's will to engage itself firmly, alongside the international community, in the maintenance of peace and security in Africa. This also demonstrates Beijing's responsible attitude to world peace and stability and its support for the vision and purpose of the UN Charter. While deserving to be more publicized, China-Africa cooperation in the fields of peace and security is just at its very initial stage, with the following distinctive characteristics:

This cooperation is mainly focusing on traditional security issues. The 2006 *China's African Policy* white paper addresses that,

> In order to enhance the ability of both sides to address non-traditional security threats, it is necessary to increase intelligence exchange, explore more effective ways and means for closer cooperation in combating terrorism, small arms smuggling, drug trafficking, transnational economic crimes, etc.[15]

The second policy paper also focuses on traditional security issues, especially traditional peacekeeping activities. For example, in Liberia, Chinese peacekeepers were active in supervising the implementation of the ceasefire agreement by the country's various parties, and ensured civilian protection, supported police reform, and provided training to the local police. Chinese peacekeepers, through their engineering unit, also played a decisive role in the postconflict reconstruction efforts of the country by helping local communities build and renovate some public facilities such as bridges and roads and providing free medical treatments.[16] To be fair, China-Africa peace and security cooperation has omitted non-traditional security issues such as terrorism, climate change, human security, drug trafficking, etc., to a large extent. The reasons lie in lacking of willingness, capability, experience, urgency, and so on. In one word, non-traditional security issues are not on the top of the policy priorities of both parties.

This cooperation is exclusively focused on governmental level cooperation. Due to its integral relationship with sovereignty, peace and security cooperation is clearly the priority of state-to-state relations. It is important to say that there should have been more room for nonstate actors to participate in this cooperation. For example, there are a lot of state-owned companies having a role, not always positive one due to their poor corporation social responsibility performance, in shaping the China-Africa peace and security cooperation. However, both Chinese and African governments have not made efforts to include them into the China-Africa peace and security cooperation. Another example, while there are abundant intellectual resources in both China and Africa, including universities and think tanks, governments have not explored their full potential to contribute to peace and security cooperation.

Despite a lot of regional, continental, and global level efforts, this cooperation remains primarily bilateral. Related to this is the fact that there is a debate about the nature of FOCAC. For Chinese officials and scholars, FOCAC is a collective bilateral platform for designing China-Africa relations. Its negotiation process is between China and Africa as a whole, while its implementation is bilateral, that is to say between China and individual African countries. Thus, neither the negotiation process nor the implementation process is multilateral as the foreign scholars portray it.[17] And, while FOCAC attaches importance to multilateral cooperation in terms of African peace and security, the bilateral one is the most important. And given the non-interventionist diplomacy, bilateral cooperation is more welcomed by both China and African countries.

Logics for ICACPPS

Why China proposed ICACPPS in 2012 rather than in 2006 or 2015? The answer lies in the development of China-Africa relationship itself. Entering into the twenty-first century, China-Africa has experienced a triple jump: in 2000, the two sides proposed to establish "a new long-term stable partnership of equality and mutual benefit"; in 2003, the two advocated "a new type of partnership featuring long-term stability, equality and mutual benefit and all-round cooperation"; and in 2006, the two were committed to "a new type of strategic partnership between China and Africa featuring political equality and mutual trust, mutually beneficial economic cooperation, and cultural exchanges".[18] In other words, China's engagement in Africa is becoming more comprehensive in its approach and direction: from a one-dimensional relationship that depended on emotional and/or ideological linkages through the 1950s to the early 1990s, to an all-round relationship relations with economic dimension added since 1994–1995, then social and cultural exchanges since the early twenty-first century, and most recently the peace and security cooperation. It is this triple jump that nurtures the forth jump in 2015, namely "comprehensive strategic and cooperative partnership". In sum, it is the transition of China-Africa relations that calls for greater engagement of China in African peace and security affairs.

There are significant and urgent calls for China's engagement in African peace and security. Since the end of the Cold War and especially after entering the twenty-first century, there are at least three main developments calling for China's bigger role in African peace and security affairs, from international level, African continental level, and China-Africa bilateral relationship level.

On the international level, security and development, two traditionally separate policy areas, now are gradually merging. Since the end of the Cold War, the forces of globalization and interdependence have produced an intertwining of security issues with the development issues. During the Cold War, security and development were thoroughly institutionalized as separate "policy fields" with distinct objectives and means of intervention. Schematically, one may say that the Cold War effectuated a broad geographical ordering of security and development, in which development concerned North-South relations, while security concerned East-West relations.[19] Following this, geographical ordering of world politics was an institutionalization of two distinct fields of operations, whose areas of concerns and modes of intervention diverged so as to create a conceptual and political division of labor, and a cognitive division of labor as "development studies",[20] on the one hand, and "security studies",[21] on the other hand, were linked up with and partly funded by the respective agencies in both policy fields.

This situation has been changing since the collapse of the Soviet Union. The prevalence and persistence of conflict in some of the world's poorest areas have both frustrated development efforts and inspired a desire to understand and harmonize the objectives of security and development. Now, security and development concerns have been increasingly understood as being interlinked. Governments and international institutions have stated that they have become increasingly aware of the need to integrate security and development programs in policy interventions in postconflict situations and in their relations to the growing category of failed and potentially "failing" states. Two previously distinct policy areas are overlapping in terms of the actors and agencies engaged and the policy prescriptions advocated. As former UN Secretary-General Kofi Anan says,

> In the twenty-first century, all States and their collective institutions must advance the cause of larger freedom—by ensuring freedom from want, freedom from fear and freedom to live in dignity. In an increasingly

> interconnected world, progress in the areas of development, security and human rights must go hand in hand. There will be no development without security and no security without development. And both development and security also depend on respect for human rights and the rule of law.[22]

Thus, the framework of the "security – development nexus" has been hailed as a way of cohering national and international policy-making interventions in non-Western states, which has two significant policy implications: securitization of development policy and developmentalization of security policy. Such a development asks for more consideration about the security environment, implications, and consequences of China's engagement in Africa.

Entering into the twenty-first century, African security needs have changed significantly. Africa today is more peaceful than it was a decade ago. It should be recognized that progress has been made in overcoming the twin challenges of conflict and insecurity. While conflicts continue, African security challenges have shifted from wars and conflicts in the last decade of the twentieth century to postconflict reconstructions entering into the twenty-first century. With the end of the Cold War, Africa, both governmental and nongovernmental or rebellions forces, was freed from the influence of the bipolar system, which made conflict as the main characteristics in much of Africa. As Christopher Clapham summarizes:

> As the administrative reach of African states declined, with the shrinking of their revenue base and the spread of armed challenges to their power, so the number and size of such zones increased, ... in the process creating a new international relations of statelessness.[23]

There were armed conflicts in 16 of Africa's 53 countries in 1999; most of them defying the classical definition of war occurring between states. Since the early 1990s, Africa has suffered three particularly devastating clusters of interconnected wars centered around West Africa (Liberia, Sierra Leone, Guinea, Cote d'Ivoire), the Greater Horn (Chad, Ethiopia, Eritrea, Somalia, Sudan), and the Great Lakes (Rwanda, Burundi, Zaire/DRC, Uganda). Most casualties of these conflicts have been women and children, usually killed by the effects of diseases and malnutrition intensified by displacement.[24]

Entering into the twenty-first century, with the help of the international community, Africa has ended most of its wars and conflicts. Most of the former war-torn states now turn their focus toward rebuilding their countries, the effort characterized as postconflict reconstruction. However, this task is full of obstacles. Armed conflict continues to affect several countries, including Somalia, the Democratic Republic of Congo, Sudan, and South Sudan, the most notable examples of embedded and cyclical conflicts with devastating humanitarian and economic costs. In other countries, environments of postconflict fragility continue to cast shadows of insecurity while the unforeseen political transition in Tunisia, Egypt, and Libya have cast northern Africa's stability in a different light. In other regions still, localized and communal violence, low-level insurgencies, and politically related violence occur with alarming frequency.

The very nature of China-Africa relationship is changing as well. After half-century developments and under the shadow of international system transformation, China-Africa relationship now is facing at least three transitions: from ideological/emotional-based relationship to economic interest-based one, from economic interest promotion to economic interest protection, and from asymmetrical interdependence to symmetrical interdependence.

China-Africa relationship is transforming from a kind of relationship mainly based on emotional and/or ideological intimacy to one that is based more on economic interest consideration, if not to say this process has finished. Looking back to China-Africa relationship during the period from the 1950s to the early 1990s, emotional and/or ideological linkages, to a very great extent, supported this bilateral relationship and made it one of the closest relationships of China's foreign exchanges. Meanwhile, because of geographical distance and poor economic conditions of both parties, the economic dimension of China-Africa relationship was quite weak. In 1950, bilateral trade volume was only $12.14 million; in 1989, the figure was $1.17 billion, with 9.7 times growth by 40 years. Since 1994–1995, China has paid much more attention to Africa, with specific focus on economic relations. In 1996, bilateral trade volume increased to $4.03 billion, nearly four times that of 1989.[25] Since then, the economic relation grows very fast with reaching $10 billion in 2000, $100 billion in 2010, and more than $220 billion in 2014. With economic linkages growing, bilateral trade frictions increase as well, which to some extent diminishes the emotional foundations of this bilateral relationship, along with the power shifting from the first-generation leaders to the second generation across the whole African continent.[26]

The second transition China-Africa relations facing is the economic relationship now is shifting from promoting to protecting China's overseas interest. Since the late 1990s, China initiated a "going global" policy for promoting Chinese interests, mainly economic interest, worldwide. The establishment of the FOCAC in 2000 strengthened this effort in Africa greatly.[27] Since then, we have witnessed the fast growing presence of China's economic interests across the African continent. However, at the same time, the security concerns over China's presence in Africa rose under these changing circumstances of global and African uncertainties, including mainly energy security, civilian protection, investment safety, and others. In 2009, Africa's oil exports to China represented 33% of China's total oil imports, and 60% of total Sino-African trade.[28] As has been the case with oil companies from other countries operating in Africa, Chinese oil installations, and the Chinese citizens who work on them, have been targeted in numerous countries, including Nigeria, Ethiopia, and Sudan. Since early 2011, the outbreak of the "Arab Spring" highlighted the importance of protecting China's overseas economic interests and national citizens. Based on the principle of "People First", to protect overseas Chinese and economic interests is and will be one of the top priorities of China's foreign policy in general and China's Africa policy in particular.

While the above two transitions are already in the making, the third transition in Sino-African relations is a would-be one that will happen in the next few years or decade. This transition is, from my perspective, moving from asymmetrical interdependence to symmetrical interdependence. As all know that the current Sino-African relationship is an asymmetrical interdependent one with China depends more on African natural resources and Africa depends more on opportunities along with China's rise and Sino-African relations developments. However, there are several developments that have potential for undermining the current interdependence between these two parties. The first is the slowing down of China's economic growth that it is a natural development after three decades and more rapid growth with the signs have emerged early 2013, as the growth rates in the first quarter of 2013 was about 7.5%. While China is slowing down, Africa is rising, with six African countries on the list of 10 fastest growing in the first decade of the twenty-first century, and seven African countries on the list of 10 fastest growing from 2011 to 2015. The third development that will change the interdependence between China and Africa is that Africa is returning to the traditional powers' strategic consideration and entering into partnerships with other emerging powers, as exemplified by the recovery of EU-Africa Summit and Japan's TICAD and the creation of India-Africa Summit, South Korea-Africa Summit, India-Africa Summit, and Turkey-Africa Summit.

Such three transitions call for deep thinking about the future of China-Africa relationship, especially how to maintain the current positive dynamics, and create new momentum. Among these measures, one full of promises is the peace and security affairs, which is recognised as a competitive advantage for China.

CHALLENGES FOR ICACPPS

At the FOCAC Johannesburg Summit, both China and Africa promised to implement the ICACPPS for promoting the building of peace and security pillar of China-Africa relationship. However, there are still significant challenges for ICACPPS.

There is a huge gap between the expectations of African, Chinese, and the rest of the world.

Due to its severe peace and security pressures, African does expect China to contribute a lot to African peace and stability. First of all, China is expected to provide more financial supports for African peace and security problem-solving. With its remarkable records of economic growth since the 1980s, China now has to engage proactively with a changing global order. Increasingly, since the financial and economic crisis that erupted in America in 2008, China came under enormous pressure to redefine its role in and contribution to global problem-solving, with the African continent at the core. Meanwhile, Africans seem to expect China to provide support in every policy field, including, for example, antiterrorism, antipiracy, peacekeeping, conflict resolution, crisis management, mediation, infrastructure building, postconflict reconstruction, etc.

However, there are two opposite expectations regarding China's role in African peace and security affair. The first one comes from Africans who are worried about losing ownership and controlling powers to China's hand. For them, Africa has a long memory of being enslaved by external powers, there is a potential of "second scramble for Africa" in terms of peace and security affair if Africa fully embraces China's engagement. The second one comes from the former colonials and the global hegemony of the United States. For these Western powers, China's engagement means a zero-sum game that they will be replaced by China. While the West always calls for greater contributions from

China to global public goods, the main content of what should China provide is not clear. According to my personal observation, there are only two kinds of public goods that the West welcomes. The first one is to share burden or more blatantly to pay more money, and the second is a kind of damage control in places like Sudan and Zimbabwe. However, these two kinds of public goods are negative ones from China's perspective, because there is no any added-value in providing them. China can only contribute to preventing some bad things but not to promote some good things. If China wants to expand its provision of public goods from, for example, economic opportunities to security guarantee in the Asia-Pacific region, it will be challenged by the rebalancing efforts of other countries.[29]

Under these two contrary expectations, China-Africa peace and security cooperation will be very sensitive because every step is likely to be contested and evaluated for its positive or negative impact. Thus, it will be a serious task for both China and Africa to manage this expectation gap.

Parallel to the expectation gap, there is a capacity gap between the willingness and the available resources.

While China promised to strengthen peace and security cooperation with Africa, the capability deficit is a key challenge. Generally, the resources that China can assign to support Africa, including peace and security, are limited. China is still a developing state with uneven progress between different areas, as repeatedly highlighted in various official statements; consequently, a number of Chinese citizens question the rationale for providing international assistance citing that there are still huge urgent domestic needs. As part of its effort to nurture a better international image, China continues with its tradition of sending medical teams with the best doctors, nurses, and technicians to Africa and other developing countries, which arguably increases the domestic healthcare needs and capability gap. This is a very tangible problem that Chinese citizens complain about.[30]

More specifically, China now is not well prepared to provide significant support for Africa peace and security affairs. For example, China's peace-keeping contributions are appraised by the international community, while criticized not to contribute combating troops. Before May 2013, China only provided logistic supporting troops, such as medical teams and engineering companies. The key reason for not providing combat troops lies in the lack of such capability. Chinese peacekeeping training center has been established in 2009, which is the first of its kind in the country; it is a joint project of the Ministry of National Defense and the UN.[31] To be fair, only 6 years after establishment, the center is at the very beginning stage of improving capability of Chinese peacekeepers, especially in terms of combat troops. Thus, while China is the biggest contributor of peacekeepers among the permanent members of the Security Council, its combat troops are still very small; and it is really a huge step for China to send its first combat troop to Africa when China declared to send its first security/ police troop to UN peacekeeping operation in Mali May 2013. And this fact is a real consideration behind the decision to join the new UN peacekeeping capacity readiness system, setting up a permanent peacekeeping police squad, and establishing an 8,000-strong standby peacekeeping force, declared by Chinese President Xi at the UN Peacekeeping Summit in September 2015.[32]

There is still a policy gap because China and Africa hold different views on non-interference principle.

As is well known, China officially holds as a central premise of its foreign policy that governments should not interfere in the "internal affairs" of other countries. This principle is welcomed by most African countries and people, while many Western scholars and policymakers claim that China's interpretation of noninterference and respect for sovereignty has affected, not always positively, modes of governance as well as ongoing conflicts. It is interesting to point out that in recent years, China has become somewhat more flexible in its interpretation of non-interference and has shown to be willing to take a more active diplomatic role in the resolution of internal conflicts. As already noted, Beijing eventually deployed significant diplomatic pressures on Khartoum to push the Sudanese government to accept the deployment of UN peacekeepers.

Contrary to China's flexible adjustment, Africa has gradually moved from setting conditions for non-interference policy. The AU Charter declares that The Union shall function in accordance with:

> (g) non-interference by any Member State in the internal affairs of another;
> (h) the right of the Union to intervene in a Member State pursuant to a decision of the Assembly in respect of grave circumstances, namely: war crimes, genocide and crimes against humanity.

In terms of policy, this means that African countries have agreed to pool their sovereignty to enable the AU to act as the ultimate guarantor and protector of the rights and well-being of African people. In effect, the AU has adopted a much more interventionist stance and has embraced a spirit of nonindifference toward war crimes and crimes against humanity in Africa.[33]

Interestingly, this policy gap between China and Africa with regard to the non-interference principle once again magnifies the expectation gap and capability gap between China and Africa. Thus, to understand what role China will play in future African peace and security affairs, one has to keep an eye on the evolution of China's non-interference principle.

Policy Prescriptions for ICACPPS

China-Africa peace and security cooperation has achieved significant progress in the past decades. The FOCAC Johannesburg Summit has made strong commitment to build the ICACPPS, China and Africa should join hand together, while strengthening the traditional strong aspects of cooperation, attaching more importance to the following dimensions:

To broaden the scope of cooperation to cover most non-traditional security issues.

As mentioned above, current cooperation between China and Africa in peace and security is focusing on mostly traditional ones, including military exchange, military training, peacekeeping, antipiracy, and so on. However, with the pacification of Africa conflict-torn countries and achievements of postconflict reconstruction in transitional countries, looking to the mid-long-term future, or for 20–30 years time frame, China's support to African peace and security is possibly to be changed because of the rapidly evolving environment. That is, while traditional security challenges will continue to feature in the African landscape, the non-traditional security challenges are sure to be highlighted in the near future. More and more security challenges will be linked with the development of African continent, including for example, climate change, environmental degradation, human security, poverty reduction, unemployment or underemployment, etc.

Thus, there are two policy areas China and Africa should pay more attention to, along with lasting emphasis on cooperation on traditional security. One is the peace and security cooperation under the UN 2030 Agenda for Sustainable Development (initially named as UN Post-2015 Development Agenda). As passed at the UN Development Summit in September 2015, peace and security is listed as an independent goal of the 2030 Agenda, namely Goal 16 "promote peaceful and inclusive societies for sustainable development, provide access to justice for all and build effective, accountable and inclusive institutions at all levels".[34] Under the framework of 2030 Agenda, China and Africa should jointly address peace and security issues, contributing to the realization of peace and security targets of the Africa Agenda 2063 especially the goal of "Silence the Gun by 2020" of the First Ten-Year Implementation Plan (2014–2023) of Agenda 2063.

Another is the cooperation on governance experience exchange. As we all remember that in the late 1960s and 1970s, China faced arguably more serious security challenges than most African countries today. After adopting of the reform and opening up policy in 1979, China has successfully addressed lots of security challenges through its development achievements. Thus, China now is one or two steps ahead of Africa, and China's experience of how to develop and how to solve security challenges arising in the process of developing will be of great relevance for Africa. This is the very reason why the Party School of the Central Committee, CPC held the conference on "China-Africa governance and development experience" on September 24, 2013.[35]

To motivate more nonstate actors to contribute to building of ICACPPS.

China and African countries do prefer to governmental cooperation in terms of peace and security affairs. However, given the fact of increasing diversification of actors and interests involved in the China-Africa relations, central governmental focused approach needs to be supplemented by introducing all stakeholders into, including at least the following three elements.

First of all, there should be more room for provincial and local governments to play their roles in China-Africa peace and security cooperation. As Prof. Zheng Yongnian, a famous China expert in Singapore rightly pointed out, China is a de-facto federalist state, with provincial and local governments which have lots of bargaining chips in relation to the central government. In the field of international economic cooperation, provincial and local governments have their own cost-benefits accounts, significantly different with the central governmental one.[36] This holds true as well in China-Africa relations. All 31 Chinese provinces have economic activities in Africa, 22 of them sending medical teams to Africa, and 126 sister cities with Africa between 28 provinces and African countries.[37] The First Forum on China-Africa Local Government Cooperation, held in August 2012, argues for faster development of local governmental level engagement with Africa, with number of sister cities (provinces) reaching 220 in the next 5 years.[38]

Secondly, there is an urgent need for including various companies, both state-owned and private ones, into the China-Africa peace and security cooperation process. Considering the bad reputation of some Chinese companies' corporation social responsibility (CSR) performance, how can China ensure, while doing business in Africa, that indeed its actions do not interfere with the aspiration of the populations for stability and development, by exacerbating already existing tension and does not increase inequalities in the country? In doing business in Africa, China may need to apply the *"Do no harm"* principle and principles of social corporate responsibility. Only by incorporating them, will the profit-seeking businessmen hold their responsibility.

Thirdly, China needs to develop its own private security companies to help promoting Africa peace and security. To have Chinese private security companies operating in Africa will greatly help the China-Africa peace and security cooperation. On the one hand, Chinese private security companies will improve the CSR performance of Chinese companies in Africa due to common language, culture, practice, etc. On the other hand, the presence of Chinese private companies will also help China better communicate with local actors and better understand local security situation. However, due to the very slow domestic readjustment, most of Chinese private security companies have not been market-oriented reformed, and most of the reformed ones are very weak in terms of operating abroad.[39]

Finally, to rely more on multilateral cooperation platforms.

To promote peace and security cooperation, it is important to realize a balance between engagement and noninterference. However, as mentioned above, one of the main characteristics of China-Africa peace and security cooperation is bilateral, whose risks greatly interfere into African domestic affair. Thus, a smart approach to address such a dilemma is to rely more on multilateral cooperation platforms.

First of all, African peace and security issues are multilateral in nature, to a very great extent. Because of the legacies of colonialism, African conflicts, both domestic ones and interstate ones, involve regional powers because of either ethnic considerations or border disputes or resources competition or other reasons. Thus, to participate in one country's post-conflict reconstruction, to some extent, influences the third parties, which calls for trilateral cooperation.

Secondly, as a result, peace and security cooperation in general compels consideration of expansion of trilateral or multilateral cooperation and coordination. For example, peacekeeping or peacebuilding operations normally include at least three parties: the conflict-torn country, peacekeepers sending country/countries, and UN Peacekeeping Operation Department. Currently, except for sending peacekeepers, most of China's participation in postconflict reconstruction in Africa is bilateral.

And thirdly, thanks to the fast development of China-Africa relationship, many international actors call for trilateral cooperation with China in Africa, including the European Union, the United States, Japan, South Korea, and some other international organizations – both governmental and nongovernmental. Meanwhile, these actors established their trilateral cooperation to pressure China to start trilateral cooperation with them.

It's important to note that the key to such a trilateral and/or multilateral cooperation should depend upon on African continental and regional organizations. As illustrated earlier, China has had close cooperation with African continental and regional organizations, as reflected in the ICACPPS. China should closely cooperate with African continental and regional organizations, especially in the fields of peacekeeping, peace and security financing, peacekeepers training, African Standby Force building, international arm control especially small arms and light weapons control, antiterrorism, antipiracy, transnational crimes, and so on. Promoting cooperation with African organizations will help China to overcome the dilemma posed between deepening engagement and non-interference on the one hand, and to counterbalance the pressures of trilateral cooperation from the EU, the United States, and other third parties significantly.

NOTES

1. President Hu Jintao (2012), 'Open Up New Prospects for A New Type of China-Africa Strategic Partnership,' Speech at the Opening Ceremony of the Fifth Ministerial Conference of The Forum on China-Africa Cooperation, Beijing, FOCAC website, 19 July 2012, accessed 20 July 2012, http://www.focac.org/eng/dwjbzjjhys/hyqk/t953115.htm.

2. *Declaration of the Johannesburg Summit of the Forum on China-Africa Cooperation*, FOCAC Website, 25 December 2015, accessed 26 December 2015, http://www.focac.org/eng/ltda/dwjbzjjhys_1/hywj/t1327960.htm.

3. Chinese Ministry of Foreign Affairs (2006), *China's African Policy* (Beijing).

4. *China's Second Africa Policy Paper*, Xinhua News Agency, 5 December 2015, accessed 6 December 2015, http://africa.chinadaily.com.cn/2015-12/05/content_22632880.htm.

5. 'Africa: China's Growing Role in Africa - Implications for U.S. Policy,' *AllAfrica*, accessed 1 November 2011, http://allafrica.com/stories/201111021230.html?viewall=1.

6. Various presentations at the conferences of the Saferworld-supported Africa-China-EU Expert Working Group on Conventional Arms (EWG), 2–3 July 2013, Nairobi, Kenya, and 13–14 November 2013, Brussels, Belgium.

7. ZhangWenxian and Gu Zhaomin (2013), 'China's Law Diplomacy: Theory and Practice,' *Global Review*, Summer 2013, pp. 48–50.

8. President Hu Jintao, 'Open Up New Prospects for a New Type of China-Africa Strategic Partnership'.

9. 'China, AU pledge to Enhance Friendly Cooperation,' *China Daily*, accessed 16 February 2013, http://www.chinadaily.com.cn/china/2013-02/16/content_16225150.htm.

10. *The Forum on China-Africa Cooperation Johannesburg Action Plan(2016–2018)*, FOCAC Website, 25 December 2015, accessed 28 December 2015, http://www.focac.org/eng/ltda/dwjbzjjhys_1/hywj/t1327961.htm.

11. 'Xi Jiniping Attends and Addresses UN Leaders' Summit on Peacekeeping,' Ministry of Foreign Affairs of China, accessed 29 September 2015, http://www.fmprc.gov.cn/mfa_eng/topics_665678/xjpdmgjxgsfwbcxlhgcl70znxlfh/t1304147.shtml.

12. Bates Gill and Chin-Hao Huang (2009), 'China's Expanding Role in Peacebuilding: Prospects and Policy Implications,' *SIPRI Policy Paper*, 25.

13. Zhou Bo (2015), 'Birth of Truly Global Chinese Navy,' China Daily, updated 10 April 2015, http://www.chinadaily.com.cn/opinion/2015-04/10/content_20400202.htm.

14. Gareth Evans and Donald Steinberg, 'China and Darfur: 'Signs of Transition',' *Guardian Unlimited*, accessed 11 June 2007, http://www.crisisgroup.org/home/index.cfm?id=4891&l=1.

15. Chinese Ministry of Foreign Affairs, *China's African Policy*.

16. Zhang Chun (2013), 'China's Engagement in African Post-Conflict Reconstruction: Achievements and Future Developments,' in James Shikwati, ed., *China-Africa Partnership: The Quest for a Win-Win Relationship* (Nairobi: IREN Kenya).

17. Li Anshan (2012), 'Why the Forum on China-Africa Cooperation-Analyzing China's Strategy in Africa,' *Foreign Affairs Review* (Chinese), 29:3; Sven Grimm (2012), 'The Forum on China-Africa Cooperation – Its Political Role and Functioning,' *CCS Policy Briefing*, Centre for Chinese Studies, Stellenbosch, May 2012.

18. President Hu Jintao, 'Open Up New Prospects for a New Type of China-Africa Strategic Partnership'.

19. See Geir Lundestad (1999), *East, West, North, South: Major Developments in International Politics Since 1945* (Oxford: Oxford University Press).

20. Frederick Cooper and Randall Packard, eds. (1998), *International Development and the Social Sciences: Essays on the History and Politics of Knowledge* (California: University of California Press).

21. Pinar Bilgin and Adam. D. Morton (2002), 'Historicizing the Representations of 'Failed States': Beyond the Cold War Annexation of the Social Sciences?' *Third World Quarterly*, 23:1, pp. 55–80.

22. *In Larger Freedom: Towards Development, Security and Human Rights for All*, Report of the Secretary-General, United Nations, 21 March 2005, accessed 20 June 2005, http://www.un.org/largerfreedom/contents. htm.

23. Christopher Clapham (1996), *Africa and the International System: The Politics of State Survival* (New York: Cambridge University Press), p. 222.

24. Paul D. Williams (2009), 'Africa's Challenges, America's Choice,' in Robert R. Tomes, Angela Sapp Mancini, James T. Kirkhope, eds., *Crossroads Africa: Perspectives on U.S.-China-Africa Security Affairs* (Washington, DC: Council for Emerging National Security Affairs), p. 37.

25. 'Fifty Years of China-Africa Economic and Trade Relations,' Ministry of Commerce, July 16, 2002, http://www.mofcom.gov.cn/aarticle/bg/ 200207/20020700032255.html; Li Yanchang (2003), 'The Present Situation and Prospects of the Sino-Africa Economy and Trade Relationship Development,' *Journal of Shanxi Administration School and Shanxi Economic Management School*, 17:4, p. 45.

26. Li Weijian et al. (2010), 'Towards a New Decade: A Study on the Sustainability of FOCAC,' *West Asia and Africa*, 209 (September), p. 8.

27. Kerry Brown and Zhang Chun (2009), 'China in Africa – Preparing for the Next Forum for China Africa Cooperation,' *Chatham House Briefing Note*, June 2009, pp. 5–6.

28. Such a dynamic is not unique to China. In 2008, oil accounted for 80% of all imports from Africa to the United States, the continent's second largest trade partner after China. See Standard Bank (2011), 'China and the US in Africa: Measuring Washington's Response to Beijing's Commercial Advance,' *Standard Bank Economic Strategy Paper*, 2011; Standard Bank (2011), 'Oil Price to Remain at Two-and-a-Half-Year Peak,' *Standard Bank Press Release*, 21 February 2011.

29. Zhang Chun (2013), 'Managing China-U.S. Power Transition in a Power Diffusion Era,' *Conference Proceedings, The International Symposium on The Change of International System and China*, 27–28 November 2013, Fudan University, Shanghai, pp. 176–177.

30. Zhang Chun (2010), 'Projecting Soft Power through Medical Diplomacy: A Case Study of Chinese Medical Team to Africa,' *Contemporary International Relations* (Chinese), 3.

31. 'China's Military Opens First Peacekeeping Training Center near Beijing,' *People's Daily*, accessed 26 June 2009, http://english.peopledaily.com.cn/ 90001/90776/90785/6686691.html.

32. 'Xi Jiniping Attends and Addresses UN Leaders' Summit on Peacekeeping'.

33. Tim Murithi (2009), 'The African Union's Transition from Non-Intervention to Non-Indifference: An Ad Hoc Approach to the Responsibility to Protect?' *IPG*, 1, pp. 94–95.

34. *Transforming Our World: The 2030 Agenda for Sustainable Development*, UN Document, A/RES/70/1, 21 October 2015.

35. 'Conference on "China-Africa Governance and Development Experience" Held by CCPS,' FOCAC Website, accessed 9 October 2013, http://www.focac.org/chn/xsjl/zflhyjjljh/t1086342.htm.

36. Zheng Yongnian (2007), *De Facto Federalism in China: Reforms and Dynamics of Central-Local Relations* (London: World Scientific); Zheng Yongnian (2006), 'De Facto Federalism and Dynamics of Central-Local Relations in China,' *Discussion Paper*, No. 8, China Policy Institute, Nottingham University, June 2006.

37. China International Friendship Cities Association, accessed 15 February 2015, http://www.cifca.org.cn.

38. *Beijing Declaration of the First Forum on China-Africa Local Government Cooperation*, Beijing, 28 August 2012; 'Li Keqiang Speech at the Opening Ceremony of the First China-Africa Local Government Forum,' *Xinhua News Agency*, accessed 27 August 2012, http://www.newshome.us/news-2060728-Li-Keqiang-speech-at-the-opening-ceremony-of-the-first-China-Africa-Local-Government-Forum.html.

39. Presentation by Mr. Xun Jinqing, CEO of the Shandong Huawei Security Group Co., Ltd, China, at the Conference 'Managing Security and Risk in China-Africa Relations' on 25–26 April 2013, Center for Chinese Studies, Stellenbosch University, South Africa.

Zhang Chun is Deputy Director of Institute for Foreign Policy Studies, Shanghai Institutes for International Studies (SIIS). His research focuses on China-Africa relations, African peace and security, UN 2030 Agenda for sustainable development, and international relations theory.

PART II

Case Studies

CHAPTER 8

China in International Conflict Management

Darfur Issue as a Case

Jian Junbo

Preface

After the outbreak of the Darfur crisis in February 2003, China as an emerging international player with substantive economic involvement in Sudan was expected to be involved in the resolution of the crisis and the recovery of the region. Due to China's economic and strategic interests, diplomatic philosophy, cultural and philosophical tradition, the China's positions, principles, and approaches on the Darfur issue-resolving were somewhat different from those of Western countries; China had quite a particular policy toward Sudan and approach to deal with Darfur issue, an approach which is characteristic of its international conflict management to this day.

This chapter will review China's policy on the Darfur issue in crisis period and analyze the role that China had played. Based on this analysis, the features of China's conflict management on international conflicts will be explained and concluded.

J. Junbo (✉)
Institute of International Studies, Fudan University, Shanghai, China
e-mail: jianjunbo@fudan.edu.cn

C. Alden et al. (eds.), *China and Africa*,
DOI 10.1007/978-3-319-52893-9_8

CHINESE INVOLVEMENT IN SUDAN:
AS AN ECONOMIC PARTNER

In the period of the Cold War, China-Sudan's economic relationship, from 1959 when their diplomatic relationship was established, was generally marked by politics. For instance, before the 1990s, China's support for this country (e.g., giving economic aid and sending medical groups) was echoed by Sudan's political support in international settings, such as adhering "one China" policy or refusing the accession of Taiwan to the United Nations. However, with the collapse of the Cold War and the deepening economic involvement of China in this country, Sino-Sudanese relations were marked primarily by more investment and trade, like China's relations with some other African countries, notwithstanding the emergence of some areas of political friction.

Investment and Trade

Before the onset of the Darfur crisis in February 2003, the greater part of Chinese investment in Sudan was in the field of energy, mainly invested by one Chinese oil giant – the state-owned enterprise, Chinese National Petroleum Corporation (CNPC). Since 1995, this enterprise's investment in Sudan has reached around $27 billion, linked with many oil-related businesses, such as oil-exploring, extracting, refining, pipeline-paving, and harbor-building. The CNPC was also the primary stock holder of Sudanese big oil-related corporations, exercising considerable influence over the Sudanese economy. Due to this, Sudanese government felt compelled to pursue a foreign policy rebalancing that was aimed at reducing CNPC's influence on Sudan's economy, introducing investment from other countries' companies.

Nevertheless, Sudan's economy largely benefited from Chinese investment. According to the statistics, in 2003 when crisis broke out, the total Sino-Sudan's trade volume reached $1.92 billion, more than that in 2002 ($1.55 billion), and oil trade was a main trade form between these two countries.[1] As a result from 1999, Sudan shifted from being an oil-importer to an oil-exporter.

In addition, many Chinese private enterprise entered into Sudan, investing in diverse field such as agriculture, shoe industry, beverages, and so on. Meanwhile, some companies of China invested those labor-intensive industries, such as constructing power stations, bridges, roads, houses, and harbors. It was reported that by 2009, the FDI that Sudan received from China reached at least 150 billion Chinese Yuan within only ten years.

In the meantime, bilateral trade relations developed quickly; the volume was increased from a tiny number to $81.8 billion in 2008 and to $63.9 billion in 2009, especially bolstered by the oil trade.[2] Apart from the energy sector, the trade in other fields was also grew. For example, the two government held discussions about the possibility of creatiing Free Trade Agreements (FTAs) to enhance agricultural exports from Sudan to the Chinese market as well as conducting trade settlements in national currencies (Sudanese Pound or Chinese Yuan). From 2003 to 2011, the two-way trade volume reached 59.6 billion making Sudan China's third largest trading partner in Africa and the Middle East.[3]

Aid for Development

Except for the Chinese grant aid (e.g., on 5 September 2009, one primary school that Chinese embassy to Sudan donated had finished. This school was at the capital of South Darfur state.[4]), much financial and material assistance for Sudanese was implemented by Chinese companies. CNPC, for example, the biggest investor of China to Sudan, was one of the biggest supporters of Sudanese social projects, often linked to infrastructure provisions. It helped Sudanese to build local hospitals, bridges, airports, roads, and other infrastructures. By 2006, its aid in the public affairs and facilities of Sudan reached $32.28 million, from which more than 1.5 million Sudanese people had benefited. On 31 January 2007, CNPC donated $1.9 million to Sudan, of which $0.9 million would be used for training Sudan's specialists on oil, and $1 million for promoting the living condition and medical facilities of Sudanese orphanages, old folk's homes, and some social medical institutions. In another example, in August 2008, CNPC donated $50,000 to initiate a health-related cultural campaign of pculture and medicines in the countryside".[5]

In addition, some Chinese government-controlled social organizations provided donations to Sudan. For example, in March 2010, China Poverty Eradication Award (CPEA) granted $110,000 worth of materials to two Sudanese charity organizations, including medical facilities, flashlights, and radios, which would assist hospitals and those refugees who were coming back to Sudan.[6] On 19 November 2010, Yang Qinghai, the Vice-secretary of CPEA said that CPEA would give total more than $600 million to Sudan to build 13 hospitals for maternal and child health within 3 years, as a contribution to the building of Sudan's healthcare system.[7]

China assistance also reached Darfur in the form of dams and hydropower stations, schools, hospitals, and so on. Reportedly, China provided material assistance worth $11 million to Darfur, $1.8 million to African Union, and $0.5 million to a UN fund to solve the Darfur issue.[8]

That is, as an economic partner of China, Chinese government, firms, and social organizations have donated and aided Sudanese by financial and materials approaches. This donation and aid is considered by Beijing as an auxiliary means for Sudan's development (and development is seen as the key to resolving divisive domestic issues), certainly as well as an approach to enhance the bilateral relations.

Conflict

Although China and Sudan maintained a good relationship in general, this was not always the case and certainly elements in Sudanese civil society, especially opposition political organizations, complained about aspects of Chinese cooperation and aid to the central government.

In October 2008, nine Chinese workers serving in CNPC that had business in the region near to Darfur were kidnapped by armed personnel from one rebel groups in South Sudan, and four Chinese persons were ultimately killed by this group.[9] This was a stark reminder that some rebel groups were not fond of China's deep involvement in Sudan, because this involvement were considered to be strengthening Khartoum's ruling power and encouraging its ambition of oppressing the Southern black Sudanese. Because this violence aim at Chinese in Sudan could not be stopped by Sudanese central government, the relationship between Beijing and Khartoum was challenged, which further gave rise to potential conflicts between them.

Beyond these political disputes, some conflicts occurred between Chinese private companies and Sudan's local civil society. Some Chinese private companies had a bad image amongst the local population derived from the low wages paid to local workers, absence of local environmental protection, arm sales to central government, and so forth. This people-to-people distrust and some hostility largely influenced Chinese business and also led to some misunderstandings and further tensions between China and Sudan. Yet despite these problems, these disagreements and disputes did not harm the overall relationship.

CHINESE POLICY OVER DARFUR ISSUE: FROM NEUTRALITY TO ACTIVE ENGAGEMENT

Generally, Chinese policy on the Darfur issue experienced three stages successively: indifference to crisis, persuading Khartoum, and active involvement. This policy change reflects China's adherence to its national interests, the sensitivity of the international responsibility, and the change of international politics as well.

Indifferent to Sudan's Crisis (2003–2004)

When military conflicts happened in the western part of Sudan, China didn't pay much attention to them. Even when two Chinese people were kidnapped in March 2004 in Darfur, Beijing did not seem to respond to the crisis, although this kidnapping resulted from that local unrest there.

Clearly, at that moment Chinese leaders were successfully persuaded by the Sudanese government that what happened in the western Sudan was just a local violent affair that could be controlled by government. This is despite the fact that the United States (US) considered this violence "genocide" undertaken with the authority of the Sudanese president, Omar Hassan al-Bashir.

In general, in the period from 2003 when the humanitarian crisis in Darfur began to the mid-term of 2004 when China started experiencing significant international pressure, Beijing maintained an attitude of relative indifferent toward the Darfur issue. It trusted Khartoum's account, and even supported Bashir authority in international society. For example, China appealed for the United Nations to provide African Union's (AU's) peacekeeping force in Sudan with financial support, since Khartoum refused to allow the UN peacekeeping forces to deploy in Sudan.

In addition, China refused to sanction Sudan when the UN planned to adopt a US-supported resolution that would impose sanction on Sudan. Chinese representatives in the UN explained that what was happened in Darfur was not a "genocide" but an internal conflict between different tribes who competed for resources – water, land, and oils; and according to this, the crisis should be handled by Sudanese government and its people, and not by external actors since Sudan was a sovereign state. From this explanation, it could be seen that at least in this early period of the Darfur crisis, China was convinced that Sudan government could control the situation and deal with this issue well, and large-scale external engagement was unnecessary.

Persuading Sudanese Central Government to Accept the UN's Suggestions (2004–2006)

However, China's policy toward Darfur issue had a subtle change from the indifference or neutrality to taking some constructive activities through persuading Omar Hassan al-Bashir authority to accept the UN's resolutions.

In August 2004, Lui Guijin, the Chinese special representative to Darfur, visited Sudan. There he confirmed the roles of the AU and the League of Arab States (LAS) in the dealing with Darfur crisis and stated that China hoped Sudanese government could comply with those relevant UN resolutions,[10] in order to relieve the deteriorating condition in Darfur. Meanwhile, he also declared China would provide 5 million Chinese Yuan-valued materials as humanitarian assistance to help mitigate the crisis in Darfur. Ambassador Lui Guijin's speech could be seen as the earliest efforts to persuade the Sudanese government to accept the UN resolutions.

In November 2006, Chinese Premier Wen Jiabao spoke to Sudanese President Bashir in the Sino-Africa Summit in Beijing, saying that China supported the UN Resolution 1706, hoping the Sudanese government could comprehensively cooperate with international society and the UN's resolution and Darfur Peace Agreement, to realize comprehensive peace and stability in Darfur as early as possible.[11] It was known the UN Resolution 1706 called for the imposition of sanction on Sudan since it stated that the UN would "impede implementation of the Agreement, and reiterates its intention to take, including in response to a request by the African Union, strong and effective measures, such as an asset freeze or travel ban, against any individual or group that violates or attempts to block the implementation of the Agreement or commits human rights violations".[12]

Chinese President Hu Jintao also extended the same message to Bashir and especially hoped the Sudanese government could accept the hybrid UN-AU peacekeeping force according to the UN Resolution 1769, when he met Bashir in Beijing in November 2006 and visited Sudan in February 2007. Mostly due to China's persuasion, the joint peacekeeping force entered Sudanese territory in 2007 at last, which was considered as "a great achievement in the settlement of the crisis there".[13]

Practical Activism involving the Darfur Issue at Bilateral and International Levels (2006–2011)

After 2006, China took a more active role in dealing with the Darfur issue in three ways: pressing Sudanese government to accept international resolutions; promoting to build a joint peacekeeping troop in Darfur; and coordinating with related actors in international society.

Pressing the Sudanese Government

Although from 2004, Beijing had rhetorically persuaded Khartoum to accept the UN resolutions, it became more serious and active in applying pressure on Khartoum, for instance, using more harsh language to criticize Bashier authority, supporting more stringent UN resolutions that Khartoum refused, and contacting with those rebelling groups.

In March 2008, Liu Guijin, the Chinese special representative to Darfur, in a press conference stated that Sudan's government must do much more, such as agreeing to sit at the negotiation table, and stopping armed militias competing for territorywith rebel groups.

Meanwhile, China didn't veto UN Resolution 1769, which called for the appointment of a UN-led peacekeeping mission to Sudan, working with the AU's peacekeeping force. That meant a joint peace-keeping mission led by both the UN and the AU would be deployed in Darfur, which was opposed by Khartoum because it worried that the joint army would undermine Sudan's sovereignty. However, when it became clear that China supported this resolution, Sudan agreed in principle to the hybrid peacekeeping mission.

Furthermore, Beijing also took some pragmatic actions to balance the interests of China in North Sudan and South Sudan. This produced more pressure on Khartoum. For instance, it set up a consulate in Juba, the capital of South Sudan. Furthermore, China contacted with South Sudan's leaders of the rebel groups, for example, inviting Salva Kiir, the Chairman of Sudan Liberation Movement, to visit Beijing two times.

Pushing to Build a Joint Peacekeeping Force in Darfur

In November 2006, Kofi Annan, the Secretary-General of the UN, sug-gested to deploy an UN-led peacekeeping troop with 17,000 soldiers and

3,000 policemen in Sudan, commanded by the UN and worked with the AU's peacekeeping mission. This suggestion as one part of so-called "Annan Plan" was supported by all Security Council members, including China. In July 2007, Security Council approved the UN resolution, which decided to send an UN-led peacekeeping mission to Darfur. Although China abstained from the resolution, this made the resolution effective, and the operation of joint peacekeeping force was put into practice.

Partly pushed by China, Sudan began to accept a hybrid peacekeeping force to stabilize Darfur, although some delays of the deployment happened due to Sudan's stonewalling.[14] One official in charge of Darfur issue of the LAS said that in order to help Sudan realize peace, stability, and development, China played key role in reaching a consensus on deploying a hybrid peacekeeping force in Sudan. Because of China's coordination, Sudanese government agreed to accept this hybrid force.[15]

Coordinating with International Actors

In May 2007, only two afterAmbassador Liu Guijin was appointed as the Chinese special representative to Darfur, he visited Africa wice, talked with Sudan, the AU, the LAS, and some Western powers, coordinating with them to reach some shared positions to resolve the Darfur issue through political dialogues.[16]

In Beijing's opinion, not only Khartoum should be persuaded but also those rebel groups should be given suggestions and imposed pressures. Ambassador Liu had said that Khartoum should do much more to end the violence, but rebel groups should also share responsibility. He strengthened the importance of cooperation within all related actors involved in the process. He had argued that the UN and AU should try more to jointly handle those technological issues regarding the deployment of peacekeeping force, all related countries in this region should undertake cooperative action, and the international society, including Security Council members, should work together, without sending wrong messages to Sudan and the rebel groups.

Ambassador Liu complained that the releant actors, especially those rebel groups in Darfur, were not actively to participating in the peace negotiation. In 27 October 2007, a peace conference was held, chaired by the UN and the AU, nonetheless, only few non-influential rebelling groups attended, and those important groups were absent. "This is a fundamental inadequacy", Ambassaor Liu said.[17]

In pursuit of a peace settlement, Chinese special representative to Darfur had also visited London and Paris, to coordinate with European counterparts. Meanwhile, Chinese representatives in the UN coordinated with other Security Council members in order to put forward a commonly agreed UN resolution over Darfur. Because of Chinese active cooperation with international society and dialogues with Sudan's rebel groups, a political approach in dealing with Darfur issue was finally achievable.

CHINA IN THE CONFLICT MANAGEMENT ON DARFUR ISSUE: DYNAMICS, PRINCIPLES, AND APPROACHES

It can be seen that in pursuit of a resolution to the Darfur issue, China played a special role based on special interests and principles through its diplomatic approaches. To a large extent this was because China was a different player from other powers, especially the United States and the European Union (EU).

Dynamics: Balancing National Interests and International Responsibility

Undoubtedly, like any state's foreign policy, China's policy toward Darfur and its evolution is embedded in its typical preference on national interests. Because of the deep economic ties with Sudan, China did not wish to damage the bilateral relationship. So, in the early period of the crisis, China didn't join the Western side to oppose Khartoum.

However, when the early crisis swiftly changed into a humanitarian crisis and the situation spiralled out of control, more pressure was imposed on China itself by Western world which criticised China's stance as one which indulged Khartoum which the Sudanese government killed Southern Sudanese. Facing this criticism, China began to persuade Sudan's government to accept the UN's suggestions and resolution and sent several special representatives to Khartoum to coordinate positions.

Yet this policy change resulted not only from the international pressure but also from the worry about the lasting instability and violence in Darfur, which impacted negatively upon Chinese enterprises, especially those in Darfur. China was afraid of the ineffectiveness of the bilateral agreements on those oil projects (most of them were operating in what was later to becomeSouth Sudan).

On the other hand, Beijing's policy and its alteration are also due to another, namely its global image. As a rising power, one of China's ambitions is to be accepted as a responsible actor in international society. When Darfur crisis escalated, China felt too much international pressure, and it had to care about its international image as well. With the condition in Darfur became more and more serious, accordingly Beijing became more and more active in dealing with the issue. Consequently, after a period of indifference and silence, China refused to stop the international sanctions on those individuals who were named as being culpable for the terrible Darfur humanitarian crisis[18] and, as a result, began to join the international society to handle the issue through persuasion, cooperation, and coordination.

Principles: Sovereign Independence, Multilateralism, and Development

On 2 February 2007, Chinese President Hu Jintao proposed four principles for handling the Darfur issue, when he visited Sudan after the end of Sino-African Summit. These four principles included respecting Sudan's territory and sovereign integrity, adhering dialogues and equal consultation, the AU and the UN's importance of playing constructive roles in Darfur issue, and promoting local stability in this region.[19] Generally speaking, the principles China used in Darfur issue can be classified into three dimensions: sovereign independence, multilateralism, and development.

The Chinese special representative Liu Guijin had argued that China didn't agree with dealing with with regional conflict through resort to force and coerce; and the principle Chinese government adhered was respectful of Sudan's sovereignty and territorial integrity. This principle was not only adhered in China's bilateral relations with Sudan but also used in international negotiations on Darfur issue.

The other principle is multilateralism. When the crisis began, China didn't get involved in the issue since it was considered by Beijing as a domestic problem. Then, after China decided to join international action for resolving Darfur issue, Beijing adhered to multilateralism as an important principle. It strengthened all actions aiming at finding a peaceful resolution to the crisis in Darfur, calling for Darfur to be placed under the UN's leadership and carried out through multilateral negotiations, dialogues, and cooperation, not only among international actors like

China, the United States, the AU, and so on, but also among different political groups in Sudan, including those rebels. Liu Guijin argued that it was necessary that at least "five actors" should work together to handle the Darfur issue. These five actors were Sudanese government, rebel groups, international society, Sudan's neighboring countries, and the AU, and the UN.[20]

At the same time, Chinese considered that promoting Sudan's development was a fundamental and essential principle to reduce the conflict in Darfur, since the poverty and backwardness was the root of the conflict. Zhai Jun, another Chinese special representative to Darfur, claimed that the nature of Darfur issue was in fact a development issue. In terms of it, he argued the essential road to resolution of Darfur issue was to realize the region's economic reconstruction and development. In consideration of this idea, China hoped international society would be willing provide social and financial assistance to this poor region of Sudan.

Approaches: Persuasion, Cooperation, Coordination, and Political Dialogue

The approaches that China used in the Darfur issue-resolving were political dialogue and diplomatic means. "We are against the idea of using sanctions to solve the problem," Ambassador Liu Guijin said, "because there is only one way to solve the problem in Darfur, and that's through dialogue and consultation."[21] According to this, sanctions as an approach was not preferred by China. Liu Jianchao, the spokesperson of Chinese government, had said that it was not possible to talk about sanctions resolving the Darfur issue, and each actor should take actions to reach a consensus on tackling this problem. Clearly, in Beijing's views, the diplomatic approach – persuasion, cooperation, coordination, negotiation, and so forth, rather than sanctions and unilateral action – was the best way to resolve the Darfur issue. Ambassador Liu Guijin concluded one of the principles used in Darfur issue was adherence to political dialogue.[22]

In order to operationalise the idea – political dialogue rather than sanction – China made the Security Council's resolution adopted through cooperation with other members, especially with the United States. For example, China didn't veto Resolutions 1556 and 1564 since these two resolutions sought to impose sanctions on the Sudan's oil-dependent economy, all the while knowing that these measures would, undoubtedly would harm international oil companies, including the Chinese enterprises there. That is, in order to realize peace and stability in Darfur, China chose cooperation as the main approach to realize international consensus although it didn't agree some part of the resolutions.[23]

CONCLUSION: FROM NON-INTERFERENCE TO INTERFERENCE?

At the first glance, Beijing, especially in the case of Darfur issue, had changed the longstanding non-interference policy to a some what tempered interference policy by actively persuading Khartoum to accept joint peacekeeping troops, contacting Sudan's rebel groups and inviting them to visit Beijing, supporting the UN's resolutions aiming at sanctioning Bashir regime, coordinating with Western powers, and so on. If we observe some other cases beyond Darfur issue, this temperate "interference" seems to be an approach constantly being used by Beijing. For instance, in Libya crisis in 2011 and in Syria crisis in 2012–2013, China also built links with those rebel groups or invited them to visit Beijing and actively discussed these issues with international actors.

Although the Chinese government took some different actions (e.g., hedging policy) from previous conduct in to dealing with foreign countries' domestic crisis, Beijing has not fundamentally or essentially altered the non-interference principle. As a long-existed diplomatic idea, non-interference has not changed, nor been abandoned, but just adjusted. This adjustment is still in accordance with the definition of "interference", which is considered as an enforcement of one country on another by force or fear. According to this definition, interference is a forcible action that is different from suggestions or mediation.

In terms of this, China's engagement in Darfur crisis is not interference; conversely, it is consistent with the essence of noninterference. Firstly, China didn't impose its suggestions on Bashier regime by force or threatening. When Annan Plan was accepted by international society, including by the AU, China started to advise that Khartoum should accept the hybrid UN-AU's peacekeeping troops in order to calm the situation in Darfur region. Clearly, this is not a threat or intimidation.

Second, China's engagement during the crisis was agreed or accepted, at least not refused, by both Khartoum and rebels. Because China's engagement was not a threat to the Khartoum regime, but an act of mediation, Khartoum didn't have a reason to refuse or oppose China's contacts with rebel groups. In practice, the meetings between Beijing and those rebels was not openly opposed by Khartoum.

Third, China's suggestions reflected international consensus. For example, China's suggestion that Sudan government should accept the hybrid peace-keeping troops was consistent with the position of the UN, the African Union, and the League of Arab States. From this perspective, China's engagement reflected not only China's idea, but also international society's position.

Fourth, China's engagement in Darfur issue didn't take up a partisan position. According to the Chinese understanding of interference, it means providing ssupport to one side against another in a given situation. However, China didn't overtly or covertly support Khartoum or rebels in the fight against the other side. In Beijing's opinion, the crisis was in essence a civil war and other countries and international organizations should only push them to come to a negotiation table, but not to support one side to eliminate the other. China acted as a broker rather than a teacher or a judge in this crisis.

Fifth, the objective of China's engagement was not to realize regime change or political revolution, but to bring about domestic stability and pacification in the Darfur region through political dialogue and negotiations.

In general, from this examination of the case of Darfur crisis, it can be seen that China has changed its traditional attitude to many regional and international crises from indifference to active involvement. Yet it can also be seen that this involvement in those conflicts is not an alternative to interference but a temperate engagement that requires sophisticated skills. This can be viewed as "active and smart engagement" that does not conflict with China's longstanding principle of non-interference. In other words, with the widening of China's economic interest in the world and the rising of China as an international power, non-interference with its negative response to international conflicts is gradually trans-formed into non-interference with active and smart engagement in the first half of the twenty-first century.[24] And this transformation is now a tendency that is introducing a new pattern of China's conflict manage-ment, concurrently, a novel approach to resolving international conflicts.

NOTES

1. China's Statistic Yearbook (2004), http://www.stats.gov.cn/tjsj/ndsj/yb2004-c/indexch.htm, date accessed 1 May 2004.
2. MFA (2010), 'China's Relations with Sudan', http://www.mfa.gov.cn/chn/pds/gjhdq/gj/fz/1206_45_3/sbgx/t359836.htm, accessed 2 June 2010.

3. 'Sudan's Minister of Investment: Respect for China's Contribution to the Organization in and Support for [Sino-Sudan's] Trade', http://news.hexun.com/2014-09-09/168286809.html, accessed 30 October 2015.

4. Xinhua News (2009), 'Chinese Embassy to Sudan Donated Primary School to Darfur Finished', http://news.xinhuanet.com/world/2009-09/06/c_124471.htm, accessed 6 September 2009.

5. CNPC (2010), 'CNPC in Sudan: Review of 15 Years of Sino-Sudanese Petroleum Cooperation', http://www.cnpc.com.cn/csr/xhtml/PageAssets/CNPCinSudan.pdf, p. 29, accessed 30 December 2010.

6. Hu Chi (2010), 'China Poverty Eradication Award Donated Materials to One Charity Organization of Sudan', *Xinhua Website*, http://www.xinhuanet.com/english/home.htm (home page), 10 March 2010.

7. Wu Wenbin (2010), 'China's Contributions Hospital to Sudan Had Groundbreaking Ceremony', *People Website*, http://en.people.cn (homepage), accessed 20 November 2010.

8. China makes unremitting efforts to resolve crisis in Darfur (2008), *China Daily*, 16 February 2008.

9. American Newspaper Supposed the Change of China's Policy on Darfur (2008), *Global Times*, 30 October 2008.

10. In this 1556 resolution, the UN asked Sudan's government to relieve weapons of Arabian militias in Darfur.

11. Wen Jiabao (2006), 'China-Sudan Relations are Equal and Without Any Private Interests', *China's News Website*, http://www.sina.com.cn http://news.sina.com.cn/c/2006-11-03/202211419625.shtml, accessed 3 November 2006.

12. UN meeting coverage and press release (2006), 'The UN's 1706 Resolution', http://www.un.org/press/en/2006/sc8821.doc.htm, accessed 30 December 2006.

13. China makes unremitting efforts to resolve crisis in Darfur (2008), *China Daily*, 16 February 2008.

14. Jim Yardley (2008), 'China Defends Sudan Policy and Criticizes Olympics Tie-In', *The New York Times*, 8 March 2008.

15. Chinese Central Government Website (2008), 'The League of Arab States: The Role of China in Darfur Is Transparent and Heartfelt', www.gov.cn (homepage), accessed 26 February 2008.

16. Gu Guoping and Dong Jirong (2010), 'The Positions and Policies of China and the US on Darfur Issue: Based on Each Official States and Speeches', *International Forum*, 1.

17. Shao Jie (2007), 'How Far Is Darfur from the Peace?', *International Herald Leader*, 2 November 2007.

18. Josh Kurlantzick (2010), 'China, Myanmar and Sudan: Perusable Idea', *New Republic*, 4 September 2010.

19. Hu Jintao (2007), 'Met Sudanese President Bashier', *People Daily*, 3 February 2007.
20. China Website (2008), *Chinese Representative Explained Chinese Government's Position Over Darfur*, www.china.com.cn (home page), accessed 22 February 2008.
21. Gwen Thompkins (2008), 'Chinese Influence in Sudan Is Subtle, Complicated', *NPR (2008)*, http://www.npr.org/templates/story/story.php?storyId=92282540, accessed 29 July 2008.
22. Wang Yaping (2007), 'China and Darfur Issue', *Carnegie's Perspective on China*, 8 September 2007.
23. Wang Meng (2005), 'The Darfur Crisis: the Challenge and Chance of Chinese Diplomatic Change', *World Economy and Politics*, 6.
24. According to professor Wang Yizhou, who uses the term 'creative engagement' to depict China's recent engagement in foreign affairs. He argues that the 'creative engagement' is a necessary approach to protect China's overseas interests, and is not conflicted with previous principles such as non-interference, respect for sovereignty. See Wang Yizhou (2013), *Creative Engagement: The Formation of China's Global Role* (Beijing University Press).

Jian Junbo is an Associate Professor of the Institute of International Studies at Fudan University. He focuses on Sino-European relations in Africa, Chinese foreign affairs, and European politics and external relations.

CHAPTER 9

Sudan and South Sudan: A Testing Ground for Beijing's Peace and Security Engagement

Daniel Large

INTRODUCTION

China's response to conflict in South Sudan after December 2013 attracted much attention and was touted as a foreign policy test case for China in Africa.[1] At the same time, Sudan's relations with China remained salient, confirmed when the two governments agreed a renewed 'strategic partnership' in late 2015. This continued a trend by which China's relations with Sudan and more recently South Sudan have been at the forefront of its wider continental engagement. From 1995, when Chinese oil companies first entered Sudan, China's engagement had been dominated by economic drivers and assisted by political management, but more recently the economic importance of both Sudans has been displaced by more political concerns, in which security has become a key engagement concern.

This chapter offers a short, thematic summary survey of China's peace and security engagement with Sudan and South Sudan in terms of its North-South political axis and within South Sudan from 2011.[2] What

D. Large
School of Public Policy, Central European University, Budapest, Hungary

© The Author(s) 2018
C. Alden et al. (eds.), *China and Africa*,
DOI 10.1007/978-3-319-52893-9_9

follows begins by putting China's engagement into general context. Second, it examines China's role after Sudan's 2005 Comprehensive Peace Agreement (CPA), which resulted in the secession of South Sudan. Third, it considers key aspects of China's changing role from 2011, when Beijing shifted from attempting to broker agreement between Khartoum and Juba to responding to new conflict within South Sudan. Finally, it discusses some of the thematic issues and challenges China's role has faced.

Before proceeding, a number of caveats should be noted. First, what follows can only begin to engage what are clearly a set of more complex issues and cases, even without proper discussion of Darfur. This renders any focus upon peace and security questions one part of a broader web of connections. Second, the challenge of seeking to better grasp the nature of relations confronts a basic but important methodological issue of how best to frame and approach this topic: from the perspective, broadly, of China's engagement, or from the perspectives of different Sudanese protagonists? Generally speaking, when it comes to how best to fit China in to a historically produced set of conflicts to which China made a relatively late, albeit consequential intervention, both have advantages and disadvantages, but the primacy of Sudanese politics renders any effort to understand require such contextualisation. Ideally, a different form of analysis that goes beyond such basic options would be pursued. Here, however, the approach is to foreground China but attempt to locate the various strands of its engagement in political context in order not to artificially abstract the Chinese role from that of other actors and political dynamics.

BACKGROUND

Sudanese politics has exerted by far the most influence on China's evolving engagement: China's engagement with conflict in Sudan and South Sudan, and attempts to negotiate, implement and sustain peace agreements, should be primarily located within this complex context. This primacy of Sudanese politics, elite predation, political economy of intractable conflict and extraverted use of China to pursue domestic political objectives, far from being unusual, conforms to previous historical patterns of Sudan's external relations. Anotable difference, however, with China was the instrumental and successful role Chinese oil companies had in developing Sudan's oil export industry from

1995. This intensified the long-running North-South civil war and contributed to new conflict in Darfur from 2003, but also served to incentivise the 2005 Comprehensive Peace Agreement signed between the National Congress party (NCP)-controlled government of Sudan and the Sudan People's Liberation Movement/Army (SPLM/A).

The CPA established a semi-autonomous Government of Southern Sudan (GOSS) and also, as part of a reformed architecture of North-South Sudanese politics, a government of national unity composed mainly of NCP and SPLM figures. During the CPA, the dominance of China's relations with Khartoum was progressively revised as the agreement's 'one country, two systems' framework moved ever closer to a two-state scenario. A January 2011 referendum produced an overwhelming vote in favour of Southern secession, and China's engagement was recalibrated to more actively prepare for South Sudan's independence on 9 July 2011. When this happened, there were two formally separate but practically and politically interconnected countries, exemplified by the oil sector. South Sudan's independence stripped away some 75% of Sudan's oil production and the large majority of prospective new oil discoveries. Having partly contributed to a recrudescence of conflict in South Kordofan and Blue Nile from June 2011, oil was central to the subsequent tensions between Khartoum and Juba, which then were superseded by the violent irruption of conflict in Juba and then Unity and Upper Nile in South Sudan from December 2013.

An important reason why Sudan and South Sudan matter as cases in China's evolving engagement with peace and security in Africa concerns the notable comparative longevity and evolution of engagement over time of China's relations. Having operated in Sudan for more than two decades, it is hard to regard China as an emerging power; it has emerged. It has undergone a transition from an ad hoc, emergent and expansive phase of relations into becoming an established, more structural part of the Sudanese landscape in which economic activity is inevitably politicised. With the exposure attending China's emerged status – perceived and ascribed – has come a very different set of challenges, including those external to the Sudans.

China's engagement in Sudan over the CPA period (excluding Darfur) features a number of indirect and direct roles. Most importantly, China has followed an indirect role in enabling the CPA via the economics of Sudan to expand its role in the industry as part of the dividend created by the CPA that economically enabled, via wealth sharing between Khartoum and Juba, the creation and functioning of the regional GOSS. China's role in the political economy of the CPA, mixed up as this was with the conflict in Darfur, was thus fundamental.

Beijing's own relations with Sudan after 2005 came to feature more engaged, though qualified and limited, multilateral participation, most evident in Juba towards the end of the CPA. This process, however, was accompanied by the important continuity of Beijing's predominantly bilateral relations with Khartoum, and later Juba. This was not a linear process, and partly reflected a wider shift in international policy from Darfur back to the CPA as Sudan's North-South politics, overshadowed by Darfur, belatedly received more attention. At the same time, it was indicative of China's navigation of Sudan's turbulent politics and the evolution of its more flexible, ad hoc and engaged role that came to feature a mostly discreet but nonetheless more involved political aspect

Until the CPA, and well into the agreement until they had no choice but to go against their allies by engaging the SPLM, China firmly sided with Khartoum but in time, the agreement necessitated a radical reordering of China's Sudan relations. The evolution of China's relations with the GoSS involved a strategic recalibration of relations with the NCP-state in Khartoum. A sequence of phases saw China pragmatically reassess its firm support for the unity of Sudan as its policy engagement was compelled to go South. At first, China firmly supported unity, on the basis of the CPA and its own political preference, but later hedged its bets on Sudan's political future, developing relations with the GoSS within the CPA's 'one Sudan, two systems' framework. Finally, in the face of the strong momentum towards secession, Beijing began to prepare for and look ahead to an independent state. China's consulate in Juba was opened by Assistant Foreign Minister Zhai Jun in September 2008, falling under the Chinese Embassy in Khartoum and the Ministry of Foreign Affairs in Beijing. An important pillar of China's official relations with GoSS was initiating and enhancing economic relations.

China became more involved in multilateral forums in Juba than Khartoum. It's Juba consulate was not only more active vis-à-vis GoSS or the UN, but also in such international bodies as the Donor Coordination Forum.[3] China's more involved role in Juba placed its policy engagement more within a multilateral context, enabling Beijing to minimise its past Khartoum orientation there, at the same time as continuing close bilateral ties with Khartoum. Such positioning in Juba also appeared to reflect a desire not to be singled out, a position that would carry more risk, but rather be a more – albeit partially and selectively – integrated part of the multilateral system. This also applied to China's assistance programme, which was formulated in part through consultations with GoSS and UN officials as well, and devised with at least an awareness of the need to avoid duplication.[4] China's assistance, in other words, was not designed in a vacuum but in relation to GoSS priorities and the programmes of its other international partners.[5]

Diplomatic-political engagement was a further aspect of China's role.[6] China's multilateral participation in Khartoum during the CPA's final stages, when planning about the UN's future role was also taking place, was minimal. China was widely viewed within the international aid sector in Khartoum as being mostly outside and apart from the multilateral system, reinforcing perceptions of its bilateral focus.[7] This was unsurprising and consistent, however, with wider Chinese positioning towards multilateral forums. Furthermore, there was limited select interaction with certain forums. China's participation in UN processes continued outside Sudan. China's UN Ambassador, for example, visited Sudan with the UN Security Council delegations in the CPA's latter stages. China supported the Southern referendum itself, expending political capital and providing a donation of US $500,000 to the Southern Sudan Referendum Commission in January 2011 as well as sending a team of observers. It was thus active in certain ways, despite not interacting with the office of the UN Special Representative or operating within the full international support structures.

Between 2005 and 2011, there was a marked progression in China's engagement: a convinced supporter of Sudan's unity, China nonetheless came to champion peaceful, CPA-mandated political transition. What started as a relatively marginal aspect of China's overall Sudan relations – a policy engagement substantially overshadowed by Darfur, and Beijing's support for a united Sudan – mainstreamed in a process that saw China become a notable supporter of a stable transition to two Sudans under the terms of the CPA. This reflected China's development of an all-Sudan policy framework. Having first hedged its bets about the referendum's outcome, Beijing – like CNPC – then began preparing more actively for an independent South Sudan. As January 2011 approached, Beijing became more fully cognizant with the SPLM's independence drive. Further initiatives to enhance political relations were made. China officially continued to support the CPA's principle of 'making unity attractive', and refused to overtly prejudge the referendum's outcome, but affirmed its willingness to accept the result. The bottom line was stability.

A final theme concerned the transition from the CPA to a situation of two states divided by a new international border, which led Beijing's diplomacy to seek to try to enhance relations between Khartoum and Juba. Beijing positioned itself as a friend of both Sudans. Until December 2013, China's relations with South Sudan were caught up in Juba's disputes with Khartoum. China was caught in the middle of political and at times militarised disputes between Juba and Khartoum rooted in unfinished CPA business. It was also rooted in the geography of China's oil interests. Juba used its new sovereign political power to pressure CNPC and its partners to support their position in negotiations with Sudan over pipeline transit fees. Sudan unilaterally confiscated shipments of South Sudanese oil in late 2011 as payment for undetermined pipeline fees. South Sudan then pushed the oil companies accept a new clause freeing Juba from any liability if it imposed an oil shutdown.[8]

China sought to bridge the differences between Khartoum and Juba. In face of a possible oil shutdown, its former special envoy to Africa, Liu Guijin, was dispatched to Juba and Khartoum in early December 2011 to try to find a solution to the impasse over pipeline transit fees, thereby also protecting oil interests. CNPC and its partners also put forward a plan to offer an oil package to Sudan if it allowed the South Sudanese oil to flow freely through its pipeline. Such efforts didn't work, and in January 2012 Juba shut down its oil sector. Not long after the shutdown, South Sudan's oil minister expelled the CNPC president of the Petrodar consortium, alleging complicity in Sudan's earlier confiscation of oil shipments. The oil shutdown created a major security and economic crisis, which China tried to engage politically. The shutdown halted CNPC's most profitable venture overseas; production only resumed in April and May 2013 and reached about 220,000 bpd by June 2013. Beijing's failure to avoid the shutdown through diplomacy only strengthened moves in CNPC to pursue a more risk-adverse approach in the Sudans. It was a further indication of the pronounced limits of externally perceived Chinese 'leverage' over Juba or Khartoum, demonstrating instead the decisive influence of a few leading figures around Salva Kiir.

China and South Sudan

The outbreak of conflict in South Sudan triggered in December 2013 by fighting in Juba would have severe consequences, including for China's engagement. Failure to resolve the political differences between the SPLM's top leaders – in particular, South Sudan's president, Salva Kiir Mayardit, and former vice-president, Riek Machar Teny Dhurgon– rapidly translated into a violent, inter-ethnic conflict, drawing key regional actors into both the fighting and efforts to end it. The trigger for violence was in Juba, in what the government alleged was a coup attempt but involved fighting amongst the presidential guard, which then rapidly spread to greater Upper Nile.[9] The current conflict as of late 2015 had resulted in more than 2.2 million displaced people, including over 630 000 refugees in neighbouring countries,[10] and stretched the ability of the UN Mission in the Republic of South Sudan (UNMISS), as well as other international agencies and the likes of China, to respond adequately and effectively. China's engagement has featured notable features in key areas: political relations, investment protection, military connections, peacekeeping and recalibrated economic relations, resulting in an engagement dependent upon the fate of the August 2015 peace agreement going forward.

Political relations between China and the Government of the Republic of South Sudan continued on a regular basis at the highest level.[11] China also maintained non-official links with the SPLM-In Opposition (IO). This meant that its political relations were multi-stranded, and not confined to relations with the state and ruling SPLM. In September 2014, an SPLM-IO delegation visited Beijing headed by Dhieu Mathok Diing Wol, Chairman of its External Relations Committee. They met with Foreign Minister Wang Yi and the Vice Foreign Minister Zhang Ming. Chinese media reports were at pains to underscore: 'China stressed its fair and objective stance'.[12] Wang Yi reiterated this: 'China always adheres to a just and objective position'.[13] In the SPLM-IO's headquarters, there have been reports of Chinese connections with Riek and rumours of deals over oil field security but no confirmation. China's regular and institutionalised engagement with Sudan involves coordination over the conflict in South Sudan. Nonetheless, and despite the civil war, South Sudan continued to try to court Chinese investment. In April 2014, South Sudan's embassy in Beijing hosted the first South Sudan-China Investment Forum to identify and make effective use of investment and trade opportunities. There appeared to be mixed responses from the some 200 Chinese businessmen present, with the large Chinese companies still being interested in investing in South Sudan, whereas the medium and small ones were deterred by daunting security risks.

Military support to the government of South Sudan underscored the challenges of China's mixed role and necessitated changes in Beijing's approach to its bilateral military ties with Juba. Beijing and Juba did not initially have a direct formal military relationship after July 2011. Part of the initial problem was China's longstanding close links with the Sudan Armed Forces and America's support to the SPLA. However, military links grew as a result of Juba's new needs after December 2013. The government received arms from China, something that the SPLM-IO tried to draw attention to.[14] The UN sanctions panel reported that the SPLA received a shipment of arms, ammunition and related material from China North Industries Group Corporation (Norinco) in July 2014. This weapons consignment, worth some USD 46.8 million according to the Ministry of Finance and Economic Planning, appeared to have been ordered before December 2013.[15] South Sudan has not relied solely on China for arms purchases; far from it; it has a number of more significant suppliers. However, the mere appearance of Beijing seeking to concurrently promote peace and assist UN peacekeeping in a conflict zone while a Chinese company was supplying the weapons of war to Juba was a dramatic illustration of a conflicted and contradictory Chinese role. Furthermore, when China's arms transfers to Sudan are factored in, particularly the indirect impacts caused by Khartoum's secondary retransfer of arms to allied armed groups in South Sudan, Beijing's role is more significant.[16] After the Norinco revelations, and facing not just a damaging political backlash but also possible blowback on its interests and peacekeepers, China declared a moratorium on arms sales to South Sudan.[17]

Investment protection became an important part of China's response to the fighting from mid-December 2013 and subsequent engagement. CNPC mounted a rapid security response to the fighting that started in Juba on 15 December 2013 and rapidly spread, especially in Unity and Upper Nile states. The rapid, successful evacuation of Chinese oil workers and those working for other companies like Sinohydro after 15 December 2013 ensured the Chinese government – and CNPC – did and were seen to act to protect its nationals.[18] This trigged much debate for Chinese analysts about how best to respond. From December 2013, the Unity oil fields were at the centre of fighting following the defection of the SPLA's fourth division commanded by Major-General James Koang. This caused a complete orderly shutdown of oil operations and the evacuation of most expatriate oil workers. The Unity oil blocks ceased operating completely. In Upper Nile, production was reduced but not stopped, despite intensified conflict over the oil fields. In 2014, production ran at an average of 165 000 bpd, but the figure for 2015 is likely to have been lower due to further intense oilfield fighting. This caused further threats to Chinese oil workers. In May 2015, China evacuated some 400 workers from Paloch, Upper Nile, because of fighting, but production later resumed when the SPLA regained control.

Efforts to undertake and promote investment protection assumed various responses within South Sudan and in China's diplomatic engagement outside the country. Within South Sudan, there were links attributed between oil companies and armed militias in the oil fields.[19] This concerns the Unity blocks of the oil consortium, in which CNPC features as the main partner, which were reported as being defended by fourth Division troops, and a 700-strong militia force recruited from among the Rueng Dinka youth of Pariang county and run by South Sudan's National Security Service.[20] Outside South Sudan, the timing and nature of China's immediate response to the fighting of December 2013 was noteworthy: it combined concern at the fighting with a call for restraint and negotiated settlement with measures to 'protect personal and properly safety' of Chinese enterprises and employees.[21] It is partly because of Chinese pressure that UNMISS's mandate features the aim to 'deter violence against civilians, including foreign nationals [...] in areas at high risk of conflict including, as appropriate, schools, places of worship, hospitals and the oil installations'.[22] In May 2015, a MOFA spokesperson asserted that: 'Both sides have the responsibility to protect oil infrastructure in South Sudan, as oil is a critical resource in its reconstruction and economic development during the country's peaceful transition period'.[23] Such invocation of a responsibility to protect with Chinese characteristics illustrated the combination of its economic interests linked to efforts to exert lavage on parties for whom China's economic interests – like those of other oil investors – represented fundamental part of the conflict.

China's support to UN peacekeeping in South Sudan is anotable part of its engagement. China's peacekeeping in South Sudan follows on nearly a decade after its first deployment of UN peacekeepers after the CPA. Since December 2013, however, the nature of China's UN peacekeeping has importantly evolved. South Sudan is the first case of China deploying combat troops under a Chapter VII mandate. In April 2015, the final detachment of Chinese troops was deployed to UNMISS on this basis, making a full battalion comprising three infantry companies and a supply company. Most notably, this included a civilian protection role. Amidst debate around how this was – or was not – related to China's efforts to pursue investment protection by multilateral means under multilateral UN colours, the real departure was the changed nature of what type of peacekeepers China was sending.

China's engagement in efforts to mediate peace was another prominent aspect of its political engagement. China's efforts to undertake a 'mediation' role after December 2013 drew wide attention.[24] While China has been styled a mediator, in reality, China's engagement essentially represented a diplomatic-political intervention to try to assist anegotiated settlement. In January 2014, Wang Yi held talks in Addis with the protagonists. He had been scheduled to visit Addis Ababa, but his talks with both main parties to the conflict on 6 January 2014, at which he urged them to 'seek a reasonable and rational way out', were notable. In August 2014, China advocated a four-point solution to South Sudan's civil war and subsequently supported and participated in the IGAD mediation process.[25] In January 2015, Beijing convened a meeting in Khartoum under the IGAD banner to try to bridge differences, but this did not succeed. Regardless of impact on the negotiations, however, in many ways China's diplomacy had important outward-bearing dimensions. The essence of China's role was, in Wang Yi's words, to convey the message that 'China is an active promoter of peace in South Sudan'.[26]

Humanitarian assistance came to play a greater role in China's bilateral engagement, superseding much of its previous plans to support South Sudan's development needs. The conflict severely interrupted China's then existing aid programme, including construction of hospitals in all 10 of South Sudan's state capitals. Since December 2013, China's aid has responded to the renewed conflict by a changed programme of assistance.[27] Health and medical assistance remain central to China's current assistance. In March 2015, the Chinese embassy in Juba and South Sudan's Ministry of Health signed an MoU regarding the third batch of Chinese medical assistance to South Sudan, particularly for Juba Teaching Hospital. Outside of humanitarian assistance, China's aid programme encompassed other areas, notably agriculture where, for example, in September 2014, China advanced a USD 25 million grant for 'agro-infrastructural development' reportedly 'mostly in the areas hugely affected' by the conflict.[28] However, given the spread of conflict to areas previously untouched by the fighting in greater Upper Nile, the future of such programmes were dependent upon whether or not the August 2015 peace agreement could be made to work and last.

Engaging Intractable Conflict

The eventual signing of an agreement to end the fighting in August 2015 between the government of South Sudan and the SPLM-IO was met with cautious optimism. However, the realistic prospects for a genuine and sustainable peace remained very much in the balance. At the same time, conflict continued in parts of Sudan. These various inter-locking combinations of conflict continued to connect both counties in important ways through political and military support by Khartoum and Juba to rebels and military support by rebel forces of the government of South Sudan against the SPLM-IO. A number of general themes emerge from this pointing to China's adaptation to the intractability of conflict in both Sudans.

First of all, China's diplomatic response became more prominent but evolved in a manner that appeared to indicate greater resignation towards the conflict. The new civil war was seen to accelerate 'China's evolution from a reactive and passive actor in conflict resolution to one that is more active and positive in both conflict management and conflict prevention'.[29] In reality, while becoming engaged, China's approach was ad hoc and reactive and continued to offer primary support to the IGAD-led negotiations while endeavouring to maintain reduced exposure to the fighting. After more than a decade of diplomatic involvement, China's role had become more prominent in public but in private, and notwithstanding active role, appeared resigned to reality of intractable conflict.

The second theme concerns the actual experience of China's otherwise official support for the notion of peace (understood as the absence of war) though economic development. While Beijing maintained its public support for the efficacy of economic development as the main driver of peace, its policy engagement appeared to encounter the practical limits and problems of this. This commitment, advanced prominently during the Darfur crisis, had dovetailed neatly with the predominant nature of Chinese engagement in Sudan, and as such could be seen as self-serving, but in other respects harked back to much older ideas about realising peace. The centrality of economics to peace had been first most clearly argued over Darfur, where the Chinese government argued that 'Development is the key to solve the Darfur problem continuously.'[30] This, however, followed a longer history of such claims concerning economic development was upheld as the best means to produce peace. These, notably, included political and economic programmes organised around these in Sudan.[31] Chinese arguments favouring economic development also formed the basis of a strong critique of liberal peace-building critique of aid-dependence and, by implication, the efficacy of the sustained, different kinds of humanitarian and development engagement led by Western agencies in Sudan. However, even China's own core belief and practical engagement came into question in so far as the economics of the conflict were concerned and the absence of any teleological progression from development, however understood, to a state of peace.

This is where the actual political economy of development in Sudan and South Sudan as an overriding influence on China's engagement became apparent and with this some of the reasons why economic development, manifested primarily as growth produced by oil exports, failed to result in peace and, indeed, merely fed into deeper political contestation and violent conflict. In South Sudan, prior to 2013, the country's political economy had been concentrating wealth in Juba and the various state capitals, leaving the hinterlands of Jonglei and Upper Nile out of economic development. This had contributed to insecurity and conflict even before the start of the civil war in December 2013.[32] Oil became central to arguments by anti-government opposition groups that Juba has become the 'new Khartoum', and that the new South Sudan was characterised by militarised governance, corruption, oil-based patronage and the squandering of public resources.[33] Such political realities pointed, at a minimum, to the crucial role of political management of oil resources and the fundamental differences between aspirational development and existing realities.

A third theme is how the notion of China's role in post-conflict reconstruction has had to adjust as a result of the failure to achieve a meaningful absence of conflict so far. While China had sought to engage with programmes marshaled under a post-conflict banner, varying from its engagement after the CPA, in Darfur, in eastern Sudan, or, despite conflict, in South Sudan, the reality was the absence of any linear evolution in its engagement to a situation that could be confidently deemed 'post-conflict'. In South Sudan in early 2016, the notion of post-conflict engagement essentially remained akin to a policy mirage shimmering in the distance but not faithfully representative of ground realities. The phrase 'post-conflict' may have had a certain, very broad utility but, in the face of complex, shifting range of conflicts, has been rendered virtually meaningless in Sudan and South Sudan. Above all, the teleology implicit in the notion of a progressive transition from a state of conflict to a state of peace has been severely brought into question if not dispensed with.

Beyond public pronouncements and official support for the peace agreement and efforts to establish a Transitional Government of National Unity, China's actual role in South Sudan in mid-2015 and early 2016 was far more cautious and realistic. While its previous plans concerning infrastructure or other economic interventions remained on paper, its substantive engagement has to all intents and purposes undergone a process of withdrawal to a minimal level. An attitude of watch and wait appeared to prevail. China's economic interests, affected not just by fighting but lower international oil prices, had pared down and almost in tandem South Sudan come to occupy a more important diplomatic and political status. This however meant that China was experiencing the challenges of actually achieving peace more directly, a position much in contrast to its politically peripheral role over the CPA negotiations.

China's engagement appeared unlikely to embark on any substantial economic engagement unless there was a peace that worked and lasted, but achieving that appeared at best challenging. While China's theory worked well, as experienced in practice, reality had proved otherwise. Before and at South Sudan's independence, China was widely seen – including by many international agencies and donors – as key to South Sudan's development prospects because, beyond oil, of its perceived comparative advantage rooted in its ability to rapidly mobilise finance and efficiently deliver infrastructure on a large scale. In 2016, such expectations were tempered by reality of problems and ongoing conflict and humanitarian emergency, in which the realistic prospects for meaningful development appeared unlikely.

CONCLUSION

There is a view that China's diplomatic engagement with South Sudan is a key case exemplifying a shift towards a more activist role not just in Africa more generally. This is seen, for example, in the claim that China is acting not only like a 'responsible world power' but like 'a practical great power' in its response to the fighting in South Sudan.[34] However, if anything, China's response confirmed a proclivity towards experimental attempted solutions that have been moderated and adapted in the face of direct experience of the sheer intractability of the conflict. Nonetheless, South Sudan is a salient case of Beijing's efforts to be seen to practically operationalise 'international responsibility', understood as contributing to global security public goods.[35] Besides offsetting accusations of a narrowly extractive role, or associations with arms supplies, what China has been attempting to do in South Sudan could be regarded as representing an aspect of China's 'new type of big power relations' as enacted in Africa, seen in terms of its military projection, investment protection and efforts to support a political resolution of the conflict.

Official Chinese government proclamations continue to uphold the efficacy of economic development in overcoming conflict, achieving lasting peace and security. However, set in contrast against this has been the apparent realisation deriving from grounded experience that there can be no easy linear path from conflict to peace in Sudan and South Sudan. Everything depends on politics within both countries. In this, China's external leverage – like that of other parties – remains highly constrained and unsurprisingly so in view of the strength of conflict dynamics. Rather than a linear war to peace process, rather, China appeared to have been adapting to a cycle of protracted conflict, formal peace and efforts to pursue reconstruction. This appeared to better situate China's role in the context of ongoing conflict. In early 2016, Sudan was experiencing ongoing conflict in Darfur, South Kordofan and Blue Nile, and South Sudan was experiencing conflict despite the formal peace agreement. South Sudan's peace agreement had failed to produce a meaningful reduction of violence, and a lack of political will by both parties meant minimal progress towards establishing the Transitional Government of National Unity.

NOTES

1. For example, by Special Envoy Zhong Jianhua and Foreign Minister Wang Yi.
2. For analysis of China's engagement over Darfur, see Jian Junbo's chapter in this volume.
3. Established by OCHA, this involved neighbouring states, IGAD, the US, Norway, and the AU. One UN official noted that the Chinese 'attend briefings but keep quiet'. Interview with senior UN official, Khartoum, 31 January 2011; Interview with international official, 23 September 2010, Juba.
4. Interview with Chinese official, Juba, 2 June 2011.
5. Ibid.
6. Political role is understood broadly in a restricted, often informal sense, as its involvement in Sudan's peace processes via interaction with political authorities and other actors, rather than an overt political agenda it openly pursued.
7. 'They are not absent but are extremely discrete.' Interview with UN official, Khartoum, 27 January 2011. China was not part of the Donor Coordination

Group, nor did it participate in the International Partners Forum co-chaired by UNMIS and the EU. Interview with EU official, Khartoum, 31 January 2011.

8. See ICG, 'China's New Courtship in South Sudan', Brussels: ICG Africa Report No. 186, 4 April 2012.

9. The AU Commission of Inquiry on South Sudan report found that there was no coup attempt against Salva Kiir, as the President had claimed, but that a gunfight within the Presidential Guard triggered violence. Final Report of the AU Commissin of Inquiry on South Sudan, Addis Ababa 15 October 2015.

10. UN Office for the Coordination of Humanitarian Affairs, 'Humanitarian Bulletin: South Sudan: Bi-Weekly Update', 9 October 2015.

11. In June 2014, for example, Vice-President James Wani Igga visited Beijing where he met Li Keqiang, Li Yuanchao, Li Ruogu, Chairman and President of Exim Bank of Chin, and Zhou Jiping, Chairman of CNPC.

12. 'China confirms contact with South Sudan opposition', *Xinhua*, 23 September 2014.

13. 'Wang Yi: China Sincerely Hopes for an Early Comprehensive and Proper Settlement of South Sudan Issue', 22 September 2014 via http://au.china-embassy.org/eng/xw/t1194118.htm.

14. In March 2015, for example, it claimed that a Chinese flagged vessel Da Dan Xia has brought large quantity of armaments and ammunition to the RSS via Djibouti Port. 'Claims China Shipping Lethal Weapons to Juba via Ethiopia', *Sudan Tribune*, 29 March 2015.

15. Interim report of the Panel of Experts on South Sudan established pursuant to Security Council resolution 2206 (2015), 21 August 2015, p. 17 at 61.

16. Leff and Lebrun 2014: 24, 105. China accounted for some 58% of all of Khartoum's self-reported arms imports over the period 2001–12. The GOS has angered Beijing by retransferring some imported Chinese weapons and ammunition to allied groups in Darfur, violating the UN arms embargo, and also to rebel groups in South Sudan.

17. 'China Halts Arms Sales to South Sudan After Norinco Shipment', *Bloomberg* 30 September 2014.

18. Sinohydro staff working in Malakal were also evacuated to Juba and Uganda on 21 December. Chinese UN peacekeeping police evacuated 3 nationals from Bor to Juba a week or so after the outbreak of violence in Juba.

19. Small Arms Survey

20. In addition, new partnerships were created to undertake security activities, notably though the Hong Kong registered company Frontier Services Group, whose shareholders include CITIC (formerly China International Trust and Investment Corporation).

21. 'Wang Yi: Both Parties in South Sudan Should Resolve Differences through Negotiations as Soon as Possible and Effectively Protect Personal and Property

Safety of the Chinese Enterprises and Employees', 26 December 2015 http://www.fmprc.gov.cn/mfa_eng/wjb_663304/zzjg_663340/xybfs_663590/gjlb_663594/sousu_663756/ssaa_663760/t1113182.shtml

22. Luke Patey, 'Requiem for a Dream?' *Petroleum Economist*, July/August 2014; UNMISS (United Nations Mission in the Republic of South Sudan). 'UNMISS Mandate.'

23. 'China urges immediate cease-fire in South Sudan', *Xinhua*, 22 May 2015.

24. Shannon Tiezzi (2014), 'In South Sudan Conflict, China Tests Its Mediation Skills', *The Diplomat* 6 June 2014; Zhang Chuna and Mariam Kemple-Hardy (2015), 'From Conflict Resolution to Conflict Prevention: China in South Sudan', *Saferworld CPWG Briefing*, 1, 31 March 2015.

25. See Laura Barber's chapter in this volume.

26. Wang Yi: China Is an Active Promoter, Steadfast Defender and Sincere Participant of Peace in South Sudan', 13 January 2015 http://www.fmprc.gov.cn/mfa_eng/wjb_663304/zzjg_663340/xybfs_663590/gjlb_663594/sousu_663756/ssaa_663760/t1228073.shtml

27. Zhou Hang (2014), 'China's Emergency Relief to South Sudan', *The Diplomat*, 26 October 2014.

28. 'China grant $25 million to South Sudan for agricultural purposes', *Upper Niles Times*, 5 September 2014.

29. C. Zhang and M. Kemple-Hardy (2015), 'From Conflict Resolution to Conflict Prevention: China in South Sudan', *Saferworld CPWG Briefing*, 1, p. 1.

30. Zhai Jun (2007),中国积极推动解决达尔富尔问题 *Zhong Guo ji Ji Tui Dong Jie Jue Da Er Fu Er Wen Ti* China actively pushed the resolving of the Darfur problem, 求是杂志 *Qiu Shi Za Zhi*, 11, pp. 61–63.

31. Peace through Development: Perspectives and Prospects in the Sudan (SPLM, February 2000)

32. Edward Thomas (2015), *South Sudan: A Slow Liberation* (London: Zed).

33. Alex de Waal (2014), 'When Kleptocracy Becomes Insolvent: Brute Causes of the Civil War in South Sudan', *African Affairs*, 113:452, pp. 347–369.

34. Shannon Tiezzi (2015), 'China in South Sudan: Practical Responsibility', *The Diplomat*, 13 January 2015.

35. *China's Military Strategy* (Beijing: State Council Information Office of the People's Republic of China, May 2015).

Daniel Large   is an assistant professor at the School of Public Policy, Central European University, Budapest. Before joining SPP, Dr. Large was research director of the Africa-Asia Centre, Royal African Society at the School of Oriental and African Studies (SOAS).

CHAPTER 10

Lesson Learning in the Case of China-Sudan and South Sudan Relations (2005–2013)

Laura Barber

The formulation of China's policies towards individual African states and its regional policy during the 1990s was notable for an apparent lack of input provided by the consideration of internal situations within individual African polities. As a result, Chinese actors have traditionally viewed the African context in very general terms as having a wholly positive impact on China both on the global political stage through shared opposition to liberal Western 'values' and in terms of the positive contribution of resource-rich African states to the expansion of National Oil Company (NOC)' investments abroad and Chinese energy security at home. More generally, He Wenping has stated that, traditionally, 'once official relations were formed with a particular [African] country, it seems that such bilateral relations were put in a "safebox" and sealed with "friendship" forever' (He 2010).

Moreover, perceptions of the causes of internal instability and conflict within Africa have been either externalised, through blaming Western interference, or depoliticised, through removing the role of the state within the frame of reference. According to Li Anshan (2005),

L. Barber (✉)
Political and Security Analyst, London, United Kingdom
e-mail: laurabarber84@yahoo.co.uk

one of the most extensive debates within African studies in China, and continues today, has been on the process of African democratisation. In particular, Chinese African scholars have focused on how the imposition of Western democratic political institutions on an alien culture has been disruptive of progress towards African modernisation and development through creating instability. China has therefore traditionally argued that external interference cannot fundamentally solve Africa's security problem. Within this framework, the Chinese preference has been for 'African solutions to African problems', and China has been prone to 'support a regional local consensus in response to crisis in an African state' (Van Hoeymissen 2011, p.94).

In addition to externalising the dynamics of conflict in Africa, in the post-Cold War context Chinese scholars have increasingly looked at underdevelopment and poverty in African states as a root cause of conflict, an internal factor that has been primarily caused by non-political factors such as environmental degradation and climate change (Li 2007, p. 77). However, in exclusively focusing on non-political factors of internal conflict in Africa, Chinese studies exclude several other 'permissive factors' that make organised violence more likely. As exemplified in the case of Sudan, factors include the oppressive nature between the central state and Sudan's marginalised peripheral zones; ethnic tensions between Darfur's 'Arab' and 'African' populations heightened by manipulations by Khartoums' military and theocratic elites; the long-standing system of regional conflicts developed since the 1960s between Sudan, Chad and Libya; resource struggles between Arab nomadic herders and African pastoralists and the sale of oil by the elites for its own benefit to the exclusion of the Sudanese populace (Williams 2011; Jok 2007; Carmody 2008).

Fundamentally, during the 1990s little attention was paid by Chinese oil company executives and Beijing's diplomats to the inevitable impact that Chinese investment in the context of Sudan's civil war would have upon local conflict dynamics, nor the subsequent reverberations that such an involvement may have for the security of Chinese investments on the ground nor China's wider international political interests. Until the mid-2000s, the status quo of Beijing's policy approach was therefore defined by the assumption that internal political or conflict dynamics within the Sudanese state did not have an impact on China itself.

It is asserted here that many of these key perceptions and assumptions have been challenged within the Sudanese context, and this chapter seeks to exemplify this by drawing out the lessons that have been learnt by Chinese foreign policy actors along the trajectory of change to China's foreign policy within the Sudanese context, as detailed in the previous two chapters. This is with a view to assess what Chinese foreign policy actors are learning about the African context and China's role therein more broadly.

It has been argued that, as human beings tend to continue to do what has worked, it is highly likely that forms of negative learning result in changes in state behaviour (Tang 2008, p. 148). As such, as all states including China tend to develop strong propensities towards the status quo in their policymaking processes, learning is most likely to occur in response to perceived crisis, or 'when a shocking or galvanising event highlights the urgency of the problem' and pose a specific challenge to the status quo (Bo 2010, p.145).

It is asserted here that a series of negative 'crisis points', or galvanising events, that occurred in Sudan from 2005 presented a *specific* challenge to China's previous assumptions regarding the impact of such internal events. As such, it is argued that the specific lesson learnt by Chinese foreign policy institutions has been that evolving local conflict and political dynamics within Sudan could substantially affect China itself, and subsequently Beijing's relationship with the Sudanese government. It is asserted that these crisis points sparked internal debates as lessons regarding the negative impact on Chinese interests were learnt and, in debating China's response to protect these interests, Chinese foreign policy implementers also learnt a negative lesson regarding the limitations of a 'non-interference' policy in practice. This lesson learning process will be assessed regarding, firstly, the impact of the local Sudanese context on China's broader political image interests and, secondly, on Chinese interests on the ground in Sudan.

This chapter also seeks to draw out a set of broader lessons that have been gradually learnt by Chinese foreign policy institutions along the trajectory of its deepening engagement in Sudan. Rather than occurring in response to 'crisis points' and their impact specifically on Chinese interests, it is argued that broader lesson learning is likely to occur as a result of the accumulation of experience over time. In particular, this chapter aims to assess the process whereby China's understanding of the nature and dynamics of African conflict more broadly since the 1990s, has been challenged in the Sudanese context. Moreover, it will detail how such broader lesson learning has gradually led China to reassess the nature of its own role in fragile contexts such as the Sudans, particularly regarding Beijing's contribution towards peace and security initiatives.

SPECIFIC LESSON: THE IMPACT OF DOMESTIC INSTABILITY IN SUDAN ON CHINA'S INTERESTS

Chinese International Relations scholars assert that as a direct result of evolving experiences in Sudan, China's foreign policymaking establishment has leant specifically that 'local situations in other countries such as Sudan could impact negatively on China interests'.[1] Moreover, it has been stated that the two prominent sources of lesson learning and subsequent changes in China's Sudanese policies have been firstly the realisation of the impact that its Sudan relationship could have upon China's 'broader political image interests abroad' and, secondly, in the context of local instability in Sudan, China has learnt the lesson that it 'now has considerable overseas interests that need protecting'.[2] The following two sections detail this learning process:

Wider Political Interests: Improving China's International Image

Crisis Point 1: Calling on China to Become a 'Responsible Stakeholder' (September 2005)
China's foreign policymaking institutions first began to learn the lesson that the local situation in Sudan could impact upon its wider foreign policy interests when the conflict in Darfur and China's relationship with the Khartoum government began to intersect with Beijing's US ties towards the end of 2005. This lesson presented itself in the form of 'negative feedback' from the US government regarding China's ties with 'pariah regimes' such as Sudan. This feedback was crystallised in a speech by Robert Zoellick in September 2005, during which the US Deputy Secretary of State called on China to become a 'responsible stakeholder' in the international arena.

The 'responsible stakeholder' call began to feed into broader policy debates in China that culminated in the 2005 'peaceful development' (*heping fazhan* 和平发展) slogan to sanctioned by Beijing reassure the international system of China's peaceful intentions, as Hu Jintao and the ruling Communist Party of China (CPC) elites focused on addressing domestic social, economic and environmental issues that had arisen as a result of China's rapid economic development. Wang Jisi (2005), a leading international Relations scholar with close personal ties with Hu Jintao, wrote at the time that the US was the one country that could 'exert the greatest strategic pressure' on China which must, therefore 'maintain a close relationship with the United States if its modernisation efforts are to succeed' (p. 39).

In this context, the week prior to Robert Zoellick's speech on China, President Hu Jintao stated at the UN that, according to the goal of attaining a 'harmonious world', China would seek to 'fulfill its international obligations' through cooperation within the international community (Hu 2005). However, following the US 'responsible stakeholder' call in late September, China began to learn the lesson that 'its bilateral relations with countries like the US cannot be disentangled from certain difficult third-country issues' such as the Darfur conflict in Sudan (Evans and Steinberg 2007).

According to a prominent Chinese scholar, it was such 'international pressure' and China's perceptions of 'changes in the international environment' vis-à-vis Sino-US tensions that led China to begin to learn this lesson and to change its approach towards the Darfur crisis in order to better display China's responsible role in the Sudanese context.[3] Indeed, it has been asserted that it was in late 2005, after the 'responsible stakeholder' call in September, that the issue of China's global image and the Darfur crisis first came to top the agenda for Beijing's Ministry of Foreign Affairs (MFA) and became a topic of discussion within China's Foreign Affairs Small Leading Group meetings.[4]

Chinese scholars of both Sino-US and Sino-Africa relations assert that domestic discussions at the time reflected that China's foreign policy establishment had not only learnt that Chinese ties with governments such as Sudan could negatively impact upon its wider foreign policy interests, but it was also forced to acknowledge the relative 'importance of Beijing's ties with the US over those with Sudan' within the wider context of China's international relations, and that its foreign policy approach would require adjustment in this context.[5]

It is argued here that it was the initial learning of this lesson that led to the adaptations in China's Darfur policy from mid-2006, such as the role of its MFA diplomats in delivering messages behind the scenes to Khartoum urging its cooperation with the African Union (AU) and the UN, Beijing's new focus on improving 'peace and stability' in Darfur through emerging support for a UN peacekeeping force, and its UN representatives' rare public criticism of Khartoum concerning its lack of improvement of the humanitarian and security situation in Darfur (see Chapter 8).

Crisis Point 2: Questioning Ties with 'Pariah Regimes' and the Role of China's NOCs in Sudan (March 2006)

This lesson was further compounded in the context from mid-2006 of growing frustration among many sub-Saharan African states regarding Khartoum's lack of sincerity to follow through with its commitments to alleviating conflict in Darfur. As a consensus between both sub-Saharan African and Western states regarding the need for a more robust UN force on the ground in Darfur emerged, China's ongoing support for Khartoum left China increasingly 'vulnerable to being called to account within Africa for enabling Khartoum's intransigence and impeding the AU's efforts' (Huang 2007, p. 836). China's traditional policy of non-interference was viewed to be 'contrary to the expectation of other African nations that Beijing would contribute to the stabilisation of Darfur' (Holslag 2009, p. 28).

Within this context, from mid-2006 a considerable debate was sparked among China's foreign policy elites regarding Beijing's ties with 'hardline regimes' in Africa. China's foreign policy institutions and research centres expressed anxiety over the outcome of Chinese policies towards Sudan (Kleine-Ahlbrandt and Small 2008, p. 46).[6] Such new thinking caught the attention of China's leadership in Beijing, particularly the argument that in an effort to 'burnish China's image and international reputation', China should not maintain an uncritical embrace of the Sudanese government, which had proven involvement in the ongoing atrocities against civilians in Darfur, and appeared unwilling and unable to contain the fighting at the host-state level (Robinson 2006). In this context, such foreign policy research institutions also called for an enhanced degree of cooperation with the West and stronger UN support for the AU mission in Darfur (Ahmed 2010, p. 6).

According to a senior Chinese diplomat in China's MFA, the primary reason for China's policy shift towards 'strong engagement' with the West in Darfur from mid-2006 to mid-2007 was fundamentally because it had been the 'request of the international community, including the UN and the AU and other stakeholders and regional communities such as IGAD, which all wanted China to play a more active role, and China took heed to that request'.[7] It was also articulated that, as one of the permanent five members of the United Nations Security Council (UNSC), 'we felt we had the obligation, the responsibility to do something, to use the leverage we have'.[8] This gradual shift in thinking began to be translated into concrete actions by both Beijing's MFA diplomats and

China's leadership itself to exert additional pressure on Khartoum from late 2006 (Huang 2007, p. 836) (see Chapter 8).

It is also apparent that an emergent debate within China focused on an increasing 'principal-agent' dilemma regarding the government's encouragement of Chinese state-owned and private companies to 'go out' and seek investments and new markets abroad, whilst at the same time such companies were sometimes perceived to act against China's national interests, including both its wider international image and its energy security. Indeed, there was increasing disquiet in official circles about the impact of China's overseas investments on its wider international image in the context of Darfur (McGregor 2008). This was particularly from March 2006, after the Sudan Divestment Task Force produced reports highlighting the extensive oil-based ties between Sudan and China, and as part of their divestment plan targeted US assets that included investments in Chinese companies doing business with Sudan.

Certainly, in this context, conservatives within China were quick to point out that the US was just as likely to engage in an uncritical embrace of autocratic and corrupt regimes in Africa when it suited American oil interests (Huang 2007, p. 836). However, with the dramatic decline of Chinese imports of Sudanese oil in 2006, as it emerged that the China National Petroleum Corporation (CNPC) had sold much of its oil produced in Sudan to the highest bidders on the international market, concerns were triggered in Beijing over whether lending support to NOCs overseas was in the country's national interest, particularly if the NOCs are not always seen to improve China's energy security (Houser 2008, p. 165). Highlighting that the lesson that the behaviour of Chinese companies in Sudan could have wider negative impacts on China's interests had been collectively learnt, China's MFA, Minstry of Commerce and the National Development and Reform Commission (NDRC) in March 2007 removed Sudan from its list of destinations where investment by Chinese state companies would receive the central government's support.

Crisis Point 3: The 'Genocide Olympics' as a 'Tipping Point' (May 2007)
It is argued here that the process whereby China's foreign policy establishment learnt that China's wider political interests could be damaged as a result of its ties with Sudan reached its zenith in mid-2007. US-based activists increasingly began to dub the Beijing Olympics the 'Genocide Olympics' in reference to the Darfur conflict and its links to Chinese resource and military ties with the Khartoum government. In this context, China's

Sudan ties became increasingly 'internationalised' and consequential for China's core image interests through threatening to taint the Beijing Olympics to a degree that initially caught China's leadership and foreign policy institutions off-guard (Cooper 2007).

Some Chinese policymakers and academics continued to argue that the international criticism of China's Sudan policy was no more than trying to use human rights issues to contain China's presence in Africa (Jiang 2009, p. 65). However, conversely, the 'Genocide Olympics' campaign also began to spark considerable discussion regarding the limited utility of China's strict adherence to the non-interference policy in practice if it prevented Beijing from pits international image interests. Indeed, Chinese African scholars and MFA diplomats argued with reference to China's Sudan role that, whilst China did not need to 'abandon' (*fang qi* 放弃) the non-interference principle, China's rising global power and image interests means that a policy of non-interference in practice was increasingly not seen to be synonymous with that of 'non-involvement' (*bu jieru* 不介入) or inaction (Wang 2008).[9]

Meanwhile, according to a leading African scholar at Chinese Academy of Social Science (CASS), it was the letters delivered to China's top-level leadership from US government officials in April and May 2007 endorsing the position of the 'Genocide Olympics' campaigners that provided a 'tipping point' for the Chinese government to seek to counter US criticism of its role in Sudan catalyst for further change in China's diplomatic behaviour.[10] One Chinese scholar argued that, 'if China completely ignores the Western pressure and continues to do nothing on the Darfur crisis, some significant damage could be inflicted on Chinese interests and national image worldwide' (Wang 2008, p. 14). Sudan scholars at the Institute for West Asian and African Studies at Zhejiang Normal University also reiterated the potential damage that the Chinese companies' presence in Sudan in the context of Darfur was causing for China's international image in Africa (Jiang and Luo 2008).

The most visible representation of this shift in policy in response to the learning of this lesson came in May 2007 with a change in the MFA's institutional structures and actors through which China dealt with the Darfur issue, and the creation of the position of Special Envoy for African Affairs, the first of its kind in Chinese foreign policy more broadly.[11] From this point China's Special Envoy began to apply more vocally assertive pressure on Khartoum to accept the AU-UN peacekeeping mission in Darfur and better communicate China's role to a Western non-state audience through 'briefings' with Western media. The Special Envoy also sought to convey such specific lessons that had been learnt in the context of Darfur across Chinese foreign policy implementing institutions in Beijing, for example, through relaying his experiences within meetings at the CPC's International Department headquarters.[12]

Meanwhile, in early 2008, Zhang Yunling, of the CASS, dispatched international relations specialists to Sudan to prepare a report on China's conduct there (McGregor 2008). Zhai Kun, of the China Institute of Contemporary International Relations (CICIR) in Beijing, said that large state companies such as CNPC inevitably 'now stand for economic considerations'; however, 'more and more regulations should now be created by the government to constrain their behaviour overseas' (cited in McGregor 2008).

However, it is notable that, despite such increasing awareness in Beijing regarding the need to better regulate Chinese NOCs operating in unstable states such as Sudan, CNPC's expansion into the Sudanese oil sector continued unabated, with Sudanese oil flows to China were resuming after 2007. As such, although the CNPC's dominant position in Sudan had resulted in an international backlash against Beijing's ties with Khartoum, the maintenance of Sino-Sudanese oil cooperation continued to be in the broad interests of China's senior leadership and foreign policy establishment as a whole.[13]

Moreover, it was in this context of invested Chinese interests in CNPC's Sudanese oil operations that Chinese implementing institutions and oil executives would steadily begin to learn the negative impact that socio-political instability and domestic violence within Sudan would have upon the maintenance of those very interests, which the Chinese foreign policy establishment increasingly sought to protect.

Chinese Interests on the Ground: The Primacy of Investment Protection

Crisis Point 1: Local Insecurity and the Lack of Host-State Protection of Chinese Interests (October 2007–October 2008)
Domestic disquiet within China was growing after a spate of attacks on Chinese NOCs in 2006 and 2007 in Sudan. In this context, China's state-run newspaper, *China Daily,* published an article arguing, 'China needs to consider new channels to protect overseas interests', suggesting a new realisation that China's reliance on host-state protection was insufficient

(cited in Holslag 2009, p. 27). However, it is argued here that it was not until late 2007, when such attacks became steadily more frequent and deadly in this new era of instability in Sudan, that Chinese diplomats and CNPC representatives began to learn the extent to which local insecurity was beginning to have upon Chinese economic interests and citizens in Sudan and, moreover, the limited capacity of the Khartoum government to protect those interests.

As with the attacks on oil targets before, the attacks on Chinese-run oilfields by Darfur rebel groups in October and December 2007, there was a limited impact on oil production; however, concern was growing in Beijing as Chinese policymakers began to learn that CNPC was being deliberately targeted. In recognition of this new development, in response to the attacks the China's MFA had released a rare public statement expressing elevated concern and asserted public pressure on Khartoum to protect Chinese interests: 'the safety of Chinese personnel in Sudan must be effectively guaranteed' (cited in Patey 2014, p. 196). Indeed, in adapting China's non-interference policy to directly comment on Sudan's 'internal affairs' and their impact on Chinese interests, China's MFA had learnt that domestic violence 'reduces China's ability to maintain the policy of non-interference' in practice that had facilitated the initial entrance of Chinese NOCs into Sudan (Holslag 2009, p. 28).

Senior Chinese officials within the MFA and the Ministry of National Defence, and renowned academics in Beijing reaffirmed that concerns relating to the security of China's extensive economic interests and pro-liferation of Chinese nationals on the ground in both Sudan and Chad was one of the key motivations from 2007 for China to begin to deepen its support for a more robust UN peacekeeping force in partnership with the AU in Darfur.[14] Chinese government implementing institutions attempted to enhance their capacity to better respond to security challenges that had increased during 2007, and CNPC made efforts to improve its emergency response plans and safety evaluations (Patey 2014, p. 204).

It is argued here that the learning process regarding the impact of local insecurity on Chinese interests, and that Sudanese government was no longer capable of protecting Chinese interests, culminated in October 2008 with the kidnapping of nine Chinese oil workers and the death of one that had been caught in the crossfire of a botched rescue attempt launched by the Sudanese security forces. The incident presented the reality that the Sudanese government's capacity to protect CNPC was, at best, 'wearing thin' (Patey 2014, p. 179, 200). That this lesson had been learnt was evident initially within the public statements issued by the Chinese MFA after the incident that revealed a direct note of criticism of Khartoum, and CNPC issued statements indicating that its continued oil cooperation was increasingly becoming dependent on an improved security environment in Sudan.

In response to a recognition of the declining capacity of the central government in Sudan to protect its interests and heightened local criticism of the company's role at the local and national levels in Sudan, CNPC increasingly began to attempt to improve its image through enhanced Corporate Social Responsibility activities within the local communities that could harm the company's operations from 2008.[15] As such, it is argued here that CNPC had learnt specifically through its experiences in Sudan that it 'can do well by doing good', and that, fundamentally, the more it was able to develop 'sustainable and trusting relationships at both national and local levels, the more secure its investments will be' (Downs 2008, p. 31).

With the CNPC's former executive, Zhou Yongkang's, visit to Khartoum in November 2009 to celebrate the 50th anniversary of Sino-Sudanese diplomatic ties and the 10th anniversary of Sudan's position as an oil exporter, one Chinese energy scholar at the Party School under the Central Committee of the CPC argued that Sudan continued to represent a successful model of China's NOCs' implementation of the 'Going Out' strategy in Africa (Deng 2011). However, the continued hailing of symbolic energy ties at this time belied a significant learning process that had been underway for the past few years of the engagement.

It was not only in the context of China's evolving Khartoum relations that a learning process vis-à-vis the impact of local dynamics on China's economic interests would become apparent. The shifting political landscape associated with southern Sudan's referendum on secession and the resurging instability and domestic violence emerging in the independence era would introduce a new set of risks, and negative lessons, from which Chinese diplomatic and economic actors in Sudan would increasingly begin to learn.

Crisis Point 2: Southern Referendum on Secession and South Sudan's Oil Production Shutdown (January 2011–January 2012)

It is argued here that it was not until the confirmation of the South Sudanese referendum result in January 2011, and the emerging challenges to the continuity and stability of CNPC's oil investments thereafter, that

China's business and foreign policy actors in Sudan began to learn the specific impact that the politics of southern secession would have upon Chinese economic interests. Indeed, confirmation of the reality that the majority of CNPC oil operations would be relocated south, where perceptions of CNPC have historically been negatively tainted by their role in wartime Sudan, presented the negative lesson that backing one side during the war could lead the company to lose out once the political landscape of Sudan's oil leadership changed.

This was apparent when the new government of South Sudan announced at independence that all oil contracts signed with foreign companies before the 2005 signing of the Comprehensive Peace Agreement (CPA) would be re-evaluated. The ruling Sudan People's Liberation Movement's (SPLMs) historic links with the US government introduced a new phase in China's engagement in Sudan following southern independence, as the South Sudanese oil market became open to the investment of US multinational oil companies in a way that it had not been since Chevron left in 1984. Moreover, six months into independence South Sudan had shutdown its oil production in the context of the ongoing oil infrastructure-sharing dispute with Sudan; a move that had a notable negative impact on both CNPC and the Chinese government's economic interests.

The potential implications of southern independence initially fed into broader concerns in China the context of the Arab revolutions springing up across North Africa and the Middle East since 2010 that the return of a US policy aimed at promoting local democratisation and pursuing US oil interests in the region could have a destabilising effect on Sino-US relations and Chinese economic investments on the ground (Shi 2011). It was argued that a key interest of the US to encourage southern independence was in order to gain strategic access to southern oil reserves and push Chinese oil companies out of the south in the process (Li 2011).[16]

In this context, Chinese academics and policy advisors had begun to articulate the need for an evolved Chinese role in the post-referendum period leading to the emergence of two separate sovereign states; one which would 'focus on economic reconstruction in north and south Sudan' and that China will have to 'be careful to maintain good relations with both' and not work with one 'against the interests of the other', as the future of Chinese company oil contracts following formal secession remained unclear at this stage.[17] Indeed, the tentative adaptations to Beijing's policy of reaching out to the Government of South Sudan (GoSS) prior to independence, as detailed in Chapter 9, were the result of such concerns.

In addition to the potential geo-economic competition arising from southern independence, in the context of the recent 'Arab spring' and civil war in Libya where the Chinese government was forced to evacuate 35,860 Chinese citizens in February 2011, there was growing concern in China regarding possible instability resulting from southern secession and its impact on the safety of Chinese citizens on the ground.[18] In this context, it was asserted that should the transition prove to be unstable with both sides resorting to a return to 'all out war', the Chinese government would be prepared to evacuate all Chinese workers from Sudan.[19]

As South Sudan formally gained its independence in July 2011, mainstream domestic debates within China had clearly shifted from that of claiming that Chinese oil companies had 'hijacked' Chinese foreign policy, as during 2007, to stressing the significance of CNPCs investments in Sudan to China's broader national energy security strategy of safeguarding oil supply (Yang 2011).

It was stated that the Chinese government had already begun to adapt its Sudan policy through 'attaching equal importance to its relationships with north and south Sudan' (Yang 2012, p. 90). However, going further, Chinese scholars argued that the scope of such diplomacy should be more 'flexible' (*linghuo* 灵活) towards establishing a wider array of relationships within the South Sudanese political space (Yang 2012, p. 31). It was argued that the key to ensuring China's ability to secure its oil interests in South Sudan was for China to win the 'trust' (*xinren* 信任) and 'support' (*zhichi* 支持) not only of the ruling party and central government, but also of the South Sudanese people more broadly (Yang 2012, p. 31).

Not only did CNPC step up its engagement with South Sudan's SPLM-led government following the announcement of the referendum results, but it also extended its 'corporate diplomacy' below the ruling elite level for the first time through courting the support of South Sudanese parliamentary groups representing local civil society in the lead up to independence. Moreover, it is apparent that both the company and the Chinese government learnt the negative impact on Chinese long-term interests in Sudan as a result of an unquestioning support of the National Congress Party (NCP) during wartime Sudan. Indeed, for the first time within their South Sudan engagement, following the referendum CNPC and Chinese MFA representatives in Juba admitted to senior SPLM officials that 'there had been mistakes in the past' in this regard.[20]

Despite the eventual signing of new oil contracts between CNPC and the GoSS and the enhanced efforts of Chinese diplomats to encourage Juba and Khartoum to reach an oil agreement, the CPC and the Chinese government more generally were said to be 'shocked' at the way in which the situation deteriorated from mid-January leading to the shutdown of oil production, and ultimately 'learnt we couldn't do anything' to prevent its eventuality.[21] Within this context, according to an informed Western official, Chinese diplomats had learnt that 'they could now not operate in isolation' in the Sudans.[22]

Indeed, it had been this realisation that led China's Special Envoy Liu Guijin to privately press for stronger efforts in the framework of a 'division of labour' between the West and China to encourage a swift end to the current north-south impasse, with China's focus now being on pressuring Khartoum because 'that is of course where [China] has more leverage'.[23] As such, although Beijing's diplomatic efforts had failed to prevent the shutdown, its increased engagement in partnership with the West in support of the AU-led negotiations between the Sudans illustrated how China had begun to 'redefine its role in the international community as a partner in helping to find a solution to outstanding oil issues' (Patey 2014, p. 232).

Crisis Point 3: Inter-State Conflict Between the Sudans and the Descent into Civil War in South Sudan (January 2012–December 2013)
An enhanced phase of insecurity and heightened inter-state tensions between Sudan and South Sudan emerged from early 2012 that had a specific impact upon Chinese citizens and oil interests. Firstly, 29 Sinohyrdo workers were kidnapped by the GoSS-supported SPLM-N rebels in Sudan in January and, secondly, the SPLA's invasion of Heglig wrought considerable damage on the CNPC-run oilfields there in April. These incidents also compounded concerns among Chinese embassy diplomats based in Juba regarding the stability of China's state-owned companies' investments and the safety of Chinese citizens operating in an increasingly fragile inter-state political environment.[24]

Indeed, CNPC managers learnt that the company 'was in a different situation' to the decade previously when, although in the midst of civil war, united Sudan was considered to generally have been 'a friendly country towards Chinese investors and CNPC had been assisted by the [Sudanese] government'.[25] It was in this context that CNPC increasingly began to adapt its prior investment approach vis-à-vis risk and a reliance on developing 'guanxi' 关系 ('relations') with ruling elites to protect its interests, for example, through increasingly seeking protection for its operations from private security companies in South Sudan.[26]

Within Chinese academic debates, it was suggested that the independence of South Sudan 'hasn't effectively resolved the contradiction between Sudan and South Sudan' and the heightened tensions in the region had 'brought new challenges to our country's overseas interests, which should be seriously considered in the implementation of our 'Going Out' strategy and the maintaining of China's overseas national interests' (Liu and Zhang 2012).

There was growing evidence that China was learning that deep investments within insecure and politically unstable environments were not necessarily 'win-win', particularly on the Chinese side.[27] Chinese African scholars and diplomats within China's embassy in South Sudan argued that as a result of recent experience in the Sudans, China's foreign policy elite was in the thinking process of how to 'upgrade its investment strategy' in emulation of Western multinationals, such as encouraging NOCs to invest in less unstable situations and to more effectively carry out investment environment assessments before committing to projects.[28]

Moreover, it was apparent that China's state-owned policy banks, particularly China Export Import Bank (EXIM), were becoming increasingly risk averse where it came to the extension of substantial financial assistance within insecure and politically unstable environments. According to a researcher at the CPC's Party School in Beijing who conducted research in South Sudan following the shutdown and the Heglig invasion, Chinese investor confidence had been affected as the turbulent situation forced a reduction in the scale of investments to avoid high risks (Qian 2013, p. 32). Indeed, EXIM officials in Beijing contended that they 'needed to know that security was in place' because it was 'pointless to invest if the north and south were back at war'.[29]

In adopting a more risk-averse strategy vis-à-vis the provision of loans to South Sudan, Beijing also developed a new discourse of conditionality within Chinese economic diplomacy linking economic assistance to stability within its engagement with the south. Indeed, regarding South Sudan's failed attempts to garner substantial economic assistance from China, particularly for an alternative oil pipeline, during Salva Kiir's trip to Beijing in April 2012, China's Special Envoy later recounted that 'we told President Kiir, we are very willing to help...but our experience tells us that if there is not a peaceful environment it will be very difficult to do' (cited in Martina 2012).

From May 2012 Chinese government officials had stepped up Beijing's Sudan-South Sudan mediation efforts both at the AU and the UN levels in closer cooperation with Western diplomats to support the final resolution of outstanding resource and territorial issues just as CNPC representatives became increasingly involved in providing technical advice that would lead to the oil fee agreement between Juba and Khartoum in August 2012. According to a senior CNPC manager in Juba, such enhanced efforts reflected a growing convergence of interests between the CNPC, the Chinese government and the international community regarding stability in the Sudans and averting economic collapse in both countries through a peace agreement.[30]

Chinese scholars assert that this specific lesson learning process in the Sudan case reflects a much broader trajectory of China's rise towards a global power status whereby, 'as the largest trade and investment partner for many African countries', and in the context of globalisation and interdependence, China is subsequently increasingly affected by the local situations within those countries. As such, it is asserted that China's foreign policymaking institutions have broadly learnt that China must now 'have a closer eye on local developments' within African countries that could negatively affect its interests.[31]

This lesson learning process was further compounded in the context of intra-state political violence that began to rapidly spread across South Sudan from mid-2013, when both Chinese company and foreign policy actors became increasingly concerned about the impact of protracted local violence on Chinese interests as the CNPC-run oilfields became the epicentre of the conflict between government troops and rebel factions. This concern grew not only regarding the damage inflicted upon CNPC-run oil infrastructure, its effect on oil exports and, most importantly, Chinese workers in South Sudan, but additionally the potential reverberations and spillover effects that a descent into civil war in South Sudan may have throughout the broader region in northern and eastern Africa in which there is both established Chinese economic interests and citizens operating on the ground (He 2014).

Towards an Assertive Foreign Policy Approach (2012-)

According to a senior advisor at the Sudan-South Sudan negotiations prior to 2012, although Chinese representatives had attended the talks and were described as 'discreet, straightforward, direct and helpful', they 'were not exactly proactive'.[32] However, it is asserted here that from 2012 China began to chart a new direction towards an increasingly assertive foreign policy approach focused on deepening its contribution towards peace and security in the Sudans and the broader region. According to Chinese scholars, this development has been in response to the direct learning of the lesson that Chinese interests on the ground in South Sudan would continue to be negatively affected in the long term as long as protracted violent conflict there persisted and threatened broader regional stability.[33] The learning of this lesson in turn informed a broader shift in China's Africa policy when China's leadership, for the first time, included China's intention to become more involved in African peace and security initiatives at the Forum on China-Africa Cooperation convention in July 2012.

China's direct mediation in the South Sudanese conflict from late 2013 was perceived by Beijing to mark a 'new chapter' in China's foreign policy, with its Special Envoy Zhong Jianhua displaying a new diplomatic confidence and stating that 'the need to expand China's foreign policy footprint and protect its interests are both driving China's more assertive presence in South Sudan' (cited in Martina 2014). Western diplomats also noted a deeper level of engagement by China in the international diplomatic efforts to resolve the South Sudan conflict, stating, 'it's the first time China has been so proactive in addressing a foreign crisis' (cited in He 2014).[34] It is therefore apparent that China's foreign policy elite has been learning that the protection of Chinese interests and citizens in Sudan and South Sudan could not be achieved through short-term defensive and reactive measures on the ground and reliance on limited host state capacity, only through a longer-term, deeper engagement in peace and security initiatives in the broader region.

In this context, by 2012 Chinese scholars among China's foreign policy elite also began to argue for a degree of 'flexibility' (tanxing 弹性) regarding more assertive measures such as sanctions, albeit within a framework acceptable to China with notable 'Chinese characteristics'. This shift in thinking translated into change in Chinese foreign policy behaviour in practice in the Sudans case and was particularly apparent when coercive tools were seen to provide an incentive for fragile African states to end protracted violent conflict in the short term.

In 2012 Pan Yaling asserted in the context of ongoing civil unrest in Sudan, South Sudan and Libya that China has 'gradually begun to realise' that such 'internal affairs' often have a 'harmful overflow' (不良外溢 buliang waiyi) far beyond their sovereign borders and, as such, China's traditional policy of non-interference in others' 'internal affairs' is not applicable in the context of African civil wars (Pan 2012, p. 55). Pan asserts that more assertive actions to prevent this harmful overflow of violent conflict such as 'collective sanctions' (jiti zhicai 集体制裁) by the international community, notably including China, could be justified (Pan 2012, p. 55).

Such shifting internal perceptions regarding support for more coercive tools has been increasingly evident in changes in Chinese foreign policy practice. In the context of the intensifying civil war in Libya 2011, China voted in favour of UNSC Resolution 1970 imposing sanctions on the Libyan government. Beijing also voted in favour of UNSC Resolution 2046 in 2012 calling on Sudan and South Sudan to halt fighting on the border that, significantly, had expressed intent to take measures under Article 41 on sanctions for non-compliance. US diplomats based within the UN in New York expressed their surprise at the distinct lack of resistance to the reference to sanctions that has characterised China's historic position with regards to UNSC initiatives with regards to Darfur.

It is argued here that the drivers underpinning Beijing's emerging acceptance of the imposition of sanctions by the international community are twofold. Firstly, China is increasingly disposed to accepting sanctions in cases where there is international, and particularly regional, consensus that sanctions are an appropriate measure for external actors to adopt (Van Hoeymissen 2011, p. 95). In the context of the recent upheaval in Libya and the Sudans, from the perspective of Chinese scholars and UN diplomats it was the instrumental support of the Arab League and the African Union that guaranteed China's affirmative votes for Resolutions 1970 and 2046, respectively (Yan 2012, p. 114; United Nations Security Council 2011, 2012b). Yan Xuetong notes that this reflects China's growing acceptance of the emerging 'normalisation of intervention diplomacy' in the global arena as many developing countries are now adopting the norm of intervention (Yan 2012: 113–114).

Secondly, it is apparent that China has begun to accept in certain cases that coercive measures may be necessary to encourage an end to hostilities and an improvement in the security and humanitarian situation on the ground where Chinese interests continue to be under threat from protracted violent conflict (Pan 2012; He 2014; Lee et al. 2012). As fighting between Sudan and South Sudan escalated in 2012 while the AU-led peace negotiations stalled, China's UN representative stated that China supported UNSC Resolution 2046 as Beijing was 'deeply worried about the deterioration in relations between the two countries' and hoped both sides would be encouraged to 'follow the path of peace laid out by the African Union' (cited in United Nations Security Council 2012b).

As such, it is apparent that Beijing's growing concern about the broader destabilisation of the region and the coordinated position between the UN and the AU regarding the resolution of these conflicts overrode China's traditional position of opposition to more coercive measures, particularly where the threat of sanctions could have the effect of bringing about stability on the ground.

As will be detailed in the following section, China's traditional assumptions regarding African conflicts more generally have been challenged in the context of the Sudans and driven China's foreign policy institutions to realise that a more nuanced peace and security role in the Sudans was needed.

Broader Lessons: Learning About Sudanese Conflicts

The Role of the Sudanese State and the Issue of Governance

China's official policy rhetoric continues to oppose the use of the term 'good governance' in the West as a form of 'aid conditionality' to impose Western liberal democracy on developing states. However, it is contended here that along the trajectory of China's Sudan engagement, Chinese actors increasingly began to learn the role that weak governance and the lack of central state capacity or will to provide for its own citizens has played in perpetuating cycles of centre-periphery conflict in Sudan.

At a conference hosted by the China's MFA think-tank, the China Institute for International Studies (CIIS), on peace and development in Darfur in Beijing in June 2007, Chinese government officials and scholars reiterated that China attributed the conflict in Darfur to poverty, resource scarcity and the effects of global warming, and urged the international community to avoid interfering in Darfur and not to overlook the Sudanese government's efforts to address the conflict through its acceptance of UNSC Resolution 1769. However, it was argued that 'all parties' must improve the security situation so that some semblance of governance can be established on the ground as, significantly, it was acknowledged that 'not even a minimal level of governance' currently existed in Darfur.[35]

Due to Beijing's non-interference policy and position that each state should follow its own path to development and that China would not impose its own development 'model' onto Sudan, China was prevented from directly addressing the issue of Khartoum's economic mismanagement. Nevertheless, from 2007 Beijing started to publicly push the Sudanese government as well as the international community to work for development in the Darfur region, although refraining from proposing concrete policies or funding initiatives in this regard. Such advice reflected the Chinese perspective that economic development would address poverty and provide the key to promoting peace in Sudan (Jiang and Zhang 2013a, p. 20).

China's Ambassador to Sudan, Luo Xiaoguang, stated that Chinese development and humanitarian assistance 'will provide much for the local people [in Darfur] and boost their living conditions' (cited in Xinhua 2013a). As such, these official statements acknowledge the need for the 'redistribution of resources away from the centre and towards the peripheries' which had hitherto been neglected by the Sudanese central state (Regler 2013, p. 31).

The clearest representation of this shift in understanding of the role of the state in the Darfur conflict occurred during President Hu Jintao's trip to Khartoum in February 2007 where he relayed China's 'four-point plan' on the resolution of the conflict. While the Chinese leader continued to reaffirm the principle of respect for Sudanese sovereignty in the resolution of the conflict, the fourth new principle appeared to contradict the former, as Hu's use of language stressing the 'imperative' to improve the lives of people at the *local* level reflected a dramatic shift from China's predominantly state-directed discourse, in a way that indicated acknowledgement of the absence of a positive state role in improving the humanitarian situation.

Certainly, in 2005 China had endorsed the principle of the 'responsibility to protect' (R2P), a term that was introduced within the UN in 2001 to provide a framework for legitimising the use of force against states to protect populations from egregious abuse, as Beijing sought to avoid some of the image costs of obstructing the UN effort to prevent and respond to atrocities (Teitt 2008, p. 303). However, as Huang argues, Hu Jintao's statement vis-à-vis Darfur 'was as close as a Chinese leader has come publicly to supporting the emerging notion that governments have a responsibility to protect their citizens from harm' (Huang 2007, p. 837).

A further shift in China's position occurred in 2012 when it voted in favour of UNSC Resolution 2035 (see above), which had expressed UNSC's regret that actors affiliated with the Government of Sudan (GoS) continued to perpetrate violence against civilians in Darfur. As such, it can certainly be asserted that China's vote of approval for this resolution 'formally acknowledges the dimension of state sponsored violence in Darfur conflict' (Bradbury 2012, p. 382).

While at the time of South Sudan's referendum on secession and its final independence in July 2011 Chinese scholars attributed the primary cause of the division of Sudan to the role of the US (see above), it is apparent that in the post-independence era, the Chinese assessment did also begin to acknowledge historic role of central government policies that have induced a desire in the south to secede from the north. Indeed, it was argued that in addition to external factors such as the role of the US, the north-south separation represented the 'main symbol of the failure of Sudan's nation-state building' (Wang 2012b, p. 67).

Placing an ethno-religious conflict within the broader historical Sudanese context, it was argued that since gaining independence from Anglo-Egyptian rule in 1956, successive central governments have continued patterns of 'racial discrimination' and suppression of the Christian south through 'forcing' upon it an alien Islamic culture whilst the economy was skewed towards the north, with development of the south constituting less than 10% of the national budget (Wang 2012b, p. 75). Following the CPA in 2005, it was argued that both sides were unable to reach a compromise on a shared vision north and south on the 'peace-building process' of a unified post-conflict Sudan (Zhu 2012, p. 76).

Moreover, some even acknowledged the role of resource extraction and the distribution of oil wealth as a factor in ongoing north-south disputes, as it was asserted that 'meeting the key challenge of maintaining peace and stability depends on reasonable resource allocation to various oil interests' (Zeng 2011).

In private, Chinese diplomats issued more direct criticism of President al-Bashir and the ruling NPC, suggesting that during the 6-year interim period following the CPA in 2005, a period when the south would decide on whether to separate depending on the extent of reform, the Khartoum government 'failed to make unity attractive' to the south through truly implementing the power and wealth sharing agreements through ensuring political inclusion and economic development for the south.[36] It is apparent that during the interim period, Chinese diplomats had begun to be concerned that the situation in Darfur would 'head in the same direction as the south' as Darfur groups were similarly not being provided with the political and economic incentives to commit to peace within a unified Sudan.[37]

Viewing Conflict Holistically

It is argued here that another shift in China's perception of Sudanese conflicts occurred from 2007, with an increasing recognition that civil unrest and protracted violence in Darfur, which spread across Sudan's borders into Chad, had become 'trans-national' and threatened broader regional stability. This learning process was further compounded in the context of violent conflict that erupted in South Sudan in 2013, which threatened to destabilise the broader region. These emerging realities challenged China's traditional understanding that Sudanese conflicts, and African conflicts more generally, represented the 'internal affairs' of a sovereign state.

Such concerns were reflected in the rhetoric of Beijing's diplomats who increasing asserted that 'the appropriate solution to the Darfur issue not only concerns the security and humanitarian situation in Darfur, but also bears on the peace process between the north and south Sudan, neighbouring Chad, and the security and stability of Central Africa and the sub-region as a whole' (Wang 2006). According to MFA think-tank researchers in Beijing, the Chinese government's interest in stability in Sudan here did not emanate exclusively from concerns about resource security because, 'although oil is important, it is not the only important thing to China', as a 'key interest is also regional stability' and the potential impact that deteriorating instability in the Sudans may have on China's broader economic interests and political ties in east, central and north Africa more broadly.[38]

Such a realisation of the increasingly regional dynamics of the Darfur conflict translated into concrete policy actions as, in 2007 during early consultations with France, Beijing had supported a French resolution on Chad calling for the dispatch of mainly European peacekeepers under the auspices of Chapter VII, a move which Holslag highlights as significant, as China approved the 'close liaising' with the Hybrid Operation in Darfur (UNAMID), where earlier it had objected to the development of links between UNAMID and UN missions (Holslag 2009, p. 31). One Chinese diplomat confirmed how this had reflected Beijing's evolved understanding of the urgency to address the regional dynamics of the Darfur conflict and insecurity in Africa more generally: 'our support for the resolution on Chad shows that we are prepared to cooperate to tackle security issues at a regional level and that our awareness on the increasing complexity of violent conflicts in Africa grows' (cited in Holslag 2009, p. 31).

In addition to Beijing's enhanced coordination with the West, it is apparent that China's position in relation to the Darfur peace negotiations became increasingly aligned with that of the AU as a result of Beijing's shared view on the need for economic development in Sudan in order to promote Sudanese unity and regional stability. In 2007, the AU Special Envoy affirmed that should Africa's largest country split, 'it would send shock waves through the neighbouring countries and mean a disaster for the whole continent' (cited in Embassy of the PRC in Libya 2007). According to the UN humanitarian coordinator for Sudan who worked closely with China's senior Africa diplomats, Beijing was increasingly concerned about the potential for Darfur to go in the same direction as the South in its drive towards separation and this provided a further source of inspiration for China in terms of its engagement in resolving the Darfur issue.[39]

Moreover, by early 2008 Chinese officials had become rapidly worried about increasing instability in Darfur and its potential to negatively affect both the fragile peace in the south and also wider stability in a region in which Chinese economic interests and citizens are embedded. As such, in this context it also was deemed beneficial to establish a diplomatic presence through a consulate on the ground in southern Sudan in 2008 in an effort to provide potential protection of Chinese interests in this context of inter-related insecurity.[40]

It is argued here that this lesson learning process was further compounded in the context of growing instability following South Sudan's independence. Indeed, Chinese scholars assert that internal perceptions in China regarding the potential implications of South Sudan's descent towards civil war in late 2013 for the broader region of East and North Africa provided a new impetus for China's deepened involvement in supporting regional attempts to bring about a ceasefire in South Sudan (He 2014).

The Role of the US and Mutual Interests with China
In accordance with a Marxist historical-materialist theoretical perspective, Chinese scholars and policymakers alike have also traditionally viewed African civil unrest and instability to be caused by external factors, from the legacy of arbitrarily drawn borders of the colonial era, to US efforts to

promote democracy in Africa during and after the Cold War. Chapter 8 detailed how early on in the Darfur crisis in 2004, Beijing had strongly opposed external western intervention in the conflict and preferred primarily local 'African solutions', which was in a large part based on Chinese opposition to what was viewed as a politically motivated goal of the US to utilise the vehicle of a UN force to bring about regime change or use excessive force against the government in Khartoum.

That Beijing had begun to initiate initial adaptations towards cooperation with the West vis-à-vis a UN peacekeeping force and emerging behind-the-scenes efforts to encourage Khartoum to accept the mission in support of the AU from mid-2006, notably prior to the 'crisis point' represented by the 'Genocide Olympics' campaign of 2007, it is argued here was in part the result of a lesson learning process by China's foreign policy elite regarding the US and the wider international community's goals in Sudan and the perception of increasingly shared interest of respecting Sudanese sovereignty.

From mid-2006 China's position was 'in line with the approaches of other permanent members of the Security Council' as the majority of the international community saw an external military intervention without political approval from the state to have the potential to cause further chaos in the region (Holslag 2007, p. 3). As revealed within the statement of the UNSC mission to Sudan in June 2006, the delegates conveyed the message that the Council unanimously wanted a 'stable and prosperous Sudan' and reiterated its 'respect for the sovereignty and territorial integrity of the Sudan' (UNSC 2006b, p. 9).

Moreover, it became increasingly apparent to Beijing by early 2007 that the US government was not planning military intervention to end the fighting in Darfur. Indeed, in February it was asserted during a US Senate committee hearing that while the US was pressing for progress on the Darfur crisis, it was focusing on diplomatic means. The US Assistant Secretary of Defence for African Affairs, Theresa Whelan, stated that 'we are not considering doing something militarily' and the focus of the US Special Envoy, Andrew Natsios, was on 'getting the parties back to the table' (cited in *Sudan Tribune* 2007).

Following the International Criminal Court's (ICC's) issuing of an arrest warrant, Chinese diplomats again learnt that the US was not directly seeking regime change in Sudan, which accorded with China's perception that 'the change of government is decided by their own people, by their own political structure', rather than imposed externally.[41] It is apparent that US diplomats reassured their Chinese counterparts that Beijing's concern that the issuance of an arrest warrant for President Bashir could have profound destabilising effects was well founded. Indeed, US diplomats agreed that combined with the end of the rainy season and renewal of rebel activity on both sides of the Chad-Sudan border, the ICC indictment 'could set off a chain reaction of violence and instability' in the region (cited in The Guardian 2010).

In this context, it is apparent that China's Special Envoy Liu Guijin began to learn that Sino-US perspectives on Sudan were increasingly in line, 'holding similar views on the reasons of the crisis and way for resolving the crisis...a military solution on the ground will not solve north-south issues and the same with regard to Darfur'.[42] China's leading diplomats on the Darfur issue asserted that it was the shared interests of China and the US in peace and stability in Sudan 'that provides solid ground for us to work together', and it was on this basis that the Chinese Special Envoy was able to 'established good working relations with his Western counterparts'.[43]

As detailed previously, Chinese scholars and officials had in the mainstream attributed southern secession in July 2011 to the US government's historic support for the SPLM and its interests in pursuing energy opportunities in a new southern state; interests that were seen to be inimical to China's preference for the status quo. However, in the post-independence era and the context of ongoing Sudan-South Sudan tensions, Chinese diplomats continued to learn that Beijing and Washington shared a mutual interest in stability in the region, and it was this perception of shared interests that led to enhanced cooperation between China and the international community vis-à-vis north-south issues.

It is apparent that in July 2011, days after South Sudan gained its independence, Chinese scholars attending a workshop at the Center for Strategic and International Studies on the broad issue of cooperation between China and the US in Africa, Sudan and South Sudan and security came out as the predominant areas in which cooperation would be sought (He 2014). Indeed, this was the result of growing coordination of perspectives on security issues in the Sudans.

As President al-Bashir began to face internal threats to his rule both within the ruling NCP elite and the wider population in 2011 as the loss of southern oil began to impact on the Sudanese economy, Chinese diplomats and their US counterparts concurred that the overthrow of the relatively moderate al-Bashir by the more radical Islamist wing of the NCP would be more destabilising for the region.[44] Moreover, Chinese diplomats within the Chinese embassy in South Sudan began to assert that, rather than upholding an 'all-weather' friendship with the GoSS, Washington was prepared to resort to strong criticism of ruling SPLM in Juba when it pursued more bellicose tactics, as with its army's occupation of Heglig in April 2012, as such acts of retaliation against the north threatened to undermine regional stability.[45]

Moreover, coordination between China and the US continued late into 2013 in the context of heightened internal conflict in South Sudan. In December both governments worked together to ensure the rapid adoption of UNSC Resolution 2132 to temporarily increase the overall force levels of United Nations Mission in South Sudan in a mutual effort to bring about peace and stability on the ground in the fragile new nation. Joining the efforts of US and EU special envoys, China's counterpart Zhong Jianhua also began to publicly and more assertively seek a direct mediation role between the South Sudanese government and the SPLM opposition faction.

Ultimately, China's special envoy Zhong Jianhua has stated that Beijing's public diplomatic efforts to directly mediate in the South Sudan conflict marks a 'new chapter' in Beijing's foreign policy that 'will seek to engage more in Africa's security' (cited in Martina 2014). Zhong also asserted that such a shift in policy practice emanated from an increasing acceptance within China that the country 'should be engaging more in peace and security solutions for any conflict' in the African context (cited n Martina 2014).

CONCLUSIONS

This chapter has revealed the process whereby China's foreign policy implementing actors have learnt the specific lesson that local conflict and political dynamics in Sudan and South Sudan have had specific negative impacts on both China's broader political interests in terms of its international image and also the safety and security of Chinese oil interests and citizens on the ground. In turn, China learnt that its reliance on conducting relationships primarily with ruling elites in the governments of both Sudan and, latterly, South Sudan not only has failed to result in the protection of Chinese interests but, moreover, could further damage them. In seeking to protect Beijing's political and economic interests over the trajectory of the engagement, Chinese foreign policy actors subsequently learnt the limitations of a 'non-interference' policy in practice.

Moreover, Chinese institutions have learnt that the protection of Chinese citizens and investments in Sudan and South Sudan cannot be achieved through short-term defensive measures and relying on the host state, but only through a longer-term engagement in peace and security initiatives in the region. It has been argued here that it is the learning of this lesson which has begun to drive a more assertive foreign policy approach vis-à-vis the resolution of Sudanese conflicts from 2012, which contrasts with a more limited defensive and reactive approach between 2005 and 2011.

In seeking to provide further depth to an explanation of this recent shift in the Sudanese case, it was argued that learning the need for a more assertive approach vis-à-vis conflict resolution in the Sudans from 2012 has been underpinned by a process of 'broader' lesson learning about Sudanese conflicts that have been gradually learnt along the trajectory of China's engagement, particularly after 2005.

China's traditional perceptions of local political conditions and the nature of conflict in the African context, and the set of state-centric assumptions underpinning these views, were increasingly challenged as a result of Beijing's foreign policy implementers' experiences along the trajectory of a deepening engagement in the Sudanese context. Firstly, Beijing's foreign policy implementers have gradually learnt about how the lack of capacity or will of the central Sudanese government to prevent and resolve conflict in Sudan could impact upon long-term stability. Secondly, there has been an increasing recognition that Sudanese conflict was no longer confined to the 'internal' realm within Sudan's territorial borders, with implications for wider regional stability. Thirdly, Chinese foreign policy implementing actors have gradually recognised that they share interests with the US and the wider international community in bringing about peace and stability in the Sudans.

The learning of this broader set of lessons regarding the nature of Sudanese conflicts compounded the specific lesson that instability in Sudan could negatively impact on Chinese interests on the ground. Indeed, it led China's foreign policy establishment to reassess China's own role in the context such conflicts as it sought to secure Chinese assets and personnel in Sudan in the long term. Beijing's public diplomatic efforts to directly mediate in South Sudan from 2013 has certainly ushered in a newly proactive chapter in China's foreign policy characterised by a deeper engagement in peace and security solutions to conflicts in the Sudans, and Africa more generally.

Notes

1. Interview, Peking University, School for International Studies (SIS), Beijing, China, 23 December 2010.
2. Interview, Tsinghua University, Department of International Relations, Beijing, China, 27 September 2011.
3. Ibid.
4. Interview, Renmin University, Department for International Relations, Beijing, China, 4 January 2011.
5. Interview, China Institute for International Studies (CIIS), Department for Developing Countries Studies, Beijing, China, 6 January 2011; Interview, Fudan University, School of American Studies, Shanghai, China, 30 August 2012.
6. Interview, China Institute for International Studies (CIIS).
7. Interview, Chinese Ministry of Foreign Affairs, Beijing, China, 25 June 2011.
8. Ibid.
9. Ibid., 18 November 2010.
10. Ibid.
11. Interview, Peking University, School for International Studies (SIS), Beijing, China, 4 January 2011.
12. Interview, CPCID Diplomat, London, 6 March 2013.
13. Interview, China Institute for International Studies (CIIS), Department for Developing Countries Studies, Beijing, China, 6 January 2011.
14. Interview, Tsinghua University, Department of International Relations, Beijing, China, 27 September 2011; Interview, Chinese Embassy in the US, Washington, DC, US, 4 October 2013.
15. Certainly, this process had also emerged in tandem with broader domestic developments within China since 2005. See: Zhao (2012), p. 163.
16. Interview, CPCID Diplomat, London, 6 March 2013.
17. Interview, China Institutes of Contemporary International Relations (CICIR), Institute for West Asian and African Studies, Beijing, China, 12 April 2011.
18. Interview, Peking University, School for International Studies (SIS), Beijing, China, 5 May 2011.
19. Ibid., 23 December 2010
20. Interview, Government of the Republic of South Sudan, Ministry of Cabinet Affairs, Juba, South Sudan, 20 March 2012; Interview,

Government of the Republic of South Sudan, Office of the President, Juba, South Sudan, 30 November 2011.

21. Ibid.
22. Interview, British Foreign and Commonwealth Office (FCO), London, UK, 2 February 2012.
23. Interview, Chinese Ministry of Foreign Affairs, Beijing, China, 25 June 2011.
24. Ibid.
25. Interview, Peking University, School for International Studies (SIS), Beijing, China, 27 August 2012.
26. Interview, Veteran Security Services (VSS), Juba, South Sudan, 11 May 2012.
27. Interview, Zhejiang Normal University, Institute for West Asian and African Studies (IWAAS) researcher, Juba, South Sudan, 1 June 2012.
28. Interview, Interview, Shanghai Institutes for International Affairs (SIIA), Centre for West Asian and African Studies, 14 January 2013.
29. Interview, China EXIM Bank, Beijing, 28 August 2012.
30. Interview, CNPC, Juba, South Sudan, 1 June 2012.
31. Interview, Peking University, School for International Studies (SIS), Beijing, China, 27 August 2012.
32. Sudan expert and advisor at the AUHIP negotiations between Sudan and South Sudan, email to author, 20 July 2012.
33. Interview, Shanghai Institutes for International Affairs (SIIA), Centre for West Asian and African Studies, 14 January 2013
34. Cited in Ibid.
35. Interview, China Institute for International Studies (CIIS), Department for Developing Countries Studies, Beijing, China, 6 January 2011.
36. Interview, CPCID diplomat, London, 6 March 2013.
37. Telephone interview, United Nations Special Envoy to Sudan (2006–2008), 4 October 2011; Interview, Ministry of Foreign Affairs, Beijing, China, 25 June 2011.
38. Interview, China Institute for International Studies (CIIS), Department for Developing Countries Studies, Beijing, China, 6 January 2011.
39. Telephone interview, United Nations Special Envoy to Sudan (2006–2008) 4 October 2011.
40. Interview, Chinese Embassy in the Republic of South Sudan, Juba, South Sudan, 1 December 2012.
41. Interview, Ministry of Foreign Affairs, Beijing, China, 25 June 2011.
42. Ibid.
43. Ibid.
44. Interview, Chinese Embassy in the Republic of South Sudan, Juba, South Sudan, 28 May 2012.
45. Ibid.

Laura Barber has a PhD from the Department of International Relations, London School of Economics and Political Science (LSE), on the topic of learning in Chinese foreign policy towards Africa with a particular focus on China-Sudan and South Sudan relations. She currently works as a political and security analyst based in London.

CHAPTER 11

China's New Intervention Policy: China's Peacekeeping Mission to Mali

Niall Duggan

On July 12, 2013, the People's Republic of China (China) sent 395 troops to Mali as part of a United Nations (UN) peacekeeping mission. These troops formed the 30th Chinese peacekeeping mission since China first started dispatching peacekeepers in 1989. While most Chinese peacekeepers have been engineering and medical troops sent to repair transport infrastructure and provide medical assistance. On this occasion, China, for the first time, sent combat troops on a peacekeeping mission where their mandate went beyond protection of Chinese noncombat troops. China sent a small group of combat troops to South Sudan in 2012 and a large number of troops in 2015, but their mission was limited to protecting China's own noncombat troops (Hartnett 2012). Besides this single exception, China's previous contributions to UN peacekeeping missions were support staff, such as non-combat engineers or civilian police, normally from civilian units and the People's Armed Police. Sending non-combat troops on UN missions aligned with China's traditional policy of non-inference. However, towards the end of Hu Jintao's leadership, China indicated that it would adopt a more flexible interpretation of its non-inference policy (Large 2008; Gottwald and Duggan 2012, pp. 42–44, 2011, pp. 239–242).

N. Duggan (✉)
Department of Government, University College Cork, Cork, Ireland
e-mail: N.Duggan@ucc.ie

Is the commitment of Chinese combat troops to the UN mission in Mali a sign of a new, more flexible interpretation of China's non-inference policy? Is the Mali UN mission the first step to an interventionist China? This chapter will explore these questions by examining the nature of the Mali conflict and Sino-Mali relations. The chapter will also examine the Chinese UN peacekeeping mission to Mali within the overall context of China's role in UN peacekeeping.

MALI CIVIL WAR

The 2013 French military offensive in northern Mali may have seemed like a simple case of intervention to prevent the country falling under the control of jihadist militant groups. However, the conflict is far more complex. The origins of the conflict in Mali can be found in the north of the country. The northern region of Mali has a long history of instability since the establishment of borders under French colonial rule in the late 1800s. There were notable uprisings against the French colonial administration in 1894 and in 1916–1917, and the region continued to be unsettled with further uprisings occurring in 1963–1964, 1990–1996 and 2006–2009 (Dario and Fabiani 2013).

The Tuareg people who inhabitant this region of Mali – as well as parts of Niger, Algeria and Libya[1] – was the main force behind these rebellions. French colonization of the area led to the creation of formal defined borders, which had a great impact on the nomadic lifestyle of the Tuaregs. Restriction of movement exposed them to food and water insecurity, and the fact that they became a minority in Mali led to marginalization. These factors, as well as issues over land rights, led to the first Tuareg Rebellion in the early 1960s against the Malian government. Severe droughts in the 1970s and 1980s led to further conflicts with the central government in Mali and forced some Tuareg people to relocate to Niger, Algeria and Libya (Gutelius 2007). Many of these disenfranchised Tuareg people gained combat skills – either directly from joining the Libyan army or from combat training during reintegration of Tuaregs into the Malian army during period of peace (Bøås and Torheim 2013). Using Algeria and Libya as bases of attack, the Tuareg rebels maintained an on-off conflict against the Malian government.

After a failed rebellion between 2007 and 2009, large numbers of Tuareg fighters joined the Libyan army (Steward 2012). The collapse of the Qaddafi regime in 2011 also saw the departure of many Tuareg people from the Libyan army. They returned to Mali to form the National Movement for the Liberation of Azawad (MNLA),[2] demanding that Mali's government grant independence to the northern regions of Gao, Timbuktu and Kidal (Dowd and Raleigh 2013). This group was well trained, and with weapons from Qaddafi's arsenal, they were also well equipped. However, it is important not to overstate the role of these Tuareg fighters' return from Libya, as the majority of MNLA members were Tuaregs in the Malian Army who had been veterans of previous rebel movements but had integrated into the Malian military as part of peace accords. These fighters deserted to the MNLA and took their weapons with them (Shurkin 2014, p. 5).

The group declared the independence of Azawad in April 2012, and it took control of much of the north of the country within a short period of time. Like previous Tuareg rebellions, this group was bound together by ethic and clan loyalties (Boukhars 2013). However, unlike previous rebellions in the north of Mali, this rebellion also had a hardline jihadist element (Warms 1992; Niezen 1990; Soares 2005). Indeed, a hardline northern Islamist group, Ansar al-Dine or Defenders of the Faith,[3] also took part in the 2012 rebellion. Ansar Al-Dine had strong links to Al-Qaeda in the Islamic Maghreb (AQIM) (Oumar 2011), formerly known as the Salafist Group for Preaching and Combat but renamed AQIM in 2006 (Wing 2013). This group is openly anti-Western in its nature and is known to operate not only in Mali but also in Mauritania, Niger, Libya and Chad, as well as having strong international links through Al-Qaeda. The presence of these two groups, as well as smaller groups, such as the Movement for Unity and Jihad in West Africa (MUJWA), add a hardline element, to the conflict. This hardline element had not been present in the previous conflicts in the area and has led to a rapid expansion of the areas these groups controlled.

The numbers of fighters associated with the Islamist groups prior to the French intervention are not known, although estimates generally gave Ansar Dine and AQIM a few thousand fighters each, and MUJWA perhaps under 1,000 (Shurkin 2014, p. 6). Due to the rapid success of these relatively small terrorist groups, a military coup occurred in March 2012, which ousted President Amadou Toumani Touré, destabilizing Mali further (Lecocq et al. 2013, pp. 346–347). On April 3, Ansar al-Dine had started implementing Sharia law in Timbuktu. The presence of a jihadist militant group in the famous city of Timbuktu created international pressure to intervene in Mali (Solomon 2013). By June 2012, Ansar Dine, AQIM and MUJWA turned on the MNLA and seized control of northern Mali from the Tuareg rebel group (Walther and Christopoulos 2014).

The first attempt to deal with the conflict in Mali was a peacekeeping operation by the Economic Community of West African States (ECOWAS). However, the speed of the jihadi militant group's advance took ECOWAS by surprise. ECOWAS developed a contingency plan for an intervention, which called for an ECOWAS force to deploy into Mali with backup from the international community. The European Union would support this by providing training for troops in Mali. The European Union Training Mission in Mali had a mandate to train about 2,500 Malian soldiers to retake northern Mali with the support of a mainly ECOWAS contingent (Marchal 2013, p. 7). However, ECOWAS forces were unprepared and underequipped to engage the jihadist militant groups. While the UN had placed the onus on resolving the crisis on the Malian government, it was clear that neither the UN nor the Malian government were in a position to respond to the crisis (UNSC S/2012/894).

As these jihadi militant groups advanced towards Bamako, the French military took action (Flood 2013). This action came at the request of the military junta's National Committee for the Rectification of Democracy and the Restoration of the State (CNRDRE) to prevent the capture of the Malian capital by the jihadist militant groups (Lecocq et al. 2013, p. 355). ECOWAS was left as an onlooker during the initial action (Benjaminsen 2008) after the French intervention in Mali, named Opération Serval, was launched on January 11, 2013. French and African troops quickly pushed the rebels back, recapturing key towns in northern Mali before the end of the month (Ministère de la Dèfense 2013). A peace agreement between the central Malian government and Tuareg rebels was signed in June 2013, resulting in elections in July 2013 (BBC 2013, Adam Nossiter and Peter Tinti 2013). However, the jihadist militant groups continued their attacks, often using neighbouring countries as a base of attack.

Following the creation of a peace deal between the MNLA and the central government, the UN authorized the formation of the UN Multidimensional Integrated Stabilization Mission in Mali (Mission multidimensionnelle intégrée des Nations Unies pour la stabilisation au Mali, or MINUSMA) (UN-MINUSMA 2013a). The mission was authorized in April 2013 under UN Security Council Resolution 2100 (2013)

(UN S/RES/2100), which referred to the rebels as terrorists and authorized 11,200 personnel to be dispatched to Mali under the UN umbrella. The mission of MINUSMA was the re-establishment of Malian state authority and the protection of civilians and historical sites (UN-MINUSMA 2013).

By November 2013, ongoing conflict in the north of Mali had resulted in the MNLA ending its ceasefire and renewing attacks on the Malian army. The French force remained at the forefront of the peace operation, launching Opération Hydre in October 2013, which carried out action between Timbuktu and the northern city of Gao. In August 2014, the French launched Opération Barkhane, a partnership between the key countries of the Sahel-Saharan Strip (BSS): Mauritania, Mali, Niger, Chad and Burkina Faso. Opération Barkhane included 3,000 soldiers, 20 helicopters, 200 logistics vehicles, 200 armoured vehicles, 6 fighter planes, 3 drones and a dozen transport aircraft (Ministère de la Dèfense 2014). The mandate of Opération Barkhane was to support the armed forces of the BSS partner countries in their actions against terrorist armed groups and to help prevent the reconstitution of terrorist sanctuaries in the region. However, both the MNLA and the jihadist militant groups have continued to use bases located inside Libya and Algeria to launch attacks in northern Mali.

SINO-MALIAN RELATIONS

Mali and China established diplomatic relations on 25 October 1960, and have since enjoyed a positive relationship. China provided economic and technical support to Mali throughout the 1960s, famously setting up a large sugar mill in Sègou (Snow 1988, p. 159). Sino-Malian relations also have a strong political element. During the time of the first Malian president, Modibo Keita, the Malian government took a strong pro-China policy, adopting Chinese ideology mainly driven by anti-colonial solidarity. For example, four million copies of Mao's little red book are said to have circulated in Mali, leading to calls for a cultural revolution and a great leap forward in Mali (Snow 1988, p. 102). In terms of international relations, Mali has been a strong supporter of China. Mali has had a long-standing commitment to the One China Policy and the Five Principles of Peaceful Coexistence (Esterhuyse and Kane 2014). Mali was one of the PRC's sponsor for its bid to replace Taiwan as the China seat on the UN Security Council in 1971 (Snow 1988, p. 115).

China and Mali's contemporary relationship reflects the positive relations of the 1960s and also China's overall positive relations with Africa. In 2012, the total volume of China-Africa trade reached US$198.49 billion, a year-on-year growth of 19.3%. 'Of this, US$85.319 billion consisted of China's exports to Africa, up 16.7%, and US$113.171 billion was contributed by China's imports from Africa, up 21.4%' (State Council 2013, p. 3). However, economic relations between China and Mali are small both by international standards and in the context of Sino-Africa trade (Esterhuyse and Kane 2014). As of 2014, China was Mali's main trading partner: 30.6% of Mali's imports – mainly mechanical, electric, chemical and pharmaceutical products – came from China, with 9.4% of all Malian exports – mainly gold and cotton – going to China (MFA 2015). China's overall trade with Mali in 2014 was US$369 million (European Commission 2014, p. 9).

China is also a major investor in Mali. Since the establishment of the China Investment Development and Trade Promotion Centre in Bamako in 1996 (Mofcom 2002), a number of Chinese enterprises – such as the China Overseas Engineering Group Co. Ltd, China GEO-Engineering Corporation, and China Light Industrial Corporation for Foreign Economic and Technical Cooperation – have entered Mali for contracted projects and joint ventures (Xinhua 2009). China has also been involved in building Bamako Bridge, a general hospital, a conference building, and a stadium. In 2014, China launched an US$8.72 billion project to build a 900 km railway from Bamako to Conakry in Guinea (Felix 2014). China and Mali also enjoy good people-to-people relations: more than 500 Malian students have graduated from Chinese schools and are currently working in a variety of professions in Mali (Xinhua 2009). Moreover, there is an estimated 3,000 Chinese living in Mali (Esterhuyse and Kane 2014) – a much smaller Chinese population than in other African states, such as Algeria (20,000) and Nigeria (100,000) (Park 2009, p. 4).

Although both countries have maintained a good relationship since the 1960s, Mali is not of any particular strategic importance to China. Mali, unlike other African states such as Sudan and Nigeria, is a relatively small trading partner and it does not supply China with any strategic resources such as oil. The Chinese population in Mali is small compared to the Chinese populations residing in other African countries. While Sino-Mali relations do have a strong political element, it is difficult to find any evidence to suggest that Mali is of a higher level of strategic significance to China than other African nations.

CHINESE PEACEKEEPING

Until the financial crisis in 2008, China maintained a low-profile role within global governance, and China's role in the UN is no exception to this rule (Duggan 2014a). In accordance with its low-profile role, China has employed a strategy of abstention in Security Council votes. China routinely avoids voting on disputes involving the US-led Western bloc, as well as on issues where developing nations are involved. Since a permanent member's abstention is the functional equivalent of voting yes,[4] assuming the nine remaining Security Council members vote yes, this strategy has been welcomed by the US-led Western bloc. However, this strategy has gained China the nickname 'Mr. Abstention' and the reputation of a low-level actor in the UN Security Council outside issues that are central to Chinese foreign policy, for example, the principle of sovereignty and territorial integrity of nation-states (Duggan 2014a).

Conversely, in terms of its contribution to UN peacekeeping, China has recently increased its activities. Since 2007, China has adopted a more proactive role on the UN Security Council, changing its pattern of voting from one of abstention to what Joel Wuthnow described as a 'practical cooperation' with Russia (Wuthnow 2012). For example, in 2007, China and Russia vetoed criticizing Myanmar on its human rights record, and in 2008 both states vetoed sanctions against Zimbabwe (United Nations 2014). Both cases were not a threat to the key issues for Chinese foreign policy, for example, the principle of sovereignty and territorial integrity of nation-states. Therefore, the rapid increase in China's employment of the veto and the nation's expansion of its application of the veto into areas that are not central to Chinese foreign policy highlight a marked change in China's role in the UN, moving China towards a proactive position.

The marked change in China's approach to the UN Security Council has been accompanied by a significant change regarding China's role in UN peacekeeping. The Chinese National Defence policy 2008 states that, 'as a permanent member of the UN Security Council, China has consistently supported and actively participated in the peacekeeping operations within the spirit of the UN Charter' (Ministry for Defense 2010). China first participated in a UN peacekeeping operation in 1989, when 20 Chinese military personnel took part in the UN Transition Assistance Group to help monitor elections in Namibia. Chinese military troops were first dispatched to a UN peacekeeping in 1992 to Cambodia (Gill and Huang 2009, p. 2). These steps mark a notable shift in attitude towards UN peacekeeping operations from open hostility during the 1950s and 1960s to enthusiastic supporter.

The total number of Chinese troops to contribute to the UN from 1990 to 2008 was 12,443 (China's National Defense 2009). By 2013, China had increased its level of contribution to UN peacekeeping missions. In 2013, China contributed 1,868 – more than Security Council members France (963) and the UK (282) (United Nations 2014). China's increased troop numbers indicate greater engagement in UN peacekeeping. It is clear the People's Liberation Army, through participation in peacekeeping activities abroad, benefits from important military experience (Sanzhuan 2014, p. 106). However, the main driver behind China's increased involvement in peacekeeping is a change of attitude towards the concept underpinning UN peacekeeping – that of a responsible power.

First, as China has attempted to become a great power under its peaceful development (*Zhongguo heping fazhan*) doctrine, it has adopted the concept of a 'responsible great power' (*fuzeren de daguo*), which is a state that has the capability to affect the affairs of the international community and does so in a way that ensures international peace and security (Xia 2001). Therefore, it is argued that this understanding of the responsible power is an underlying reason for the change in China's attitude towards UN peacekeeping (Jiaxiang 2014; Courtney 2011). Second, as China's economic interests rise in areas of the world where conflict levels are high, it is in China's own interests to help create more stable environments in these regions. This is best seen in Africa, where China has become the continent's largest investor, and Africa has become one of the main destinations for Chinese peacekeepers (Ayenagbo et al. 2012). China's greater engagement in peacekeeping, particularly in Africa, can been seen as evidence that, in terms of security governance, China is adopting some Western norms (Alden and Large 2015). Greater cooperation with the West – in particular, the European Union – in peacekeeping missions is also an indicator of an adoption of Western norms in peacebuilding.[5]

However, 'sovereignty and territorial integrity are still the most practical and ultimate concerns to Beijing' (Wang 2014, p. 91). Therefore, China's engagement in peacekeeping missions is limited by the will of the incumbent government and the goal of maintaining the territorial integrity of a state. For example, China backed the Security Council's decision to send peacekeepers to intervene in the Democratic Republic of Congo (DRC). The DRC Force Intervention Brigade was the first UN peacekeeping mission specifically tasked to carry out targeted offensive operations (Whittle 2015). China's decision was made against the back-drop of the Peace, Security and Cooperation Framework for the DRC and the approval of 11 regional stakeholders, as well as an invitation from the legitimate government of the DRC (Xue 2014, p. 11). As highlighted by Xue Lei, 'this demonstrates China's acceptance of the legal implications of recognizing legitimate governments under international law' and it also shows 'China's preference for a policy of maintaining stability and continuity in the countries or regions affected' (2014, p. 11).

As such, while China has moved towards a greater level of engagement in the peacekeeping process and, therefore, has moved away from its non-interference policy, it is still bound by the principle of sovereignty and territorial integrity. As a result of this bounded interference policy, China has adopted two approaches to peacekeeping. First, China engages with the regional bodies, pushing these bodies to the fore of the decision-making process (Duggan 2015). In the case of Africa, China has developed strong cooperation with a number of regional and sub-regional bodies and has appointed representatives to Southern African Development Community, ECOWAS and Common Market for Eastern and Southern Africa and the African Union (AU) in 2005 (Van Hoeymissen 2010). There is a belief that African regional bodies are better placed than the wider international community to deal with issues of sovereignty and internal conflict among their regional members (Alden 2011, p. 58, Herman 2015, p. 27). In the 2006 China-Africa White Paper, China highlighted the AU's role in safeguarding peace and stability and promoting solidarity and development (People's Daily 2006). China has recommitted its support for regional organizations in the 2009 FOCAC Sharm el-Sheikh Action Plan, which outlined that China supports 'the efforts of the AU, other regional organisations and countries concerned to solve regional conflicts' (FOCAC 2009). During a speech at the African Union headquarters in Addis Ababa, Ethiopia on 5 May 2014, Chinese Premier Li Keqiang outlined China's support for regional organizations' positions within the African security architecture by stating that:

> No peaceful and stable environmental development was possible without China's firm support...We will further implement the China-Africa partnership on peace and security...help support the building of African collective security mechanisms...expand training, intelligence sharing, joint exercises, joint training, and other aspects of personnel together to help

strengthen the capacity for peacekeeping, counter-terrorism, and combating piracy. (Zhang Lei and Jun Ma 2014)

The second approach is the adoption of a comprehensive strategy towards peacekeeping (Duggan 2014b). A comprehensive security approach does not deal just with the conflict but with the underlining issue that created the conflict – for example, lack of economic development, food security or water security. This can be considered peacebuilding rather than peacekeeping. Marcus Power, Giles Mohan and May Tan-Mullins, highlighted that 'China has yet to play a significant role is in peacebuilding, i.e. the use of a wider spectrum of security, civilian, administrative, political, humanitarian, human rights and economic tools and interventions to build the foundations for longer term peace in post-conflict countries' (2012, p. 252). Nevertheless, there is a clear aim within Chinese foreign security policy to adopt elements of a comprehensive security approach (Duggan 2014b). Even China's new comprehensive security approach is bound by the principle of sovereignty as it is state-centric, funnelling their efforts via incumbent governments rather than civil society.

Chinese Peacekeeping in Mali

As highlighted by Yun Sun, the Chinese response to the French intervention in Mali was one of concern about a potential abuse of the UN mandate, as was the case in Libya (2013, p. 2). Yun also highlighted that 'Chinese analysts have further attributed France's intervention to Hollande's desire to boost his image and popularity at home given the failure of his domestic economic policies' (ibid.). Although the French obtained the support of the UN Security Council members for the intervention, the Chinese believed that the French mission went beyond the African-led International Support Mission in Mali stipulated by UNSCR 2085. Yun outlines that the fact that this was done under the banner of fighting terrorism was seen in China as particularly alarming because it legitimizes 'fighting terrorism as justification for foreign intervention in a civil war of a sovereign country' (ibid.).

For China, a country with a key foreign policy of non-interference in the internal affairs of other states, this was a dangerous precedent. It was Beijing's hope that France would pull out soon and hand over the military responsibility to the African-led mission. Despite China's concerns, that the French would not hand over control of the mission to African leadership, Beijing dispatched troops to Mali in what Foreign Minister Wang Yi described as a 'comprehensive security force' (Hille 2013). The authorized strength of MINUSMA was 12,680, comprising of up to 11,240 military personnel and 1,440 police, and as of March 31, 2015, 11,510 peacekeepers had been committed (United Nations 2015b). These peacekeepers come from 52 countries, including China.

China first dispatched a 170-member peacekeeping guard detachment to the Mali mission area in West Africa at the request of the UN to guard the UN headquarters in Gao (Ministry for Defence 2014a). In total, China dispatched 395 officers and soldiers, including 170 members in guard detachment, 155 in engineer detachment and 70 in medical detachment (Ministry for Defence 2015a). These troops were dispatched from Army Corps of Engineers and the Army Corps and a medical team from the Joint Logistics Department of the Shenyang Military Region, (Hu 2014), and had both a guard and support function. There was a clear understanding among the troops that this was not just a peacekeeping operation but also a reflection of China's attempt to adopt a responsible great power role. This is evident from a statement made by Vice Captain Zhao Guangyu: 'we have confidence and ability that we will fulfil our mandate in accordance with the relevant requirements of the UN peace-keeping operations, showing China role as a protector of international peace and a responsible great power' (Hu 2014, p. 1).

"In the first 180 days, these troops organized 145 armed patrols, but came under 31 rocket projectiles while operating in the West African country (Ministry for Defence 2015b). By the end of September 2014, the guards had carried out 600 patrol tasks and more than 200 escort tasks in the area of responsibility of the MINUSMA (Ministry for Defence 2014b). The Chinese engineer detachment successfully completed multiple tasks (Ministry for Defence 2015a), including 100 construction and support tasks, such as road construction, bridge erection, ground levelling and building of makeshift housing (ibid.). The medical detachment had treated 1,281 persons and hospitalized 84 patients (Ministry for Defence 2015a).

The combination of troops and their activities was a reflection of China's attempt to develop a comprehensive security force that would allow China to contribute to peacebuilding. Kaba Diakité, a leading supporter of the Malian president's party, highlighted that a lack of transport infrastructure in the north of Mali had been seen as a reason for the conflict, both in terms of rebels' grievances against Malian authorities and the Malian army's inability to deploy quickly in the north (Diarra 2014). Diakite also asserted that the involvement of Chinese peacekeeping in the reconstruction of Malian transport infrastructure as well as China's wider investment in developing Mali's road network[6] would help to deal with the underlying causes of the conflict.

The Chinese comprehensive security approach also included targeting Malian food and water security problems, which had been one of the main driving forces of the current and previous conflicts in northern Mali. Under the Food and Agriculture Organization of the United Nations 2013–2017 Country Programming Framework, a South-South Cooperation project was set up to enhance Mali's agricultural production through the provision of Chinese technical assistance. During this project, the Chinese team successfully introduced 13 new technologies and 28 new crop varieties (FAO 2014). The Chinese experts demonstrated new seedling varieties, new transplanting and close planting methods, bagging, water-saving irrigation and ecological disease prevention (FAO 2014). It is clear that in Mali, China is taking a wider approach to dealing with many of the non-traditional security threats that are the underlying causes for much of the conflict in Mali. This, combined with a contribution of peacekeeping troops, including combat troops, is a reflection of China's attempt to adopt a comprehensive security approach to international peacekeeping. It is also a reflection of China's desire to play a responsible great power role in international relations.

According to Chen Jian, head of the UN Association of China, 'this [China's mission to Mali] is a major breakthrough in our [China's] participation in peacekeeping' (Hille 2013). However, the question remains: why did China choose to send troops to Mali? Three main factors can explain China's actions. First, China's new foreign policy of intervention bound by the principle of sovereignty and territorial integrity made Mali a suitable case for China to send combat troops. The UN mission to Mali had a mandate to protect the Malian incumbent government. Therefore, the mission protected the territorial integrity of Mali and prevented the fall of the state, maintaining Mali's sovereignty, which is in line with China's new foreign policy.

Second, the fact that the rebels from northern Mali contained both religious extremists and separatist elements was also a factor behind China's decision to send combat troops. Domestically, China also has problems with religious and separatist extremists, giving the Chinese a common cause with the Malian government. This was highlighted by

Marc Lanteigne, who pointed to 'the fact that the adversaries in Mali were largely religious extremists seeking to dismember a sovereign state through force, an issue to which Beijing could relate given the ongoing problems in China's far-Western region of Xinjiang' (2014, p. 11). As such, while China may have feared that France was setting a dangerous precedent by intervening in order to fight terrorism, there was an underlying advantage in China setting a precedent in the use of force against religious extremists who seek independence for a particular region of a state.

The third and final factor that can explain why China contributed combat troops to Mali lies within the context of Sino-Mali relations. Although Mali enjoys a positive relationship with China, Mali is not a key African economic partner. Trade between the two countries is relatively small compared to trade between China and other African nations. Mali does not supply China with a strategic resource, such as oil, as would be the case in Sudan or Angola. China's investment and assets in Mali are also relatively small compared to other African nations. Politically, Mali is also a small actor compared to African states such as South Africa, Ethiopia and Nigeria. The fact that Mali is not a key partner for China may be a driver behind China's decision to send combat troops to the West African country. China has been accused of being a neocolonialist predator in Africa (Zhao 2014; Jian and Frasheri 2014). Indeed, China's large-scale investment in Africa and the presence of a large number of Chinese companies and migrants have led many in the West and among African civil society to fear that China was developing a colonial relationship with African states. If China was to send combat troops to an African state that was a key trading partner with a large amount of Chinese-owned assets or that supplied China with strategic resources, this may reinforce the narrative of China as a neocolonialist predator in Africa. However, sending combat troops to act as peacekeepers to Mali, a state that does not hold any key political or economic interest for China, goes against the narrative of China as a neocolonial power in Africa.

CONCLUSION

Dispatching 395 troops from the world's largest military force may not seem like a sea change in Chinese foreign policy. However, committing combat troops to a peacekeeping mission in Africa does demonstrate China's willingness to play a greater role in reinforcing international peace. This may be the first sign that China is willing to assume a responsible great power role in international affairs and may also indicate China's adoption of some Western norms in international peacekeeping. China's adoption of a comprehensive security approach to the peacekeeping mission in Mali by targeting the underlying causes of the conflict, such as water and food insecurity, is evidence of the adoption of some Westerns norms. This is line with a wider engagement in terms of security governance, particularly in Africa, and the adoption of Western concepts such as peacebuilding by China (Alden and Large 2015).

However, despite the adoption of these new roles and norms, the case of Chinese combat troops as part of a UN peacekeeping mission to Mali also demonstrates that China's new intervention policy is bound by the principle of sovereignty and territorial integrity. The conflict in Mali was driven by religious extremists and Tuaregs separatists, who threatened the sovereignty and territorial integrity of Mali. Thus, China could set an international precedent that incumbent governments should be protected by the international community against religious extremists and separatists. The conflict in Mali, a country that is not a key partner of China, was also an opportunity for China to demonstrate that it is a positive partner to the continent rather than a neocolonialist predator. The wider implication of the presence of Chinese combat troops in a UN peacekeeping mission to Mali is that China is now willing to commit troops to underwrite its view of the role of UN peacekeeping – the protection of the principle of sovereignty and territorial integrity of nation-states. The case of Mali also shows that China is willing to commit troops to states where it does not have a key economic or strategic interest.

NOTES

1. Small communities can also be found in Burkina Faso, and a small community in northern Nigeria
2. Mouvement National pour la Libération de l'Azawad (MNLA), formerly National Movement of Azawad Mouvement national de l'Azawad (MNA)
3. Ansar al-Dine is led by Iyad Ag Ghaly, one of the most prominent leaders of the Tuareg rebellion in the 1990s with links to the Algerian and Libyan governments.
4. As each permanent member of the UN Security council has a veto an abstention is the functional equivalent of voting yes as the permanent member is allow the vote to be carried.
5. See He Yin.
6. According to the Malian minister of investment, Moustapha Ben Barka, China will build a 900 km (560 miles) railway between Mali and

neighbouring Guinea Conakry. This project will cost $8 million. An old railway between Mali and Senegal, measuring 750 km (466 miles) (Diarra 2014).

Niall Duggan is a lecturer in the Department of Government, University College Cork. He has previously worked as a lecturer in Department of East Asian Politics at Ruhr-Universität Bochum and has also been the Chair of Economy and Society of Modern China in the Centre for Modern East Asian Studies, Georg-August Universität, Göttingen. His research includes global governance reform, non-traditional security issues in East and Southeast Asia and interregional studies with a particular focus on Sino-Africa and Sino-EU relations.

CHAPTER 12

China and Liberia: Engagement in a Post-Conflict Country (2003–2013)

Guillaume Moumouni

INTRODUCTION

Once labelled by the international community as a failed state, Liberia, has enjoyed something of a renaissance since it held its first truly democratic elections in October 2005. Emerging out of the ravages of civil war, the country has given itself and Africa in general, a reason for pride by electing as its president Ellen Johnson-Sirleaf, joint winner of the 2011 Nobel Peace Prize and the first woman in Africa to hold presidential office.

Working mainly through the Economic Community of West African States (ECOWAS), the African Union, the UN, Bretton Woods Institutions and global donors, the international community has played a proactive role in Liberia's regeneration. International involvement in the Liberian government's priority sectors, including reform of security and justice, and national reconciliation and healing is of particular interest.[1]

Among Liberia's bilateral relationships, the link with China has been a major factor in its renewal since diplomatic relations between the two countries were restored in 2003. China's involvement ranges from participation in the UN Mission in Liberia (UNMIL) to its social, productive

G. Moumouni (✉)

Faculty of Law and Political Science, Abomey-Calavi, Republic of Benin

e-mail: atmoug@yahoo.fr

© The Author(s) 2018

C. Alden et al. (eds.), *China and Africa*,

DOI 10.1007/978-3-319-52893-9_12

and commercial role in the revival of the country's fragile socio-economic structures. Both within the framework of UNMIL and at the bilateral level, Beijing has shown itself to be an important stakeholder and development partner in Liberia as in most national post-conflict situations on the African continent.

Within the broad body of China-Africa literature on security issues, case studies are scant because the issue area is quite new. The existing works include: chapters in Section III in Berhe MG and, H Liu (eds.), *China-Africa Relations: Governance, Peace and Security* (2013, pp. 166–246), which analyse situations of China in Sudan, Ethiopia, Zimbabwe and Nigeria; Wang SL, 'Non-Interference and China's African Policy: The Case of Sudan' (2013, pp. 13–18); Anthony R and Hengkun J, 'Security and Engagement: The Case of China and South Sudan' (2014, pp. 78–97); Attree L (2012), *China and Conflict-Affected States: Between Principle and Pragmatism. Sudan and South Sudan Case Study*; Jian J, 'China in the International Conflict-Management: Darfur as a Case' (2012, pp. 7–11); Large D, 'China and the Contradictions of *"Non-interference"* in Sudan' (2008, pp. 93–106); Large D, 'China's Sudan Engagement: Changing Northern and Southern Political Trajectories in Peace and War' (2009, pp. 610–626).

However, there is so far almost no research work on China's role in Liberian post-conflict reconstruction.

This chapter focuses on the 10 years of Chinese-Liberian cooperation from 2003 to 2013, following on the resumption of diplomatic relations. It is a multidimensional study as we understand the need to stabilise a post-conflict country has to go beyond reliance on security pillar, but to be consolidated by other pillars including aid, infrastructure, trade, investment, governance, etc. The study starts by exploring the political relations between China and Liberia, then examines the Chinese involvement in UNMIL, analyses various aspects of bilateral relations and concludes by balancing the complex interactions between both actors and making a set of recommendations to address key issues.

Political Relations: From Unstable to Stabilising

With the full support from the US Navy, the American Colonization Society (ACS) founded Liberia as an American colony in 1822. The intention of the ACS was to send 'back to Africa' former slaves who were now viewed as rebels.[2] Conversely, some of the freed slaves also wished to return 'home' to Africa. The territory became a federal state in 1838 and in 1847, 'to reduce the administration cost of the colony and limit the responsibility of the US government (USG), Liberia was granted independence'.[3] Although the new state remained heavily under US influence, at the end of the 19th century Liberia and Ethiopia were the only independent states on the African continent.[4] There followed a period of slow growth and relative political stability in Monrovia that lasted until the late 1980s.

In September 1990 the murder of President Doe (who had himself assumed power through coup d'état) was the brutal outcome of years of dictatorial rule which had generated opposition among both the elite and the rural population. Indeed Doe's rule (1980–1990) set off a chain of events leading to an extended civil war. Although Charles Taylor, the leader of the main rebel group, was elected democratically in 1997, his tenure proved to be even more destructive than that of Doe. In 2003 through the combined efforts of the international community and ECOWAS, Taylor was forced to step down, paving the way for a political transitional period and general elections in 2005. The election of President Johnson-Sirleaf, a technocrat with extensive experience in macro-economic management, to all appearances has ushered in a period of stability and is laying the foundation for national rejuvenation. In this context China's part in post-conflict reconstruction is especially significant.

For a considerable time prior to President Sirleaf's election, Beijing's role in Liberia had been subject to the shifting tides of diplomatic recognition washing between the People's Republic of China in Beijing and the Republic of China in Taiwan. Beijing's diplomatic relations with any state mainly depend on the other party's acceptance of the principle of non-recognition of Taiwan. In Liberia's case the back and forth movement between the 'two Chinas' started in February 1977, when Liberia abandoned Taiwan in favour of Beijing, after a 20-year honeymoon with Taipei. In October 1989 Monrovia switched back to Taiwan but 4 years later restored its ties with Beijing. In 1997 President Taylor attempted 'diplomatic incest' by advocating the recognition of both, upon which Beijing once again cut its diplomatic links with Monrovia. Finally, in October 2003, Liberia's provisional government signed a Joint Declaration and a Memorandum of Understanding in which it once again recognised China. This move could be interpreted as an attempt to prevent another Liberian defection to Taiwan, because at that time the issue remained unresolved in Monrovia; although in reality even before

China participated in UNMIL Liberia clearly understood that stable diplomatic relations and access to Liberian resources were vital issues for Beijing.[5] On 19 August 2005 the Liberian Senate and House of Representatives each passed Resolution No 001 of the 52nd Legislature, which 'confirms and reaffirms [its] total unwavering commitment to the...one China policy'. This resolution made the new policy irreversible,[6] so much so that in July 2006 when former house speaker Edwin Melvin Snowe hinted at a possible severance of ties with China, Sirleaf promptly denied the allegation and Snowe was eventually forced to resign.[7] From the Chinese side the need to show commitment and shore up the relationship was illustrated by visits by former minister of foreign affairs Li Zhaoxing to Monrovia in January 2006, followed by a visit from President Hu Jintao a year later.

From Monrovia's perspective, China's position as a permanent member of the UN Security Council (UNSC) made it indispensable in helping to pass UN resolutions designed to promote a normalised socio-political environment in Liberia. Beijing's status as an emerging power with global reach and its expanding levels of investment in, and development aid to other developing countries were additional incentives. Liberia has enjoyed a long history of special relations with the West. The changing global environment and a newly assertive Chinese position in Africa have, however, encouraged Liberia's exploration of closer ties with China and are reflected in the priority accorded a more pragmatic approach to foreign affairs in the transitional government's so-called 'development diplomacy'.[8] For its part the Chinese government signalled the importance it attached to relations with Liberia by building an imposing embassy in Monrovia in 2009, fuelling hopes that it would play a concomitant role in the construction.

PARTICIPATION IN UNMIL

Civil War: Background

The Liberian civil war began on 24 December 1989 when Charles Taylor entered the country from Côte d'Ivoire to lead his National Patriotic Front of Liberia (NPFL) against President Doe's brutal dictatorship. In essence the conflict was a by-product of the Cold War; Taylor was trained and armed by Libya's then President Muammar el-Qaddafi with the aim of ousting Doe, regarded as a Western puppet.[9] The NPFL eventually split into two and Prince Johnson became head of the splinter faction. Due to

Taylor and Johnson's siege to Monrovia in June 1990 and fearing an overspill of Liberian revolutionary dissidence, among other factors (including impose a ceasefire, set up an interim government and protect civilian life), ECOWAS decided in August 1990 to deploy a joint military intervention force, the ECOWAS Monitoring Observer Group (ECOMOG) under Nigerian command. The force comprised some 4,000 troops from Nigeria, Ghana, Sierra Leone, The Gambia and Guinea, which were later joined by non-members such as Tanzania and Uganda. Before ECOMOG could be fully operational Johnson's forces arrested Doe and slaughtered him in gruesome circumstances in the presence of Johnson himself in September 1990. Also, as ECOMOG prevented Taylor from taking over Monrovia, he revenged by launching the Mano River war starting from Sierra Leone, a rear base of ECOMOG. He actually armed and trained the Revolutionary United Front (RUF) led by Foday Sankoh.[10] The situation eventually was resolved by the Abuja Accord of 1995, as a result of which in July 1997 Liberia held an election, won by Taylor. The latter's bad governance coupled with his continued support of the RUF led to an armed coalition against him led by a group calling itself Liberians United for Reconciliation and Democracy (LURD), supported by Guinea, and later by the Movement for Democracy in Liberia backed by Côte d'Ivoire. Continual peace talks notwithstanding, fighting was brought to a halt only with the deployment of ECOWAS peacekeepers in August 2003, after which a weakened Taylor was forced to agree to exile in Nigeria. The various warring factions signed the Comprehensive Peace Agreement in Accra in September 2003, bringing the civil war to a close.

China in UNMIL

Following China's 'open and reform policy' adopted in 1978 and its ensuing rapid economic growth, Beijing's foreign policy has become broader and more international in nature. The transformation has brought with it multi-tiered initiatives such as the recent advocacy by President Hu Jintao of a 'harmonious world' (he xie shi jie). This ideal reflects China's renewed expectations vis-à-vis the new international order, the purported aim being:

> to enjoy together the opportunities of development, advance the noble task of human peace and development ... [H]and in hand, the people from each state should push forward peace, common prosperity and a harmonious

world. Henceforth, we should respect the aim and principles of the UN Charter, abide by the international law and universally admitted norms of international relations, and propagate democracy, friendship, cooperation and win-win spirit in international affairs.[11]

As a result China has been increasingly active in UN peacekeeping operations in Africa, particularly West Africa. It has struggled to come up with a theoretical construct of non-interference in its foreign relations and has adopted in practice a limited consultative intervention (LCI).[12] For Beijing, LCI represents a way to embark on collective action with other states, abandoning the old principle of revolutionary unilateralism.

The increase in China's participation in UN peacekeeping operations rests on a combination of factors. First, its ever-growing socio-economic development has made available extra human, material and financial resources for peacekeeping operations. Secondly, the attack on New York's World Trade Centre in 2001 helped reshape China's understanding of national sovereignty and its allegiance to the struggle against terrorism. Thirdly, involvement in peacekeeping operations is a way of improving China's image as a system warrantor or stakeholder rather than as a threat to global peace; it is also part of Beijing's 'historic missions' for the 21st century and a trial run for the so-called 'harmonious world'. Fourthly, peacekeeping missions can enhance the skills base of China's armed forces.[13] Beijing has been building its peacekeeping architecture step by step. For example the Civilian Peacekeeping Police Training Centre based in Langfang, Hebei Province, was established in 2000 as an adjunct to the longer-established Nanjing International Relations Academy, while in 2009 a new peacekeeping training centre was established in Huairou near Beijing. The latter is aimed at helping the army's Peacekeeping Affairs Office better centralise and coordinate Chinese peacekeeping operations and to serve as a venue for international exchanges, including seminars and training for foreign peacekeepers.[14] The fifth reason is that peacekeeping operations are the best possible illustration of Beijing's preference for multilateral rather than unilateral measures in solving peace and security problems; they also offer a practical platform for China's advocacy of what is or is not legitimate UN intervention.[15]

Against this backdrop China's participation in UNMIL was facilitated by a combination of two factors. The first was UNSC Resolution 1509 of September 2003, which authorised the deployment of UNMIL consisting of up to 15,000 military personnel, including 250 military observers, 160 staff officers and 1,115 civilian police officers[16]; the second was the resumption of diplomatic ties between Monrovia and Beijing in October of the same year. Also in October, UNMIL began its operations by 're-hatting' the troops of the ECOWAS mission in Liberia as UN personnel. UNMIL's mission was to support implementation of the Comprehensive Peace Agreement, provide backing for humanitarian and human rights assistance, and to support security sector reform and the implementation of the peace process. The second factor also concerns Resolution 1509, which mandates UNMIL to assist the National Transitional Government of Liberia (NTGL) in the formation of the new and restructured Liberian military, in cooperation with ECOWAS and international organisations. Beijing dispatched its first contingent of troops as early as November 2003.

A 724-strong 15th Chinese peacekeeping task force was dispatched to Liberia in July 2013; it comprised 564 military personnel including infantry, engineer and medical units, 158 police and 2 experts on mission. At the end of 2013 the Chinese total contribution to UNMIL was estimated at 8,370 troops,[17] a significant share in total UNMIL contingent.

China's participation evinces several specific characteristics. First in 2013, China is the fourth largest troop contributor after Pakistan, Nigeria and Ghana (with 2,013, 1,610 and 742 respectively). Secondly, it operates as a unified command comprising transportation, civil engineering and medical units. Thirdly, in terms of 'force enablers' China provides mainly logistical support, including humanitarian aid and other deliveries to UN contingents, engineering services and a field hospital.[18] Finally the Chinese contingent is focused more on hardware and much less on software, a policy that justifies the need for greater collaboration with other foreign entities involved in capacity building, institutional reform and so on.

Engineering and Logistic Support
The Liberian road network is one of West Africa's worst. Liberia covers 111,370 km2 but the total length of its road system is only 10,600 km, of which just 657 km are paved. Due to heavy rains and poor maintenance, the road system suffers from continued and substantial deterioration. Most roads are inaccessible during the rainy season and less than 10% of the system is classified as all-weather road. The country is crossed only by the north–south highway from Monrovia to Nimba via Kakata and the west–east highway from the Sierra Leone border at Bo Waterside to Buchanan.[19]

As noted earlier China's contingent in UNMIL includes medical, civil engineering and transportation components. The engineering unit has renovated and ensured the maintenance of more than 500 km of road, particularly the Zwedru–Tappita, Zwedru–Greenville and Zwedru–Webo highways, and the Toe Town road to the Côte d'Ivoire border.[20] Together with their Pakistani and Bangladeshi counterparts the Chinese have rehabilitated 2,000 km of road networks and built or repaired a number of bridges.[21] The transportation unit provided water, oil, construction materials, apparel and medical products – donated by the World Health Organization – to peacekeeping units from 37 countries while the Chinese medical team has diagnosed and treated thousands of patients.

Interaction with the Donor Community

The Chinese UNMIL contingent has been fairly active in empowering local communities, particularly around its base in Zwedru. It organises training in the use of agricultural tools and in cultivation techniques for crops such as rice and vegetables. It also promotes some features of Chinese culture. Its relationships with other UNIML elements are sporadic and mainly linked to special functions organised by the special representative of the UN secretary-general, such as the UN Day; seemingly it does not favour consistent interaction with contingents from other countries.[22]

BILATERAL INVOLVEMENT

Development Aid

China's development aid to Liberia ('technical assistance' in Beijing's diplomatic vocabulary) covers several socio-economic sectors.

Education

Although the two states signed a cultural cooperation agreement in 1982, until relatively recently their cultural and educational exchanges were very limited in scope. By the end of 2008 only 108 Liberians had been trained on regular programmes in China.[23] The situation has greatly improved, over the 5 years that followed, however. By end 2013 an estimated 500 Liberian students either had received or were receiving formal education in China, and close to 2,000 civil servants and journalists have had some form of training there.[24] Fendell Campus, a branch of the University of Liberia covering 11 ha, with 124,800 m^2 of floor space, was built entirely by the Chinese at a cost of $23 million (against an initial budget of $21.5 million) and handed over in July 2010. China has also built three rural schools.[25]

Health

China built the Jackson F Doe Memorial Regional Referral Hospital in Tappita, opened in 2011, at a cost of $10 million and provided training to 25 Liberian medical personnel in China for the effective use and maintenance of its modern equipment. Three shifts of medical teams were dispatched to other hospitals. China has also built an anti-malaria centre in Monrovia and renovated Liberia's Ministry of Health headquarters building for $4.7 million.[26]

Agriculture

Following on the 2006 Forum on China–Africa Cooperation (FOCAC) and as a direct consequence China undertook the construction of a $6 million China Agricultural Technology Demonstration Centre in Maryland County in the far south, one of 10 such centres in Africa. It also provided $1 million in agricultural equipment and sent Chinese experts to the Booker T Washington Agricultural and Industrial Institute in Kakata to train Liberians in rice cultivation.

Infrastructure

Since first establishing a diplomatic presence in Monrovia China has undertaken a number of social and economic infrastructure projects, including a sugar factory and a sports complex. It has also provided hospital maintenance and medical assistance (having sent more than 60 Chinese medical staff to Liberia since 1984). It also put together the Gbedin rice development project in Saniquellie and founded the Liberia Sugar Corporation (Libsuco).[27] Other infrastructure projects include renovation of the $7.6 million Samuel Kanyon Doe multi-purpose sports stadium in Monrovia; the construction of Tubman cantonment, a military installation in Bong; and assisting in the establishment of countrywide network coverage for radio and television.

Debt Cancellation

China has cancelled $16 million in debt while granting annual aid of $20 million to Liberia in the wake of the 2006 meeting of FOCAC. As a participant in the Liberian Reconstruction and Development Committee, an outcome of the UN Development Assistance Framework for Liberia, China had completed all its pledged obligations by 2011 (see Table 12.1).

Table 12.1 China's contribution to poverty reduction strategy programme 2006–2011 ($ million)

Pillars	Pledged	Disbursed	Remaining
Peace and security	6.2	6.2	0
Economic revitalisation	14.2	14.2	0
Governance and rule of law	0	0	0
Infrastructure and basic services	68.0	68.0	0
Total	88.4	88.4	0

Source: ACET, December 2009. Interview with former Chinese Ambassador to Monrovia Zhou Yuxiao, 3 December 2010

As Table 12.1 shows, China has disbursed nothing for the governance and rule of law pillar, evidence of Beijing's indecisiveness in addressing those issues. Though its discourse on non-interference has developed somewhat[28] China still has no clear-cut position on governance and the rule of law in countries beyond its borders. Nonetheless, it is clear that the complexity of China's evolving interests in Africa, taken with an increasing governance and rule of law deficit in several African countries, will soon make it impossible for Beijing to continue to evade the issue.[29]

TRADE

In terms both of the classes of goods and the overall imbalance, trade between Liberia and China reflects China's business profile with the West Africa sub-region as a whole. In 2001, trade between the two countries was $141.5 million; China's exports totalled $113 million and its imports from Liberia a mere $29 million.[30] By 2006, 3 years after the resumption of diplomatic ties, the volume had risen to $532 million with China's exports at $530 million but imports down to $2 million. The Chinese imported only iron ore and timber whereas most of its exports took the form of foodstuffs, electrical machinery and ships. In 2009 two-way trade had increased 65% over the previous year to $1.88 billion, up but Liberian exports, mainly rubber, timber and scrap metal, had fallen 33%, to just $4 million.[31]

According to Chinese customs statistics two-way trade in 2012 totalled $3.67 billion, with a balance of $3.44 billion in favour of China, indicative of a record $200 million in imports from Liberia.[32] This trend continued over the first nine months of 2013, during which Liberia's exports to China accounted for $165 million of $1.92 billion in total trade.[33]

The fact that ships comprise up to 70% of Chinese exports to Liberia might seem anomalous but[34] most of these vessels, although registered under the Liberian flag, are owned by non-Liberians including Germans (who own 1,185 vessels), Scandinavians and other Western Europeans escaping their own countries' more stringent regulatory and taxation regimes. With 2,771 vessels under registration, Liberia was second only to Panama among operators of flags of convenience in 2012. In that year Liberia was one of 10 flag countries that together accounted for more than 70% of the world's registered tonnage of cargo ships.[35]

As Table 12.2[36] shows, in 2011 two-way trade reached a peak of $5 billion; Liberia earned nearly $50 million, an increase of 84% over the previous year[37] but in real terms meaningless, representing as it does less than 1% of total volume. Overall the situation in Liberia replicates that of Africa in general, where Chinese traders flood markets with counterfeit and poor-quality goods whose comparative advantage is to be affordable for the many.[38] It is therefore important for Monrovia to devise a policy sufficiently aggressive to enable it to claim a more equitable share of the Chinese market. Such a programme would include capacity building, access to financial markets, all-round information workshops and multi-tiered incentives for joint ventures, particularly in processing raw materials

A further challenge for President Sirleaf's government is to bring under its jurisdiction the activities of Chinese companies engaged in smuggling

Table 12.2 China's trade with Liberia ($ billion), 2006–2013

Year	Total volume	Chinese exports
2006	0.53	0.52
2007	0.80	0.80
2008	1.14	1.13
2009	1.88	1.87
2010	4.41	4.39
2011	5.00	4.96
2012	3.67	3.44
2013[a]	1.92	1.75
Total	19.35	18.86

Source: Chinese Ministry of Commerce (http://www.mofcom.gov.cn) and Embassy of China, Monrovia
[a] January to September

iron ore and timber in collusion with corrupt Liberian officials. Prior to the demise of the Taylor regime in 2003, commercial logging was a significant component of the economy, in 2002 accounting for one-quarter of gross domestic product and 65% of foreign-exchange revenue.[39] In 2003, after logging and diamond mining had become a source of extra-budgetary revenue for Taylor and others to fuel conflict in Liberia and its neighbours the UNSC passed Resolution 1521 to impose sanctions on those industries, until such time as the central government took full control of Liberia's natural resources.[40] (The timber business was controlled mainly by a company owned by Gus van Kouwenhoven, a Dutch citizen and a known associate of the Taylor regime.)[41] The UN embargo on timber exports was lifted only in June 2006. In a 2005 survey the International Tropical Timber Organization (ITTO) testified that China was the destination for 75% of Liberia's log exports, while Europe took 80% of sawn timber.[42]

To address issues pertaining to trade and economic relations the respective governments held the first China-Liberia economic and trade cooperation forum in Monrovia in April 2010, attended by about 100 representatives of Chinese and Liberian companies. Although concrete results from the forum have yet to materialise, its main merit lies in attempting to structure an increasingly deep relationship between the two states. China's agreement to build a free trade zone in the coastal city of Buchanan was one eagerly anticipated outcome; another was the establishment of the Chinese Business Association of Liberia (CBAL) in March 2011, with 15 Chinese companies as founding members. CBAL is headed by the chairman of Sino-Liberia Mining Company. Among other motivations the establishment of CBAL was in response to former Chinese Ambassador Zhou Yuxiao's plea that his countrymen be involved only in legal businesses.[43]

INVESTMENT

The Bong Mine Agreement

In the initial post-conflict period Liberia registered negative capital flows of $479 million in 2005 and $82 million in 2006 but investor confidence is recovering slowly following the election of President Sirleaf.[44] It is an open secret that Beijing is being intensively wooed by the Liberian government to tap into Monrovia's abundant natural resources and according to the Chinese vice-minister of commerce China's investment in Liberia had reached $9.9 billion by 2010.[45]

Solicitations for exploration and mining bids for the iron ore deposits in the Bong Range 150 km north of Monrovia had been published by the Liberian government in January 2008. China Union Investment Company Ltd, a Monrovia-represented affiliate of the Hong Kong-based China Union Mining Ltd, submitted a tender and received approval notification in May 2008. In December 2008 President Sirleaf announced that China Union Mining was the highest bidder to renovate and mine the Bong Range deposit. With a total package of $2.6 billion, China Union promised a preliminary payment of $40 million, which the Liberian government intended to use as part of its Poverty Reduction Strategy (PRS) portfolio.[46] The Bong Mine Agreement was signed between the government of Liberia, China Union (Hong Kong) Mining Company Ltd and China-Union Investment (Liberia) Bong Mines Company Ltd.[47] Mainly due to the global financial crisis, the agreement was signed only on 19 January 2009.[48]

The total concession area (including the 'Goma Deposits or Initial Concession Area' of 24,000 ha and the 'Non-Goma Deposits Area or Additional Concession Area' of 15,375 ha) is 62,000 ha, and is signed over for 25 years with exploration rights limited to 5 years. Government estimates that the concession area offers 304 million tonnes of iron ore reserves with a high grade of 36.5%, on which the concessionaire is committed to concentrate at least 64.5–65% into iron ore fine grade, which has a higher added value. According to the agreement,[49] the main objective of the Liberian government is for the mining companies' operations

> to benefit regions in which Minerals are developed, including facilitating growth centres and education for sustainable regional development, to create more employment opportunities, to encourage and develop local business and ensure that skills, know-how and technology are transferred to citizens of Liberia, to acquire basic data regarding and relating [to] the country's Mineral resources and to preserve and rehabilitate the natural environment for further development of Liberia.

The agreement with China Union is comprehensive and in some way affects most productive sectors in Liberia. It encompasses the following aspects[50]:

- Financial: Royalties and surface rent are to be paid to the government. Royalties comprise 3.8% of index price.[51] Surface rent is paid against two time frames: the rate is $100,000 a year for the first 10 years and $250,000 for each of the following 15 years. A second financial component relates to a set of allocations such as: a mineral development and research fund (one payment of $50,000 then $100,000 a year starting from the first payment date) and general education funding for scholarships, worth $200,000 annually. The initial payment comprises $20 million to be paid three days after the effective date and the remaining $20 million within 120 days thereafter.
- Environmental and social norms: An environmental impact assessment and environmental management plan seek to minimise harm from eventual plant closure and ensure that the mining area is restored to a productive state. A social impact assessment and social assessment plan aim to manage any potential adverse impact on local communities of the construction and operation of mining plant and equipment, if necessary by relocating those communities. China Union will provide annual social contribution, medical care for employees and their families as well as for community members, at reasonable cost, and arrange appropriate housing for employees.
- Compliance with the Extractive Industries Transparency Initiative (LEITI), an international standard to which 14 other countries in sub-Saharan Africa subscribe.
- Labour: Apart from giving preference to Liberians for unskilled positions, the agreement extends to all management positions. At least 30% of total skilled posts (including 30% of the 10 most senior) should be filled by Liberians within 5 years and at least 70% (including the 10 most senior positions) within 10 years. This provision seeks *inter alia* to ensure technology and skills transfer.

The agreement also contains a provision for primacy to be given to the purchase of Liberian goods and services when these are comparable in quality, quantity, price, terms and delivery to those from other sources. (Table 12.3)

Table 12.3 Benefits estimates for Liberia

No.	Designation	Amount ($ million)	Observations
1	Compensation for landowners relocation	0.1	
2	Social contribution	87.5	3.5 × 25 years
3	General education funding	5	0.2 × 25 years for scholarships
		1.25	50,000 × 25 years for a mining and geology institute
4	Payment of custom user fees	10	Capped at 0.4 annually
5	Royalties	1155.2	Estimated mine volume (304 million tonnes) × average index of 3.8% × 100[a]
6	Income tax rate	760	25% of estimated 10% of total sale
7	Surface rent	4.75	100,000 × 10 years + 250,000 × 15 years
8	Mineral development fund	0.5	Single payment
9	Scientific research fund	2.5	100,000 × 25 years
Total		2028.8	

[a] Average price of iron ore fine between 2003 and 2013. The figures are as follows:

$/tonne	2003	2004	2005	2006	2007	2008	2009	2010	2011	2012	2013
	30	36	62	73	80	145	97	146	168	128	135

Source: www.statistica.com/statistics/282830/iron-ore-prices-since-2003/, accessed 25 February 2016

Subsequent to the agreement, competitive pressure has also had some positive collateral effects. As a result of the agreement the Indian company Arcelor Mittal, also involved in mining in Liberia, declared in February 2010 that it too would engage in social responsibility activities, including:

- a community development fund worth $3 million a year to benefit local communities;
- producing the first biodiversity map of parts of the unique rainforest of the Nimba mountain range;
- establishing a compensation programme for communities affected by the rehabilitation of an Arcelor Mittal-built railway;

- creating an annual scholarship fund of $200,000 for advanced studies for Liberian college graduates;
- supporting the development of a mining and geology department at the University of Liberia;
- providing free medical care and education for all Liberian employees and their dependents as well as allowing the local community easy access to its schools and hospitals and
- compliance with LEITI.[52]

These developments might appear to demonstrate positive outcomes from the Bong Mine agreement. As might be expected, however, there are a number of shortcomings detrimental to Liberian government and society. First, China Union took more than a year to make payments supposed to be made three days after the effective agreement date and in particular to comply with the provision relating to the first $20 million of the initial payment. It was reported that before China Union finally made the payment the Liberian government had threatened to repeal the agreement. The second half of the initial payment was not paid until January 2011[53] and in fact the Fourth Extractive Industry Transparency Initiative (EITI) Report for Liberia, published 15 May 2013, mentioned an aggregate payment of only $13.7 million as of June 2011. On the positive side of the ledger China Union made a contribution in kind of $5.6 million for renovating 11.4 km of road from Bong Mines to Hendy and 30 km from Bong Mines to Kakata.[54]

A second flaw is that the agreement exempts China Union from any surtax on high-yield projects, an exemption linked to the fall in iron ore prices due to the 2008 financial crisis. This overlooks the likelihood of a price recovery within a few years at most – which was already the case only a few months after signature of the contract. Over a 25-year contract term this exemption makes for a substantial shortfall for the Liberian state; one might expect some pressure on the government to renegotiate the surtax.[55]

Thirdly, it is not clear why in this case the government relinquished its right to claim the 10–15% free equity stake prescribed in Liberia's Minerals and Mining Law for all mining operations.[56]

Fourthly, China Union has been granted a zero withholding tax on dividends to non-residents for the first 12 years, while the relevant legislation sets a rate of 5%. Similarly the Bong agreement provides stabilisation of the corporate income tax rate at 25%[57] although the relevant legislation sets the particular tax rate at 30% (which is the rate applied to Arcelor Mittal's mining contract).[58]

Fifth and most important, close scrutiny of the expected benefits to both sides reveals $2.02 billion for Liberia and $7.6 billion for China Union, assuming that costs and losses for China Union represent up to 75% of anticipated gross income, which is a much pessimistic forecast for the company. Hence the expected benefit ratio between Liberia and China Union is almost 1 to 4.[59] It would seem that regardless of the many social contributions promised by China Union, the Liberian government should have secured the thoroughgoing implementation of relevant provisions in the law.

Contracting

Fewer than 10 Chinese construction companies have moved into the Liberian contracting sector. The most notable are China Henan International Cooperation Group Company Limited (CHICO), China Chongqing International Construction Corporation (CICO), Qing Dao Construction Group, Riders Incorporated and Vic Liberia Development Corporation (see Table 12.4).

Although CHICO and CICO appear to be major international road contractors and compete for almost every road project, there seems to be no fundamental difference between Chinese construction companies in operating in Liberia and most of their counterparts elsewhere on the continent. This applies in particular to low pay, poor working conditions, almost no subcontracting to local businesses and a policy of outbidding competitors at any cost, irrespective of its impact on the standard of work.

CHICO was in the spotlight in the last quarter of 2010 when it was accused of substandard work on refurbishment of a 15 km section of the Cotton Tree–Bokay Town road, budgeted at $9.2 million. A few months after completion, the road began to deteriorate. CHICO claimed that both the World Bank and the Liberia Reconstruction Trust Fund (LRTF) knew that the budget was inadequate for high-quality work and also argued that turnaround times for completion were too short. As the then Chinese ambassador put it, however, it was up to CHICO to refuse to execute the project if it knew that the quality of work could not be guaranteed.[60] It is true that the project was a shared responsibility, as both the World Bank and LRTF attended the completion ceremony and indeed praised CHICO for delivering quality work on deadline.[61] In any event, CHICO was given a 10 km continuation section of the road, for an aggregate sum

Table 12.4   Major Chinese contracting companies in Liberia

Company name	Business area	Location
China Union Liberia	Mining	Congo Town, Monrovia
CICO	General construction	Vai Town Monrovia
CHICO	General construction and mining	Bong County
Qing Dao Liberia Construction Corporation	General construction and mining	Paynesville, Monrovia
Riders Incorporated	General construction and mining	Clara Town, Monrovia
Vic Liberia Development Corporation	General construction and mining	24th Street, Sinkor, Monrovia
Global Koream Trading Corporation	Construction services	Point Four, Monrovia
Liberia Yong Dong San Sen Corporation	Construction services	Jamaica Road, Monrovia
Qing Dao Construction Group	Construction services	Congo Town, Monrovia

Source: Extracted from *Names of Chinese Businesses-2008* of the Ministry of Commerce and Industry. CHICO and CICO added by author

of \$16.5 (including the budget for the first section), as well as being granted other road construction contracts.

CICO entered the Liberian construction sector in 2008. It then won a \$34 million tender funded by the World Bank to refurbish Monrovia roads and restore the 240 m bridge known as Old Bridge that connects the 'industrialised' Bushrod Island with commercial and diplomatic centres and with the heart of the Liberian capital.[62] Critics of the government have argued that it deliberately delayed the restoration of the bridge so that it could be completed just before the October 2011 elections to attract votes for the incumbent president; hence CICO unknowingly found itself part of the presidential campaign.

CICO Liberia employs nearly 470 local staff (including part-time workers) and some 30 Chinese. Liberian employees have launched several strikes in pursuit of higher pay. Trade unionists insist that the minimum wage should not be lower than $150 a month whereas the Chinese believe that a $60 offer is above the national minimum. CICO does not pay skilled workers, including engineers, more than $300–400 a month, a very low rate compared with other multinational companies operating in Liberia. Paradoxically CICO embarked on a social responsibility project by repairing roads and lending heavy equipment to the police and the Ministry of Public Works at no cost.[63] Given that Chinese companies often favour low wages, implying poor living conditions for their workers, corporate social responsibility projects rather lose their full meaning. Unsurprisingly some observers are reluctant to view China as a benevolent actor.[64]

Generally speaking China is more interested in 'design, build and transfer' turnkey projects rather than output and performance-based contracts, which may imply for instance a 10-year maintenance requirement. It may be desirable for the Liberian government to combine Chinese hardware with Western software in running such infrastructure. There is a hint of such a move in the establishment by USAID of a 'centre of excellence' for engineering and road maintenance at the School of Engineering in the Fendell Campus.[65]

Balancing Chinese Contribution

China is a key factor in the post-conflict reconstruction programme and it is critical to determine what Beijing has brought in, and what it has taken out. In 2003 the NTGL inherited a chaotic situation at the socio-economic level and on the diplomatic front. The latter included a break from Beijing, the immediate impact of which was felt in the interruption of all Chinese-assisted projects. Those Chinese businessmen who remained in Liberia succeeded in weaving their own connections within Taylor's governing network, some of them through the highly profitable business of illegal logging, albeit in the face of UN prohibition. With the resumption of diplomatic relations with Beijing one might speculate that China has been instrumental in the waiving of the UN ban on timber exports and the subsequent resumption of logging on a commercial basis – which would be only one of the many factors involved in evaluating China's role in Liberia's post-conflict reconstruction.

Balancing complex interactions involves both quantifiable and non-quantifiable variables. Even the former cannot be entirely divorced from some marginal undetermined factors, which for present purposes can be set aside in the interests of clarity. Table 12.5 represents an attempt to balance quantifiable variables in a rough time frame 2003–2013.

It is important to note that China's nearly $18 billion favourable balance may not be an accurate real aggregate sum insofar as it derives partly from what are effectively barter transactions, in which Chinese goods and services are exchanged for imports from Liberia. Even so one cannot disregard the fact that the Chinese trade surplus is 15 times its total contribution to Liberia's post-conflict reconstruction. When this component is added to an expected profit margin for Chinese mining operations of nearly $8 billion it becomes obvious that the relationship between China and Liberia is less a win-win partnership, more a 'relative win–absolute win' situation.

Liberia's 'relative win' is based on general satisfaction of its expectations vis-à-vis China. This arises from China's support for UNMIL including its operational extension; its diplomatic support for Liberia's attempt to lift sanctions on diamond mining and the ban on timber trade; and China's all-round contribution to Liberian post-conflict reconstruction. The last includes socio-economic infrastructure, technical assistance, cancellation of debt, multiple donations, much-needed investment in a mining sector with an important social impact and rhetorical backing for foreign investment in Liberia.

Table 12.5   China's quantifiable input–output 2003–2013 ($ million)

No.	Designation	Input to Liberia	Balance for China
1	Contingent expenses	255.45[a]	−255.45
2	PRS	88.3	−88.3
3	Debt cancellation	16	−16
4	Development aid[b]	200[c]	−200
5	Socio-economic infrastructure[d]	49.25	−49.25
6	Scholarship	4	−4
7	Training in China	20	−20
8	Trade	490	18,860
9	Investment (Bong Mine)[e]	–	–
10	Others	100	−100
Total		1,223	17,637[c]

[a] Taking the average UNMIL annual budget of $650 million over 10 years (2003–2013) multiplied by China's 3.93% contribution to UN peacekeeping operations
[b] Including $20 million in annual aid
[c] Excluding benefits from extractive industries, e.g. $7.6 billion net income from Bong Mine over 25 years
[d] Including $4.65 million renovation cost for the Ministry of Health and $3 million estimate for Monrovia Vocational School and Monrovia Weaving Centre
[e] The Bong Mine Agreement indicates a moderate expected income that leaves China Union with revenues of $10.6 billion over 25 years, whereas Liberia is expected to get roughly $2.7 billion
Source: Author's own elaboration based on official data, including data from China's ministry of commerce, Bong Mine agreement, etc.

China's 'absolute' win derives not only from its success in relative terms (such as Liberia's irreversible commitment to the 'one China' policy and its broader political support for Beijing in the international arena), but also from its overwhelming advantage in quantifiable aspects of the bilateral partnership.

CONCLUSION

China's participation in UNMIL is part of a global effort to help normalise the political and socio-economic situation in Liberia. In this, the UN mandate has met with some success. The civil administration component of the mission has succeeded in bringing about a degree of capacity building, although only in part; most reconstruction programmes are financed from outside sources, making it hard to claim that Liberia 'owns' its post-conflict reconstruction agenda or has invested it with local spirit.[66]

Furthermore, Liberia appears as a missed opportunity for a move towards an eventual re-shaping of China-Africa cooperation methods. The same shortcomings that threaten China's presence elsewhere on the continent are evident in Beijing and Monrovia's bilateral relations. Among them the most notable include poor pay and labour relations exacerbating grievances that find expression in sporadic riots and strikes (already evident at Bong Mines), counterfeit and low quality goods, unreliable delivery and unsafe production practices. The Liberian experience exemplifies many, if not most, of these facets of China's relations with Africa and might perhaps indicate the desirability of a more guarded and aggressive attitude by African countries towards their apparent benefactor.

If the Liberian government wishes substantially to increase the benefits it derives from Chinese involvement, it should move to further formalise bilateral relations with China by establishing permanent platforms for political consultation. These might include a bilateral commission, city twinning and decentralised cooperation. Given its still precarious security situation, Liberia should also join China in pushing for a much slower pace of UNMIL withdrawal, at present scheduled to take place by 2016.

Liberia should also engage China in a comprehensive implementation of its various projects, including those within the UNMIL framework. It should complement the hardware content with a substantial dosage of software, if necessary by involving other stakeholders (such as the EU, US, international institutions and neighbouring African countries) that have the advantage of greater familiarity with Liberia's cultural, ethnic, political, linguistic and other complex realities.

In spite of the many advantages expected to accrue from mining contracts with Chinese companies such as that with China Union, there is evidence that Liberia could get much more. Monrovia should find ways to invite China Union to the negotiating table so that parts of the existing agreement on such a high yield project as the Bong Mines contract could be revised – particularly those that may be challenged after the end of President Sirleaf's incumbency (including the aspects noted earlier of excessive royalties, a free equity stake and zero surtax and withholding tax on dividends to non-residents for the first 12 years).

Perhaps most importantly, Liberia needs to take real ownership of its reconstruction agenda. Apart from security and stability issues there remains an important challenge: to reverse Liberians' general expectations concerning foreign input rather than domestic output. In addition, there is a very substantial need for capacity building, not only at government level but also in areas such as civil society, education, public service and security. To this end, among other things Liberia should press Chinese construction companies commit to sub-contracting part of their work to local concerns. Moreover, it is the Liberian government that is entirely responsible for acceptance of sub-standard work and for this reason the supervisory aspect of public construction, whatever the sources of finance, should also be reinforced.

One may assume that China is gaining much from its involvement in Liberia and sees no need to change its approach. If so, the Chinese may miss the many opportunities at hand and lose longer-run benefits unless they address key issues pertaining to their presence in Liberia. China should seek partnerships with other actors to better handle the software dimension of their delivery, particularly in the field of security training. Put bluntly, the vast majority of Liberians are still pro-American; even so the USAID-built police academy could well be a venue for China-sponsored security training programmes. China, in fact, can still make its involvement in Liberia stand as a model in Africa for success in controlling product quality, avoiding sub-standard work, encouraging better pay through tax incentives at home and undertaking corporate social responsibility programmes as part of a formal policy.

As a major power that contributes to global reconstruction efforts, China is not supposed to be passive in regard to governance and rule of law issues in Liberia. Indeed, the governance and rule of law pillar of the PRS is the best single guarantee that the Liberian government is accountable for the resources that are being pledged and disbursed for reconstruction. In addition, governance and rule of law have been on China's domestic reform agenda for years; hence Beijing is quite aware that there is no way Liberia can succeed in its reconstruction efforts without implementing these core values.

NOTES

1. L. Gberie (2010), *Liberia: The 2011 Elections and Building Peace in the Fragile State*, situation report. Pretoria: Institute for Security Studies (ISS), p. 1.
2. Niels Kahn (2014), 'US Covert and Overt Operations in Liberia, 1970s to 2003', *ASPJ Africa & Francophonie*, 1st quarter, 5:1, p. 19.
3. *Ibid.*
4. R. Goff et al., eds. (1998), *The Twentieth Century: A Global Brief History* (Boston: McGraw Hill), 5th edition, p. 42.
5. Personal interview, Mohammed BOS Kenneth, Minister Counsellor at the Liberian Embassy Beijing, 14 January 2009.
6. Liberia (2005), *Resolution No 001 of the 52nd Legislature of the Republic of Liberia Liberian Embassy, 'Liberia–China Relations'* (Beijing: Liberian Embassy), p. 3.
7. Snowe was removed from office in January 2007 following a vote of no-confidence for 'taking an interpreter on a trip without permission and meddling in Liberia's diplomatic policy on China'. The Supreme Court later overturned Snowe's removal; he was reinstated on 27 January 2007 only to resign a few weeks later. See 'Ex-Taylor Ally Sacked as Speaker', *BBC News*, 18 January 2007, http://news.bbc.co.uk/2/hi/africa/6276391.stm, accessed 20 September 2012. See also G. Sneh (2006), 'The Honourable House Deserves a Better Leader', *The Perspective* (Monrovia), 19 July 2006, http://www.theperspective.org/articles/0719200601.html, accessed on 27 December 2007.
8. Personal interview, George Wisner, Assistant to the Minister of Foreign Affairs, in Charge of Africa–Asia Department, Ministry of Foreign Affairs in Monrovia, 23 November 2010.
9. International Crisis Group (ICG) (2002), *Africa Report No 43* (Brussels: ICG), pp. 1–2.
10. *Ibid*, p. 2.
11. Xinhuanet (2009), Report on 'Pushing for the construction of a peaceful; prosperous and harmonious world' ('Bao gao jie du tui dong jian she chi jiu he ping, gong tong fan rong de he xie shi jie') http://news.xinhuanet.com/newscenter/2008-01/20/content_7455216.htm, accessed on 12 May 2009. Author's translation.
12. This concept is developed further in the author's forthcoming book on the dialectic of China's international responsibility and the non-interference principle in Africa.

13. Yin He (2007), *China's Changing Policy on UN Peacekeeping Operations* (Stockholm: Institute for Security and Development Policy (ISDP)), pp. 9–10.

14. B. Gill and C.–H Huang (2009), *China's Expanding Peacekeeping Role: Its Significance and Policy Implications*, Stockholm International Peace Research Institute (SIPRI) Policy Brief. (Stockholm: SIPRI), p. 3. Also, Safer World (2011), *China's Growing Role in African Peace and Security* (London: Safer World), p. 75.

15. Safer World, *China's Growing Role in African Peace and Security*, London: Safer World, 2011, p. 76.

16. United Nations Security Council, Resolution 1509 (2003), p. 3.

17. 'Chinese peacekeeping contingent in Liberia has completed its 14th shift' ('zhong guo fu li bi li ya wei he bu dui wan cheng di 14 ci lun huan'), http://military.people.com.cn/n/2013/0725/c1011-22326123.html, accessed on 5 January 2014. See also 'UN Mission's Summary Detailed by Country. Month of report: 30 November 2013'.

18. 'UN envoy meets visiting military delegation from the People's Republic of China; praises China for contributing military personnel to UNMIL', http://reliefweb.int/report/liberia/un-envoy-meets-visiting-military-dele gation-peoples-republic-china-praises-china., accessed on 10 January 2014.

19. Based on T. Schweitzer and M Kihlström (2009), 'Logistics Capacity Assessment' – Liberia, Version 1.05, p. 49, http://safersurgery.files.word press.com/2012/04/liberia-country-assessment.pdf.

20. A. Kaure (2006), 'Peacekeepers from China, with Love', *UNMIL Focus*, September–November 2006, p. 35.

21. Safer World, *op. cit.*, p. 75.

22. Personal interview, Rory Keane, Advisor on Security Sector Reform to the Special Representative of the UN Secretary-General, UNMIL HQ Monrovia, 24 November 2010.

23. Personal interview, Mohammed BOS Kenneth, *op. cit.* A total of 41 students received training 1981–1995; and a further 67 had participated in regular studies by end 2008. Since then China has been offering roughly 70 government scholarships and 200 training opportunities. See also 'China Outlines Achievements in Liberia', http://www.thenewdawnliberia.com/index.php?option=com_content&view=article&id=9271:china-outlines-achievements-in-liberia&catid=25:politics&Itemid=59, accessed 4 January 2014.

24. Calculation based on note 19 above.

25. Chinese Ambassador Zhou Yuxiao 'Remarks at the Handover Ceremony of the China-aided Fendell Campus of the University of Liberia', http://lr.china-embassy.org/chn/dszc/jianghua/t718566.htm.

26. Personal interview, Chinese Ambassador to Monrovia, Zhou Xiaoyu, China's embassy in Monrovia, 3 December 2010.

27. Chinese Embassy, Monrovia, http://lr.china-embassy.org/chn/sbgx/jingji/default.html, accessed 28 January 2008; Liberian Embassy, Beijing, 'Liberia–China Relations', *op. cit.*, p. 1; Personal interview, Mohammed BOS Kenneth, *op. cit.*

28. See C. Alden and D. Large (2013), 'China's Evolving Policy Towards Peace and Security in Africa: Constructing a New Paradigm for Peace Building', in M. G. Berhe and H. Liu, eds., *China-Africa Relations: Governance, Peace and Security* (Ethiopia: Institute for Peace and Security Studies Addis Ababa University), pp. 16–25.

29. M. K. Admore, 'Africa and China's Non-Interference Policy: Towards Peace Enhancement in Africa', in M. G. Berhe and H. Liu, eds., *ibid.* p. 43.

30. Liberian Embassy, Beijing, 'Liberia–China Relations', internal document, January 2008.

31. 'China-Liberia two way trade increased by 65% in 2009' (2009 nian zhong li shuang bian mao yi e tong bi shang sheng 65%'), http://lr.mofcom.gov.cn/aarticle/zxhz/tjsj/201003/20100306802801.html, accessed 22 March 2011.

32. Beijing: Ministry of Foreign Affairs, 'China-Liberia Relations', http://www.mfa.gov.cn/fzs/sbgxdsj/t6599.html, accessed on 4 January 2014.

33. *Ibid.*

34. See note 28.

35. The Basement Geographer, 'Flags of Convenience', http://basementgeographer.com/flags-of-convenience/, accessed on 19 January 2014.

36. See 'Zhong guo tong li bi li ya de guan xi' (China-Liberia relations), www.chinanews.com/gj/zlk/2014/01-16/25982.shtml, accessed 10 February 2016.

37. A. M. Johnson (2012), 'Chinese Business Association of Liberia Launched, As China's Trade with Liberia Passes US$5 Billion in 2011', http://www.liberianobserver.com/index.php/business/item/1105-chinese-business-association-of-liberia-launched-as-china%E2%80%99s-trade-with-liberia-passes-us$5-billion-in-2011, accessed 24 April 2012.

38. Personal interview, Thomas Jaye, Liberia, 22 November 2010.

39. International Tropical Timber Organization (ITTO) (2005), Achieving the ITTO Objective 2000 and Sustainable Forest Management in Liberia, ITTC (XXXVIII)/6, p. viii, http://www.itto.int/mission_reports.

40. UNSC, S/RES/1521 (2003), Liberia, Adopted by the Security Council at 4,890th meeting, 22 December 2003, http://www.un.org/ga/search/view_doc.asp?symbol=S/RES/1521%282003%29.

41. Global Witness (2006), *Cautiously Optimistic: The Case for Maintaining Sanctions in Liberia*, Briefing Document, June 2006, p. 7. Van Kouwenhoven was arrested March 2005 and tried the following year at The Hague indicted on violation of UN Resolution (788) on arms embargo

on Liberia. See the Geneva Academy of International Humanitarian Law and Human Rights, 'The Trial of Charles Taylor', http://www.adh-geneva. ch/RULAC/international_judicial_decisions.php?id_state=127.

42. ITTC, *op. cit*, p. ix.

43. See Chinese Business Association of Liberia is born ('Li bi li ya zhong guo qi ye shang hui cheng li'), http://lr.mofcom.gov.cn/aarticle/jmxw/ 201103/20110307458315.html (Chinese economic and commercial office's website).

44. UN Conference on Trade and Development (Unctad) (2007), *World Investment Report 2007: Transnational Corporations, Extractive Industries and Development* (New York & Geneva: Unctad), p. 36.

45. *AllAfrica* (2010), 'Liberia: China's Investment Reaches US$9.9 Billion', 26 April 2010, http://allafrica.com/stories/201004280378.html.

46. *Ibid.*

47. The agreement was signed by the Minister of Land, Mines and Energy, the Minister of Finance and the chairman of the National Investment Commission on the one side; and by China Union (Hong Kong) Mining Company Ltd and China Union Investment (Liberia) Bong Mines Company Ltd on the other.

48. The Liberian government was advised in part by Joseph Bell and Lorraine Sostowski, partners in Hogan & Hartson LLP. Bell also chairs the Advisory Board of the Revenue Watch Institute.

49. See document signed 19 January 2009: 'Mineral Development Agreement Between the Government of the Republic of Liberia, China-Union (Hong Kong) Mining Co., Ltd., and China-Union Investment (Liberia) Bong Mine Co., Ltd.', p. 1.

50. *Ibid.*

51. Royalties (R) are calculated according to the following formulae: (a) when the index price is $100/m³, R= 3.25%; (b) when the index price is greater than $100/m³ and less than $125, R= 3.5%; (c) when the index price is greater than $125/m³ and less than $150, R= 4.0%; and (d) when the index price is $150/m³ or more, R= 4.5%. The index price should be the Vale spot price FOB Brazil for shipment to China for iron ore of the same grade and quality produced at Bong Mine.

52. P. Wrokpoh, 'Liberia's Mining Sector: Stimulating Post-War Reconstruction?', *Pambazuka News* (Nairobi) 481, http://www.pamba zuka.org/en/category/africa_china/64411.

53. Personal interview, Matenokary Tingba, Director of Mines at Ministry of Land and Mines, Monrovia, 25 November 2010.

54. V. Gborglah et al., *4th EITI Report for Liberia*, PDF document edited by Ernst & Young, 15 May 2013, pp. 36–51.

55. 'Draft Analysis of China Union Contract Fiscal Framework', Revenue Watch Institute and Colombia University, 25 February 2009, p. 2.
56. *Ibid*, p. 4.
57. Bong agreement, Section 14.3.a. See 'Mineral Development Agreement Between the Government of the Republic of Liberia, China-Union (Hong Kong) Mining Co., Ltd., and China-Union Investment (Liberia) Bong Mine Co., Ltd.', p. 47.
58. 'Addendum: Draft Analysis of China Union Contract Fiscal Framework', Revenue Watch Institute and Colombia University, 13 March 2009, p. 1.
59. China Union's expected net income is then: 304,000,000 tonnes × $100 × 25% = $7,600,000,000.
60. Personal interview, former Chinese Ambassador, Zhou Yuxiao, *op.cit.*
61. See Minutes of the Oversight Commission meeting of the Liberia Reconstruction Trust Fund (LRTF), 3 March 2011, p. 1.
62. Personal interview, Xie Xudong, CICO, Monrovia, 4 December 2010.
63. *Ibid.*
64. Comment by Zambian citizen during public debate on Chinese involvement in Africa. Lusaka, Mulungushi Center, 2 March 2010.
65. Chinese Embassy Monrovia, 'Chinese engagement in Liberia', 16 February 2010, http://www.cablegatesearch.net/cable.php?id=10MONROVIA188, accessed 17 September 2011.
66. K. Bajzíková (2010), 'Distribution of Power Within Post-Conflict Reconstruction Concept (Liberian Case)', paper presented at the seminar 'AFRICA: 1960–2010–2060 A Century (Re)visited: What Next?', University of Pécs (Slovakia), 27–29 May 2010.

Guillaume Moumouni is an assistant professor at the University of Abomey-Calavi, Benin, and a former vice-head of the department of political science at the faculty of law and political science. He is either a member or a research associate of several academic institutions, including Alioune Blondin Beye Academy for Peace (ABBAP), Benin, South African Institute of International Affairs (SAIIA), etc. He holds a BA, an MA and a PhD in international relations from Peking University, China. Dr Moumouni has worked as an interpreter, public relations officer, and general manager for a number of Chinese companies in Benin, his native country.

CHAPTER 13

Security Risks facing Chinese Actors in Sub-Saharan Africa: The Case of the Democratic Republic of Congo

Wang Duanyong and Zhao Pei

Background

Most countries in Sub-Saharan Africa have been experiencing instability due to low levels of development, poor economic situations and bad governance in the past decades. The security situation has become even worse since 2008. Meanwhile, there has been increasing reports on security threats toward Chinese with more and more Chinese businessmen, laborers and enterprises 'going out', especially in some Sub-Saharan African countries with rapidly growing Chinese investment. In 2011, we conducted a fieldwork in the Democratic Republic of Congo (DRC) to investigate Chinese investment and security risk toward Chinese there. We interviewed 37 Chinese there including senior diplomats, management of Multinational Corporations, businessmen and residents in four cities. At the same time, we also visited dozens of local people and foreigners and collected additional secondary source material as well.

Although there is widespread agreement that Africa is a 'higher security risk compared to other parts of the world'(Xia 2012), we will nevertheless present a short summative description of the African security circumstances

W. Duanyong (✉) · Z. Pei
Shanghai International Studies University, Shanghai, China
e-mail: wangduanyong@gmail.com; zp@shisu.edu.cn

C. Alden et al. (eds.), *China and Africa*,
DOI 10.1007/978-3-319-52893-9_13

253

as background to help assess and understand the DRC situation. Based on our previous research experience, some generally agreed information on public security can be utilized as a data resource (Wang 2013). By comparison, 'Foreign Travel Advice' released by the U.K. Foreign & Commonwealth Office (FCO) is considered as an optimal information source based on its comprehensive, concise, timely and standardized features. In this chapter, we make an overall text analysis on FCO's 'Foreign Travel Advice' toward all of 48 Sub-Saharan African countries in 2013 so as to draw a distribution map of security risk in these countries (Fig. 13.1).

According to data analysis of 'Foreign Travel Advice', 38.5% of total population in the Sub-Saharan Africa live in the countries where crime rate is high and 33.4% in moderate level (Table 13.1). Accordingly, the land area involved account for 32.6% and 44.9% of total area separately. The top three among criminal activities there are mugging, stealing and armed robbery.

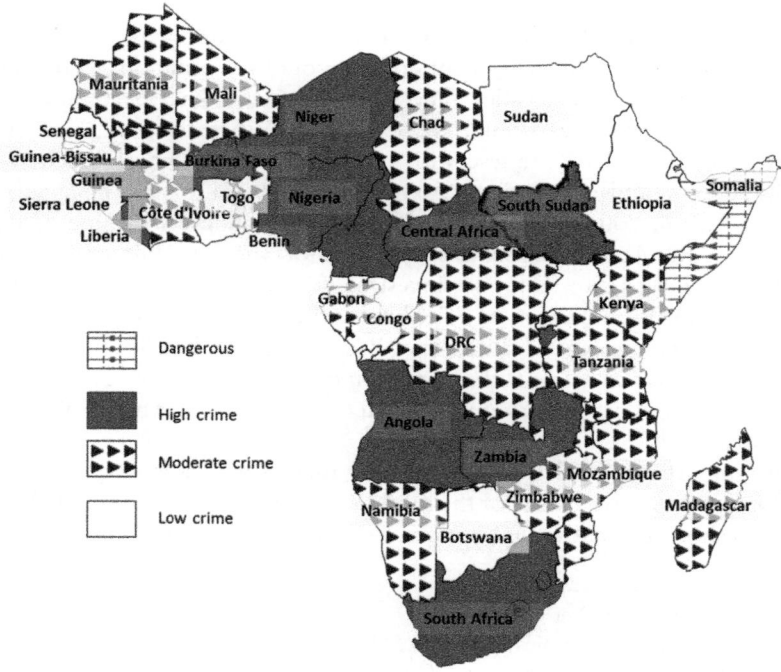

Fig. 13.1 The distribution map of security risk in Sub-Saharan Africa countries

Table 13.1 The classification of the Sub-Saharan African countries in terms of the level of crime rate

The level of criminal activities	The number of countries involved	Population impacted (million p.)	Area involved (1,000 km²)
Dangerous	2	168.38	682
High level	12	351.09	7,758
Moderate level	17	304.18	10,662
Low level	17	239.02	4,669

Source: World Bank, World Development Indicators in 2012

The other frequent-occurring crimes include car-jacking, violent assault, scam and rape, etc. Moreover, 'Foreign Travel Advice' observed an increasing crime rate and a deteriorating security situation in many countries of Sub-Saharan Africa for their remaining in poverty and underdevelopment (UK FCO 2013). In fact, local Chinese residents generally believed that it would be very dangerous to go out alone, at night, or by foot in the DRC and some parts of South Africa.[1]

THE MAIN THREAT SOURCES TOWARD CHINESE IN THE DRC

For a long period, terrorist activities in Sub-Saharan Africa had been not rampant and religious extremism not active. Attacks by rebel forces, kidnapping and other severe criminals had been the main security threats to Chinese institutions, businesses and citizens. With the rebels' diminishing in the recent years and Chinese rare involvements in the eastern part of the DRC, there are few reports on the rebels' attacks against Chinese currently.

In fact, according to Chinese interviewees in the DRC by contrast, 'legitimate harm' from local official security forces such as the police and the military is relatively common threat against Chinese. Soldiers, policemen and governmental officials of the DRC are low-paid, and most of them are poorly trained and managed. A majority of security forces and many governmental authorities such as Immigration Service, Bureau of Justice, National Safety Authority, Customs, Procuratorate, Court, Bureau of Labor and Tax Bureau have the right to carry out fines, collecting fees, detention and arbitrary arrest in a variety of names. Sometimes they even openly extort or ask for 'a tip'. Most of the Chinese interviewees believed that Chinese citizens and businesses are primary victims. From their viewpoint, on the one hand, there was a higher incidence corrupted or criminal acts aimed against Chinese citizens. Moreover, there was a popular belief that Chinese diplomatic missions had never made earnest effort to provide consular protection to Chinese citizens. Based on this, the Chinese community held a firm consensual belief that Chinese were likely to be bullied by local officials. However, interviewees from diverse third-party sources argued that these harmful actions were not aimed specially at Chinese but 'favored' nearly all foreigners.[2]

In addition to corruption of local authorities, there was also a particularly noteworthy source of risk from Chinese community itself. In fact, some Chinese deliberately made use of local authorities and criminals to attack or threaten the property and personal safety of their competitors coexisting in the same Chinese business circle.[3] This effectively signfied how business competition was transformed into security risk, highlighting how generalised breakdowns in law and order induce unexpected risks.

Overall, investors experience greater levels of security risk in so-called failed or failing states. Generally, Westerners working or traveling in these countries are cautioned or even are subject to the legal restrictions from their home governments. What's more, the enterprise itself will carry out a detailed assessment of the security environment and develop as a result more stringent safety precautions. The experience of Western countries shows that the home government should take primary responsibility for securing and preventing risk of 'going out' of its citizens and businesses. The home government should provide some basic public goods such as investigating security situation, assessing risks and publishing early warning information on the host country, as well as protecting and rescuing citizens while security events occurring.

SOURCES OF RISK: FROM THE HOST COUNTRY SIDE

Firstly, as 'Travel Warning' on the DRC released by the US Department of State in 2013 stated, 'Poor economic conditions, high unemployment, and low pay that is often in arrears for the military and police contribute to criminal activity in Kinshasa and throughout the country' (U.S. Department of State 2013). Fundamentally, poor economic conditions were blamed as the source of crime in the DRC. A United Nations Environment Programme report in 2011 called the DRC as the poorest country in the world. The Gross National

Income per capita of this country was only US$400 in 2013 and ranked 181 among 184 countries of the world (World Bank 2013a).

The long-term situation of extreme poverty and underdevelopment is always linked with bad governance and social disorder. By Country Policy and Institutional Assessment Index of World Bank, the DRC was rated at the lowest levels in terms of three key indicators of public management including 'Public Sector Management and Institutions Cluster Average' and its sub-indicators 'Quality of Public Administration' and 'Transparency, Accountability, and Corruption in the Public Sector' (World Bank 2013b). The mixed effect of under-development and bad governance provides enormous rent-seeking opportunities for the power as the scarce resource. As a result, the disorder in the public management always appears in the form of corruption. In terms of the 2013 Corruption Perceptions Index of Transparency International, the DRC was ranked 154 among 177 countries and regions (Transparency International 2013). According to a survey conducted worldwide by World Bank, there was up to 50.4% firms to be 'expected to make informal payments to public officials to "get things done" with regard to customs, taxes, licenses, regulations, services, and the like'. The figure was one of the highest among 223 economies surveyed (World Bank 2013c).

Overall, the security risk in Sub-Saharan African Countries including the DRC primarily arises from some interactional crises of the severe insufficiency of economic viability and the fragment of the state. These crises originated to the failures of development and governance as the basis features of failed states.

Secondly, political struggles between domestic interest groups in the host country often have 'spillover' impact on the external actors, especially at the time of transferring governments. In recent years, the topic about China is increasingly popular and contentious during elections in some Sub-Saharan African countries. If some country in this region has kept good or even close relations with China, some interest groups or opposition parties always claim that it is harmful to the state and then the situation should be changed. This kind of argument could be translated into real risk or threatens toward local Chinese.

In Zambia, for example, in the lead up to the country's 2011 presidential election, the opposition presidential candidate criticized China and claimed he would take harsh attitude toward investment and imports of goods from China should he win the election (Gettleman 2011; Anonymous 2011). At that time this matter had a strong impact on Chinese, many Chinese people and Chinese enterprises temporarily withdrew or suspended operations in the country in order to avoid accidents. Although the ultimate success candidate of the campaign did not actually produce an unfriendly policy toward China, however it indirectly caused economic losses and to a certain extent damaged the social atmosphere, allowing negative attitudes towards Chinese and China to strengthen.

This event produced negative demonstration effect on neighboring countries, to some extent fostering a 'broken window effect' phenomenon, causing Chinese residents and Chinese companies to have negative expectations of the future security situation. It is very likely to be a common trick to play the 'China card' for some Sub-Saharan African authorities in the future. On this occasion, the security and interest of local Chinese will also face increasing threats.

Thirdly, interstate conflict and tension is still an active factor threating toward local Chinese in Sub-Saharan Africa. It is believed that the active anti-government armed forces and occasional firefights in the eastern provinces of the DRC have been supported by other countries. The point is that the defense force of the DRC itself has been not capable enough to meet the challenges taken by the rebels and foreign military forces.

In fact, according to defense professionals who are familiar with Congolese military affairs,[4] the Armed Forces of the Democratic Republic of Congo (FARDC) can hardly meet the basic task of providing for national defense in terms of size, equipment, training, command system and the unity of military orders. The number of FARDC members is only about 120,000–150,000 and is significantly insufficient to the huge territory of 2.34 million square kilometers. The equipment of FARDC is mostly consisting of small arms without proper maintenance so that much of the equipment is non-operational. The training level and mobilization capacity of FARDC are so low that the force members can't master basic martial skills and learn to disciplines. Moreover, the commanding system inside FARDC is in a mess and some garrisons especially in the eastern part aren't always obedient. For these reasons, the armed force of the DRC has remained woefully ineffective.

In essence, from the host country side, the severe security situation in some Sub-Saharan African countries is just a result of the failed state which features weak legitimacy of government, the social order in chaos, a huge proportion of population in extreme poverty and the strong external inference on domestic affairs. The real question is why some foreigners and foreign investment still come to these countries at any cost and whether they have sufficient safety measures to protect themselves.

SOURCES OF RISK: FROM CHINESE SIDE

Although there is high security risk, Chinese are still increasingly enthusiastic to invest, trade and build in Sub-Saharan Africa. From 2004 to 2013, the average annual growth rate of trade between China and Sub-Saharan Africa reached up to 24.9% which was far more than the average of China's total trade, 15.3% (National Bureau of Statistics of China 2015). From 2003 to 2012, the average annual growth rate of China's direct investment in this region was 51.7% which was far more than the average annual growth rate of China's total Foreign Direct Investment (FDI), 36.1% (MOFCOM 2013). From 2002 to 2012, the average annual growth rate of the value of turnover for Chinese contractors in Sub-Saharan Africa was 37.0%, again which was higher than by Chinese contractors in any other region of the world. At present Sub-Saharan Africa account for 29.8% of China's total contracting business abroad (National Bureau of Statistics of China 2004–2014). In general, the attraction of Sub-Saharan Africa in fact is remains considerable for Chinese firms especially to investors and contractors, most of whom are state-owned enterprises (SOE).

Based on our field study in the DRC, most of the Chinese large and medium-size enterprises, especially SOEs, always had adequate preparation for security and risk prevention (National Bureau of Statistics of China).[5] Generally these enterprises have stringent security systems in the plant, the office area and the living quarters (in most productive enterprises, the living quarters is always adjacent to the plant area), such as full closure of all areas, all-around monitoring, strict management of staff going out, high-sensitive access control system, 24-hour armed security guards, etc. When tensions rise, enterprises will strengthen the armed security forces by hiring local private security companies or asking for assistance from the police and military forces of host countries, or even some enterprises will evacuate their Chinese employees home or to safer neighboring countries.

As for those individual merchants, small businesses or institutions, their ability to prevent risks is far less than those large and medium-size enterprises mentioned earlier. They are unlikely to adopt sufficient measures such as hiring security guards and equipment as those large businesses do and their social networks within the local community are limited. Therefore, the individual merchant and small institutions are always more vulnerable when faced with a local security situation. Obviously such groups deserve more public goods provided by the Chinese government, embassies and consulates including early risk warning, safe guide and emergent rescuing, which are the basic obligations of the home country government to citizens abroad.

Apart from prevention and relief measures for 'extraneous risks', it is necessary for overseas Chinese to avoid generating 'endogenous risks' taken by misunderstandings or due to their own misconduct.

First, there are recorded incidents of improper behaviour by some of the Chinese institutions and citizens in those Sub-Saharan African countries with severely social disorders. The usual misconduct include entry without proper documents, unlawful labor practices and illegal wildlife trade. These incidents almost certainly give rise to huge risks which are susceptible to legal punishment of the host country and making space for rent-seeking of local officials.

Second, some Chinese lack of the necessary awareness of avoiding risk. It happened that two Chinese were robbed, shot and eventually badly hurt in Kolwezi, Katanga Province, in June 2011. In that case, the two bare-handed Chinese victims combated with two gunmen and such brave behavior was clearly unwise.

Third, it is difficult for many Chinese to integrate into the local society. Although Chinese are widespread in Sub-Saharan Africa, most of them have kept a low level of interaction with the local community. Forreasons of security management, Chinese employees in the same Chinese enterprise usually are asked to reside in the same living quarters so that in fact most Chinese have rare opportunities to get in touch with the local people. Moreover, on account of language barrier and in order to avoid unnecessary misunderstandings, many Chinese have limited and often poor contact with their local colleagues.

Therefore, for many Chinese people's points of view, there is unfair unbalance between the Chinese contributions to local community and the esteem Chinese deserve from local people. Many Chinese in the DRC believed that most of the local people, including the government, acknowledged the emerging growth and prosperity taken by Chinese investment and businessmen coming, while these beneficiaries didn't seem to result in a basic friendly attitude to the Chinese.

In fact, a senior official in charge of Chinese affairs in the DRC government repeatedly emphasized that his government will always consider friendly relations with China as a long-standing policy, not a temporary expedient for that China provided irreplaceable assistance and development model worthy of learning.[6] However, some diplomats from other countries thought maybe it was not the case. They believed that the relationship between China and some Sub-Saharan African countries, including with the DRC, was only based on commercial transactions rather than friendship. This kind of bilateral relationship would likely to be unstable and African countries would as a result change their diplomatic attitude toward China with the development of the situation.[7]

RETHINKING THE NATIONAL CAPABILITY OF PROTECTING CITIZENS ABROAD

Based on our fieldwork in the DRC and the comparative research afterward, we hold that there is a critical deficiency in China's capability to protect its citizens abroad.

A Serious Insufficiency of Basic Information

In the case of the DRC, there is so far the biggest China's largest single investment project in Sub-Saharan Africa. It is just called 'the Minerals-for- infrastructure Deal', whose contract value is up to US$ 6 billion. In fact, the DRC is one of the major copper-producing countries in the world and has been attractive to global extractors and investors. Although there have been dozens of Chinese mining companies and 6,000–8,000 Chinese in Katanga Province, it is difficult to get any systematic and comprehensive presentation on the situation of the country in Chinese domestic information databases. In China's current research system, there are hardly any scholars focused on the DRC studies.

No Understanding and Not Being Understood

One of the popular misconceptions on Africa in China is that Africa is a uniform continent. In fact, the continent with 54 countries is extremely sophisticated. For Sub-Saharan Africa with over 2,000 languages

(UNESCO 2016) and thousands of tribes, there is remarkable diversity even within a single country. In the case of the DRC, even some Chinese business-men with long-standing local experience always consider it difficult to under-stand and figure out the investment management regime of the country.[8]

In fact, the institutional differences and conflicts with host countries have been the prominent risk of Chinese outward FDI (Wang 2011). It is worth reminding that China itself had ever been long-term incompatible with some international conventions, and that up until this day many Chinese are not familiar with basic international rules and practices. It deserves to be pointed out that there is a trend in China to neglect or even look down upon some international rules with 'Chinese Miracle' in recent years. When Chinese deliberately refuse to learn, understand and accept some international norms, it means that we ourselves will be difficult to be understood by local people. It will ultimately harm our own overseas interests.

The Serious Shortage of Hard and Soft Powers

Embassies and consulates of the home country should bear primary responsibility for protecting citizens abroad. However, Chinese in the DRC deeply dissatisfied with the Chinese embassy in Kinshasa for its capacity and attitude to provide protection to Chinese citizens. The common complaints about the Chinese embassy are the difficulty of getting contact with the embassy, its always slow response and inability to assist Chinese asking for assistance.

However, from the embassy side, there are some severe constraints for its willingness and capacity to provide assistance to Chinese citizens. Given that the DRC has a huge territory with thousands of Chinese there, obviously it is far from enough for China to keep only one embassy in the capital. However, due to institutional constraints at home and abroad, it is very difficult to set up more official institutions in this country. In a word, objectively, there is gravely insufficient hard power and official resource for China to protect its citizens in the DRC.

On this occasion, unfortunately, there is little soft power and social resources available that could be applied to protect Chinese citizens. There was hardly any cultural exchange that could contribute to the growth of friendship between China and the DRC, as is the case in much of Sub-Saharan Africa. Compared to the size of Chinese citizens and investment, Chinese cultural communication with local community is almost negligible. In the case of the Confucius Institutes with rapid development in recent years, by updated available data, there are only 46 Confucius Institutes and 23 Confucius Classrooms in Sub-Saharan Africa that holds 13.1% of the world's population, accounting for 8.8% and 2.1% of the totality separately (Hanban 2016). Under the circumstances, it is hard to say that Chinese will have remarkable soft power matching its economic power there.

CONCLUSIONS AND RECOMMENDATIONS

On the whole, the security risk toward Chinese in Sub-Saharan African is to a large extent from the disconnection between China's rapid marching into this region and its insufficient preparation in knowledge and institutions. In brief, it could be called as 'the eyes falling behind the feet'. Compared to Western European countries and the US, Chinese learning and studies on Sub-Saharan Africa is far less.

According to our fieldwork in the DRC, China's national capacity to protect its citizens there is insufficient. In spite of huge investment and economic contribution widely acknowledged to local communities, China is still lacks of enough hard power for protection of its citizens there. As to soft power, there is effectively none.

In our opinion, it is unfair and meaningless to just blame China's official department in charge of consular protection. In fact, the Foreign Ministry is the biggest ministry in Chinese government and the Consular Department is also the biggest department in the Foreign Ministry. Despite this, it cannot meet requirements of protecting Chinese citizens abroad yet. Faced with this difficult situation, maybe we should have some innovative ways. According to some successful experiences from various powers, it is more efficient to mobilize a diversity of social resources than to only depend on the officially monopolistic way.

For example, regarding the collection of information on host country conditions, Chinese current management system has an excessive reliance on formal research institutions such as governmental institutes, universities and colleges. Chinese long-term experiences in the past planned economy showed us how inefficient the highly centralized resource distribution system was. Unfortunately, Chinese current research management operates in this 'traditional way'. Under this central-planning mindset, researchers usually pay more attention to the preference of the government or 'leaders' and neglect the practicability and academic value of a study. As a result, most of the international studies lack of first-hand information and are highly repetitive and therefore have poor efficiency and quality. As a result, it is crucial for China to build an information community which consists of widespread social resources such as independent researchers, business institutions and non-governmental organizations, etc.

Moreover, social resources are not limited to domestic resources. The international and local resources could be more helpful sources in international affairs. As the UK FCO annual report states, of over 14,000 employees in nearly 270 British embassies and consulates worldwide, only one-third are British, and local employees account for two-thirds of total staff. By this highly international and localized structure, the UK FCO supported British nationals making nearly 60 million overseas trips a year, and nearly 5 million British nationals live and work abroad. In 2013, the FCO's consular network dealt with more than 450,000 consular customers. (UK FCO 2014) It is intriguing for a country to build a highly localized foreign affairs team to provide protection to its citizens abroad. There is something in management, institutions and loyalty China can learn.

Notes

1. Interviews with local Chinese residents: (1) 19 September, Lubumbashi, DRC. (2) 25 September 2011, Kolwezi, DRC. (3) 17 September, Kinshasa, DRC. (4) 4 November, Likasi, DRC. 5. 8 December 2013, Johannesburg, South Africa.
2. (1) 20 September 2011, Lubumbashi, DRC. (2) 18 October 2011, Kinshasa, DRC. (3) 15 March 2012, Washington, DC, USA.
3. (1). Interview on 6 October 2011, Lubumbashi. (2) Interview on 19 October 2011, Kinshasa.
4. (1) 8 June 2011. Nanjing, China. (2) 26 October 2011. Kinshasa, DRC.
5. Field studies and interviews on from 25 to 29 September 2011 in Kolwezi, the DRC, on from 6 to 10 October 2011 in Lubumbashi, and on 3 November 2011 in Likasi.
6. 19 October 2011. Kinshasa, DRC.
7. (1) 5 October 2011. Johannesburg, South Africa. (2) 15 March 2012, Washington, DC, USA.
8. Interview with Chinese businessman, on 21 October 2011, Kinshasa.

Wang Duanyong is the Director of the Centre for China's Overseas Interests Studies and an associate professor at Shanghai International Studies University, China. In recent years his research focuses on Chinese investment and infrastructure projects in Africa and the security risk of Chinese citizens abroad.

Zhao Pei is the editor of International Review, Shanghai International Studies University. He obtained his PhD degree in Political Science at Fudan University, Shanghai, China. He has conducted fieldwork on Chinese investment and infrastructure projects in the D.R. Congo, Myanmar and Pakistan.

PART III

Regional and Global Perspectives

CHAPTER 14

Ethiopia, China, and the West

Aaron Tesfaye

Ethiopia is a pivotal state in the Horn of Africa, which includes Djibouti, Eritrea, and Somalia. The 'greater Horn' also consists of Kenya, Sudan, South Sudan, Uganda, and Yemen across the narrow strait of *Bab-el-Mendeb* in the Red Sea. The importance of Ethiopia is not in its mineral deposits, the fate of democracy, or even the politics of the Nile River: it is simply its geography. Ethiopia exists in a region where a complex set of historical, ideological, political, social, economic, humanitarian, geographical, territorial, and environmental factors has created tensions within and between states. This is because the problems in the Horn of Africa are interlinked; events in one state affect others, and the problems of one can often be solved only with the involvement of others. The area has been called a 'security complex,' where for any of the countries, social, economic, and political development can only be achieved in a climate of enhanced security and stability for all.[1]

Ethiopia is a pivotal state in the Horn of Africa because from its mountainous redoubts has kept its independence and, more importantly, has projected its power to the borderlands and beyond in its national interest. It is important also because Addis Ababa is a political, economic, and diplomatic hub, headquarters to the Africana Union (AU), the United Nations Economic Commission to Africa, and the African Standby Force

A. Tesfaye (✉)
Political Science Department, William Paterson University, Wayne, NJ, USA
e-mail: tesfaye.aaron@gmail.com

(ASF). The ASF is an international, continental, African multidisciplinary peacekeeping force with military, police, and civilian contingents that acts under the direction of the AU and can be deployed in times of crisis in Africa. As a consequence of the above, the West – namely the European Union (EU) and the United States – and now China have been actively engaged with Ethiopia. Ethiopia's strategic position in the unstable, terrorism-prone Horn of Africa makes it a key state in the region, playing important roles in mediation in the South Sudan conflict, as a member of the Intergovernmental Authority for Development (IGAD), and in helping in the reconstruction of the state of Somalia.

EMERGENCE OF TRIANGULAR RELATIONS

Ethiopia has had a long relationship with the West. Europeans, first the British and later the French and Italians, all with various motives, were formidable diplomatic players not only in Ethiopia, but also in the greater Horn. The United States followed suit, establishing formal diplomatic relations in 1903. The highlight of Ethiopia's relations with the West came in a 1935 speech by the Emperor Haile Selassie at the League of Nations in Geneva, Switzerland, when Ethiopia, a founding member, sought assistance in the aftermath of Mussolini's invasion. Unfortunately, the request fell on deaf ears. It was only after World War II, at the beginning of the Cold War, that Ethiopia and the West, particularly the United States, began to have a meaningful relationship.[2] In 1953 Ethiopia and the United States signed a mutual defense assistance agreement whereby the latter would provide military assistance for Ethiopia to achieve internal security and meet external threats.[3]

This agreement was to become a major challenge for China in developing its relations with Ethiopia. In 1955, at the first Asia-Africa conference held in Bandung, Indonesia, China found an ideal opportunity to develop relations with participating countries, including Ethiopia. China was later to use the Bandung experience to deepen relations with Ethiopia, leading to cultural exchange between the two nations. In 1958, after the Accra Summit that focused on anti-colonial struggles, Ethiopia broadened its relations from the confines of the western colonial powers and diversified its relations to include the Eastern Bloc, which was supporting anti-colonial movements in Africa.[4]

But it was not until 1963 that Ethiopia invited a Chinese delegation – led by Zhou Enlai, who was announcing a five-point guideline and eight principles of foreign aid during a tour of Africa – to Ethiopia. The delegation was not well received by the United States, which was at that time conducting an indirect war with China in Vietnam.[5] Ethiopia invited the Chinese delegation to Asmara (now the capital city of Eritrea) with the intent of not displeasing the United States, which at that time was a major donor of military aid, and Zhou accepted the invitation based on practical, long-term Chinese interests. Ethiopia was a major player in African politics and China wanted to gain political support and establish relations with African nations.

But during this period, China's relationship with Somalia was to prove a stumbling block to Ethio-China relations. Somalia was publicly supporting China in its ideological battle against the Soviet Union and China was providing economic assistance to Somalia in a variety of fields. Although Ethiopia during this period was decidedly in the western camp, it could not afford to ignore a key member of the non-aligned movement and the most populous nation in the world. In 1970, following the Soviet-Chinese border dispute over the Damansky Islands (or Zhen Bao) and fear of Soviet expansion in Asia, the United States began a rapprochement with China. This thawing eventually led to Ethiopia establishing full diplomatic relations with China. In October 1971, the Emperor Haile Selassie visited Beijing, where he was received by Mao Zedong.

In the 1960s, in the waning years of Emperor Haile Selassie I's rule, a pro-Ethiopia foreign policy led the United States to recognize Ethiopia as the most important state actor in the Horn of Africa. Ethiopia had survived the Cold War and was playing a major role in shaping US policy in the region.[6] The importance of Ethiopia to US foreign policy was evidenced at the height of the Cold War. The two countries entered a tenuous but unusual relationship in which the United States 'committed substantial resources to Ethiopian famine relief, spending over $500 million and delivering over 800,000 tons of food.'7 But when Ethio-Soviet relations were strengthened, particularly with the flow of arms and eventually advisors from East Germany and later from Cuba, Ethiopian-US relations deteriorated, leading to the termination of the mutual defense agreement signed in 1953.

After the revolution overthrew the Empreror in 1974, Ethiopia's relations with the Western countries, particularly with the United States, became strained when the nation, under the leadership of the nationalist military regime led by Colonel Mengistu Haile Mariam (1974–1990), came under the sphere of influence of the Soviet Union. The regime's objectives, once it consolidated political power, were to win its wars in Eritrea and with Somalia and achieve internal political stability by creating a framework for 'socialist' development. These required increasing military strength, which led to alliances that would ensure the immediate and massive inflow of armaments. The regime's foreign policy was based on the principles of 'proletarian internationalism,' non-alignment, and solidarity with socialist countries.

During the initial years of the Ethiopian Revolution (1974–1977) there was a good relationship between Ethiopia and China because both countries recognized their uniqueness in terms of their imperial histories and revolutions against ancient orders. At that time there were frequent exchanges of delegates in a number of economic fields. The regime's embrace of socialism, particularly in its land reform, interested China. This interest led to Ethio-China cooperation in the field of agriculture, but overall relations were not smooth.

Specifically, after a delegation led by Mengistu Haile Mariam visited Beijing in 1977, relations between China and Ethiopia began to deteriorate as a result of Somalia's invasion of Ethiopia. Although officially China announced that it adhered to the decision made by the UN and Organization of African Unity (OAU) founded in 1963, (now the African Union) regarding the mediation of the conflict, this did not sit well with Addis Ababa. In time, Ethiopia began to strengthen its relations with the Soviet Union, which was providing Ethiopia with material support to oppose Beijing. In 1979, the Ethiopian regime, bedeviled in wars on two fronts – with Eritrea and Somalia – condemned 'imperialist' countries, identifying China as 'reactionary,' and began to closely identify itself with the causes of the Soviet Union and its socialist allies.[7]

In 1991, with the defeat of the military regime, consolidation of power by the Ethiopian People's Democratic Revolutionary Front (EPDRF), and the emergence of a federal republic under the leadership of the late Meles Zenawi, Ethiopia began a new era of Sino-Ethiopian cooperation. The impetus for the closer relationship came around 1995 when the EPDRF wanted to re-calibrate its relations with the West and re-calibrate its policy toward Russia and China. Ethiopia-China cooperation differs fundamentally from the Western type of relations; it is multilayered. First, the traditional relationships of Ethiopia with the industrialized nations are North to South whereas its relationship with China is South to South, allowing for a two-way approach and, at least in theory, is mutual. Second,

China's development assistance to Ethiopia, ranging from infrastructure construction to development loans, comes with no official conditions, perhaps a legacy of its own experiences and ideology of equity. Third, relations between China and Ethiopia are bilateral, with the Forum on China-Africa Cooperation (FOCAC) serving as a multilateral forum for engagement in areas related to economic, diplomatic, and social agendas. The importance of the forum was underlined by a white paper released by the Chinese state in 2006 that set forth its long-term strategic plan for deepening cooperation and consultation with African countries.

China's relationship with Ethiopia is also multilayered because of the latter's relationship with the West, particularly with the EU. Ethiopia is the largest EU aid recipient in Africa, and aid is the major instrument in European cooperation. Ethiopia is one of the key countries in reforming the highly fragmented European aid system.[8] For China, in contrast, Ethiopia is not primarily an aid recipient, but an important economic and political ally in its new Africa policy. Contrary to widespread assumptions that China primarily engages in resource-rich countries, Ethiopia has become one of the largest recipients of official Chinese flows. This is evidenced by the newly built gleaming steel and glass tower in Addis Ababa funded by China at a cost of $200 million as a gift to the African Union, which continues to strengthen Beijing's influence in Africa.

In addition Ethiopia offers political stability (the ruling regime has been in power since 1990), a large market (the population is expected to be 170 million by 2050), and a strategic location in the Horn of Africa. For Ethiopian leaders, China is a model of a late industrializer practicing a 'socialist market economy' from which Ethiopia wants to glean important lessons.[9]

In 1995, the late prime minister of Ethiopia, Meles Zenawi, visited China and subsequently President Jiang Zemin stopped in Addis Ababa as part of an extensive tour of Africa. The visits culminated in the signing of a trade, economic, and technical cooperation agreement between the two nations. The agreement bestowed on Ethiopia most-favored-nation status and Addis Ababa was chosen to host the first FOCAC, in 2000. Since then China has been actively engaged in Ethiopia's economic development, offering loans and skilled manpower and helping to build highly visible infrastructures, roads, and railway systems in Addis Ababa and elsewhere. In short, for Ethiopia, China's rapprochement to Africa coincided with the efforts of the ruling party, led by then-Prime Minister Meles Zenawi, to implement its Growth and Transformation Plan, which was part and parcel of its agriculture-led industrial development strategy for transforming the ancient policy.[10]

Ethiopia's political system has been labeled by some scholars as semi-authoritarian.[11] Be that as it may, China's relationship with Ethiopia is not based, as one scholar claimed, on 'authoritarian affinities,'[12] but rather on strategic pragmatism. After all, China has also formed relationships with African nations that are not authoritarian, such as Botswana, Mauritius, and Tanzania and, for that matter, with Mexico and Australia. But then again, the United States also has a good relationship with Ethiopia because it considers the African country a strong security partner; the two nations collaborate on issues of counterterrorism and regional conflicts in Sudan and South Sudan and US drones patrol East Africa, especially Somalia.

ETHIOPIA'S MODERNIZATION INTERESTS IN CHINA

Ethiopia's interest in China is based on pragmatism and is primarily economic. While there are historical parallels between China and Ethiopia in the evolution of their indigenous states and revolutions – successful in the former and not so in the latter – Ethiopia sees in China what it can become with the right mix of political-social control and state-led development in a mixed economy. Deng Xiaoping's economic reform was not lost on Ethiopia's state leaders, who as guerrillas had once adopted a Marxist ideology but became practical with the end of the Cold War and new challenges of globalization.

But Ethiopia also shares certain characteristics with China. Both were empires, both underwent a violent revolution, and both practiced similar forms of social control led by a vanguard party; in Ethiopia that party was the EPDRF, which has been in power since 1991. There have been reforms and the Ethiopian state does not have a monopoly of the commanding heights of the economy, but certain sectors, such as banking and communications, are off limits both to private and foreign capital although there are now hints of liberalization of communication.

Chinese-Ethiopian cooperation is manifested at several levels. First, Ethiopia sees China as a source of economic assistance and investments as well as inexpensive technologies that would lift millions of small entrepreneurs out of poverty through access to farm machinery and transport. This is because state policymakers in Ethiopia have grasped that economic growth cannot be achieved without sustained technological and industrial upgrading and structural transformation of the country's economic activities. As a result, China's investments in Ethiopia's infrastructure projects – highways, railways, bridges, and inputs into power generating plants – are transforming the ancient polity. Finally, Ethiopia considers China a vast market for its agricultural commodities and thus a vehicle for improving the lives of the peasantry.

Economic cooperation between the two nations has been assisted by political support and economic support from both governments. Ethiopian policymakers seem to grasp the fact that East Asian Tigers, who achieved rapid economic growth in the past three decades due to a combination of export-led growth, the discipline of labor, and state investment in key industries, are slowly losing their comparative advance due to increased costs of production in terms of land, stricter regulatory compliance, and high labor cost. Ethiopia, with abundant labor, domestic and regional markets, and access to high income markets, seems poised to step in and fill the breach and promote itself as an alternative hub for Chinese to find new and favorable production centers.[13] Such prospects are very attractive because China is graduating from low skilled manufacturing to a higher stage, freeing jobs into which Ethiopia with it huge population and labor cost can step.[14]

Ethiopia sees its agriculture sector playing a key role in the acceleration of the country's industrial development. The rationale is that since the sector accounts for over 50% of GDP, the development and expansion of agriculture will act as a catalyst in driving growth in trade and industry through its strong forward linkages. That is, an increase in food production implies a greater supply of raw materials for production and higher incomes for the agricultural population; higher incomes, in turn, mean increases in consumption of industrial goods, which will boost economic growth as well as capital formation. Thus while China is active in Ethiopia's agriculture sector, Ethiopia's leaders for their part are carefully looking into the Chinese model that involves a combination of policy reform; state support; access to and development of new technologies, irrigation systems, seed varieties, and fertilizers; and the use of hybrid crops that have aided China in feeding its growing population. Although Chinese cannot legally own land in Ethiopia, they have brought in bulldozers and trucks to improve already-existing roads and build new ones, an action that has earned them good will with Ethiopian policymakers and peasant farmers because better roads allow farmers to get their goods from farm to market more easily. In northern Ethiopia the Chinese have built more than 93 miles of roads and provided cell phone coverage to peasant farmers, allowing them for the first time ever to check prices before they go to market and call ahead for supplies and materials.[15]

US Strategic and Diplomatic Interests in Ethiopia

US strategic interests in the Horn of Africa center on preventing any country in the Horn of Africa from becoming a safe haven for al-Qaeda or other transnational jihadist groups. In pursuing its counterterror strategy, the United States has found common cause with Ethiopia and the African Union's Peace and Security Council (PSC) but also China, which is keenly interested in peace and stability in order to pursue its long-term interest in the region. The Ethiopian government has long feared the renewal of Somali irredentist claims on its eastern border or that a powerful Islamist movement may stoke unrest among its own large Muslim populations; it feels beset both by a powerful indigenous separatist movement in its Ogaden region and an unresolved border dispute with its northern neighbor, Eritrea.

The AU PSC peace interventions in Somalia were complex. The UN intervened to address the insecurity in the country with the deployment of the UN Operation in Somalia (UNOSOM) in May 1992 and UNOSMO II in 1995, which was not successful. An IGAD peacemaking initiative in 2004 laid the foundations for the election of members of the Somali Transitional Federal Parliament, which subsequently went on to draft the charter of the Transitional Federal Government (TFG), which was adopted in November 2004. A number of Western governments recognized the TFG as legitimate.[16] In 2006, Ethiopia intervened in Somalia in order to assist the fledgling government wrest control in most of the nation's conflict zones from the Islamic Courts Union, which had emerged during the anarchic period of the civil war and further fueled instability in the country. This led AMISOM to initially attempt to stabilize parts of Mogadishu, in which it established its operations in 2007. It sought to create the security conditions that would enable the complete withdrawal of Ethiopian troops from the country.[17] The upshot was the 2008 resignation of the president of the Transitional Government, who claimed that Somalia had been overrun by armed militia and that he could not legitimately exercise power.

Somalia is still in a condition of insecurity.[18] Its continuing instability has created fertile ground for a range of armed militia, which are often clan-based, to wield significant power and control over sections of the country. Regional and international security has been affected by the spillover of refugees and armed militia into neighboring countries, particularly Ethiopia and Kenya, as well as the hijacking of seafaring vessels in the Indian Ocean.[19]

CHINESE STRATEGIC AND DIPLOMATIC INTERESTS IN ETHIOPIA

There are several variables to consider in China's strategic interests in Ethiopia. One obvious fact is that Addis Ababa is increasingly becoming an intercontinental diplomatic hub hosting (a) the African Union, whose headquarters facility was built by China, (b) the UN Economic Commission for Africa, (c) the IGAD located in nearby Djibouti, and (d) various important international non-governmental organizations. These organizations offer China an opportunity for close contact with African leaders as well as with eminent personages who influence individual African nations' domestic and foreign policies.

A second variable is the reality that Ethiopia, with the largest standing army in sub-Saharan Africa, 130,000 strong, is a force for stability in the Horn of Africa. Although Ethiopia is still influential in Mogadishu, having helped establish the Federal Government of Somalia, it also has close relations with Somaliland, with its capital city Hargeisa, which has been an unrecognized, self-declared de facto sovereign state since 1991. Somaliland is not internationally recognized as an independent state but is considered an autonomous region of Somalia. Ethiopia's interest in Somaliland is tied to the port of Berbera, which it needs in order to reduce its dependence on Djibouti,[20] and its close relations with Hargeisa may have opened the opportunity for a major Chinese business group to visit Somaliland and engage in talks regarding expanding the port on the Indian Ocean.

Furthermore, Ethiopia is deeply involved with its western neighbors in the Republic of South Sudan, which is now plagued with conflict between Dinka and Nuer ethnic groups.[21] Ethiopia has concerns for the security of its federal form of governance due to a rebel Nilotic ethnic group straddling the Ethiopia-South Sudan border, the *Anuak* militants. This group, which lives in western Ethiopia and South Sudan, has established a liberation front.[22] China and Ethiopia thus have a common interest in political stability in South Sudan. The oil that is being refined there by China and is critical for its energy needs is also critical to Ethiopia, which is landlocked and would like to acquire it through a cross-border pipeline. But both China and Ethiopia have had to contend with the politics of two Sudans because South Sudan's oil flows through Port Sudan in the north.[23]

Thus Chinese and Ethiopian interests in the Horn of Africa have led to a close partnership that includes military cooperation, with Beijing supplying Ethiopia with artillery, light armored vehicles, and troop transport. These relations have also resulted in a number of Ethiopian officers visiting China for training. This military relationship was cemented when Ethiopia signed a military cooperation agreement with Beijing in 2005 for training, exchange of technologies, and joint peacekeeping missions.[24] This close cooperation is underlined by the presence of a military attaché, one of the few on the continent, in the Chinese embassy in Addis Ababa.

China is also interested in Ethiopia because of the latter's influence on the Republic of Sudan and Egypt due to its control of the Blue Nile River, whose flow generates some 80% of the water that reaches the Republic of Sudan and Egypt. Ethiopia's Grand Renaissance dam is expected to revitalize the impoverished region with 6,000 GWh annually and Ethiopia intends to exploit its invaluable water sources to achieve the status of a middle-income country. In order to achieve its long-term objective of becoming a regional energy supplier to nations such as Djibouti, Kenya, Sudan, and Yemen, Ethiopia initiated its 25-year Master Plan, building hydroelectric dams along the nation's vast waterways in 12 river basins. Five of the six proposed dam projects are with Chinese firms; the sixth, the Grand Renaissance dam, is solely an Ethiopian project.

At present Ethiopia is building the Grand Renaissance dam 25 miles east of its border with Sudan. At a projected production of 6,000 Mega Wat annually, the dam will be the largest hydroelectric power plant in Africa when completed. The potential impacts of the dam and the methods Ethiopia will use in sharing the waters of the Nile have been sources of basin-wide cooperation as well as regional controversy.[25] However, the Republic of Sudan is increasingly siding with Ethiopia's plan and wants good relations. Egypt, too, recognizing the facts on the ground, seems to have acquiesced, has toned down its belligerence, and appears to be seeking amicable arrangement with Ethiopia.[26] Although China is not entirely financing the construction of the dam, the Chinese Electric Power Equipment and Technology Co., Ltd., is covering 85% of the cost of the transmissions lines while the balance is being financed by the Ethiopian Electric Power Corporation.[27]

THE WEST, ETHIOPIA, CHINA, AND REGIONAL SECURITY

The Horn of Africa region is affected by four main ongoing conflicts: (a) the fragmentation and now recovery of Somalia and the effects of the military intervention of its neighbors and global actors, (b) the separation of South Sudan from Sudan (c), the unsolved dispute between Ethiopia and Eritrea, and (d) the recent internal conflict in South Sudan. The reconfiguration of Ethiopia (with Eritrea's independence) and Sudan and the creation of two new states (Eritrea in 1993 and South Sudan in 2011) changed state borders in the Horn of Africa and left two new landlocked countries – Ethiopia and South Sudan – to consider alternative routes to the sea. Ethiopia has been particularly engaged in the effort to find peace in Somalia, where global, regional, and local dynamics sustained a war for decades and brought about the emergence of one of the most aggressive Somalia-based terrorist organizations.

The TFG of Somalia was formed in 2004 in Kenya under the auspices of IGAD and with heavy support from both Ethiopia and Kenya. Despite its recognition by some international bodies such as the AU and the UN, the government lacked any meaningful control of Somalia. The TFG was on shaky grounds and Ethiopia as well as the West had significant concerns about political stability not only in Somalia, but also throughout the Horn of Africa. After the attack on American embassies in Kenya and Tanzania by al-Qaeda-affiliated Somali nationals and similar but smaller-scale attacks by Islamists in Ethiopia, both the United States and Ethiopia considered the Islamic Courts – a union of Sharia courts that presented itself as a rival to the TGF – a threat that had to be dealt with. Hence, Ethiopia pre-emptively invaded Somalia in 2006 with the goal of helping enforce the authority of the TFG and lessening the power of the Courts. The unfortunate consequence was not only huge devastation in Mogadishu, which had begun to stabilize under the rule of the Courts, but also the fragmentation of the Courts and the evolution of an offshoot, the *Al-Shabaab*, a terror organization that has been responsible for many subsequent attacks including on the Westgate Mall in Kenya in 2013, in which 65 were killed.

Meanwhile, China was also busy exploring for minerals and oil in Ethiopia's Ogaden region near Somalia. In 2007, separatist rebels stormed a Chinese-run oil facility, killing more than 70 people including nine Chinese workers; the Ogaden Liberation Front, a militant group fighting for independence for part of eastern Ethiopia, immediately took responsibility. While Ethiopia's intervention in Somalia may have sparked the rebel attack, the Chinese have not left the region. In 2011, after a Chinese delegation visited Somaliland, a trilateral agreement worth $4 billion was signed between China, Ethiopia, and Somaliland with PetroTrans Ltd. of China. The agreement permitted the Chinese company to explore and develop gas and oil reserves in the Ogaden region of Ethiopia and ship them through Berbera.[28] The port of Berbera sits at a strategic location at the mouth of the Red Sea, at the center of Asia, Africa, and the Middle East. The government in Hargeisa, Somaliland, is interested in leasing the port to Hong Kong-based Hutchison Port Holdings with Ethiopian Shipping Lines becoming one of the main shareholders. Berbera is expected to become the main port for Somaliland and Ethiopia, a land-locked nation. Many in the region believe that if the port of Berbera is well managed by China and given a full facelift, it could exceed its rival neighbor, Djibouti.

But China is also making its presence felt in Djibouti. The Republic of Djibouti is wedged between Ethiopia, Eritrea, and Somali. What is more, it is strategically located in the Red Sea and oversees the narrow *Bab al-Mandeb* straits, the channel separating Africa from Arabia and one of the busiest shipping lanes in the world, leading into the Red Sea and north-wards to the Mediterranean. Camp Lemonnier hosts US Special Forces, fighter planes, and helicopters and is a major base for drone operations in Yemen and Somalia in the War against Terror. In 2014, Somali al Qaeda-linked militants attacked Djibouti, saying the attack was to punish the East African state for contributing to an AU force in Somalia. In 2015, the United States renewed the lease of the base the base for 10 years with an option to extend for another ten.[29] But the United States was in for a surprise; Djibouti and Beijing signed a military agreement in February 2014 allowing the Chinese navy to use its port, and China later made its presence felt when its warship docked at the port and a senior Djibouti military official toured the ship.[30]

Djibouti's links with China are strong. Former president Hassan Gouled Aptidon made four trips to the PRC during his tenure in office which was reciprocated by Chinese Deputy Foreign Minister Ji Peiding's visit to Djibouti in 1999 to discuss economic to Djibouti. In March 2001, President Guelleh made his first trip to the China to strengthen economic and trade cooperation and addressed the China-Djibouti Economic and Trade Seminar in Beijing attended by about 100 Chinese and Djibouti entrepreneurs. This was followed in 2002, with President Guelleh meeting Chinese vice Foreign Minister Qiao Zonghuai in the capital city of

Djibouti on bilateral relations. President Guelleh's visit to China last year ushered their relations to a new stage.

Since then China and Djibouti relations have been on a fast track. In 2015 China has now announced that it will establish its first military base in Africa in the strategic port of Djibouti, raising the prospect of US and Chinese bases side by side in the tiny Horn of Africa nation.[31] It is obvious that in its dealings with Djibouti, China has a much stronger strategic advantage. This is because maritime ports are Djibouti's only major economic asset, apart from its military and logistical facilities currently in use by France and the United States. Thus China's plan to spend significant capital on upgrading its ports and infrastructure is an offer that Djibouti cannot refuse.

France also bases members of its armed forces in Djibouti, the 5th Overseas Interarms Regiment of the French Army is based in the country. It also has bases fighter aircraft bases at Ambouli airport, the main airport in Djibouti. The presence of France in Djibouti ensures its strategic presence in the Horn of Africa, as well as along the crucial sea lines of communication between the Persian Gulf and the Mediterranean Sea because the Red Sea carries the bulk of France's energy imports. However in 2009, France opened its first foreign base in the Middle East, Camp de la Paix (Peace Camp), in Abu Dhabi, United Arab Emirates.[32]

As for the United States, although it was at first very concerned about the China-Djibouti pact and the former's intention to build the base in Obock, Djibouti's northern port city, it understood the tremendous financial incentive China offered Djibouti, namely, the purchase by China Merchant Holdings, an important state-owned enterprise, a majority share in vital Port of Djibouti, spending $185 million in addition to the $429 million contract awarded to China State Construction Engineering Corporation redesign the infrastructure of the port which includes a vital link rail link to Ethiopia. At this stage it is hard to gauge Chinese intention whether the Obock region will serve as a full blown military base or a facility designed as a staging ground to project its power in the Horn of Africa. But for now it is believed that China hopes the center could ease difficulties in refueling and replenishing Chinese navy ships and provide recreation for officers and sailors taking part in anti-piracy missions in the Gulf of Aden. This does seem plausible as China has sent more than 60 ships to the waters of the coast of Somali on 21 separate missions since December 2008.[33]

CHINA AS UN PEACEKEEPER IN AFRICA

China is a permanent member of the UN Security Council. Although in the past it had adopted the principle of peaceful co-existence, which was one of the main pillars of the 1955 Bandung Conference, its modernization in the post-Cold War era has necessitated that it be engaged in constructive intervention. This policy has resulted in involvement in UN peacekeeping operations.[34] It is important to note that Africa is not high in terms of security concerns for China, but its importance to China as a trading partner has grown. In any case, China's policy of constructive intervention has been buttressed by official cooperation between China and Africa in several agreements between 2003 and 2006, culminating in areas of cooperation under the 2009 Sharm El-Sheik Plan, and fleshed out in the Beijing Action Plan 2013–2015 adopted at the 5th Ministerial Conference of FOCAC. China also launched the China-Africa Cooperation Partnership for Peace and Security initiative, which includes financial assistance to the AU PSC.

In the Horn of Africa, China is beginning to strengthen its relationship with IGAD. The body was established in 1983 by Djibouti, Ethiopia, Kenya, Somalia, Sudan, and Uganda for development and drought control in their region, with Eritrea becoming a member in 1993 after attaining independence. In 1996 a revitalized IGAD expanded into areas of regional cooperation. In 2011, China contributed $100,000 to the secretariat in Djibouti to support the organizational cost of the institution.[35] IGAD is deeply involved in helping reconstruct the state of Somalia and mediating in the South Sudan conflict, an area in which China has substantial investments. IGAD is important in terms of peace and security because there is an international consensus that regional organizations should play a key role in maintaining international order.[36]

China's diplomatic efforts seem designed to work within the overall IGAD peace process. This was made evident in 2006, when African Affairs Ambassador Zhong Jianhua held talks with officials in South Sudan and Ethiopia to appeal for the protection of Chinese nationals and investments in rebel-held areas in South Sudan.[37] Such efforts become more important to China after the IGAD talks in Addis Ababa, Ethiopia, on March 5, 2015, failed to obtain a lasting ceasefire in South Sudan, leading one scholar to suggest China was attempting to upstage Western powers in the peace process, namely the United States, the United Kingdom, and Norway.[38]

It is thus apparent that China is expanding its peacekeeping operations in Africa, an effort that coincides with its commercial and civilian presence on the continent. In 2015, China has more than 2,000 peacekeepers posted around the world. But nearly all are engineers, medical and transport workers, and security guards. China's peacekeeping operation in Africa is a significant shift from its stated policy of non-interference in African conflicts. Since 1989 China has been involved in peacekeeping operations with the UN Transition Assistance Group in Namibia, and since 1991 China has sent military observers in 15 UN peacekeeping operations in Africa.[39] China plans to be a major player in UN peace-keeping efforts. In 2015, China's President Xi Jinping informed the UN General Assembly it had 'decided to lead in setting up a permanent peacekeeping police squad and build a peacekeeping standby force of 8,000 troops.'[40] He also pledged that China would provide $100 million in military assistance to the African Union to support the ASF in boosting its capacity for crisis response.

The ASF came into being after the establishment of the AU Peace and Security Architecture and provides regional standby brigades with the East African Standby Brigade, headquartered in Addis Ababa, Ethiopia. Thus Chinese deployment of troops under the UN flag, while modest, highlights its aim to strengthen its position within the United Nations and in UN peacekeeping. Its long-term objective may be the build-up of a military presence under UN command, which may eventually open up new possibilities for protecting citizens and economic assets in Africa.

CONCLUSION

The triangular relationship between the West, Ethiopia, and China has evolved and is based either on economic or security interests or both. The interests of the West in Ethiopia are multifaceted. For the EU, Ethiopia is an important economic and political ally in its Africa policy and is the largest aid recipient on the continent. EU and Chinese financial flows to Ethiopia are largely complementary and assist the African nation in obtaining resources greatly needed to implement its ambitious development strategy.[41] But more importantly, China is an alternative partner to the Ethiopian government, providing alternative development strategies. The United States is also very much engaged with Ethiopia. Although the United States is not building roads, railways, or schools and Americans are not very visible in Ethiopia because of security issues, the United States has provided Ethiopia with much needed assistance for its agricultural growth program, food security, and nutrition as well as in combatting HIV/AIDS.[42] In addition, the United States considers Ethiopia an important ally in its War against Terror, countering the influence of al-Qaeda fighters in Somalia and the region. For China, its past involvement with Ethiopia was based on geopolitical values as it needed Ethiopia's support in its quest for African solidarity and alliances against Western imperialism. But China has embarked on a path to great power status, and its traditional ideological policy is being replaced with instruments that facilitate its new aims and that befit an emergent power. China is interested in Ethiopia because the African country, with an estimated population of 90 million people, offers a huge market. It is the most stable nation in the region with a large and reputable military force. But more importantly, China's deepening of relations with Ethiopia is also driven by political reasons: Addis Ababa is the headquarters of the African Union, the UN Economic Commission for Africa and thus offers China an entrée to the African diplomatic Community. Finally, while the establishment of relations between China and Djibouti in many ways is similar to its relations with many African countries, one difference is that the latter offers China not only to become an important international maritime player at the chokepoint of the narrow strait of *Bab-el-Mendeb* in the Red Sea but also to project its military presence in the Horn of Africa and eventually the Middle East.

NOTES

1. Barry Buzan and Ole Waever (2003), *Regions and Power: The Structures of International Security* (Cambridge: Cambridge University Press), pp. 230–231.
2. Getachew Metafria (2008), *Ethiopia and the United States: History, Diplomacy, and Analysis* (New York: Algora Press).
3. Meraheiwot Gebremariam (1995), 'Ethio-US Relations,' *EthioScope*, January.
4. Arka Abota (2006), 'Ethiopia's Foreign Policy under Emperor Haile Selassie I: An Appraisal' (master's thesis, Addis Ababa University).
5. He Wenping (2006), 'Moving Forward with the Time: The Evolution of China's African Policy' (paper presented for Workshop on China-Africa Relations: Engaging the International Discourse Hong Kong University of Science and Technology Center on China's Transnational Relations, 11–12 November 2006).

6. See Peter J. Schraeder (1996), *United States Foreign Policy Towards Africa: Incrementalism, Crisis and Change* (Cambridge: Cambridge University Press), pp. 114–188.

7. Amare Tekle (1989), 'The Determinants of the Foreign Policy of Revolutionary Ethiopia,' *Journal of Modern African Studies*, 27:3, pp. 479–502.

8. See Christine Hackenesch (2011), *Competing for Development? The European Union and China in Ethiopia* (discussion paper, Center for Chinese studies, University of Stellenbosch, South Africa, November).

9. Seifudein Adem (2012), 'China in Ethiopia: Diplomacy and Economics of Sino-Optimism,' *African Studies Review*, 55:1, pp. 143–160.

10. Federal Republic of Ethiopia, Ministry of Finance and Economic Development (2010), *Growth and Transformation Plan*, Volume I (Addis Ababa, Ethiopia).

11. Lovise Aalen (2006), 'Ethnic Federalism and Self-Determination for Nationalities in a Semi-Authoritarian State: The Case of Ethiopia,' *International Journal of Minorities and Group Rights*, 13, pp. 243–261.

12. Jean-Pierre Cabestan (2012), 'China and Ethiopia: Authoritarian Affinities and Economic Cooperation,' *China Perspectives* 2012, 4.

13. 'Ethiopia Draws Asian Manufacturing Interests (2014),' *Voice of America*, 4 August 2014 http://www.voanews.com/content/ethiopia-drawing-asia-manufacturing-interest/1970953.html.

14. 'Interview: Ethiopia Keen to Bolster Cooperation with China in Manufacturing Sector, Ethiopian President Mulatu Teshome,' *Xinua News Agency*, 5 June 2015.

15. Author's field work in northern Ethiopia, February 2011 and June 2013.

16. Tom Maliti (2014), 'IGAD and Somalia: Now and Then,' *Horn of Africa Bulletin*, 26:3.

17. Awol K. Allo (2010), 'Ethiopia's Armed Intervention in Somalia: The Legality of Self-Defense in Response to the Threat of Terrorism,' *Denver Journal of International Law and Policy*, 39, p. 139.

18. Mwangi S. Kimenyi, John Mukum Mbaku, and Nelipher Moyo (2010), 'Reconstituting Africa's Failed States: The Case of Somalia,' *Social Research*, 77:4.

19. Maliti, 'IGAD and Somalia'.

20. Mahlet Mesfin (2011), 'Ethiopia: Chinese Firm Eyes Gas Export from Calub Through Berbera,' *All Africa.com*, 25 July 2011, http://allafrica.com/stories/201107270752.html.

21. International Crisis Group (2015), 'South Sudan: Keeping Faith with the IGAD Peace Process,' *Africa Report*, 228, 27 July 2015.

22. See John Young (1999), 'Ethiopia's Western Frontier: Gambella and Benishangul in Transition,' *Journal of Modern African Studies*, 37:2, pp. 321–346.

23. 'South Sudan Delays Shutdown of Oil Pipelines to Ethiopia,' *Reuters*, 26 July 2013.

24. Joshua Eisenman and Joshua Kurlantzick (2006), 'China's Africa Strategy,' *Current History*, 105:691, p. 219.

25. See Aaron Tesfaye (2012), 'Environmental Security, Regime Building and International Law in the Nile Basin,' *Canadian Journal of African Studies*, 46:2.

26. William Davidson (2013), 'Egypt, Ethiopia and Sudan Mull New Probe Nile Dam Impact,' *Bloomberg News*, 21 October 2013.

27. Daniel Berhane (2013), 'China Provides $1 Billion for Renaissance Dam Transmissions Lines,' *Horn Affairs*, 26 April 2013, http://danielberhane.com/2013/04/26/nile-china-finance-billion-dollar-renaissance-dam/.

28. 'Somaliland, Ethiopia and China to Sign Trilateral Deals,' *Somaliland Press*, 14 August 2011.

29. John Lee (2015), 'China Comes to Djibouti: Why Washington Should Be Worried,' *Foreign Affairs*, 23 April 2015.

30. Jiang Anquan and Zhang Jianbo (2013), 'Djibouti Welcomes China to Build a Military Base,' *Global Times*, 11 March 2013, http://www.chinaafricaproject.com/djibouti-welcomes-china-to-build-a-military-base-translation.

31. Jane Perlez and Chris Buckley (2015), 'China Retools Its Military with a First Overseas Outpost in Djibouti,' *New York Times*, 26 November 2015.

32. Bruno De Palva (2011), 'France: National Involvement in the Indian Ocean Region,' *Future Directions International, Strategic Analysis Paper*, 5 December 2011.

33. Christopher Boden (2015), 'China in Talks with Djibouti on Establishing Logistics Base,' *Associate Press*, (AP), 26 November 2015.

34. Yin He (2007), *China's Changing Policy on UN Peacekeeping Operations* (Stockholm: Institute for Security and Development Policy).

35. Intergovernmental Authority on Development (2011), 'Cooperation with China,' 21 November 2011, http://igad.int/index.php?option=com_content&view=article&id=370:cooperation-with-china&catid=46:executive-secretary&Itemid=123.

36. Sally Healey (2011), 'Seeking Peace and Security in the Horn of Africa: The Contribution of Intergovernmental Authority on Development,' *International Affairs*, 87:1, pp. 105–120.

37. Hang Zhou (2014), 'Testing the Limits: China's Expanding Role in the South Sudanese Civil War,' *China Brief*, 14:19.

38. George Akwaya Genyi (2015), 'South Sudan: Resolving Conflicts in Africa – A Test Case for China,' *Conflict Studies Quarterly*, 13, pp. 17–28.

39. Kay Mathews (2013), 'China and UN Peacekeeping Operations in Africa,' In Gebrehiwot Berhe and Liu Hongwu, eds., *China-Africa Relations: Governance, Peace and Security* (Institute for Peace and Security Studies, Addis Ababa University and Zhejiang Normal University.)

40. Michael Martina and David Brunnstrom (2015), 'China's Xi Says to Commit 8,000 Troops for U.N. Peacekeeping Force,' *Reuters*, 28 September 2015, http://news.yahoo.com/chinas-xi-says-commit-8-000-troops-u-160032557.html

41. See Lars Christian Moller (2015), '*Ethiopia's Great Run: The Growth Acceleration and How to Pace It*' (working paper, Washington, DC: World Bank Group).

42. USAID (2015), 'Agriculture and Food Security,' accessed 1 December 2015, https://www.usaid.gov/ethiopia/agriculture-and-food-security.

Aaron Tesfaye is Professor in the Department of Political Science, William Paterson University, Wayne, NJ, USA. He is the author of *State and Economic Development in Africa: The Case of Ethiopia* (NY: Palgrave-Macmillan, 2017), *The Political Economy of the Nile Basis Regime in the Twentieth Century* (New York: Edwin Mellon 2009), and *Political Power and Ethnic Federalism: The Struggle for Democracy in Ethiopia* (Lanham, MD: University Press of America, 2002). He is a former Fulbright Scholar at the Department of Political Science and International Studies, Addis Ababa University, Ethiopia (2010–11). He is a visiting professor at the Institute of Peace and Security Studies, Addis Ababa University, Ethiopia, and has also taught at Universidad de Sao Jose, Macau, S.A.R. Peoples Republic of China (2011).

CHAPTER 15

Beyond Symbolism: China and the African Union in African Peace and Security

Charles Ukeje and Yonas Tariku

INTRODUCTION

By far the most visible testimonial to China's presence in Africa was the decision by Beijing to singlehandedly build, furnish and handover the towering Secretariat and modern Conference Centre to the African Union Commission (AUC) in Addis Ababa, Ethiopia, January 2012. Amidst criticisms[1] that African government could not mobilize resources internally to build a befitting structure for the AUC, the obvious symbolism of the $200 million gift should not be lost. Put to use the same month for the 18th AU Summit, it pointed to China's keen interest in the affairs of the African Union (AU); the institutional arrowhead of pan-Africanism. In a broad sense, also, the gesture was evidence that China was determined to score further politico-diplomatic mileage while consolidating the already substantial economic inroads made across Africa in little less than two decades.

In terms of longevity, scale and intensity of support to the AU, it might be an ambitious mismatch to place China at par with other bilateral and multilateral development partners.[2] There is no doubt, however, that Beijing is slowly but steadily increasing its engagement with the AU in several critical

C. Ukeje (✉) · Y. Tariku
Institute for Peace and Security Studies, Addis Ababa University, Addis Ababa, Ethiopia
e-mail: c.ukeje@ipss-addis.org; yonas.tariku@aau.edu.et

© The Author(s) 2018
C. Alden et al. (eds.), *China and Africa*,
DOI 10.1007/978-3-319-52893-9_15

sphere, including in peace and security that seems to have become the dominant – but by no means the only – focus of the continental body since it transformed from the Organization of African Unity (OAU) to the African Union (AU) in 2002.

This chapter focuses on three key themes. First is to trace the genealogy of China's decades of engagements with the OAU, and its new reincarnation, the AU. In doing this, the chapter casts a retrospective glance into the rearview mirror to examine how changing institutional and policy contexts, and several other imperatives that accompanied the transition from the OAU to the AU also informed, conditioned and determined Beijing's relationship with the AU, for good or otherwise. Second, the chapter takes a closer look at the evolution of Africa's peace and security landscape and how the AU is grappling with changing threats as an inter-governmental institution. The section essentially aims to situate the broad and contrasting roles of key external actors involved with and supporting the AU on peace and security matters on the continent. Given this involvement and support, it is important to interrogate some of the salient points of divergences and similarities in the disposition of external partners towards the AU on matters relating to continental peace and security. By doing this, it becomes easier to gain better understanding of how those differ from that of China in terms of outlook and content. It is, in the latter regard, possible to appreciate why in spite of the steady increase in its financial commitment to the AU on an equally growing range of issues, China is still in relative – if not strategic – terms less visible compared to other external partners with equally extensive engagements with the AU.

The third section of this chapter will focus on some of the identifiable thrusts or aspects of China's policy toward the AU on peace and security matters, including how those are articulated and defined within the broader framework of the Forum on China-Africa Cooperation (FOCAC). The argument in this section is partly that FOCAC, in distinctive as well as substantive ways, provides an omnibus 'organizational' umbrella around which China's engagement with the AU is anchored. The concluding section will offer alternative, even if tentative, future perspectives for China vis-à-vis the AU in the area of peace and security; not just in terms of resourcing the Union and its activities (an area in which Beijing is playing a lead role only after the EU and the World Bank) and on agenda setting (where the potential for China to exercise stronger leverage is still limited).

In interrogating the above issues, this chapter solicits answers to a number of key questions. What factors, for instance, account for the content and upswing in the tempo of relationship between China and the AU on peace and security issues? How is such relationship captured within broader strategic interests of China vis-à-vis the AU on peace and security issues? What, if any, are some of the substantive differences between China and other external 'development' partners in relation to support to the AU on peace and security issues? In what areas have China focused on in peace and security matter in relation to the AU, and why?

Despite the quantum of Chinese involvements with the AU that seems evident today, there are contrasting views on whether or not they represent a set of well-conceived and implementable instrument rather than merely ad hoc and reactive diplomacy. Along with the United States, which established its mission to the AU in December 2006, China is the only other country at the time of writing this chapter with a dedicated diplomatic delegation to the AU that was set up only in May 2016.[3] This followed the memorandum of understanding (MoU) signed during the official visit of the Chairperson of the AUC, Dr. Nkosazana Dlamini-Zuma, to Beijing in January 2015 which approved the exchange of ambassadors. Although barely 2 years since the signing of the MoU, a number of logical questions should follow; first, what does this new diplomatic rapprochement at the multilateral level mean for China and the AU in terms of the pursuit of peace and security in Africa? To what extent might this development translate into regular, tangible and cumulative relationships between the two parties regarding a common understanding of the peace and security imperatives for Africa and China? Furthermore, what specific resources (in terms of funding, training, logistics or others) have China placed at the disposal of the AUC in the pursuit of continental peace and security priorities? Finally, in considering the alternative futures for China and the AU on peace and security issues, some of the questions to ask relate to long-term (or future) perspectives on their relationship, including how both sides perceive the evolving engagements in terms of best and worst case scenarios now and in the near future.

CHINA AND THE AU: THE EVOLUTION OF A BELATED RELATIONSHIP

Although it falls within the broader scope of China-Africa relations, the intention here is only to focus on specific institutional dimensions of Beijing's relationship at the multilateral level; first, with the OAU, and then with its successor, the AU. The broad aspects, however, need not detain us here; given that other chapters in this volume have already taken up several facets of China-Africa relations in terms of development-oriented peacekeeping, military diplomacy, cooperative partnership, crisis management, mediation, post-conflict reconstruction, new peacekeeping interventions, protection of overseas interests in Africa, to name a few.

An important footnote in benchmarking the evolution of China's engagement with Africa would be to acknowledge that because it was not a colonial power on the continent in the classical sense, Beijing did not enjoy the same 'early-bird' advantage and deeply embedded economic and political privileges that countries such as Britain and France; and to a lesser extent, Portugal, enjoyed on the continent. By extension, also, its late arrival (even though historical evidence suggested a longer engagement dating far back) meant at least that China could not have had direct and substantive engagements with African institutions that only began to sprout after the wave of independence in the 1960s. Regardless of this caveat, it is impossible to ignore how the revolutionary ideologies that coincided with and attended the cultural revolution in China during the 1960s, the same time that many African countries were gaining independence, might have influenced the mindset of several leaders of post-independence Africa in ways that made them to see and respond differently to the imperatives of establishing inter-governmental institutions to complement fledgling bilateral relations amongst themselves, and that between them and the rest of the world.

In the later regard also, a parallel is partly evident in how the Marxist-communist ideology that gained ascent following communism in China not only shaped the worldview of elites in many countries around the world, particularly those in many African countries that provided the intellectual power and contrasting visions on pathways to achieving continental unity. In actual fact, there is an inescapable linkage between the divisions and compromises that produced the ideological blocs that argued for continental unity from divergent positions, and eventually shaped the form that the OAU took when it was inaugurated in 1963.[4] Thus, whereas a number of scholars have captured the emergence of the Monrovia, Casablanca and Brazzaville groups whose compromise produced the OAU. In the prevailing circumstance of the Cold War rivalries between the East and the West, it was clear that the divide went further and deeper and was fueled by broader global contestations between capitalism and communism championed by Washington and Beijing. At the ideological level, then, a link could be 'established' in the pattern of influence exercised by China in the build-up and circumstances leading to the establishment of the OAU. What is perhaps necessary to explain, in some detail, was how the ideology of communist China did not immediately translate into Beijing's direct and concrete involvement in the affairs of the OAU in its formative years, and beyond.

One key explanation for this would be that following the communist revolution led by Chairman Mao Zedong, the People's Republic of China quickly opted for a policy of autarky that required looking inwards to tackle urgent and myriad developmental challenges at home than have to pursue an outward-looking policy of engagement with the rest of the world. Even if it had wished to embrace the rest of the world, Africa would in all likelihood be too distant and far-fetched for China. In any case, direct engagement with Africa would have pitched it against established European powers that have grown accustomed to centuries of substantive presence across Africa. Since it neither had the same kind of reach, depth and *de jure* presence in Africa, painstakingly cultivating new relationships at bilateral or multilateral levels – would have been unnecessary or at best too costly.

It was not coincidental therefore that it was only after the gains of the communist revolution and of impressive socio-economic development at home that China began to test the waters through a policy of cautious engagement with the rest of the world, including newly independent African countries. In sum, that any direct and tangible relationship between China and Africa, and by extension, with African inter-governmental institutions, did not exist for much of the first decade of independence in the 1960s should be understood in terms of Beijing's limited colonial presence in Africa; the imperative of the communist revolution that made it to look inwards rather than outwards; and finally, the initial reluctance of China to engage major European colonial powers in contestations over spheres of influence during the initial periods of the Cold War up to the 1970s when it found a compelling rationale to open up.

Be it in the context of the late 1960s or today, China's relation with African inter-governmental institutions such as the OAU/AU cannot be extricated from broader (and changing) imperatives of China-Africa relations. With the establishment of the OAU in 1963, however, relationship with China became more focused, even if it was still mainly expressed within the context of the Cold War. Due to the prevailing ideological war between the United States and Soviet Union, China's relation with African states and the OAU was throughout that period decidedly shaped by ideology than other substantive economic and political or geostrategic considerations. The only exception to the ideology-driven disposition of China would be that over the contested issue of Taiwan which Beijing considers as part of mainland China. China have consistently made the 'one-China' policy a precondition for bilateral or multilateral diplomatic relationship with African states and institutions.[5]

Zhang Chun (2013) identifies three phases in China-Africa relations over the past six decades. First was the period between the early 1950s and the late 1970s dominated by expectations of mutual supports between China and Africa on matters related to the struggle against colonialism and imperialism. During this phase, China openly supported liberation movements in Africa; partly aware that the unraveling of European colonial enterprise on the continent would, inevitably, create new opportunities for direct and unfettered engagements. The second phase, during the 1980s, was marked by greater openness and reform in China, developments that encouraged the country to open up to the world. Having become emboldened and relatively confident on the home front, China realized the need to go beyond demands imposed by its own circumstances at home and within its 'near-abroad' to one that places premium on pragmatic engagements with the rest of the world based on her enlightened national interest. Indeed, it was since the 1980s that China began to promote its 'Four Principles' (of 'equality and mutual benefit, emphasis on practical results, diversification, and economic development') guiding her evolving relations with Africa. The last phase, which followed the end of the Cold War after the collapse of the Soviet Union in 1989, and the emergence of the United States as the sole superpower still standing, witnessed a more active, robust and broader China-Africa relations. From then, onwards, Beijing began to deploy a repertoire of human and material resources to 're-engage actively' with Africa.[6]

In another instance, Liang (2011) has discussed the ebbs and flows of China-Africa relations, and the far-reaching implication for China-OAU/AU relations. According to him, China's relation with Africa, in general, and with the OAU, in particular, was complicated by the undue rivalries between the two super powers during the Cold War era. Although China at that time was an ardent supporter of liberation movements in Africa and actually maintained both ideological and substantive relationship with the defunct OAU-Liberation Committee located in Dar es Salaam, Tanzania, its rivalry with the Soviet Union which had been involved for longer in African affairs and in the activities of the OAU during its formative years, seriously hampered progress toward the incubation and consolidation of a viable relationship between Beijing and the OAU.

It was only from the 1970s that China's relations with African states and the OAU showed signs of improvements; only for it to fizzle out again during the 1980s following China's reform policy which attached limited importance to ideology as a factor determining bilateral and multilateral relations. To quote Liang, again, China-OAU relations declined in the 1980s due to '...China's switch of interest from unconditional internationalism to the prioritization of national interest and its resulting sharp decrease in her devotion for ideological issues and liberation struggles.' Yet, another peak period came in the 1990s, following the end of the Cold War essentially characterized by the development of broader Sino-African relations.[7] With the termination of the Cold War came a major global reconfiguration of power, notably one in which the former Soviet Union lost its global strategic advantage. Certainly, China did not only benefit immensely from the demise of the Soviet Union but also quickly pushed itself to the forefront of global power play in Africa and around the world. Beijing was able to do so for at least two related reasons. First, it had come out of the Cold War with a more formidable economy and stronger military capability. Second, it became much more willing and determined to engage more with the rest of the world on its own terms.

Thus, whereas it was a timid and naïve power before the 1990s, China thereafter gained the economic, political, military clouts to become a budding superpower in a matter of time. When it flexed muscle in the past, it was almost always within her 'near abroad' in the Asian continent. As far as Beijing was concerned at that time, Africa was only of distant and limited geo-strategic importance. The paradox that brought China closer to Africa, and vice versa, could not be further from her quest to sustain the momentum of its own domestic growth. The only way to do so was to step up its global engagements, especially with resource rich countries in the so-called 'new frontiers' that Africa now represents. In other words, if the quest for natural resources to feed the economy at home brought Beijing closer and deeper into Africa, it is likely to keep it on the continent for a long time to come given the manner in which global contestations over – and around – natural resources have become both politicized and securitized. One outcrop of China's new quest to gain access to and maintain foothold in Africa's resource-rich countries was therefore that Beijing quickly realized the urgency to redefine and recalibrate several aspects of its relationships with African states and their continental institutions such as the OAU/AU. In the same regard, Beijing stepped up its engagements with Africa's regional economic communities.

Before closing this section, it is important to note that the circumstances that pushed China toward Africa, and by extension, toward African inter-governmental institutions, were not entirely unidirectional. It is also instructive that African states and institutions were, for most of the first three decades after independence, also overly preoccupied with myriad state-building and development challenges of which China featured only from a distance. It would be recalled, for instance, that the core mandates of the OAU when it was established in 1963 were to promote continental unity, terminate the vestiges of colonialism and white minority rule on the continent, tackle the challenges of nation-building and economic development, and generally provide a pan-African platform to project Africa's international relations. Further, it was evident that the circumstances of the Cold War era during which the wave of independence occurred in Africa was such that majority of African states found a greater urge to retain cordial relationship with their former European colonial powers and Western allies; in particular, the United States. Even when the Cold War imperative required African countries (and their Asian counterparts) to maintain safe equidistance between the two superpowers in what could be described as the 'spirit of Bandung' espoused by the Non-Aligned Movement, only a few African countries looked eastwards; either toward the other major superpower, the Soviet Union, or toward communist China.

In many ways, then, the circumstances that surrounded the birth and existence of the OAU during much of its first three decades were also such that the felt-need to have any tangible and sustained engagement with China was either uncalled for or outright unnecessary. Clearly, also, just as individual African states were understandably preoccupied with consolidating the gains of independence, the OAU was also fixated with broader pan-African challenges linked to the pursuit of the core mandates previously highlighted. With some justification, the successful pursuit of those mandates (especially that of degrading colonialism and white minority rule) required the OAU to engage more vigorously at political and diplomatic levels with European colonial powers than with China (or even Russia). If at all, what the OAU might have required from China (and the other two superpowers – the United States and the Soviet Union), none of them could give because they had no direct colonial presence in Africa. At best, they could only offer symbolic expressions of solidarity with their yearnings and aspirations to end colonial and white minority rules. Indeed, from Washington, Beijing and Russia, there was never a shortage of mostly vague expressions of solidarity with the OAU when it comes to the collective pan-African struggle to break away from the yoke of colonialism. Whether or not such omnibus expressions of solidarity, in turn, translated into concrete support for the organization was another issue entirely. The conclusion to make, in drawing the curtain on this section, would be that beyond occasional expressions of solidarity, neither China nor the OAU needed each other tangibly and sufficiently enough during much of the first three decades (1960–1990). The scenario described, however, changed dramatically during subsequent decades, particularly since the late 1990s, for a number of reasons to be discussed next.

CHINA AND AFRICA: THE CHANGING IMPERATIVES FOR PEACE AND SECURITY IN POST-COLD WAR AFRICA

A constellation of developments altered China-AU relationship in several substantive ways from the late 1990s onwards; the same period that coincided, at the global or systemic level, with the collapse of the Soviet Union and the unraveling of the Cold War order. It is outside the scope of this chapter to dwell in any detail on the spread, or multiplier, effects of the end of the Cold War for the international system, in general, and for Africa, in particular.[8] The point to make, however, was that the emergent post-Cold War order quickly created new – in some cases, unanticipated – impulses that changed the tempo and content of China-Africa relations as well as brought the imperative for greater and closer engagements between Beijing and the AU to the fore. For China, the post-Cold War dispensation meant that the once overbearing influence exercised by the two superpowers and their allies was no longer as formidable to hinder 'new' external actors from consolidating their engagements with African states and institutions.

A corollary to the first was that the post-Cold War dispensation meant that China could extend and deepen her presence in places where it previously held back due to complicated diplomatic, economic, political and security exegeses. It simply did not wanting to 'upset' established major powers by starting a 'tuft war' in African countries where European colonizer have maintained structural and embedded interests. It had further become obvious to China from the late 1990s onwards that the way to meet up with the geometrical growth in industrial (economic) demands at home was to change tactics; from that of a timid and elusive interlocutor around the world to one that pursues vigorous and assertive economic diplomacy abroad. China needed resources to feed its industries, open new markets for its huge industrial output, and find labor outlet for her teeming population, the largest in the world. It was by a twist of providence, therefore, that Africa became the new, one-stop, frontier for China to pursue her three prong ambitions, and more. What was perhaps more distinctive was that Beijing did not have to pursue any of its ambitions mindful of the circumstances, limitations and implications of its brand of engagement with Africa.

For the newly formed AU, on the other hand, the post-Cold War era created a number of ripples across the African continent that required it to respond quickly and decisively; even if it lacked the financial and human resources to back up emerging ambitions. If the OAU was relatively ad hoc in terms of the infrastructure put in place to respond to peace and security challenges up until the end of the 1990s, the successor institution, the AU, could not afford the same luxury of not putting adequate measures in place to promote peace and security in Africa in the post-Cold War dispensation. It is important to recall that in substantive and irreversible ways, the peace and security landscape in Africa changed considerably with the advent of the post-Cold War era. Whereas conflicts during the preceding era were typically inter-states in nature, their sources and scope have mostly become internal, even when they spillover across national borders to create heavy and complex humanitarian exegeses. Such new conflicts result from festering governance deficits, ethno-religious contestations, the activities of insurgent and terrorist movements, and those around zero-sum electoral contestations as well as festering socio-economic inequalities, to name a few. As the continent's strategic importance to major powers waned in relative terms, so too did the amount of time and resources key external actors were willing to allocate to peace, security and developmental issues on the continent. The paradox from the nature, and impacts, of new conflicts in Africa is partly that the AU found itself unexpectedly having to take the lead in resolving them despite its own inherent human, institutional and financial limitations. It is not surprising, then, that the AU have had to rely on external partners, including China, to pick the huge bills for maintaining its core mandate of maintaining peace and security in Africa.

That the African peace and security landscape has changed in numerical, qualitative and mostly irreversible ways in the new post-Cold War dispensation inevitably created additional impetus to revamp and transform the OAU into the AU in 2002. Whereas the defunct OAU was preoccupied with five key issues[9] of critical importance at the time it was inaugurated in May 1963, the Constitutive Act of the African Union that was adopted in Lome, the capital of Togo, in 2000, to replace it considerably expanded the scope into 14 areas. For this purpose of this chapter, the additional mandates emphasized were to promote peace, security and stability on the continent; promote democratic principles and institutions, popular participation and good governance; promote and protect human and peoples' rights in accordance with the African Charter on Human and Peoples' Rights and other relevant human rights instruments; establish the necessary and minimum conditions which enable the continent to play its rightful role in the global economy and international negotiations; and finally, promote sustainable development at the economic, social and cultural levels as well as the integration of African economies. Apart from reflecting the new and critical exegeses that the continent faces in the post-Cold War period, the additional responsibilities that the AU places upon itself required even with the best of intentions much more than its member states could singlehandedly implement without the support and goodwill of the international community.

The expansion of its mandate required that the AU must considerably increase its resource base to be able to adequately and effectively respond to existing and emerging peace, security, governance, human rights, sustainable development, regional integration, challenges. It also implied that the AU must rethink, revamp and update the overall policy and institutional architecture required to respond to such new imperatives. In terms of peace and security, the AU adopted the African Peace and Security Architecture (APSA) to capture the unique nature, taxonomy and spectrum of conflicts in Africa and also established different mechanisms of response. The five key pillars of the APSA are the Continental Early Warning System, Panel of the Wise, African Standby Force (ASF), the Peace and Security Council and the Peace Fund. The different components of APSA could either standalone or serve as integrated parts of the process for conflict prevention, management and resolution. Regardless of whether each component is standalone or parts of an integrated menu of response, the cost (and politics) of establishing, validating and implementing them is considerably beyond what member states of the AU can manage without robust and continuous external support.

THE 'NEW' FRAMEWORK FOR CHINA-AU ENGAGEMENTS ON PEACE AND SECURITY IN AFRICA

The focus of this chapter is on China's engagement with the AU in the sphere of peace and security. There are a number of reasons why it is important to dwell on this. Notably, China-AU relationship distinctively reflects an interest in multilateral diplomacy; an arrangement that has gained traction since the end of the Cold War when key countries began to recognize the economies of scale inherent in engaging with different regions to complement traditional bilateral relations. Before interrogating the framework for China-AU engagements on peace and security in Africa, however, it is useful to provide a bit of context that should help to put in better perspective how Beijing perceives and understands the continent and the myriad security challenges it faces. In principle (if not in reality), China has been adamant in its insistence that relations with Africa – and by extension, with the AU – are to be guided by the principles of 'non-interference.' From either side, however, what constitutes 'non-interference' remains largely contested and controversial. The principle, on the one hand, implied that Beijing focuses on the real content rather than the side distractions of her relationship with African government and institutions. By 'side distractions', the chapter refers to the baggage of issues that typically raises concern in and attracts opprobrium to African governments and institutions: especially human rights abuses, suppression of political opponents, indiscriminate use of military force, poor environmental records, to name a few.

Several exegeses have made the principle of non-interference less and less sacrosanct in China-Africa/AU relations, especially with Beijing rapidly growing and expanding her involvement in Africa's extractive and non-extractive industries in virtually every parts of the continent. In less than two decades, China's interests in Africa have blossomed to the extent that it must consciously be in a position to protect and defend such interests, or be seen to be doing so. This, in part, has led China to actively court major African actors – states and institutions – capable of reflecting, defending or simply echoing its interests within the continent and beyond. Thus, whereas it would have been unthinkable many years ago for China to be involved in the growing range of peace support operations on the continent by evoking the principle of non-interference, the situation has changed considerably now. China has demonstrated increasing commitment to support peacekeeping missions in Africa; as evident in her becoming the third largest source of funding, after the European Union and the World Bank, to the activities of the AU. It is also evident from her funding support to enhance the rapid deployment capabilities of the African Standby Force (ASF)[10] as well as the appointment of a standalone delegation to the AU (different from Beijing's mission to Ethiopia). Almost every year, China contributes – financially and logistically – to the AU peace and security endeavors; and in late 2015, it pledged an additional $100 million toward AU peace operations and for the strengthening of the ASF.[11]

Still, China is relatively a newcomer into the African peace and security sector when compared with the United States and major European countries. In many ways, then, China's engagements cannot be expected at par but largely a fledgling work-in-progress. It is not surprising that there is still on ongoing- and mostly unsettled- debate as to the essence of China's role in African peace and security. Wang Xuejun (2014) identified two diametrically opposite views in this regards. First, is that which proposes that 'China will maintain a conservative stance in African security affairs and will adapt to the unstable situation in Africa rather than trying to reshape it' while the second one suggests that 'China will construct a new paradigm of peacebuilding and play an increasing role in peace and security affairs in Africa.' While both perspectives have their proponents in China as well as across Africa, Xuejun argues for the latter by acknowledging how the outlook that Beijing eventually pursues will be shaped by its own domestic experience of 'developmental peace' (distinct from the dominant liberal peace paradigm privileged by the West).[12] An additional point to emphasize is that China might, in time, find itself oscillating between the two extremes; on the one hand, conservatively adapting to the realities of peace and security without seeking to shape it in any substantive ways while also playing a secondary role in redefining existing peace and security paradigms on the continent.

In essence, China's policy toward African peace and security is not only ideologically different from that of the West; but it is opposed to the more established liberal interventionist policies the later privileges in bilateral and multilateral responses to African issues. To quote Xuejun, again, China's policy '...puts special emphasis on the effect of autonomy and social economy development on conflict resolution and post-conflict reconstruction, so it can be termed *sovereignty plus development model*.'[13] There are several implications from this brand of Chinese policy toward Africa. Based on China's own domestic experiences, the model places premium on the long debate that the peace and stability in Africa should be linked as much to socio-economic development as to political or geo-strategic imperatives.[14] The policy also seats well with the quest to identify, establish and exercise African agency, as well as leadership, in determining the peace and security priorities of the continent. The Chinese model, invariably, supports notions around 'African ownership' and that of 'African solutions to African problems' on matters related to peace and security.

Having made these preliminary observations, a good point of departure for understanding and situating China's current engagement with the AU should be to trace it to the umbrella cooperative initiative known as the Forum for China-Africa Cooperation (FOCAC). The focus in this section is however not on FOCAC *per se* but to explore how China-AU relations have been captured and given practical expression within that multilateral framework. Although FOCAC was launched in October 2000, it was only in 2011, slightly over one decade after, that the status of the AU changed from that of an observer to full membership. It was specifically to align China-Africa cooperation with that of the strategic objectives and priorities of the AU that the change in status should be appreciated.[15] FOCAC is held every three years, alternating between Beijing and different African cities, the most recent being in Johannesburg, in December 2015. In-between FOCAC summits, senior Chinese and AU officials meet twice a year. At the ministerial level one or two meetings are also held; the first one, to prepare for FOCAC, the other to follow-up on implementation of decisions.

Since the First Strategic Dialogue took place in 2008, six China-AU Strategic Dialogues have been held, most recently in May 2015.

Generally aimed at further '...consolidating and deepening relations between China and the Commission'[16] as the former Chairperson of the AUC, Jean Ping, had underscored 4 years earlier during the 4th China-AU Strategic Dialogue in May 2011.[17] In 2012, and following the change of AU's status in FOCAC to full membership the previous year, President Hu Jintao stressed that China has keen interest to work with and deepen commitments to the AU. He also expressed his country's willingness to provide financial support for AU's peacekeeping missions, as well as toward the development of the ASF and to train security officials and peacekeepers for the AU. Further, out of the five priority areas to boost China-Africa tie announced by President Hu Jintao, one directly pertains to peace and security in Africa. The President was emphatic that '...we should promote peace and stability in Africa and create a secure environment for Africa's development'[18] by China focusing on (a) launching of the 'Initiative on China-Africa Cooperative Partnership for Peace and Security' (ICACPPS); (b) deepening of cooperation with the AU and African countries in maintaining peace and security in Africa; (c) providing financial support for AU peacekeeping missions and the development of the ASF and (d) training more security officials and peacekeepers for the AU.[19] It was to further give concrete institutional expression to the evolving relationship that China and the AU committed to establishing and exchanging full-fledged missions and ambassadors following the official visit of the Chairperson of the AU to Beijing in 2014.

As of August 2016, then, China had engaged in at least three major peace and security issues that have direct and immediate bearing on Africa. By that period, Beijing had deployed an estimated 2,639 troops and other personnel in nine peacekeeping missions across Africa.[20] The latter development has made China the largest troops contributing country among the permanent members of the United Nations Security Council. In addition to sending peacekeepers to Africa, China had played a pivotal – and decisive – role in the mediation efforts involving the Government of Sudan, the AU and the United Nations which led to the deployment of the hybrid UN-AU peacekeeping mission in Darfur, UNAMID, in 2007. Last but not the least, China played a major role in the multinational coalition against piracy off the coast of Somalia; not just by actively conducting 400 successful missions between 2008 and 2011, but also escorting 4,300 vessels and rescuing 55 ships.[21]

In all, the launch of ICACPPS and other FOCAC-inspired initiatives marked a conscious decision to reinvigorate China's engagements with the AU on African peace and security issues which had, until then, only tangentially been touched upon in China's African policy. However, one of the challenges this initiative may face has to do with that of multi-dimensionality. According to Zhang Chun (2014: pp. 55–58), three major challenges confront the successful implementation of ICAPPS, namely (a) the huge, and growing, gap between the expectations of Africa vis-à-vis what China can realistically provide; (b) the gap between China's willingness and availability of resources at its disposal to support and satisfy Africa/AU's thirst for assistance; and finally, (c) the point raised earlier relating to the policy disconnect between China and Africa/AU in terms of their divergent views as far as underlying the principle of 'non-interference' is concerned.

Even though it came entirely as a Chinese initiative, FOCAC is widely considered as the joint platform through which China and Africa, might enhance their relations through regular consultations. By inviting it into full membership of FOCAC, then, China recognizes the status of the AU in Africa's international relations as the premier pan-African institutional actor in relation to peace and security matters. The flipside, of course, is that China is also widely seen as an indispensable partner in terms of capacitating the AU to carry out its responsibility. These sentiments were re-echoed, with equivocation, in the Johannesburg Action Plan of FOCAC (2016-2018) which recognizes:

> ...the important role of the African Union in safeguarding peace and stability in Africa, promoting the development of Africa, and advancing the integration process of Africa. The two sides, furthermore, acknowledge with appreciation the efforts and contributions made by China to support Africa's peaceful and stable development and integration.[22]

Section 6 of the Johannesburg Action Plan further reiterated that China will continue '...to support the African Union, its Regional Economic Communities and other African sub-regional institutions that play a leading role in coordinating and solving issues of peace and security in Africa and further continues to support and advocate for African solutions to African challenges without interference from outside the continent.'[23] In the same Plan, China committed to providing the AU with free military assistance worth over US$60 million during the following three years as well as supporting the operationalization of the APSA, including that of the African Capacity for the Immediate Response to Crisis and the ASF.[24]

There are, of course, several angles through which the density of high-level exchanges between China and the AU within the framework of FOCAC might be situated and understood. From the Chinese perspective, it is better and more expedient in the short and long runs to deal with a single – if not necessarily unified – entity capable of realigning the priorities and interests of diverse actors than have to maintain a complex (and complicated) tapestry of relationship with 54 separate African countries. Embedded here is also the prospects that growing its engagement with the AU will bring about some economies of scale in terms of following up on and supporting pan-African agenda, including those around peace and security issues that have now assumed greater salience and urgency. Further, no matter the empire of circumstances it currently faces, the AU has in several distinct ways become the institutional face of Africa's international diplomacy; a major interlocutor whose voice and decisions can no longer be discounted, sidelined or ignored by the international community.

With some justification, the AU sees itself as an indispensable platform – or channel – through which the international community, including China, might contribute meaningfully to peace and security in Africa. On the sides of the December 2015 FOCAC summit in South Africa, Madam Dlamini-Zuma and President Xi Jinging held a bilateral meeting to further discuss possible areas of cooperation between the AU and China. The meeting itself came barely one month after the Chairperson had paid an official visit to China. At both events, the two leaders identified several areas of cooperation, such as the capacitating of the newly established Africa Centre for Disease Control (Africa-CDC), tackling adverse climate change outcomes and supporting the 10-year implementation plan of Agenda 2063 on 'silencing the gun' in Africa. As if to underscore the win-win nature of FOCAC and other avenues opened for China-AU relations, the Deputy Foreign Minister of China, Zhang Ming, reiterated during the 6th Strategic Dialogue held on 16 May 2015, that:

> China always views China-AU relations from a strategic and long-term perspective, and sincerely wishes a united Africa and a strong AU. China is willing to deepen exchanges and cooperation with the AU and vigorously promote an all-round, multi-level and three-dimensional cooperation pattern by giving high-level contacts a leading role and taking mechanisms such as the Strategic Dialogue as pillars.[25]

The Future Prospects and Challenges of an Evolving Relationship

At least four changes in China's policy toward the AU in relation to peace and security in Africa are already self-evident. The first is captured in what might be described as sector-focused expansion, as demonstrated by China's visible and tangible involvements in a range of 'hard' as well as 'soft' supports to different spectrums of peace operations; from peace-keeping to peacebuilding. What is perhaps missing in this aspect, especially when compared to the deep-reaching involvements of key Western governments, is that China is still far away in terms of deepening, regularizing and routinizing her engagements by embedding Chinese experts within the AU as other Western governments have done. In key units within the AU Peace and Security Department, it is not unusual to find Western consultants on short-term or fairly longer tours of duty unlike their Chinese counterparts who only make occasional appearances. It might be difficult, for now, to quantify the importance or impact of such regular engagements between Western experts and key AU officials. What is not disputable is that by maintaining fairly regular presence and engagement with AU officials involved in peace and security related issues, Western experts are better able to gain and maintain critical access and relevance when it comes to advancing the interest of their respective countries. By working (and socializing) together, for instance, AU officials and Western experts they engage with on regular basis are in a reasonably better position to develop shared values or dispositions essential for mobilizing consensus, or that are critical to the evolution of a community of practice around African peace and security issues. This view, however, does not discount the fact that the frequency of exchanges between AU and Chinese officials has grown in recent times, almost always funded by Beijing and mostly involved one-way visits to China.

Second, given especially that China's influence in, and engagements with, the AU has grown in qualitative and quantitative terms over the past decades, it is unlikely that Beijing will be contented with merely playing the exchequer role on matters that involve AU peace and security activities in Africa. Indeed, as China commits itself to providing more resources (with relatively little or no strings attached) in pursuit of Africa's peace and security agenda led or supported by the AU, it may sooner begin to demand greater participation in shaping outcomes favorable to its interest on the continent. In short, what is likely to happen in the near future is that China would not be contented with 'downstream' involvements in which it is only called upon to contribute resources to peace and security activities but one in which her contributions begin 'upstream', as a norm-setter, at the stage of conception, planning and deployment of key peace and security initiatives. This is particular so in view of the fact acknowledged earlier that China has her own franchise on ways of approaching African peace and security issues.

The third aspect likely to influence the extent and degree of China's engagement with the AU on peace and security matters would have to do with the involvement of a plethora of actors with keen interest in African peace and security issues whose sources and character have become diverse and complex. This might portend a double-edged sword for China, especially as certain controversial aspects of its engagements might raise concerns and apprehensions from state and non-state actors aware of how Beijing exercises itself in Africa; including how it continues to maintain deep and opaque relationship with African governments with international notoriety. By pursuing steps that open her to greater public scrutiny, either subjecting to criticism or commendation, China would have to decide what public image to cultivate with key African constituencies.

The final point to make is that while the AU is for now seen by China as the arrowhead of its peace and security engagements in Africa, it is uncertain for how long such a disposition would last given some of the institutional limitations, or inertia, that make working with/through inter-governmental frameworks difficult. There are already so many contentious issues that border on peace and security (e.g., terrorism, impacts of climate change, migration, piracy and maritime security, to name a few) that the AU is experiencing difficulty mobilizing broad pan-African consensus. Invariably, the prospect that Beijing might for the same purpose lead and/or work within the framework established by other multilateral institutions, including regional arrangements, or even occasionally rely on specific countries or regional institutions to take the lead when her interests are better served, cannot be foreclosed. Invariably, the only guarantee that China-Africa/AU relationship will blossom in the decades to come would largely depend on the recognition by both sides that they need each other to advance critical politico-diplomatic, economic and security interests within Africa, and globally.

NOTES

1. Reuters (2012b), 'Glitzy new AU headquarters a symbol of China-Africa ties', http://www.reuters.com/article/ozatp-africa-china-idAFJOE80S00K2012012.
2. In the presentation to partners on 30 September 2016 titled 'Transforming the Finance Function 2016–2018, the AU PBFA Directorate identified China as third, only after two multilateral partners (the European Union and the World Bank), on the top 10 contributors to the overall AUC budget, including peace and security, in the period between January and August 2016
3. 'China Opens a Permanent Mission to AU' http://www.chinadaily.com.cn/world/2015-05/08/content_20656451.htm.
4. A. Sesay, Orobola Faseun and Sola Ojo, eds. (1984), *OAU After Twenty Years* (Boulder, CO: Westeview).
5. Pan Liang (2011), 'A Historical Survey of China and Africa OAU/AU Relations to 2011' (MA Thesis, Addis Ababa University, Addis Ababa, Ethiopia).
6. Zhang Chun (2013), 'The Sino-Africa Relationship: Toward a New Strategic Partnership', *Emerging Powers in Africa*, http://www.lse.ac.uk/IDEAS/publications/reports/pdf/SR016/SR-016-Chun.pdf.
7. *Ibid.*
8. S. Akinrinade and A. Sesay (1998), *Africa in the Post-Cold War International System* (London: Pinter).
9. The section of the OAU Charter on purposes identified the promotion of continental unity and solidarity; cooperation to achieve better life for African citizens; defense of sovereignty, territorial integrity and independence; eradication of all forms of colonialism from Africa; and international cooperation, as core issues.
10. During the FOCAC VI Summit in December 2015, China pledged to '...provide the AU with US$60 million free military assistance over the next three years, support the operationalization of the African Peace and Security Architecture, including the operationalization of the African Capacity for Immediate Response to Crisis and the African Standby Force' (Johannesburg Action Plan (2016–2018) Combined Draft Version of Africa and China, Forum on China-Africa Cooperation, December 2015).
11. The People's Republic of China extends financial support to the African Union Mission in Somalia http://www.peaceau.org/en/article/the-people-s-republic-of-china-extends-financial-support-to-the-african-union-mission-in-somalia.
12. Wang Xuejun(2014). 'Developmental Peace: Understanding China's Africa Policy in Peace and Security', *Global Review*, Spring 2014.
13. *Ibid.*

14. *Ibid.*
15. 'China-Africa Cooperation Forum (FOCAC)', http://au.int/en/partner ships/africa_china.
16. 'Opening Remarks by H. E. Dr. Jean Ping, Chairperson of the Commission of the African Union At the Opening of the 4th China-Africa Strategic Dialogue, 2011/05/06', http://et.china-embassy.org/eng/zfgx/t821017.htm; http://rw.china-embassy.org/eng/gnzyxw/t820459.htm
17. Ibid
18. 'President Hu Proposes New Measures to Boost China-Africa Ties', http://www.gov.cn/english/2012-07/19/content_2187416.htm.
19. 'Chinese President's Speech at Opening Ceremony of Fifth Ministerial Conference of Forum on China-Africa Cooperation', http://news.xinhua net.com/english/bilingual/2012-07/19/c_131725872.htm.
20. United Nations Peacekeeping: Contributions by Country http://www.un.org/en/peacekeeping/resources/statistics/contributors.shtml.
21. Wang Xuejun, Developmental Peace.
22. The Forum on China-Africa Cooperation, Johannesburg Action Plan (2016–2018) (Combined Draft Version of Africa and China), http://www.dirco.gov.za/docs/2015/focac_action_plan2016_2018.pdf
23. *Ibid.*
24. *Ibid.*
25. 'Sixth China-African Union Strategic Dialogue Held', http://www.fmprc.gov.cn/mfa_eng/wjbxw/t1265421.shtml.

Charles Ukeje Professor of International Relations, is a Senior Researcher with the Institute for Peace and Security Studies, Addis Ababa University. He holds a doctorate in International Relations from Obafemi Awolowo University Ile-Ife, and has held academic and fellowship positions at Oxford University and the School of Oriental and African Studies (SOAS).

Yonas Tariku is on leave from his position at the Institute for Peace and Security Studies (IPSS) of Addis Ababa University to pursue doctoral training on the Security and International Studies Program (SSIP) of the National Graduate Institute for Policy (GRIPS), Tokyo, Japan.

CHAPTER 16

Comparing China's Approach to Security in the Shanghai Cooperation Organization and in Africa: Shifting Approaches, Practices and Motivations

Rudolf du Plessis

China's modern engagement with Central Asia started with the establishment of diplomatic ties between itself and Kazakhstan, Kyrgyzstan, Tajikistan, Turkmenistan and Uzbekistan in 1992. Following the collapse of the Soviet Union in 1991, China has become the largest economic actor in the region and has made various investments in infrastructure, energy and hydrocarbon extraction. These endeavours have led to the establishment of railways, flight routes, gas pipelines and road networks which have contributed to the almost 100-fold increase in trade between China and the five Central Asian states since 1992. However, increasing security challenges have prompted China to forge closer bilateral and multilateral ties in order to combat threats of terrorism, extremism and separatism in Central Asia and China's Xinjiang Uyghur Autonomous Region (新疆维吾尔自治, hereafter referred to as Xinjiang). China and Central Asia has thus moved from regional military

R. du Plessis (✉)
South African Institute of International Affairs (SAIIA), Johannesburg, South Africa
e-mail: rudolf.duplessis@wits.ac.za

C. Alden et al. (eds.), *China and Africa*,
DOI 10.1007/978-3-319-52893-9_16

311

tension of the Sino-Soviet split, to cooperation in order to jointly combat Non-Traditional Security (NTS) threats emanating from Xinjiang, the five Shanghai Cooperation Organization (上海合作组织, hereafter the SCO) states and Afghanistan (India and Pakistan have also had membership applications approved in July 2015 and are expected to become full members sometime in 2016).

In contrast to its 20-year involvement in central Asia, over the past decade China has emerged as a new actor in Africa providing various forms of investments free of political conditions in exchange for access to scarce resources. Initially, China's non-interventionist approach gave it access to markets such as Angola and Sudan, relatively free of more established Western competitors. However, it soon became apparent that China can no longer remain uninvolved in regional peace and security – damages to Chinese assets, incidents of kidnapping Chinese oil workers in Sudan in 2012 and 2013, the beating of Chinese miners in Ghana in 2013, the deaths of three Chinese railway workers in Mali in 2015 and increased incidents of crime perpetrated against Chinese citizens in South Africa and Kenya. This has increasingly led to growing disillusionment within China and is putting increased pressure on the Communist Party of China (CPC) to act more decisively in protecting its citizens.

The purpose of this chapter is to examine China's long-term security engagement with Central Asian states, specifically members of the SCO, and to compare it with China's peace and security engagements in Africa. China has been actively involved in forging close diplomatic ties with its resource rich, yet politically unstable central Asian neighbours for more than two decades. In contrast, China is a relative newcomer on the African stage and is yet to demonstrate the methods it wishes to employ in order to safeguard its citizens and interests. The definition of security utilized here will be narrowed down to the measures taken to ensure protection to Chinese workers and assets in areas with high incidents of crime and violence against Chinese citizens. The examination of how security measures have been institutionalized and operationalized in Central Asia and whether these security measures are specific to their environment or can be considered emblematic of China's stance on peace and security in Africa and beyond will feature as well. A closer look will be taken at the influence of other multinational organizations such as the United Nations (UN) and African Union (AU) in Peacekeeping Operations in areas with high security risks and increasing Chinese involvement in these organizations. Also to be examined are the lessons African actors can draw from Central Asian actors in their engagements with China in issues of development, infrastructure projects, peace and security.

This comparison will thus investigate congruencies between China's engagement in Africa and Central Asia, specifically around issues of peace and security in the twenty-first-century Economic Belt and the Maritime Silk Road. The comparison will thus seek to investigate whether China's role in Peace and security in the SCO region and Central Asia can be viewed as emblematic of China's current and future engagements in the African peace and security landscape.

CHINA, CENTRAL ASIA AND THE SHANGHAI COOPERATION ORGANIZATION

Over the past 20 years, China has forged powerful diplomatic and military ties with its Central Asian neighbours. The primary vehicle for regional cooperation is the SCO – founded in 2001 as a re-branded version of the Shanghai Five, subsequently renamed SCO after the inclusion of Uzbekistan in 2001. The Shanghai Five was initially created with the signing of the Treaty in Deepening Military Trust in Border Regions in Shanghai by the five heads of state of the People's Republic of China (PRC), Russia, Tajikistan and Kazakhstan. An auxiliary purpose of the original five grouping organization was in order to reduce residual cold war era military build-up in Eurasian border regions, culminating in the 1997 Treaty on Reduction of Military Forces in Border Regions, signed in Moscow. In July 2005, the fifth SCO summit held in Astana, Kazakhstan, representatives from India, Iran, Mongolia and Pakistan were allowed observer status with the future possibility of allowing member status to observer members.[1] At the July 2015 joint SCO-BRICS summit in Ufa, Russia, it was announced that Pakistan and India will accepted as full members of the SCO in 2016. This could potentially lead to the strengthening of Sino-Indian ties and joint efforts by the two regional powers to find solutions to growing security risks emanating from Afghanistan and provide reconstruction and development aid in that region.[2] This move echoes President Xi Jinping's call that 'SCO members have created a new model of international relations — partnership instead of alliance'.[3]

In 1991, Central Asian nations sought rapprochement with China after a decades-long hiatus in relations. The primary focus of the SCO, the Shanghai Five, was to demilitarize the former Sino-Soviet border which had been the source of decades of military build-up amidst breakdown of relations after Khrushchev condemnation of Stalin's policies, and later the warming of Sino-American relations in the late 1970s. Therefore, there was a need to demilitarize the borders between China and the Central Asian states along its border in order to create a more stable region and more favourable conditions for investment and cooperation.[4] During this period, it took China and its newly independent Central Asian partners (primarily Kazakhstan, Kyrgyzstan and Tajikistan) a mere 10 years to resolve decades-old territorial disputes it had with the former Soviet Union.[5]

Central Asian nations were in search for new allies amidst an economic vacuum left by the termination of Soviet subsidies and trade. Similarly, China had an interest in regional stability in order to manage its borders in the case they were settled and demarcated. In doing so, it was hoped that it would be easier to identify terrorist threats to on either side of the Chinese or Central Asian states' borders by means of military cooperation. Between 1994 and 2002, long-standing territorial disputes were settled with Kazakhstan (Treaty for negotiations signed in 1994, settled in 1999), Kyrgyzstan (Treaty for negotiations signed in 1996, settled in 1999), Tajikistan (settled in 2002) and Russia (settled in 2008, demarcated in 2009). This came as an effort to unite the region in pursuit of common security goals and to unite Central Asian states in fighting terrorism and emerging separatism.[6]

With the most contentious issues hampering regional cooperation tended to, China began investing in security and strategic affairs and moved from merely securing borders to investing manpower and resources to promote regional stability. China and its Central Asian partners thus identified common security concerns needing cooperation in the region namely Separatism, Terrorism and Extremism, thereafter known as the 'Three Evils' (三股势力). The SCO was thus not designed to serve as a supranational organization, but rather a regional forum for the promotion of stability, security and economic cooperation. The efforts of military and intelligence cooperation thus culminated in the establishment of Regional Anti-Terrorism Structure (RATS) in Tashkent, Uzbekistan, in 2006. The purpose of RATS is not to serve as a regional police force, but rather a platform for finding common approaches in dealing with separatism, extremism and terrorism.[7] On 28 November, 2013, Premier Li Kejiang conducted the opening speech of the SCO annual meeting in Uzbekistan. In his speech, he stated that the SCO should strive to be an organization specifically focused on regional economic development with a large part of the organizations efforts used to combat the 'Three Evils' in Central Asia.[8]

The mandate of the SCO has undergone different phases since the founding of the Shanghai Five on 26 April 1996. The first half of the 1990s sought to the demilitarization of borders and to settle long-standing territorial disputes in order to curtail the emergence of separatism in the region. The latter half of the 1990s and early 2000s saw the focus of the SCO shifting towards the exploration and discovery of possible energy reserves located in the previously disputed territory and the establishment of a joint security framework to deal with issues of terrorism and separatism arising in the region. The latter half of the 2000s turned its attention to increasing regional economic activity and interdependence with the view that joint economic ventures could be a vehicle to lessen political tensions amongst Central Asian nations.

Since 2005, the SCO has continued past policies of economic cooperation, but has expanded to include increased scholarships to study in China in order to increase regional cohesiveness. It has also promoted increased Chinese-language training and has created initiatives to educate political elites in Chinese economy and models of leadership.[9] The 2012 Meeting of the Council of the Heads of the Member States on the SCO in Beijing highlighted the importance of regional energy and information safety and security. The 13th Meeting of the Council of Heads of Government (Prime Ministers) of the SCO Member states in 2013 emphasized economic cooperation, sustainable energy practices and regional infrastructure linkages in order to promote trade. Also notable during the meeting, delegates welcomed China's 'Silk Road Economic Zone' initiative and launched consultations with SCO member states. During the 2015 joint BRICS-SCO summit, heads of SCO member states approved India and Pakistan's bid to become full members by 2016. Belarus was elevated from Dialogue Partner to Observer status and announced Azerbaijan, Armenia, Cambodia and Nepal as new dialogue partners. It was during this summit that the SCO Development Strategy was approved, which sets detailed targets for the bloc's development by 2025.[10]

However, potential tensions between members continue to act as an obstacle to enhancing further cooperation. Russia has shown concern regarding China's proposed free trade agreements with other SCO members as it fears that this might undermine Eurasian Economic Union Russian has in place with Kazakhstan and Belarus. Russia is also putting economic pressure on Kyrgyzstan and Tajikistan in order to join the customs union. In 2015, however, what was at first perceived as an inevitable collision course changed direction when during Russia's victory day celebrations in Moscow in May 2015, Russia's Putin and China's Xi agreed to formally link China's Silk Road Economic Belt (SREB) and Russia's Eurasian Economic Union. Putin stated that 'The integration of the Eurasian Economic Union and Silk Road projects means reaching a new level of partnership and actually implies a common economic space on the continent', which will link China to the Middle East and Europe through Central Asia.[11] As a precursor to further cooperation, China agreed to extend the Moscow-Kazan high-speed railway into China at a cost of USD 5.8 billion (Tiezzi 2015).[12]

Another factor that potentially complicates matters in the SCO grouping is tensions over territorial disputes and natural resources. Military clashes along the Kyrgyzstan-Uzbekistan border and growing suspicion between the long-standing leaders of these countries make cooperation a difficult consideration,[13] not to mention increasing terrorism threats emerging from growing Uighur separatist groups such as the East Turkestan Independence Movement.

In order to overcome disputes amongst individual actors, China has taken up a policy of bilateral cooperation between individual actors of the SCO. This model has been applied to railway, road and pipeline projects that transverse multiple borders. As an organization, the SCO has made some achievements as a multilateral institution: joint military drills, the establishment of an anti-terrorism bureau and has established itself as a forum that makes it possible for the leaders of smaller states to interact with larger actors such as China, Russia and Kazakhstan on a regular basis.[14]

Contrary to perceptions in Western circles, the SCO was thus created as a vehicle for cooperation and the promotion of regional stability rather than a vehicle for anti-Western policies and actions. The SCO aims for stability in the region, economic stability and increased cooperation a potentially unstable region. The SCO has changed economics in the region with its promotion of cooperation and friendly competition. Initial security cooperation in the early 1990s has led to social and economic development that has seen to investments in a region ignored by Western investors for fears of being too unstable. These investments have been broad in scope and big in scale. For example, in Kazakhstan, China National Petroleum Corporation (CNPC) made the largest foreign purchase by a Chinese company in history when it acquired PetroKazakhstan in for USD 4.2 billion in

2009; in Turkmenistan, China has constructed a 1,830 km gas pipeline, completed in December 2009, which resulted in the purchase of over USD 15.72 billion of natural gas by China since 2009; in Kyrgyzstan, various Chinese actors have invested in the construction of power lines, railway ties and road infrastructure; In Uzbekistan, bilateral trade volume has increased to USD 2.87 billion in 2012, 50 times the volume of trade since the establishment of diplomatic relations in 1992; and in Tajikistan, historically the least prosperous of the five Central Asian states, China has developed road infrastructure such as the Dushanbe-Chanak highway and have constructed hydro- and thermal power plants amongst various other investment and development loan projects. This has improved the lives of individuals in the region and has aided Kazakhstan, Uzbekistan and Tajikistan to successfully submit applications and be admitted to the World Trade Organization (WTO).[15]

The role of the military in the SCO and Central Asia has moved from the settling of border disputes on the border of the PRC and the former Soviet Union to a unifying force in the region. Where military force was traditionally used as an instrument of coercion, under the SCO it has become a policy tool used for cooperation, securing regional stability of the demarcation of borders and the creation of a safe environment for energy exploration and transportation, business and economic cooperation. Military force is no longer the primary policy tool used to ensure goals are attained outside of states' borders, but rather a tool amongst a range of tools used to ensure cooperation and increased bilateral ties in order to combat NTS threats. That being said, thus far, security cooperation still lags behind the trade ties operating between Central Asian nations and China. However, closer security cooperation continues to create an ever more favourable environment for investment and regional economic cooperation and trade.

Since its establishment, the SCO has expanded to become the preeminent multilateral forum for regional security matters in Central Asia. With the emergence of the economic and infrastructure projects including railway links from China to Europe under the One Belt One Road (OBOR) strategy, the SCO has grown past being a military cooperation organization to becoming a vehicle for both economic and security cooperation in a region that will see an increase in Chinese interests.

THE OBOR STRATEGY

In September 2013 during a state visit to Astana, Kazakhstan, President Xi Jinping announced ambitious plans to establish a 'Silk Road Economic Belt' that will 'open the strategic regional thoroughfare from the Pacific Ocean to the Baltic Sea, and gradually move towards the set-up of a network of transportation that connects Eastern, Western and South Asia'. This announcement marked China's first declaration of its projection of foreign affairs, and at the same time, President Xi Jinping's first public foreign policy. Under the auspices of President Xi, China has launched the ambitious action plan to revive its historic Silk Road. The initiative will potentially cover 55% of world GNP and 70% of the world's population and 75% of confirmed global energy reserves and is expected to cost up to USD 300 billion.[16] The initiative is envisioned to take up to 35 years to complete, in time for 100th anniversary of the establishment of the PRC in 2049. This will see to a dramatic rise in Chinese civilians and personnel in the region.

The SREB is aimed towards creating land-based trade networks across the Eurasian continent, linking China's developed east coast to markets in the Middle East, Russia and Europe. The maritime component, termed the '21st century Maritime Silk Road', is envisioned to link the South China Sea to Indian Ocean, the Red Sea and the Mediterranean as well as enhancing Chinese ties to developing markets in South Asia, Southeast Asia, the Middle East and East Africa. This initiative, collectively known as 'One Belt One Road', is aimed at constructing road, railway and port infrastructure along various main lines and branches. On the 28th of March 2015, an Action Plan was launched by the Ministry of Foreign Affairs, the National Development and Reform Commission and the Ministry of Commerce. The document envisions an initiative that fosters seamless trade flows between the various regions that transverse OBOR, using Chinese-built infrastructure and streamlined customs administration. In order to demonstrate its seriousness and devotion to the OBOR initiative, China has pledged USD 40 billion to Silk Road Fund, USD 50 billion to the Asian Infrastructure Investment Bank (officially launched on 26 December 2015, due to begin operations by mid-January 2016)[17] and USD 10 billion to the BRICS New Development Bank (People's Republic of China, National Reform and Development Commission et al. 2015).[18]

During President Xi Jinping's tour of Kazakhstan, Russia and Belarus, trade deals were signed in Almaty, Moscow and Minsk including a deal with Russian president Putin which aims to create linkages with the Russian-led Eurasian Economic Union. The initiatives also include China-Pakistan and Bangladesh-China-India-Myanmar Economic Corridors. The former aims to link the port of Gwadar with Kashgar in Xinjiang. This project comes after President Xi's April 2015 visit where he pledged USD 46 billion over the next 15 years towards the construction of roads, pipelines and railway linkages between China's remote western periphery and the Arabian Sea.[19] The latter comes after Premier Li Keqiang's December 2013 visit where he announced ambitious plans to connect China's Yunnan Province to Kolkata in India, passing through Myanmar and Bangladesh. The initiative aims to increase trade in the region through the construction of a network of roads, railways, waterways and airways.[20] Both these initiatives will likely form vital parts of the twenty-first-century Maritime Silk Road.[21]

In January 2016, China's state council assigned the first batch of USD 40 billion of an expected USD 300 billion to be used to fund OBOR projects. These funds were raised from the insurance sector and forms part of stable capital that will spearhead China's infrastructure development projects.[22] At the 15th SCO Summit in July 2015, President Xi also mentioned the possibility of addressing the shortage in capital with the creation of an SCO development bank.[23] The initiative could lead to massive investments and development gains in the region. However, the potential also exists for substantial security risks in various regional hotspots such as Xinjiang, Pakistan and the five Central Asian states. For instance, the occasional kidnappings and killings of Chinese workers have taken place in Pakistan's Baluchistan, itself experiencing a separatist insurgency. Separatists have also called for the abandonment of the Gwadar Port construction project until their calls for Baluchistan's independence come to realization.[24] In Kazakhstan, risks of popular protests and mounting Sinophobia also pose security risks for Chinese individuals in the region.[25] It is thus imperative that China find solutions in the region that can ensure the security of its infrastructure and citizens whilst adhering to its policy of non-interference. It is therefore possible, according to Kucera (2015), that OBOR, particularly the overland route through Central Asia, will serve a dual purpose in that it will not only cater to commercial and civilian interests, but also aid in bolstering China's security in the region through improved infrastructure.

SECURITY IN CHINA'S BACKYARD

In order to contextualize the SCO's role in the SREB, the role of security in Xinjiang needs to be highlighted. China's Xinjiang province is the largest province in China and occupies roughly 17% of its total landmass. The region possesses vast natural resources ranging from approximately 40% of China's high-quality coal supply, natural gas (shale and conventional) and oil. The region's agrarian sector is also a major contributor to the global tomato supply. Although Xinjiang is home to only 1.5% of China's population, ethnic tensions have also led to major security issues emerging from the region. The region's native Uighur populations, making up roughly 60% of the total population, feel increasingly marginalized by the Beijing government and increasing Han migration to the region. This led to the July 2009 Urumqi riots that lead to the deaths of an estimated 200 Han Chinese and subsequent anti-government protests by Urumqi-based Han Chinese.[26]

Tensions between Xinjiang's Uighur population, the majority Han Chinese population and the Beijing government were further strained with groups of Uighur individuals travelling abroad to Afghanistan and elsewhere in Central Asia in order to connect with Jihadist groups and receive training to carry out acts of terror in the PRC. China has experienced numerous terrorist attacks, the most recent being the March 2014 Kunming Railway station knife attack that killed 29 and injured 143,[27] and the October 2013 Tiananmen Square motor vehicle rampage that left 38 people injured.[28] Both these attacks reportedly originate from Uighur separatist groups.

In the aftermath of growing tensions and the Urumqi riots in May 2010, the CCP Central Committee and the State Council hosted the Xinjiang work conference in Beijing. The main premise of the conference was to create new policy initiatives that would lead to further economic development and ultimately solve the region's issues of inclusion and ethnic tensions. Initiatives included development aid from Shanghai and the establishment of the Kashgar Special Economic Zone with the help of Shenzhen. More significantly, although relatively little emphasis was placed on its importance at the time, Beijing helped in transforming the Urumqi trade fare into the Eurasian Expo. This initiative sought to encourage investors and business people from Central Asia to invest in Xinjiang by the use of tax incentives and other benefits in special economic zones established around Urumqi and the Kazakhstan border. In a further attempt to bring development to the province, ex-Premier Wen Jiaobao announced the allocation of funds towards the development of road-and-rail infrastructure to further tie Xinjiang to the Eurasian landmass. During the second Eurasian Expo in Urumqi, the ex-premier announced plans for Xinjiang to emerge as 'a gateway for mutually beneficial cooperation between China and other Eurasian Countries'. Adding to this, Beijing has announced that through the OBOR initiative, it plans to create one million textile jobs in Xinjiang by 2023.[29] The focus of the CPC is thus not only to further 'export' development to Xinjiang, but to bring prosperity to the region by means of creating linkages between Central Asia and China's more developed East, fostering the notion of Xinjiang as a 'gateway' between Central Asia and Eastern China. This fits into Beijing's broader vision of shifting labour-intensive manufacturing industries towards its interior in order to 'export' stability by means of tackling unemployment, whilst lessening competitive pressures with its South East Asian neighbours. China therefore aims at creating sustainable industries through favourable government subsidies and reliable infrastructure.[30] China's move to increase investments in its western regions, particularly Xinjiang, comes with an increased sense of urgency due to threats on China's immediate periphery. Beijing has thus sought a two-pronged approach to regional development and stability.

Firstly, Beijing has prompted the Xinjiang government to spend approximately USD 130 billion to develop infrastructure and build stronger infrastructure links (particularly high-speed rail and road networks) to increase trade and investment originating from China's more developed coastal regions.

Secondly, by means of multilateral institutional approach through the SCO, China is developing regional economic and security infrastructure in Central Asia. This has taken various forms: at a local level, by regional security chiefs in Urumqi and Beijing establishing links with their counterparts in Central Asia; and at a multilateral level through the SCO. By and large, China's bilateral and multilateral forays into Central Asia have come in response to threats of extremism, separatism and narcotics trade, which is perceived to emanate from a low degree of social and economic development on its western periphery. With the formation of the SCO, China, Russia and its Central Asia partners aim to decrease the influence of separatist groups by targeting the regional narcotics trade, increasing the capacities of local police and security forces as well as strengthening ties and military capacity building by means of joint military exercises. This, in a wider sense, creates a safer environment for Chinese nationals both in China and in Central Asia and aims to address issues of Sinophobia and terrorism through military means and cultural diplomacy efforts.

Additionally, as mentioned in a recent report by the U.S.-China Economic and Security Review Commission, it has been highlighted that even though China's influence in the SCO region remains primarily economic, the SCO serves as a vehicle for the People's Liberation Army to gain much-needed experience by means of joint military and anti-terrorism exercises – approximately half of all China's military activities abroad involve Central Asian states and/or the Russian military. This allows China to carry out cross-border security operations with the approval of the host SCO nation.[31]

And, as noted above, military force has emerged as a form of regional cooperation in the founding of the SCO, of which one of the stated goals are to fight the 'Three Evils' of separatism, extremism and terrorism. The region has a long history with the above-mentioned issues plaguing regional security. It is thus that increased security by means of military cooperation has created a safer arena for economic initiatives such as the OBOR and has made it possible for increased economic prosperity to improve the lives of individuals residing in Central Asian nations signatory to the SCO.

CHINA IN AFRICA

China's modern post-Maoist historical engagement with African actors has been characterized as largely non-interventionist. In an attempt to diversify its diplomatic relations with non-Western actors and to find a stable, constant source for raw commodities, China had to form stable relations with governments shunned by the West for their non-democratic systems. Starting in 1991, China moved towards economic engagement in all parts of Africa – specifically resource-rich regions. This led to various forms of investments and engagements, including investments by smaller private firms and entrepreneurs and resource for infrastructure (R4I) deals. These R4I deals have allowed cash-strapped yet resource-rich African states to pay for large infrastructure deals with future commodity exports (Konijn 2014). Through these various engagements of non-interference, Beijing has through its state-owned enterprises (SOE)-funded various infrastructure projects, extractive operations and have actively encouraged private Chinese firms to set up operations in states in states such as Sudan, Chad, Ethiopia, Angola, Liberia, Sudan and South Sudan – states long neglected by Western investors and donors due to sanctions and volatile political and security environments.[32] However, increased numbers of Chinese firms have seen to a rise in security threats in areas such as Ghana, South Africa, Sudan and the Democratic Republic of the Congo (DRC). In states with weak regulatory environments and ineffective governance, these Chinese entities often operate outside the reach of the host government. For this reason, security risks are both numerous and persistent. China therefore faces the challenge of addressing concerns of Chinese actors operating in unsafe areas, whilst maintaining its non-interference stance which forms the very basis of China's engagement with many governments in the region. China therefore had to strike a balance between maintaining regional peace and security and maintaining its stance on African states' rights to sovereignty.

Threats to Chinese citizens' security have been manifold. Ranging from increased hostage taking of Chinese workers in South Sudan and Nigeria, increasing incidents of crime perpetrated against Chinese businesses and tourists in South Africa, Ghana and Zambia; and in Libya and Yemen, the dissolution of state authority and, ultimately, civil war. More recently, for example, in November 2015, three employees of China Railway Construction Corporation were killed in a terrorist attack on the Radisson Blu hotel in Bamoko, Mali.[33]

According to Alden and Large,[34] the problems of post-conflict African countries have not featured prominently on the Chinese foreign policy agenda, even though Chinese backed loans and investments have proven tantamount to the reconstruction of post-conflict African states. This has made Chinese entities visible and active, and therefore at higher risk of security threats that exist in these environments. In order to mitigate political, social and economic risks, China has over the past decade gradually broadened its once purely economic engagement to a more assertive engagement in the African peace and security sphere through greater involvement multilateral peacekeeping operations. This new approach for Chinese foreign policy gained further recognition and support with the announcement of the China-Africa Cooperative Partnership for Peace and Security in 2012, which adds a peace and security aspect to the Forum on China Africa Cooperation (中非合作论坛, FOCAC) framework.[35] During FOCAC VI held in Johannesburg in December 2015, President Xi pledged USD 60 million to support the building and operation of the African Standby Force and the African Capacity for the Immediate Response to Crisis. It has also pledged to continue to participate in UN peacekeeping missions in Africa and support African countries' capacity building (in areas of defence, counterterrorism, riot prevention customs and immigration control).[36] Still, exactly how China aims to address security issues through this forum remains uncertain.

China's engagement with numerous initiatives by both African and Western actors has seen to the establishment of different forms of peace and security architecture in the region through the guise of the UN and AU. By and large, China's involvement in the African peace and security arena has taken place either through UN missions or multilateral cooperation. China has thus approached the African peace and security environment with caution and has rather chosen to both partake and contribute to multilateral fora such as the UN, choosing to cooperate with other state actors more experienced in the African peace and security sphere. It could therefore be argued that China chooses see its engagement in Africa as an effort geared at learning and gaining experience in protecting its citizens and assets in high-risk environments.[37]

Over the past 25 years, China has become the biggest contributor of non-combatant peacekeeping troops amongst the five permanent members of the UN Security Council, providing approximately 2,720 peacekeeping personnel by 2015, with over 1,800 in Africa alone.[38] China's peacekeeping budget also comes in as the sixth largest globally. Since the majority of issues that come appear to the UN Security Council are Africa related, China has increasingly involved itself with African Peace Keeping Operations in order to protect Chinese economic interest whilst maintaining a policy of non-interference and avoiding Western criticisms for not being involved enough. China's involvement has since taken various forms, ranging from the establishment of three peacekeeping training centres and the contribution of troops in Liberia, the DRC, Darfur and South Sudan and since 2008 and escorting missions in the Gulf of Aden as part of the UN's anti-piracy operations.[39]

In December 2014, in an unprecedented move, China announced the deployment of an infantry battalion to South Sudan to take part in UN missions in 2015. This move was a departure from the usual approach of deploying non-combatant personnel such as engineering, transportation, medical service and security guard corps. In March 2014, in line with China's healthcare cooperation priorities in Africa, China deployed a 140 member peacekeeping contingent to protect UN staff and transport hubs to ensure the safe transportation of healthcare workers tending to the Ebola crisis. During this time, China also established a medical centre in

Liberia consisting of two doctors and five nurses in order to further aid in alleviating the crisis.[40]

During a state visit to the AU in May 2014, Premier Li Keqiang announced that China will establish a permanent mission to the AU, in line with China's endeavours in multilateral diplomacy. On the 7th of May 2015, this came to fruition when Vice Foreign Minister Zhang Ming and AU Chairperson Nkosazana Dlamini-Zuma inaugurated the opening of the Chinese permanent mission to the AU and the accreditation of China's Ambassador Kuang Weilin as permanent representative to the AU. The purpose of the Mission is to create new channels for communication with the AU and its institutions. More importantly, during the inauguration speech in May 2015, AU Chairperson Nkosazana Dlamini-Zuma stated that the Mission will aid in the implementation China's 'Six Major Cooperation Projects' and cooperation on 'Three Networks and Infrastructure Industrialization' initiatives.[41]

These initiatives, also known as the '461 Framework', refer to four principles for deepening cooperation, six areas to promote new projects and one platform for cooperation. The four principles are treating each other with sincerity and as equals; enhancing solidarity and mutual trust; jointly pursue inclusive development; and innovate on practical cooperation. The six areas to promote new projects are industrial cooperation projects; financial cooperation projects; poverty reduction projects; ecological and environmental protection projects; cultural and people-to-people exchanges; and enhancing peace and security. Finally, the 'One Platform' refers to the FOCAC.[42] In January 2015, in line with this initiative, China has committed to a plan to link all 54 African countries with railway, air and highway links as well as industrialization.[43] Reportedly, work is already underway in Nigeria where an agreement has been signed between the Nigerian government and a Chinese SOE to build a USD 12 billion, 1,400 km railway line along the Nigerian coastline.[44]

The Signing of this Memorandum of Understanding, if this ambitious plan is to come to realization, will undoubtedly aid in regional economic cooperation, job creation, industrialization and capacity building. However, this will also lead to further security risks for Chinese workers and business people in Africa's high-risk zones such as South Sudan, Central Africa and North Africa. China will therefore look to furthering its engagement in multilateral fora such as the AU and UN in order to make Africa safe for Chinese economic interests.

CONCLUSION

China has approached security in Central Asia and Africa in varying ways, both distinct and similar to one another.

In Central Asia, China has entered the regional security sphere as a 'norm shaper' rather than a 'norm follower'. China has opted for this approach for two main reasons. Firstly, since the fall of the Soviet Union in 1991, once dominant Russian investment, subsidies and military presence declined precipitously. In light of this, Central Asian nations have been open to various forms of Chinese investment, ranging from energy and infrastructure, to financial services and consumer goods. This has led to China rapidly resolving long-standing military and territorial disputes with newly independent Central Asian nations in the space of less than 25 years. Secondly, since the fall of the Soviet Union, China has experienced relatively little competition from the Russian Federation and has therefore used its favourable geopolitical and economic position to shape the region in a way that compliments China's broader vision of multilateral security and economic cooperation. China has used this advantageous position to form the SCO in spite of ethnic and political tensions between Central Asian nations. This role as instigator of a regional security organization provides China with an opportunity to shape the initiative in accordance with its own norms and values regarding trade, investment, security cooperation and other anti-terror activities in the region without risking relations with other actors already established in the region. Beijing has chosen to establish its own multilateral forum rather than utilizing existing frameworks for cooperation as laid out by longer established fora such as the UN and WTO. This also is behind its decision to strengthen the SCO and OBOR instead of integrating its efforts with the Russian-led Eurasian Economic Union. In a sense, China has approached Central Asia through a range of bilateral engagements that have since involved in a China lead multilateral security cooperative. An added advantage of this model is that China can maintain flexibility in dealing with individual SCO members in order to mitigate the possibility of collective action against Chinese interests in the region.

In contrast to its engagements in Central Asia, China has opted for following established norms in Africa through more actively engaging with established multilateral fora such as the UN and the AU to address peace and security issues. China has opted for this form of engagement for two reasons. Firstly, China enters the African peace and security sphere in the presence of longer established actors such as France, the USA, the UK, amongst others. Similarly, China faces economic and political competition not only from long-established actors, but also other emerging economies such as India, Brazil, Russia and South Africa. This leaves China with less room for shaping institutions and cooperative frameworks. Even though China has forged strong bilateral economic ties with states that have seen a decline in Western investors such as Angola, Chad and Sudan, it has primarily engaged the African peace and security sphere through UN missions such as United Nations Mission in South Sudan, United Nations Organization Stabilization Mission in the Democratic Republic of the Congo and the United Nations Mission in Liberia. This strategy ensures China operates within the parameters of established norms and values whilst at the same time seeing to the security of its citizens and interests in Africa. China has also pledged significant aid to the building and strengthening of African Institutions such as the AU and its various cooperative peace and security mechanisms. Unique to Africa, China has approached the peace and security sphere almost exclusively through established multilateral fora and has chosen to approach issues of economic cooperation primarily through bilateral agreements, or the China-led FOCAC.

Utilizing this analysis, it becomes clear that China chooses to engage peace and security matters in Africa and Central Asia through a multilateral approach. This method provides China with ample opportunities for institutional learning, whilst at the same time shaping norms and values around peace and security issues. It is therefore clear that China's preferred approach in dealing with peace and security is multilateral; whilst it at the same time chooses to engage economic and political matters bilaterally, with the exception of agreements and pledges made at FOCAC. However, exactly how china chooses to behave within these fora varies significantly. Within the SCO and the OBOR strategy, China views itself as a regional leader and more independently sets the agenda of how and which issues of peace and security are to be dealt with. Within Africa, China's engagement with peace and security issues has primarily occurred within established UN Missions and African Union Peace and Security mechanisms which have left China with less responsibility over the sustainability of such peace missions, whilst at the same time actively contributing to areas of risk to Chinese interests. This also comes with the effect of bolstering China's global image as a responsible power.

As China constantly increases engagements in the Central Asian and African spheres, it will have to continue to operate within regional norms and contexts in Africa, whilst it has the political autonomy to shape and create its own institutions. It is for this reason that China's peace and security engagements in Central Asia are shaped by the security context of its outlying border regions and Xinjiang rather than a broader geopolitical vision. However, China's engagements in Central Asia should not be discarded for this reason, but rather be viewed as emblematic of China's commitment to multilateral diplomacy as a panacea for regional security issues. This commitment to multilateral security strategies is also applied to Africa, albeit within the context of long-established institutions, actors, norms and values.

Notes

1. M. de Haas and F. van der Putten (2007), 'The Shanghai Cooperation Organisation: Towards a Full-Grown Security Alliance?', *Netherlands Institute of International Relations*, 9–10.
2. A. Panda (2015), 'India and Pakistan are Set to Join the Shanghai Cooperation Organization. So What?', *The Diplomat*. 7 July, accessed 23 October 2015. http://thediplomat.com/2015/07/india-and-pakistan-are-set-to-join-the-shanghai-cooperation-organization-so-what/.
3. Xinhua (2014), 'Deeper SCO Cooperation Promises Regional Peace, Development', *China Daily*. 11 September, accessed 15 November 2015. http://www.chinadaily.com.cn/world/2014xisco/2014-09/11/content_18583977.htm.
4. Stephen Aris (2011), 'Eurasian Regionalism: The Shanghai Cooperation Organisation', In *Eurasian Regionalism: The Shanghai Cooperation Organisation* (New York: Palgrave), pp. 54–59.
5. de Haas and van der Putten, 'The Shanghai Cooperation Organisation', pp. 7–8.
6. Ibid.
7. Ibid., pp. 8–11.
8. Embassy of the People's Republic of China in the Sultanate of Oman. 2013. 'Premier Li Keqiang Arrives in Tashkent for the 12th Prime Ministers' Meeting of the SCO Member States', accessed 22 October 2015. http://om.chineseembassy.org/eng/xwdt_2_1_1/t1104499.htm.
9. de Haas and van der Putten, 'The Shanghai Cooperation Organisation', pp. 29–30.
10. CCTV English (2015), 'Spotlight: Just-concluded BRICS, SCO Summits in Ufa Highlight China's Constructive Role', 12 July, accessed 15 July 2015. http://english.cntv.cn/2015/07/12/ARTI1436680950900480.shtml.

11. The BRICS Post (2015), *Working to Join Eurasian Union, Silk Road: Putin.* 3 June, accessed 15 October 2015. http://thebricspost.com/work ing-to-join-eurasian-union-silk-road-putin/#.VipBRn4rLIV.
12. Shannon Tiezzi (2015), 'At Russia's Military Parade, Putin and Xi Cement Ties', 9 May, 1ccessed 23 October 2015. http://thediplomat.com/2015/ 05/at-russias-military-parade-putin-and-xi-cement-ties/.
13. Ria Novosti (2012), 'Uzbek Border Guards Killed in Shootout on Kyrgyz Border', 23 July, accessed 23 October 2015. http://en.ria.ru/ world20130723/182380466.html.
14. F. Tolipov (2006), 'Multilateralism, Bilateralism and Unilateralism in Fighting Terrorism in the SCO Area'', *Eurasia Forum Quarterly*, 4:2, pp. 153–169.
15. Y. Chen (2014), 'China's Westward Strategy', *The Diplomat*, 15 January, accessed 24 October 2015. http://thediplomat.com/2014/01/chinas-westward-strategy/1/.
16. Godement (2015), 'One Belt, One Road': China's Great Leap Outward', *China Analysis, European Council on Foreign Relations*, pp. 1–3.
17. Yangpeng Zheng (2015), 'China Daily.' *AIIB Officially Launched, to Become Operational in Mid-January*, 25 December, accessed 15 January 2016. http://www.chinadaily.com.cn/business/2015-12/25/content_ 22808685.htm.
18. PRC National Reform and Development Commission; Ministry of Foreign Affairs; The Ministry Commerce: State Council (2015), *Visions and Actions on Jointly Building Silk Road Economic Belt and 21st Century Maritime Silk Road.* First Edition (Beijing: People's Republic of China).
19. Akhilesh Pillalamarri (2015), 'The China-Pakistan Economic Corridor is Easier Said Than Done', *The Diplomat.* 24 April, accessed 23 October 2015. http://thediplomat.com/2015/04/the-china-pakistan-economic-corridor-is-easier-said-than-done/.
20. Pravakar Sahoo and Abhirup Bhunia (2014), 'BCIM Corridor a Game Changer for South Asian Trade', *East Asia Forum*, 18 July, accessed 25 October 2015. http://www.eastasiaforum.org/2014/07/18/bcim-corri dor-a-game-changer-for-south-asian-trade/.
21. Godement, 'One Belt, One Road'', p. 3.
22. Xinhua (2015), 'Belt & Road Initiative Drives Economic Rejuvenation of SCO Countries', *China Daily.* 12 December, accessed 10 January 2015. http://www.chinadaily.com.cn/business/2015-12/12/content_ 22695699_2.htm.
23. CCTV (2016), 'First Batch of 40 bln yuan Assigned to Belt & Road Projects', *CCTV English.* 4 January, accessed 10 January 2016. http:// english.cntv.cn/2016/01/04/VIDE1451878202655671.shtml.

24. The Economist (2015), 'Dark Corridor', *The Economist*, 4 June, accessed 23 October 2015. http://www.economist.com/news/asia/21653657-con flict-balochistan-must-be-resolved-trade-corridor-between-pakistan-and-china-bring.

25. China Digital Times (2014), 'Amid Mounting Criticism in Kazakhstan, Beijing and Astana Seal New Deals – Marat Yermukanov', *China Digital Times*, 23 December, accessed 26 December 2015. http://chinadigital times.net/2007/01/amid-mounting-criticism-in-kazakhstan-beijing-and-astana-seal-new-deals-marat-yermukanov/.

26. B. Mariani (2013), *China's Role and Interests in Central Asia* (Saferworld Briefing, Saferworld), pp. 3–5.

27. Xinhuanet (2013), 'Kunming Terrorist Attack Suspects Captured', *Xinhuanet*, 3 March, accessed 16 July 2015. http://news.xinhuanet. com/english/china/2014-03/03/c_133157281.htm.

28. Reuters (2013), 'China Suspects Tiananmen Crash a Suicide Attack-Sources', *Reuters*. 29 October, accessed 16 July 2015. http://www.reu ters.com/article/2013/10/29/us-china-tiananmen-idUSBRE99S02R20131029.

29. Reuters (2016), 'Xinjiang Cotton at Crossroads of China's New Silk Road', *American Journal of Transportation,* 12 January, accessed 16 January 2016. https://www.ajot.com/news/xinjiang-cotton-at-crossroads-of-chinas-new-silk-road.

30. Ibid.

31. Joshua Kucera (2015), 'Report: Central Asia Key Site for Chinese Military Training', *Eurasianet*, 8 December, accessed 15 January 2015. http://www.eurasianet.org/node/76481.

32. J. C. Alden and D. Large (2015), 'On Becoming a Norms Maker: Chinese Foreign Policy, Norms Evolution and the Challenges of Security in Africa', *The China Quarterly*, 221, pp. 123–142.

33. Jane Perlez and Neil MacFarquhar (2015), '9 Foreigners Killed in Mali Are Identified', *New York Times*, 21 November accessed 13 January 2015. http://www.nytimes.com/2015/11/22/world/asia/3-chinese-execu tives-killed-in-mali-attack-company-says.html.

34. Alden and Large, 'On Becoming a Norms Maker", p. 124.

35. J. C. Alden (2014), 'Seeking Security in Africa: China's Evolving Approach to The African Peace and Security Architecture', *Norwegian Peacebuilding Resource Centre Report*, pp. 1–2.

36. DIRCO; MOFA (2015), 'Declaration of the Johannesburg Summit of the Forum in China-Africa Relations', *Declaration of the Johannesburg Summit of the Forum in China-Africa Relations.* Johannesburg, p. 10.

37. Xinhuanet (2015), 'Spotlight: China's Peacekeeping Contribution to UN Missions in Africa Shows Growing Sense of Responsibility', *Xinhuanet*, 27

March 27, accessed 20 October 2015. http://news.xinhuanet.com/eng lish/2015-03/27/c_134104184.htm.

38. Global Times (2015), 'China's 25-Year Engagement in Overseas Peacekeeping Missions', *Global Times*, 1 August, accessed 20 October 2015. http://www.globaltimes.cn/content/934954.shtml.

39. Alden, 'Seeking Security in Africa', pp. 5–6.

40. Ibid.

41. Ministry of Foreign Affairs of the People's Republic of China (2015), 'Chinese Mission to the African Union Holds a Grand Opening Ceremony', *Foreign Ministry of the People's Republic of China*, 8 May, accessed 25 October 2015. http://www.fmprc.gov.cn/mfa_eng/wjbxw/ t1263538.shtml.

42. The China Story (2014), 'Li Keqiang's "461 Framework" for the China-Africa Strategic Partnership', *The China Story*, 25 June, accessed 1 September 2015. https://www.thechinastory.org/dossier/li-keqiangs-461-framework-for-the-china-africa-strategic-partnership/.

43. South African Broadcasting Corporation (2015), 'AU, China Sign Transport Infrastructure Deal', *SABC*, 27 January, accessed 2 September 2015. http:// www.sabc.co.za/news/a/38ad5d004716ed3db484b4686e648436/AU,-China-sign-transport-infrastructure-deal-20152701.

44. Reuters (2014), 'China Railway Construction Wins $12 Billion Nigeria Deal: Xinhua', *Reuters*. 20 November, accessed 2 September 2015. http://www.reuters.com/article/2014/11/20/us-china-railway-construc tion-nigeria-idUSKCN0J40C420141120.

Rudolf du Plessis is a Researcher at the South African Institute of International Affairs (SAIIA) Economic Diplomacy Programme. He holds a degree in International Relations from the University of Pretoria and a Masters in China Studies from Nanjing University.

CHAPTER 17

China, Africa and the Arms Trade Treaty

Bernardo Mariani and Elizabeth Kirkham

INTRODUCTION

Through financial assistance and development projects, China is playing a positive role in conflict-affected and fragile environments in Africa. China has also been praised for playing a progressive diplomatic role, for example, because of its mediation efforts following the outbreak of conflict in South Sudan in December 2013, as well as its provision of peacekeepers to a variety of conflict-affected countries. However, one of the areas where China is sometimes perceived to play a more ambiguous role is with regard to arms transfers.

Africa is particularly affected by the uncontrolled flow of arms. While illicit trafficking and the re-circulation of arms within Africa is a major challenge for African governments to address, reducing additional transfers of arms and ammunition from external suppliers into conflict-affected regions and human rights crisis zones in Africa is nevertheless a critical element in preventing conflict and promoting peace on the continent. Achieving this will require better and more transparent regulation of the international arms trade by producers and exporters of arms based on responsibility and restraint.

B. Mariani (✉)
Head of China Programme, Saferworld, London, United Kingdom
e-mail: bmariani@saferworld.org.uk

E. Kirkham
Small Arms & Transfer Controls Adviser, Saferworld, London, United Kingdom
e-mail: general@saferworld.org.uk

© The Author(s) 2018
C. Alden et al. (eds.), *China and Africa*,
DOI 10.1007/978-3-319-52893-9_17

On 24 December 2014 the Arms Trade Treaty (ATT), the first international instrument establishing legally binding obligations for the trade in conventional arms, ammunition, parts and components, came into force. Starting out as an NGO campaign for an 'International Code of Conduct on Arms Transfers in the mid-1990s, the international movement received a boost in 1997 when a group of Nobel Peace laureates called for an International Code. But it was not until 2006 that the proposal for an ATT was first addressed in the United Nations when the UN General Assembly adopted resolution 61/89 'Towards an Arms Trade Treaty: establishing common international standards for the import, export and transfer of conventional arms'. After six years of preparatory work, negotiations were held at two Diplomatic Conferences in 2012 and 2013, both of which could not achieve consensus for the adoption of the Treaty's text. However, political support for a final agreement grew and at the end only three states decided to block consensus: Iran, North Korea and Syria. The final draft text of the Treaty was then set before the UN General Assembly and adopted on 2 April 2013 by a vote of 154 to 3, with 23 abstentions.[1] At the time of writing, 80 states have ratified the ATT, and a further 50 states have signed but not ratified it.[2]

Over the past two decades, proponents and supporters of the ATT initiative have shown different motivations and interests in promoting the ATT. Civil society organisations, such as Amnesty International and the Control Arms coalition, have sought to extend the application of human security principles, especially norms based on human rights and international humanitarian law (IHL), in the field of arms transfer controls and to oblige states to adhere to these principles in their arms transfer activities. In this regard, the Treaty built on previous efforts in the field of 'humanitarian arms control' – in particular the Ottawa Treaty banning anti-personnel mines. African and Latin American states, which had suffered for many years from the irresponsible and illicit trade in conventional arms, saw their future security and prosperity as being supported by the ATT and voted at the UN overwhelmingly and consistently in support of the Treaty. A key motivation for these countries was to curb the proliferation of conventional arms, especially small arms and light weapons (SALW) within their territories. For their part, when in the mid-2000s European Union member states decided to support the ATT initiative they had been committed to applying human security principles to arms export controls since the late 1990s. EU member states therefore saw the ATT as an opportunity to universalise the standards they had adopted and also to create a 'level playing field' on which their defence industries could compete internationally.

The enshrinement of the ATT into international law is a major stepping stone towards the reduction of irresponsible arms transfers that fuel instability, corruption and human rights violations in Africa, as well as in other conflict-affected regions of the world. The Treaty obliges state parties to abide by a common set of criteria for the regulation of the international trade in arms (from battle tanks and warships, to missiles and SALW), ammunition, weapons parts and components. With effective implementation, the ATT will help to protect civilians by limiting the flow of arms to terrorists, rebel forces and other problematic non-state actors (NSAs), as well as to irresponsible governments, all of whom would use these arms to exacerbate armed conflicts and/or commit atrocities. The ATT includes explicit prohibitions of arms transfer authorisations if states have knowledge that the arms would be used to perpetrate genocide, crimes against humanity, grave breaches of the Geneva Conventions, attacks against civilians, or other war crimes.[3] Where the prohibitions do not apply, States Parties are obliged to assess whether there is an over-riding risk that a proposed arms transfer will be used for or contribute to committing serious violations of international human rights or humanitarian law; contravening conventions relating to terrorism and organised crime; or facilitating gender-based violence or violence against women and children. If so, the arms must not be transferred.[4]

China's position towards the ATT and its content shifted significantly over the span of the negotiations, from initial suspicion, if not rejection, of the initiative mainly due to state security concerns, to gradual acceptance. Heeding the call from numerous African states, China consented to the inclusion of SALW in the scope of the Treaty; and it acquiesced to the exclusion of a ban on the transfer of weapons to NSAs, even though preventing transfers to NSAs is one of its chief concerns and a stated principle in its own national arms export control policy. It also accepted that human security principles have a place in conventional arms control and dropped its opposition to the inclusion of human rights and IHL criteria in the treaty. After the April 2013 UN vote, especially in the months leading up to the Treaty's entry-into-force, governments and non-government organisations around the world waited with keen interest the outcome of an internal inter-agency analysis of the Treaty text, which was co-ordinated by the Chinese Ministry of Foreign Affairs (MFA), in the hope that China would cement its position as an ATT supporter and interlocutor by signing the Treaty. At the end, however, China decided against signing the Treaty before its entry into force.[5]

This chapter reflects on China's growing arms trade, especially with Africa and the evolution of China's arms export controls; it proceeds to examine China's engagement with the international ATT process and its policy shift in the years leading up to the final vote on the ATT; it then discusses the procedural, diplomatic, commercial, institutional and security factors that influenced China's decision not to sign the ATT; finally, it outlines the prospects for and factors shaping future Chinese engagement with the ATT and the key issues for continued debate with China on responsible arms transfer controls.

China's Growing Arms Trade

According to the Stockholm International Peace Research Institute (SIPRI), the volume of Chinese major conventional arms (including tanks, aircraft, radar, artillery, rockets, missiles and ships)[6] sales soared by 143% between 2005 and 2014.[7] In the 2010–2014 period, China was the world's third largest exporter of major conventional arms, behind the USA and Russia and slightly in front of Germany and France.[8] During 2010–2014, African arms imports increased by 45% compared to the previous 5-year period. It is worth highlighting a few aspects regarding the available data on Africa's arms imports and China's arms exports upward trends.

Firstly, no matter how accurate, arms export data needs to be taken with caution as it lends itself to be interpreted differently depending on the emphasis placed on or sought from certain data. Increasing arms imports in Africa have to be put in the context of the welcome involvement of certain countries, such as Uganda, Ghana and Kenya, in peacekeeping operations mandated by the African Union and the UN, which has also contributed to an increased demand for arms. Moreover, while some African countries used rising oil revenues to buy weapons, it is likely that the sharp drop in the price of oil during the past two years will decrease, at least in the short term, their ability to continue heightened defence spending. From other countries, however, for example, Cameroon and Nigeria that are fighting the rebel group Boko Haram, the demand for weapons is likely to remain high. Moreover, despite efforts at mapping policies and practices related to SALW transfers, reliable data on SALW frequently remains patchy.

Governmental transparency in international transfers of SALW varies considerably across the globe and it remains inferior to the transparency levels of other types of conventional arms particularly because the principal international transparency mechanism of the past two decades – the UN Register of Conventional Arms – encourages, but does not require, states to provide information on SALW imports and exports. China, one of the most significant suppliers of SALW,[9] 'is also among the least transparent'.[10] This is particularly problematic in relation to Africa where SALW are the weapons of choice and cause the most instability and human suffering across the continent.

At around 5% of the global arms trade, China still lags well behind the leading exporters (the USA and Russia) who account respectively for 31% and 27% of worldwide arms exports.[11] A significant proportion of Chinese arms go to neighbouring countries. For example, between 2010 and 2014, the bulk of Chinese arms exports (over 68%) went to Pakistan, which bought 41% of China's arms exports, including 50 JF-17 fighter jets, Bangladesh and Myanmar, which together totalled 28% of China's arms exports.[12]

But China is also one of the leading exporters of arms to Africa, a continent where it continues to build economic, diplomatic and political influence. Between 2010 and 2014, China exported major conventional arms to 18 African states.[13] Notable sales included three frigates to Algeria and a number of unmanned aerial vehicles to Nigeria while China also found markets in Egypt and Morocco, all of which have larger defence budgets than most other African countries. There are signs of China wanting to provide more sophisticated military equipment and services to African countries. For example, in October 2015 there were reports that International Aero Development Corporation, a subsidiary of Aviation Industry Corporation of China, had ambitious expansion plans in Africa aimed at promoting sales and maintenance for Chinese-made aircraft. This included setting up an aviation training centre in South Africa, two regional marketing offices, two maintenance and support centres in Tanzania and the Republic of Congo, and three spare-parts warehouses in Kenya, Zimbabwe and the Congo.[14]

However, numerous buyers of Chinese weapons are states with a low technological base and limited military professionalism that cannot afford very advanced weapons systems, but are willing to acquire low technology type of equipment such as SALW, especially inexpensive assault rifles and ammunition. During 2006–2010, African states accounted for the largest share of military SALW that were exported by China to at least 46 countries around the world.[15] Despite reassurances by the Chinese authorities that China takes a cautious approach to arms exports and is committed to the implementation of agreements aimed at tackling the illicit trade in SALW, some Chinese arms transfers to Africa are highly problematic and have raised concerns because of their potential negative impact on peace, security and stability. Some of the African recipients of Chinese arms are regimes, such as Sudan and Zimbabwe that other leading producers and exporters do not feel comfortable to deal with.

Others are countries in conflict. For example, in 2014 China was the only leading arms exporter to sell weapons to South Sudan, a country engulfed in civil war. In July 2014, it was reported that the North Industries Group Corporation (Norinco), China's biggest arms manufacturer, had shipped a consignment of weapons, including anti-tank missiles, grenade launchers, assault rifles, machine guns and ammunition worth $38 million, to South Sudan via the Kenyan port of Mombasa.[16] There is ample evidence that armed NSAs in sub-Saharan Africa are using SALW made in China. While such arms may have been stolen from government holdings or taken from government forces in battle, it appears that in many cases African governments that had legally imported SALW from China had then re-transferred them to NSAs.[17] The problem is compounded by the secrecy surrounding China's SALW exports. There is no official Chinese data on the size and destination of Chinese SALW exports, which has already suggested that 'China is probably the country with the largest quantity of undocumented exports'[18] and 'one of the least transparent arms exporters'.[19]

Despite the controversy and criticism surrounding some Chinese arms transfers, China is by no means alone in supplying arms to Africa. There are plenty of other countries, including several Western European nations, Russia, Belarus, Ukraine and others[20] that see arms exports as a major foreign policy and revenue-generating tool and are willing to supply military hardware to a range of countries in the continent. Weapons from such countries carry the same potential risk of exacerbating existing tensions, fuelling conflicts and undermining efforts to contribute to peace, stability and development in Africa. Indeed between 2010 and 2014, Russia sold the largest amount of arms to African countries, mainly to Algeria, while France's sales to Morocco made it the second-largest arms dealer to the continent.[21]

China's Arms Export Controls Norms and Policy

Over the past 20 years, China's arms export control policies towards weapons of mass destruction and conventional arms have experienced drastic changes and improvements.[22] From being viewed as a proliferator in the 1990s and early 2000s, China has put in place a comprehensive transfer controls system based in law and official regulations. As China has become more engaged abroad, more appreciative of the risks of proliferation and more willing to improve its international standing, it has gradually adopted many of the international export control standards, including: a registration and licensing system; control lists of equipment, materials, and technologies; end-user and end-use certifications; catch-all principles; customs supervision; and punishments and penalties for export control violations.[23]

The normative framework for transfer controls on sensitive goods in China is based on four laws, five administrative regulations and one control list.[24] The Foreign Trade Law, which was promulgated in 1994 and then revised in 2004, provides the state with the explicit power to regulate imports and exports. Under Articles 16 and 17, for example, the state can restrict or prohibit the import and export of goods for reasons of 'safeguarding national security and public interests' and 'under the international treaties or agreements signed or acceded to by the People's Republic of China'; Article 18 requires the creation of control lists; and Article 19 provides for licensing authority of items with 'special requirements'. The Customs Law establishes the legal basis of China's system of customs inspection and verification for import and export trade controls, and has provided the foundation to pursue a further legal basis for export controls and specifically for export control enforcement, including the Administrative Punishments Law and the 2001 Amendments to the Criminal Law.[25]

Additionally, there are several regulations that further formalise and legalise China's export control system. In particular, the *Regulations of the People's Republic of China on the Administration of Arms Exports*, established in 1997 and its subsequent 2002 amendment, the *Administrative List of Export of Military Products*, specifically address transfers of conventional arms. They cover the scope and parameters of military items, decision making structures and management procedures for the export control of conventional arms. The Regulations set out the three principles guiding decision making on Chinese arms transfers:

- the self-defence capabilities of recipient states;
- the arms' impact on regional and world peace, security and stability; and
- whether they could interfere with the internal affairs of the recipient country.

In addition to these three principles, Chinese experts have also pointed out that the Chinese government's risk assessment is also based on five policy guidelines[26]:

- international obligations and commitments to other countries;
- compliance with international non-proliferation efforts and China's foreign policy;
- whether the recipient country is under a UN arms embargo;
- whether the recipient country supports terrorist activities or has contact with terrorist groups; and
- whether the recipient country has an effective export control system.

Finally, Chinese national policy is that arms and military equipment are only exported to states; transfers to NSAs are prohibited. For the Chinese government, arms transfers to NSAs are seen as constituting interference in the internal affairs of another state, while arms transfers to a government are not.

The Chinese government and the military have strong centralised controls over arms exports. There are currently only 12 state-owned companies in China that are allowed to engage in the conventional arms trade.[27] The State Administration of Science, Technology and Industry for National Defense (SASTIND) is the main licensing body in charge of administering conventional arms export controls. Before issuing an export licence, SASTIND consults with the General Armament Department of the People's Liberation Army (PLA) and with the MFA. An ad hoc inter-agency consultation mechanism was also established in 2004 to manage transactions that draw significant internal disagreements. The mechanism allows for all of the key agencies involved to voice their concerns and to submit their deliberations to the State Council and the Central Military Commission for further review and final adjudication.[28]

However, the interpretation and application of China's arms export control principles has been a source of controversy with other countries who have argued that they are too vague and broad and do not specify criteria for a risk assessment process to determine whether an arms transfer should proceed. Moreover, there are different views and opinions between China and other leading producers and exporters of conventional arms concerning the legitimacy and conditions under which arms transfers should be authorised or not. There is, in particular, the challenge of incorporating human rights and humanitarian provisions into Chinese law and practice; at the same time there is a lack of clarity and consensus in the international discourse as regards what actually constitutes a 'legal' transfer on the one hand and an 'illicit' transfer on the other. High-profile, controversial cases in recent years include China's export of arms to Zimbabwe in 2008 and the more recent arms exports to South Sudan. China is on the record defending its decisions on the basis that it does not interfere in the internal affairs of other states; however, a decision to supply arms to a government where authority is highly contested and/or tensions are extremely high is frequently seen by other countries in a very different light.[29] Crucially, the process of creating the ATT was an opportunity to bridge this gap, to get a clearer sense of what is, and is not, internationally acceptable and to try to raise common standards in the field of conventional arms exports.

China in the ATT Negotiations

At the beginning of the ATT process (2006–2010), the Chinese government had deep reservations about the necessity and appropriateness of an international treaty regulating the arms trade and tended to emphasise the security concerns of arms exporters and importers. In explaining China's reservation about supporting the 2006 draft resolution that requested the UN Secretary General to seek the views of Member States on the feasibility, scope and draft parameters of a potential treaty,[30] the Chinese delegation declared that

> Legal arms trade is related to the security, defence need[s] and economic interest[s] of every country. How to conduct this kind of trade should be decided by arms exporters and importers. Whether it is necessary to establish shared rules or international laws to regulate the arms trade is very complicated and sensitive.[31]

Later that year, while 153 states voted in favour of a resolution towards an ATT, China abstained, along with 23 other states (including Russia and India); the USA was the only state to vote against the resolution. In 2008, China abstained from voting on UN draft resolution L.39 (2008), 'Towards an Arms Trade Treaty: Establishing Common International Standards for the Import, Export and Transfer of Conventional Arms', pointing to differences between the resolution and a report by a UN Group of Government Experts earlier that year, which had been reached by consensus. The Chinese delegation also expressed concerns that the ATT process would weaken the authority and function of the moribund Conference on Disarmament as the only multilateral arms control negotiation institution.[32] China raised this concern throughout the ATT negotiation process, and it eventually became one of the reasons mentioned by China as to why it abstained from the final vote.

Between 2010 and 2012, as it saw a growing number of supporters of the treaty, especially from Africa, China gradually warmed up to the ATT and started to place emphasis of the need to agree an ATT through a very gradual process. At the General Debate of the 65th and 66th Sessions of the United Nations General Assembly (UNGA), Chinese Ambassador Wang Qun stated: 'The negotiation of [the] Arms Trade Treaty should proceed step by step and in an open, transparent and consensual manner'.[33] Beginning in 2012, China dropped the term 'step by step', signalling that it shared the view that the ATT was coming to its final phase of negotiation and agreement. China also made important concessions on substantive issues related to the scope and criteria of the treaty.

At the beginning of the UN process, China had insisted that the scope of the treaty should conform to the seven major categories of weapons under the UN Register of Conventional Arms and opposed the inclusion of SALW and ammunition. In 2010, the Chinese Ambassador at the UN emphasised that only reducing poverty and developing a nation's economy could help 'eliminate the breeding ground for illicit transfer of SALW from its root'[34] suggesting that in the long term – the solution lies in development, not in regulating the arms trade. But in later statements, emphasis on economic development was set aside and the focus began to centre solely on regulating the arms trade itself. China's position changed from 'sharing the view that the international community should take proper measures to regulate relevant arms trade and combat illicit arms trafficking'[35]; to 'subscribing itself to international efforts to adopt proper measures to regulate relevant arms trade and combat illicit arms trafficking'.[36] At the July 2012 diplomatic conference, China did not insist on the exclusion of SALW from the scope of the treaty. Its position became: 'the scope of ATT should be defined properly by covering as a priority those conventional arms that have been clearly defined internationally and accepted universally'.[37] The new position gave much more flexibility on the final acceptable scope of weapons to be covered by the ATT. It is widely acknowledged that this shift was influenced, in part, by China's close relations with a significant number of developing countries and the pressure exerted by African states in ensuring that SALW should be included within the scope of the ATT.

As to the Treaty's criteria, China gradually softened its opposition to the inclusion of human rights and IHL in the draft treaty text. After abstaining from previous ATT resolutions, in December 2012 China voted in favour of the resolution calling for a final negotiating conference in 2013 and did not raise any specific objections or reservations to the draft text that was discussed in the diplomatic conferences in 2012 and 2013, which included human rights and humanitarian law criteria. Whatever concerns China still had, it did not want to defend them at any cost against the will of the majority of UN member states.

However, China was willing to defy the majority, and even block consensus if necessary on what became its two 'red lines'. These were: preventing the inclusion of a regional integration organisation (RIO) clause, which would have allowed regional organisations to become formal parties to the treaty, and the exclusion of any language in the Treaty covering military gifts. With regard to the RIO clause, China's main concern was to block the EU from becoming a party to the ATT as long as it maintained an arms embargo on China. On the other hand, the gifts issue concerns the fact that gifts and donations are subject to PLA's procedures which are separate from national arms export controls. Gifts are regarded as an element of military assistance, which is itself part of wider bilateral aid relations, friendship and solidarity with other developing states. The PLA insisted that military aid is therefore not a trade matter to be regulated through an international agreement and such area should be excluded from the treaty. It has been pointed out that by showing flexibility on certain aspects related to the scope and criteria of the Treaty, China was able to protect its red lines despite strong opposition from the EU and others. 'China's opposition to a RIO clause carried more weight than the EU's support and the clause was excluded from the ATT text'.[38] Whether the treaty applies only to sales or also to gifts was left deliberately ambiguous, allowing China to argue that it interprets the Treaty as covering only commercial activities and not gifts.

FACTORS INFLUENCING CHINA'S DECISION NOT TO SIGN THE ATT

There are a number of possible explanations for China not signing the ATT. While it is difficult to say exactly what considerations lay behind this decision, the reasons are likely to be complex and based on a variety of factors and influences – both domestic and international – and shaped, in part, by Africa's response to the ATT's adoption in 2013.

In its after-vote statement at the Diplomatic Conference in April 2013, China's main reason for abstention was the conclusion of the treaty by non-consensual means, rather than the substance of the Treaty itself. As explained by Foreign Ministry Spokesperson Hong Lei 'avoiding consensus may lead to wider differences and even confrontation. Neither is helpful for the effectiveness and universality of the treaty'.[39] This consideration would also have weighed heavily upon China's decision not to sign the Treaty before its entry into force, both because of the potential negative effect of a lack of consensus on effective implementation of the treaty, and because of the possibility of majority voting displacing consensus as the norm for passing agreements in multilateral arms control negotiations. However, there is some precedent for China to remain engaged in an international treaty process without consensus. In 1996, when the negotiation of the Comprehensive Nuclear Test Ban Treaty (CTBT) was held up by one state, India, but favoured by all other states, Australia took the draft text to the UN General Assembly, where it received a clear majority of votes. China was one of 158 states that voted in favour of a UNGA resolution on the adoption of the CTBT.

Another explanation appears to rest with China's emergence in recent years as a major arms exporter, with a growing share of the global arms market. Chinese arms companies will certainly be concerned to maintain this position and may have been nervous of placing their activities under the additional international scrutiny that might have followed any decision to sign, let alone ratify, the ATT and of any restrictions to their arms trade that may have emanated as a result of it. Like with all other producers and exporters of arms, the factors influencing China's arms exports also include commercial considerations. At a time when there are clear signs of a slowdown in the Chinese economy, making sustained export earnings from arms sales is an important consideration for the government and its state-owned enterprises.

Thirdly, although China has made progress in developing and updating its export controls and officials claim that China's arms exports are already well regulated and thus fulfil the basic requirements of state responsibility under the ATT, the normative basis of China's controls remains limited in comparison to the criteria set out in the ATT. The human rights and IHL provisions of the ATT would have posed a normative challenge for the Chinese government, if it had signed the Treaty[40] and even more so in case of ratification. China does not have legal or policy requirements for arms exports to be assessed against human rights criteria; nor does it include humanitarian considerations such as war crimes or crimes against humanity. Moreover, there is no specific requirement in Chinese export control regulations to consider whether an arms transfer could fuel trans-national organised crime, gender-based violence or violence against women and children. So while its arms transfers are regulated, they do not currently meet the standard set out in the ATT, which could have been a factor in the decision not to sign the ATT.

Fourthly, although the swift signature of the ATT by the USA, the world's largest arms exporter, must have given the Chinese authorities pause for thought, China's decision not to sign the ATT may well have been shaped by the reluctance of other global and regional powers to support the Treaty. In particular, the importance of China's relationship with Russia, the second biggest player in the global arms trade, which in 2010–2014 also accounted for 61% of Chinese arms imports,[41] may have played a role in China's final decision. Throughout the UN ATT negotiation process, Russia's position was hardly ever constructive. It raised several substantive objections to the draft treaty text and its signature was never seriously anticipated. India's stance may also have contributed to shift China's position. Its potential support for the Treaty was compromised by a few specific sticking points on issues such as how defence cooperation agreements were addressed in the Treaty and the absence of a ban on transfers to NSAs, which meant that India too was never on any list of 'likely signatories'.

Finally, China was never a key target for any concerted lobbying by African states seeking to promote the ATT and to ensure that China signs it. There has always been a tension in the Sino-African relationship between, on the one hand, overt criticism of China's arms export controls with calls for restraint and, on the other, deep satisfaction with the status quo in the arms trade relationship. The Chinese government has often had to weigh up the demands from clients such as Sudan for ongoing supplies of weapons, against the demands of other African states for tougher measures on arms regulation (such as Nigeria and Mali, which have both signed and ratified the treaty). But, generally speaking, from an African perspective, China is seen as a country that is trustworthy, respectful of sovereignty and which does not interfere. China's weapons are cheap, effective and easy to operate, and suitable for the military capabilities of many African states; its arms sales come without critical strings, which is also for many African governments a major advantage. Moreover, some African states are dissatisfied with Western countries' behaviour, including their arms sales, and this anti-Western sentiment pushes them towards China. No African country is willing to undermine its military and security cooperation with China.

Africa's response to the ATT since its adoption has not been as overwhelmingly positive as might have been expected – given that to date (as of February 2016), out of 54 states only just over two-thirds (37) have signed and exactly one-third (18) have ratified or acceded to the Treaty. While the pace of signature and ratification of the ATT has been quite fast in Western Africa, elsewhere across the continent it has been very disappointing, particularly in the Eastern Africa region. At the time of writing, Djibouti remains the only country in East Africa to have signed the ATT. No other country has ratified or acceded to the Treaty despite Kenya having played a leadership role during the negotiation process at the United Nations. The very slow pace of signature and ratification in Africa did not pass unnoticed in China and may also have been a contributing factor in China's decision not to sign the ATT.

Factors Shaping Future Chinese Engagement with the ATT

The fact that China has not signed the ATT does not mean that its potential to engage with the Treaty has ended.[42] Now that the ATT has come into force, several factors, both external and internal, will shape how China engages.

The first is strategic, in terms of which other states have signed and ratified. Traditionally, the USA's position on any arms control agreement has wielded significant influence over Chinese decisions and it is likely that it will remain a key factor in shaping Chinese engagement. The Chinese government has watched closely, albeit with scepticism, how the USA slowly changed its position towards the ATT. There was interest among the Chinese press towards Secretary of State John Kerry's signing of the ATT in September 2013, although some media outlets were also quick to note that the treaty was unlikely to be ratified by the US Senate, and therefore would not lead to any practical policy changes that would affect US arms sales.[43] While it is true that there is little prospect of the US government ratifying the ATT any time soon, it should also be noted that a new US Presidential Directive, issued in January 2014, includes language of human rights and IHL, regional stability and peaceful conflict resolution, counterterrorism and transnational organised crime – all key elements of the ATT.

Another factor relates to China's rapidly growing interest in stable international, regional and national environments. More and more, Chinese personnel and businesses are at direct risk of physical and commercial harm through operating in zones of insecurity. Ready access to arms, including Chinese-made weapons, by competing groups in these contexts increases the risks faced by these Chinese actors. The same applies to Chinese peacekeepers, who increasingly find themselves in harm's way from armed groups. China therefore has ever more interest in supporting an international regime that prevents international transfers of arms that are not subject to effective control by authorised and responsible actors, both by acceding to and observing the Treaty in its own right and encouraging others to join as well and implement it robustly.

It is possible that domestic security concerns might compel China to seek tighter arms trade regulations, especially as this relates to less sophisticated weapons. In recent years China has experienced a growing threat from terrorist groups operating within its borders. As a result, the question of how to prevent such groups gaining access to weaponry is an important concern for China. The ATT (under Article 7.1.b.iii and Article 7.3) addresses exactly this question, and its full implementation by States Parties will contribute to the strengthening of international safeguards against support for, and arming of, terrorist groups. Clearly, the more states that join the ATT and implement the provisions of Article 7, the greater the impact will be.[44]

There are, however, competing definitions of the national interest and institutional imbalances in play, which will shape the Chinese decision to engage with the ATT process and will impact upon the likelihood, or otherwise, of China acceding to the Treaty in the future. Specifically, internal power dynamics inside China's military-defence establishment, and between this establishment and China's MFA, will be significant. The MFA appeared to be in favour of China signing the ATT after the Treaty was adopted by the UN General Assembly, while the PLA, which has close ties to the state-owned corporations which are licensed to export conventional weapons, was more sceptical. While corporations and the military authorities benefit economically from arms sales and are therefore unlikely to be in favour of any internationally-mandated restrictions on them, the MFA traditionally seeks to avert China's arms sales to conflict areas for the potential harm that such actions could have on China's broader reputation and the ensuing international pressures. However, the MFA often finds itself not quite the equal in making these decisions, with business interests and economic concerns enabling corporations and the military to have the final say.[45]

Another factor relates to China's military modernisation process. There are on-going efforts to grow and increase the technological sophistication of the Chinese defence industrial base in pursuit of military modernisation, through processes of liberalisation and access to private capital. In this, being seen as a responsible exporter may increase the possibility of better access to Western technology – although as long as the USA and EU embargoes remain in place, this is problematic. One reason the Chinese government may wish to engage with the ATT, then, is to improve its reputation as an arms exporter and open up dialogue about its access to military technologies and the arms market.

Key Issues for Continued Debate on Responsible Arms Transfer Controls

There are a number of controversial arms transfer issues on which continuing dialogue with China would be beneficial. Chief among these is the inclusion of human security principles into arms transfer controls, especially the challenge of incorporating human rights and humanitarian provisions into Chinese law, regulations and practice; efforts to pursue agreement as to what constitutes an 'illicit' transfer would also be welcome.

For many proponents of the ATT within governmental and non-governmental communities, human rights and humanitarian law criteria form the basis of the legitimacy of arms transfers. As envisaged by the ATT proponents, a transfer is legitimate in the terms of the ATT if it is regulated by the state in line with human rights and humanitarian standards as set out under international law, including the UN Charter, global human rights treaties and customary law. However, this interpretation is not fully shared by China and other states, such as Russia, India and Pakistan, none of which have signed the ATT. These countries argue that human rights and humanitarian criteria are subjective and liable to political manipulation. But others would retort that these principles are costly and inconvenient for them. As such, further policy dialogue and diplomatic work is required in order to gain wider acceptance of the way that the universal legal imperatives of human rights and humanitarian criteria should apply to arms transfers.

China has deep concerns with regard to arms transfers to NSAs, which it considers as illicit by definition. The question of arms sales to Taiwan, seen by China as a NSA, is key among such concerns. But there is also the concern related to another category of NSAs, that is, non-state armed groups who threaten the security and stability of countries and regions, including Africa, where China is engaged. During the ATT negotiations there was deep disagreement between states over the legitimacy of transfers to NSAs. A number of states, including China, Russia and India, proposed the inclusion in the ATT of language calling for prohibition on arms transfers to NSAs, but that clashed against one of the 'red lines' of the US government, which adamantly opposed such a ban as it would 'unduly interfere with our ability to...transfer arms in support of our national security and foreign policy interests'.[46] Eventually the ATT contained no clause banning transfers to NSAs, much to the disappointment of China and other states. The restrictions of the ATT are based on the end-use to which controlled equipment will likely be put, not on the identity of the end-user (be it a state or a NSA).

However, while the ATT does not specifically ban transfers to NSAs, it is clear that, if properly implemented, it would prevent the vast majority of arms transfers to NSAs. Under Articles 6 and 7, which set out the prohibitions and the criteria for national risk assessment, if there is an 'overriding risk' that a proposed transfer could be used to 'commit or facilitate a serious violation of international humanitarian law', the exporting state is obliged not to authorise it – regardless of whether the proposed recipient is a state or a NSA. In this way, the existing provisions of the treaty could be operationalised to protect against some of the risks posed by NSAs. The ATT provisions are a 'floor, not a ceiling'. Therefore states are free to implement a more restrictive policy and have a ban on transfers to

NSAs in addition to a national control system that assessed the risks set out in Articles 6 and 7. Were it to accede to the ATT, the Chinese government would be free to maintain its ban on transfers to NSAs.

As noted above, the fact remains that even if transferred to states, weapons from China, as well as other countries, end up in the illicit market or in the hands of NSAs, or are being used in violations of international obligations, international humanitarian and human rights law. This is particularly obvious in the case of Sudan. There is no evidence to suggest that the Chinese government has knowingly or deliberately transferred weapons to NSAs in the form of militias, armed civilians or rebel groups operating within Sudan. Yet government-backed militia groups operating in Darfur are known to have used Chinese-made weaponry and ammunition, including some that has been manufactured since the 2004 embargo on arms transfers to Darfur.[47] China has a system of end-user certification in which companies have to provide evidence that the end-user is reliable and that the equipment will not be transferred to a third party. But, in practice, the Chinese national authorities find it difficult, or are not willing, to undertake a thorough prior risk assessment of Chinese arms transfers and then monitor the use of the exported weapons, including asking questions to the recipient governments as to their whereabouts. While the treatment of diversion in the ATT is weaker than that of other criteria,[48] states parties throughout the arms transfer chain are all required to take measures to prevent diversion. This is reinforced by the obligation upon states parties not to transfer weapons if they have knowledge at the time of authorisation that the arms would be used to commit genocide, crimes against humanity or war crimes, or if its risk assessment demonstrates an overriding risk that the weapons could be used to commit or facilitate serious violations of IHL or international human rights law. The internal logic of the ATT is such weapons that are likely to be diverted and used for proscribed purposes should not be transferred. These issues could provide the basis for further discussion with the Chinese authorities on strengthening the efficacy of end-use verification and risk assessment.

CONCLUSIONS

The ATT has the potential to profoundly impact upon the international trade in conventional arms. If implemented to its fullest extent, it will ultimately benefit the safety and security of people in China, Africa and everywhere else in the world. At a minimum, and in the short term, the

ATT will shape the international discourse on conventional arms transfers; indeed this is already happening through both formal and informal channels that are bringing governments and civil society experts together to discuss ATT ratification and implementation issues. In the longer term the ATT has the potential to shape the arms transfer policies and practices of all states by creating an environment whereby the principles enshrined by the Treaty are widely accepted and adhered to.

There is a variety of interests and concerns within China in relation to the arms trade and its regulation. As such, there are choices for the Chinese government to make, which may lead in different directions in terms of conventional arms control, including but not limited to the decision to remain constructively engaged in the ATT process. But, as China's global status, economic influence and commensurate responsibilities grow, competing definitions of national economic and political interest will need to be reconciled with its stated desire to contribute to international peace and security and to act as a partner of good faith in Africa and other regions. Greater Chinese compliance with international standards in arms transfer control, such as the provisions of the ATT, would begin to address the longer-term issue of Chinese arms transfers to conflict zones and the balance to strike between the profitability of arms sales against their potentially far-reaching negative consequences.

NOTES

1. United Nations, meetings coverage and press releases (2013), 'Overwhelming Majority of States in General Assembly Say "Yes" to Arms Trade Treaty to Stave Off Irresponsible Transfers That Perpetuate Conflict, Human Suffering', 2 April 2013, http://www.un.org/press/en/2013/ga11354.doc.htm.
2. United Nations Office for Disarmament Affairs (2016), accessed on 1 February 2016, http://www.un.org/disarmament/ATT/.
3. The Arms Trade Treaty, article 6 (3).
4. The Arms Trade Treaty, article 7.
5. Now that the Treaty has come into force, signature is no longer an option for China or any other non-signatory. China can only accede to the Treaty, which means becoming a full State Party with the responsibility to implement all of the Treaty's provisions in full.
6. SIPRI's Arms Transfers Database does not cover imports and exports of SALW, with the exception of portable guided missiles such as man-portable air defence systems (MANPADS) and guided anti-tank missiles.

7. Pieter D. Wezeman and Siemon T. Wezeman (2015). 'Trends in International Arms Transfers, 2014', Stockholm International Peace Research Institute (SIPRI), March 2015.
8. Ibid.
9. Mark Bromley, Mathieu Duchâtel, and Paul Holtom (2013), 'China's Exports of Small Arms and Light Weapons', SIPRI Policy Paper 38, p. VI, Stockholm International Peace Research Institute, October 2013.
10. Ibid.
11. Ibid.
12. Ibid.
13. Ibid.
14. Oscar Nkala (2015), 'Chinese Company Builds Growing African Presence', Defence News, 10 October 2015.
15. Bromley et al., Op. Cit. p. VII.
16. Ilya Gridneff (2014), 'China Sells South Sudan Arms as Its Government Talks Peace', *Bloomberg Business*, 9 July 2014.
17. Bromley et al., Op. Cit. p. VII.
18. Small Arms Survey (2009), *Shadows of War* (Cambridge University Press), p. 31.
19. Bromley et al., Op. Cit. p. 36.
20. Mark Caldwell interviewing Pieter Wezeman (2015), 'China's Arms Trade with Africa at Times Questionable', *Deutsche Welle*, 16 March 2015.
21. Mark Anderson and Achilleas Galatsidas (2015), 'Global Weapons Trade Targets Africa as Imports to Algeria and Morocco Soar', Conflict and Development Datablog, *The Guardian*, 20 March 2015.
22. China Arms Control and Disarmament Association (CACDA), Saferworld (2012), 'The Evolution of EU and Chinese Arms Export Controls', March 2012.
23. Saferworld (2015), 'Expanding and Sustaining Dialogue Between China and the Wassenaar Arrangement', January 2015, p. 3.
24. Bromley et al., Op. Cit. p. 20.
25. Saferworld, Op. Cit. p. 3.
26. Wu Jinhuai (2014), 'Military Products: China's Export Control Mechanism and Practices', presented at an international seminar on 'Contributing to International Security and Stability: Strengthening Dialogue between China and the Wassenaar Arrangement', Vienna, 10 June 2014.
27. Saferworld, Op. Cit. p. 7.
28. Ibid., p. 5.
29. Elizabeth Kirkham and Roy Isbister (2014), 'The Time Available to Sign the Arms Trade Treaty Is Shrinking Fast: Why Should China Sign the Treaty', *ATT Update 7*, Saferworld, September 2014.

30. 'Towards an Arms Trade Treaty: Establishing Common International Standards for the Import, Export and Transfer of Conventional Arms', *UN Draft Resolution* A/C.1/61/L.55 (2006).

31. Chinese Delegation at the First Committee of the 61st Session of UNGA in Explaining its Position after the Voting of Draft Resolution Titled 'Towards an Arms Trade Treaty' (L. 55). www.fmprc.gov.cn/mfa_chn/ziliao_611306/zyjh_611308/t309158.shtml.

32. Chinese Delegation at the First Committee of the 63rd Session of UNGA in Explaining its Position after the Voting of Draft Resolution Titled 'Towards an Arms Trade Treaty'. www.fmprc.gov.cn/mfa_chn/wjbxw_602253/t521632.shtml.

33. Statement by H. E. Ambassador Wang Qun (2011), Head of the Chinese Delegation at the General Debate of the First Committee of the 66th session of UNGA, 7 October 2011. www.fmprc.gov.cn/eng/wjb/zzjg/jks/jkxw/t865572.htm.

34. Statement by H.E. Li Baodong (2010), Permanent Representative of the People's Republic of China to the United Nations, at UNSC open debate on 'The Impact of Illegal Sales and Transfers of Arms on the Peace and Security of Central Africa', 19 March 2010.

35. Statement by H.E. Ambassador Wang Qun (2010), Head of the Chinese Delegation at the General Debate of the First Committee of the 65th Session of the United Nations General Assembly, 7 October 2010.

36. Statement by H.E. Ambassador Wang Qun, Head of the Chinese Delegation at the General Debate of the First Committee of the 66th Session of the United Nations General Assembly, 7 October 2011.

37. Statement by the Chinese delegation at the General Debate of United Nations Conferences on the Arms Trade Treaty, 9 July 2012.

38. Mark Bromley (2013), 'China's Arms Trade Treaty Diplomacy', Stockholm International Peace Research Institute (SIPRI), paper presented at the SIPRI conference 'The HU Jintao Decade in China's Foreign and Security Policy (2002–12): Assessments and implication', *Stockholm*, 18–19 April 2013.

39. Foreign Ministry Spokesperson Hong Lei's Regular Press Conference, 3 April 2013, www.fmprc.gov.cn/eng/xwfw/s2510/2511/t1028801.shtml.

40. Being an ATT signatory, does not bind a state to every provision of the Treaty; the only concrete obligation is that it does not act in a way that defeats the object and purpose of the Treaty. However, this would probably mean that very controversial transfer decisions (for example, those that violate Article 6) would certainly be seriously questioned.

41. SIPRI, Op. Cit.

42. Elizabeth Kirkham (2015), 'China and the ATT: Prospects for Future Engagement', *ATT Update 8*, Saferworld, 21 January 2015.

43. Anna Stavrianakis and He Yun (2014), 'China and the Arms Trade Treaty – Prospects and Challenges', p. 7, *Saferworld*, May 2014.

44. Saferworld, 'The Time Available to Sign the Arms Trade Treaty (ATT) is Shrinking Fast'.

45. Stavrianakis and He, Op. Cit. p. 8.

46. US Department of State (2013), 'United States Signs Arms Trade Treaty on September 25, 2013', https://2009-2017.state.gov/t/isn/armstrade treaty/index.htm.

47. Mike Lewis (2009), 'Skirting the Law: Sudan's Post-CPA Arms Flows', HSBA Working Paper 18; Amnesty International (2012), *Sudan: No end to violence in Darfur. Arms Supplies Continue Despite Ongoing Human Rights Violations.*

48. Under Article 11 of the treaty, states parties must seek to prevent the diversion of weapons through risk assessment as part of a national control system. States parties are obliged to consider mitigation and prevention measures that include, but do not require, the refusal of an authorisation. This is in contrast to the criteria included in Article 7, in which states parties are required not to authorise exports if there is an overriding risk of the negative consequences set out there.

Bernardo Mariani is a conflict and security analyst who has focused for 15 years on enhancing the capacities of governments and civil society to prevent conflict and support cooperative approaches to international security. Since 2008 he has managed Saferworld's China Programme, which undertakes research, raises awareness and promotes international dialogue on China's growing international role, particularly relating to conflict prevention, arms control and addressing peace and security challenges in conflict-affected and fragile states. He has authored/co-authored more than 30 publications.

Elizabeth Kirkham is a Small Arms & Transfer Controls Adviser. She has been working on arms and security issues at Saferworld since 1993. Her areas of interest include national, regional and international arms transfer control policies and practices and global and regional efforts to stem the proliferation and misuse of small arms and light weapons. She has produced numerous publications for Saferworld on a wide range of related issues such as how an international Arms Trade Treaty could be monitored and verified.

CHAPTER 18

Conclusion: China and African Security: A Glimpse into the Future

Zhang Chun and Chris Alden

At the Johannesburg Summit of the Forum on China-Africa Cooperation (FOCAC) in December 2015, Chinese President Xi Jinping recommended to upgrade the bilateral relations between China and Africa from 'the new type of strategic partnership' into a 'comprehensive strategic and cooperative partnership', which wins positiveresponses from African countries. One of the five pillars of this partnership is to 'remain committed to mutual assistance in security'.[1] In the *Declaration of the Johannesburg Summit of the Forum on China-Africa Cooperation*, both parties agreed to 'continue to support each other on security matters and maintain peace and security' and 'to solve African problems through African solutions'; to implement the 'Initiative on China-Africa Cooperative Partnership for Peace and Security' and to 'support the building of the collective security mechanism in Africa'.[2] The signing of

Z. Chun (✉)
Institute for Foreign Policy Studies, Shanghai Institutes for International Studies, Shanghai, China
e-mail: zhangchunster@163.com

C. Alden
Department of International Relations, London School of Economics and Political Science, London, United Kingdom
e-mail: j.c.alden@lse.ac.uk

© The Author(s) 2018
C. Alden et al. (eds.), *China and Africa*,
DOI 10.1007/978-3-319-52893-9_18

this Declaration symbolizes that China-Africa cooperation in peace and security is stepping onto a new stage, which calls for fresh ideas and new routes for future cooperation.

To open this new chapter of China-Africa peace and security cooperation, there are three important aspects for consideration: the changing Africa's peace and security context that calls for fresh ideas to address these new challenges; the evolution of China-Africa cooperation epitomized by the expansion of Chinese interests to the protection of thoses interests[3] that generates new requirements for China's involvement; and the adoption of new ideas, approaches and methodologies by the rest of the international community.

New Challenges for African Peace and Security

Although the Syrian crisis, Europe's refugee crisis and Korean nuclear issue draw most of the attention of the international community, Africa still remains one of the most important regions for global security considerations. According to statistics from Armed Conflict Location & Event Data Project (ACLED), there were 14,640 conflicts in Africa in 2015 alone.[4] Certainly the spread of jihadist armed violence and other sectarian militants across the Sahel in recent years has captured the concern of the international community, while other conflicts in Central Africa and the Great Lakes region sputter on with disturbing intractability. However, given the fact that Africa is a diversified continent with 54 countries and a vast land of more than 30 million square kilometres, one has to be cautious about drawing any overarching conclusion about African peace and security situation.

Declining Armed Conflicts...

One overall development is that the African continent is becoming more stable in terms of the frequency of traditional armed conflicts, even if it is difficult to state unequivocally that the root causes of these conflicts are being adequately addressed as the recent renewal of violence in some countries seems to testify. Nonetheless, since the end of the Cold War, there has been an overall drop in serious interstate and even intrastate conflicts in virtually all corners of the continent.[5] This is particularly the case in Southern Africa, a bastion of war and insurgency since the 1960s that only came to an end with the death of Unita's Jonas Savimbi in

Angola in February 2002. The prospect of an extensive period of peace and stability has translated directly into the growing economies, new investment and measurable improvements in human development. In Mozambique, a country racked by foreign intervention and a brutal civil war throughout the 1980s, the onset of peace in 1994 marked the beginning of a period of prosperity that saw double-digit growth, foreign investment into mining, agriculture and a concomitant rise in incomes amongst the population. This progress has been marred since 2015, however, by politically inspired violence in the central provinces, driven by the governing elites' corruption and self-serving management of Mozambique's natural resources.[6]

Even places where conflict threatens stable countries, Africans are taking a greater role in managing these conflicts through an activist approach to peace and security through continental and regional institutions. This is evident in cases like Burundi, where the deployment of Southern African peacekeepers is widely believed to have staved off an outbreak ethnic violence (a point emphasized by the more recent failure of the African Union (AU) to act in 2016).[7] And though the situation in Darfur eventually required a hybrid peacekeeping force with UN backing, the fact that the African Union engaged in diplomacy that isolated the Omar Bashir regime and even marshalled resources for a peacekeeping force marked a significant departure from past practices. While African countries may have to call in resources from the UN and primarily Western sources to supplement their own limited means, it is often the case that they retain a leading position in negotiations, decision-making and deployment of peacekeeping operations in the region.

Rising Terrorism and Extremism

At the same time that conflicts are scaling back in some areas, in recent years regional terrorism and extremism are on the rise and becoming more dangerous. On the Horn of Africa and West Africa, terrorism and 'traditional' armed conflicts are becoming visibly more entangled. In the Great Lakes region, though the Lord's Resistance Army has not been completely stamped out, its presence and operational capacity have been severely curtailed as the US military targeted attacks. Equally, since 2012, the sustained military actions of Kenya and Africa Union Mission in Somalia (AMISOM), coupled alongside the establishment of the new Somali government, have been increasingly successful in limiting the reach of Al-Shabaab and its militant activities. However, these positive developments have inspired new strategies and tactics on the part of the militants which include forging an alliance with international jihadist forces and the launching of more frequent and destructive terrorist attacks in neighbouring countries, especially Kenya. In June 2016, Al-Qaeda in the Islamic Maghreb (AQIM) attacked the Chinese UN Peacekeeping encampment, killing one peacekeeper and injuring four.

To the western part of the continent, since 2014 Boko Haram's 'growing lethality and tactical sophistication' and its ability to concentrate its position in Nigeria's more remote boarder areas is being reversed.[8] The progress made since that time by the Nigerian army in tackling Boko Haram has done much, however, to reduce their ability to operate in the country.

Finally, the Darfur crisis, coupled to separatist movements in east Sudan and Nubian mountains along the border with South Sudan, all pose continuing challenges to regional security. The peace process in South Sudan faces huge challenges that expose the weaknesses of the government structures and the inability of the international community to bolster either its capacity or legitimacy amongst the population. These problems find their echo in the Great Lakes region where traditional armed conflicts have periodically shattered the peace in the Democratic Republic of the Congo (DRC) and, more recently, the Central African Republic.

Prolonged Piracy

The problem of piracy off the African coastline is assuming new proportions. While declining in east, piracy activities are becoming notably threatening off the western reaches of the continent. Figure 18.1 shows that piracy in both Gulf of Aden and Guinea Gulf has declined dramatically; however, as warned by International Maritime Bureau, piracy is still a threat to waters of these regions, especially in the Gulf of Guinea, where Nigerian pirates are increasingly well-armed and able to capture freighters with relative ease.[9] Making the situation more complicated, the international community's militarized response to piracy is in itself inadequate, ignoring the other factors involved in driving communities to piracy such as the destruction of offshore fisheries or collapse of local authority. What's more, there are chaotic definitions and statistics in reports from different institutions about regional piracy activities.[10] Instead of simply focusing on costs and solutions, Africa needs to focus on creating the conditions for a safe, secure and sustainable blue economy, and conduct peace and state building to cut the grass from the root.[11]

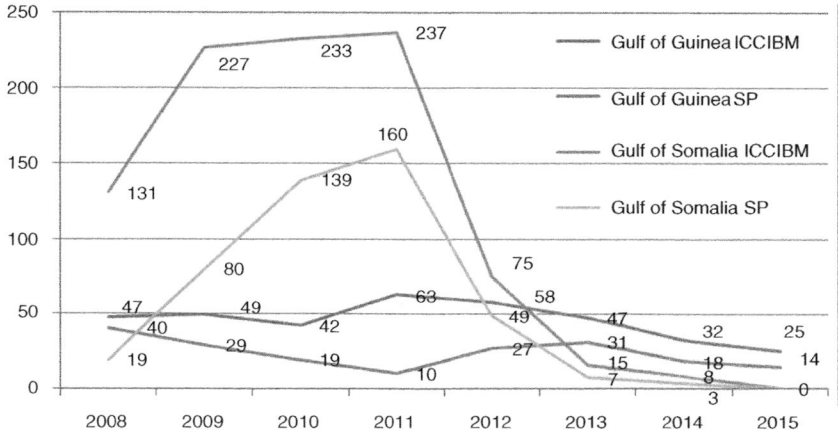

Fig. 18.1 Piracy activities in Somalian and Guinean waters, 2008–2015

Source: ICC International Maritime Bureau (IBM), *Piracy and Armed Robbery against Ships,* Reports from 2008 to 2015, London: ICC IBM, January 2016; 'Number of Actual and Attempted Piracy Attacks in Nigeria from 2008 to 2015.'
The Statistics Portal, February 2016, http://www.statista.com/markets/419/topic/491/logistics/; 'Number of Actual and Attempted Piracy Attacks in Somalia from 2008 to 2014', The Statistics Portal, February 2016, http://www.statista.com/markets/419/topic/491/logistics/.

Third-Term Crisis

The third-term crisis and gerontocracy phenomena amongst African leaders is eroding the roots of democracy in Africa. This is all the more worrying because accountable and legitimate governance, underpinned by institutional resilience and robust legal frameworks, are seen to be the necessary backbone to stable and sustainable political systems. To cite three recent examples, at the end of 2014, president of Burkina Faso, Blaise Compaoré, attempted to amend constitution to prolong its presidency but was overthrown. In 2015, Burundian president Pierre Nkurunziza successfully sought for his third term after the amendment of constitution. And the longstanding succession crisis in Zimbabwe is back in the spotlight as the country's 90-plus-year-old president, Robert Mugabe, vigorously resists transitions of any kind which threaten his personal interests and political authority.

Certainly many sub-Saharan countries are continuing to encounter an inability to successfully move beyond the existing regime and, as a consequence, are enmeshed in a 'third term (presidency) crisis'. However, it is important to note that there are four types of third-term challenges in sub-Saharan countries: those countries with two terms de jure but 'life-long tenure' de facto, including, for example, Angola, Equatorial Guinea and Chad; those countries with failed third-term attempts, for example, more than 10 leaders in African countries have sought for prolonged terms since 2000, with half of them failed; the countries 'third term' is potentially welcomed for various reasons, the example is Rwanda and Sierra Leone; and finally, those countries where third term might intrigue national turbulence or even crisis, including the prolonged Burundi crisis, and two Congos where the situation raised wide international concern.[12]

Complicated Development-Security Nexus

Finally, the development-security nexus is attaining increasing importance. All types of challenges described above are closely linked with the effectiveness of development and governance, in fields such as food security, climate change, environmental protection, cross-border security, etc. According to Food and Agriculture Organization of the United Nations (UNFAO) report of July 2016, latest estimates by Southern African Development Community (SADC) indicate that 39.7 million people are projected to be food insecure by the peak of the 2016/17 lean season. Regional cereal balance sheet analysis (excluding DRC, Madagascar, Mauritius, Seychelles and Tanzania) shows overall cereal deficit of about 9.3 million tonnes. Lesotho, Malawi, Swaziland and Zimbabwe have declared drought emergencies. The forecast continues to indicate drier than normal conditions.[13] One phenomenon of the increasingly complicated development-security nexus is the so-called 'mosaic development' in Africa. That is, developing regions and those unstable ones have crossed the boarders, and merging at continental, regional and domestic levels. Therefore, governing crisis in Africa is heading to a more complicated direction: on one hand, economic growth does not guarantee a more secured Africa; on the other hand, any deterioration of security may result in a big shock in social development and economic growth.

NEW DEVELOPMENTS OF AFRICAN SECURITY GOVERNANCE

Despite being confronted by these security concerns, on the whole Africa has not done enough to improve its governing capacity so that it might successfully address these challenges. All above-mentioned challenges imply the necessity of adopting new ideas or innovative approaches to African security governance. However, not only is existing governance capability inadequate as it stands today, furthermore the international community still looks to traditional approaches based on the assumption that all security challenges are largely static. As a result, when this old mind-set meets new realities, three mismatches emerge in African security governance, namely means-ends mismatch, willingness-capability mismatch and needs-supports mismatch; and two 'highly uncertainties' emerged along with these mismatches: the uncertainty of Africa's future security and the uncertainty of how African countries will address this dilemma.

Means-Ends Mismatch

When speaking of this means-ends mismatch, African countries remain locked in traditional ways of thinking and largely resort to military solutions when confronted by the rise of non-traditional and non-structural violence. This is despite the fact that, 25 years after the Cold War, Africa has undergone three phases of security challenges: in the decade after 1990, African countries were still mired in domestic turmoil and conventional conflicts arising from the Cold War; the first decade of the twenty-first century witnessed conventional conflicts subsiding, and the region enjoyed a relatively peaceful period; and entering into 2010s, the situation was changed substantially again, as non-structural violence became a major challenge for African security. Responding to each of these distinctive conflicts requires tailored approaches and often non-conventional strategies that focus on origins of violence as much as on stemming the outbreaks of conflict itself.

'Structural violence' is violence launched by countries against others or domestic upheavals including overseas aggregation, interference, domestic suppression, etc. In a word, it is violence waged by the state. In contrast, non-structural violence is waged by non-state actors, such as some specific groups or persons, adopting bottom-up approach, in forms of upheavals, religious and ethnic conflicts, unrest before or after elections, organized crimes, piracy, terrorism, etc. Though non-structural violence is not necessarily organized or used for anti-government purposes, its consequence is far more dangerous than structural ones. With wider social influence, non-structural violence erodes governments' legitimacy bases. There are various explanations for the growth of non-structural violence, including, for example, worldwide political awakening due to the contemporary human rights and democratization movements; massive grievances due to the uneven economic development; vast religious and ethnical confrontations whose origins may be rooted in or even predate the colonial era; and external interference armed with advanced communication techniques especially social media.[14]

ACLED divides the violence in Africa into three major types: conventional armed conflicts, violence targeted on civilians and all other violence, protests, and social unrest. Although in conventional conflicts and violence against civilians some of these actions are not initiated by government (belong to non-structural violence), but as a whole they can be regarded as structural violence. However, upheavals, protests and other social violence are basically non-structural violence. Thus, since 2010, traditional structural violence (armed conflicts and civilian-targeted violence) has declined from 81.1% in 2010 to 51.9% in 2015, by more than 30%. Meanwhile, all kinds of riots, protests and other conflicts have risen from 18.9% to 48.1% (Fig. 18.2). Hence, it is safe to say, non-structural violence has become the most challenging factor for African security.

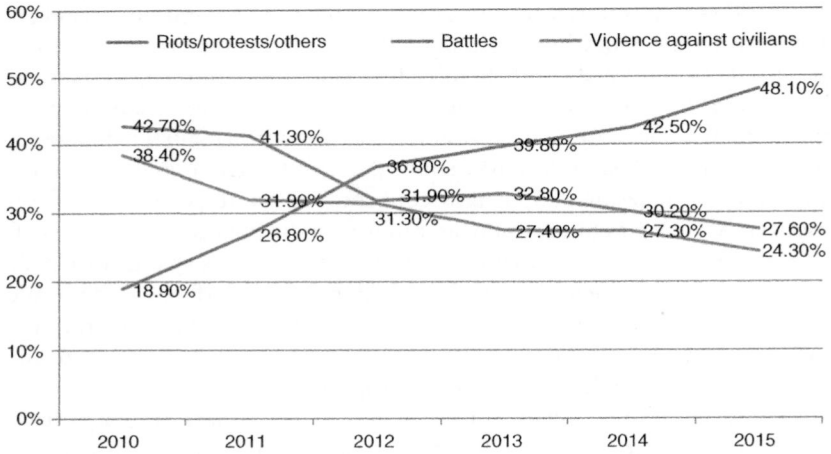

Fig. 18.2   Percentage of all kinds of violence in Africa, 2010–2025

Source: ACLED, 'Real-Time Analysis of African Political Violence', Conflict Trend, No. 46, January 2016; ACLED, 'Real-Time Analysis of African Political Violence', Conflict Trend, No. 33, January 2015; ACLED, 'Real-Time Analysis of African Political Violence', Conflict Trend, No. 22, January 2014; ACLED, 'Real-Time Analysis of African Political Violence', Conflict Trend, No. 10, January 2013; ACLED, 'Real-Time Analysis of African Political Violence', Conflict Trend, No. 1, April 2012.

Studies from the Institute of Security Studies (ISS) in South Africa echo ACLED's findings. In 2014, for instance, non-structural violence witnessed a dramatic increase in Africa. Egypt, South Africa, Nigeria, Libya and Kenya all experienced greater numbers of riots and protests, though there were few deaths in these incidents. In 2014 alone, of all conflicts happened in Africa, 90% of them involved unrest, protests and violence against civilians.[15]

Willingness-Capability Mismatch

African governments' willingness to address domestic security challenges is significantly different from its approach to dealing with external security challenges. It is important to note that all security challenges have their specific root-causes in development, or, put another way, the development-security nexus is at work behind all security challenges. To address this nexus and realize stability and peace, strong political commitments is necessary from all African leaders. However, in Africa, most countries are themselves still under construction, nation-building and state-building processes are still undergoing, and most countries are authoritarian in conduct if not name. Therefore, *realpolitik* calculations are still dominating security governance in both domestic and regional contexts. When addressing domestic security problems, most African governments prioritize the security of its own regime survival, which consequently induces disputes on power and public goods, and often produces more challenges for regional security. Against these domestic challenges, most African countries are very active in participating regional and sub-regional security governance. Some of them even set aside domestic troubles for regional and sub-regional issues. For example, while facing various domestic security challenges, including Boko Haram in the north and Emancipation of Niger Delta (MEND) in the south, and piracy in Gulf of Guinea, the Nigerian government still contributes significantly peacekeeping and mediation efforts of Economic Community of West African States (ECOWAS). An exception is the diminishing role played by South Africa in regional security governance, once a paragon of activism in expanding the continent's peace and security capacity under Nelson Mandela and Thabo Mbeki.[16] Since the advent of the Zuma presidency, South Africa's foreign policy has reflected an increasingly inward-looking foreign policy orientation and, as evidence increasingly validates, one which is oriented towards personal interests.

At the same time, security governance faces a capability deficit at both regional and sub-regional levels. With the putative rise of Africa, the continent is more conscious of the need to put into practice 'African Solutions to African Problems', which adds complexities to security governance. Hungering for external support, growing awareness of ownership at national, sub-regional and regional levels creates new dilemma for Africans. For example, the financial support document of the Africa Agenda 2063 says that Africa can mobilize 75%–80% of funds from its own national sources to realize this vision.[17] However, there are clear questions as to whether African governments are willing to make the necessary investments in capacity to improve security governance in regional and sub-regional Africa to meet these challenges.

Needs-Supports Mismatch

It is important to note that national interests are at the core of all relevant actors' calculations when engaging into African peace and security, thus whatever supports provided by international community, it is not necessarily matched to the real needs of Africa. Together with an outdated understanding of the nature of security challenges Africa is facing, such supports have no contribution in promoting African security governance at the best, making matters even worse in many cases.

NEW THINKING ON CHINA-AFRICA SECURITY COOPERATION

Chinese President Xi announced 'ten cooperation plans' for the next three years on the Johannesburg Summit in December 2015. Among them, 'China will provide US$60 million of grant to support the building and operation of the African Standby Force and the African Capacity for the Immediate Response to Crisis'. Moreover, 'China will continue to participate in UN peacekeeping missions in Africa and support African countries' capacity building in areas such as defence, counterterrorism, riot prevention, customs and immigration control'.[18] In the UN Peacekeeping Summit in last September, Xi also made a promise that China would provide free military aid of US$100 million to the African Union to support the building of the African Standby Force and the African Capacity for Immediate Response to Crisis. China would also send the first peacekeeping helicopter squad to UN peacekeeping operations in Africa, etc.[19] Hence, it is safe to say that China has a concrete commitment for expanding Sino-Africa cooperation in peace and security in this next phase. However, there is still considerable scope for more strategic and theoretical thinking to ensure that Sino-Africa security cooperation is sufficiently systematic, predictive and achievable.

Updating the Mind-Set

Given the rapidly changing security challenges and governance difficulties experienced in Africa, an unavoidable question is: what distinctive approach could China offer to improve the current situation in Africa? The most important challenge may be how to achieve a better balance between principles of non-intervention and non-indifference which still influence Chinese debates on African security questions. The Chinese approach of solving so-called 'hot issues', advocated by Chinese Foreign Minister Wang Yi, is more of a practical concept rather than a theoretical or academic one. From the authors' point of view, the balance between non-interference and non-indifference should embrace four principles:

(1) *Non-discrimination*. Namely, it is needed to stick to the tradition of 'treating all states equally' – no matter it is big or small, rich or poor, peaceful or conflict-affected. This is in accordance with the international principles established by Westphalia System, and it avoids moral judgement of different countries.

(2) *Non-intervention*. Because resolutions and actions of UNSC have collective legitimacy and will not be regarded as intervention, China should participate in more collective actions taken by UNSC while insisting on non-intervention bilaterally. Through sticking to the core role of UNSC, China can also take part in regional and sub-regional levels solutions, according to the situations, just as the way China did in mitigating the civil war in South Sudan.

(3) *Non-securitization*. It is clearly better to stick to political dialogues and diplomatic solutions in addressing conflicts and tensions, and keep military approach as the last choice. This is based on an affirmation that the coercive use of the military instrument can aggravate problems as much as it may be seen to resolve them.

(4) *No interruption of development support*. To solve the deep roots of insecurity, it is needed to promote transformations of those countries in conflicts and sustainable development afterwards, and to realize security in the long run. This means avoiding wherever possible, the withdrawal of support for economic development especially in countries operating under fragile security conditions.

Re-Prioritizing Policies

Guiding the re-prioritization of Sino-Africa peace and security cooperation should, from the author's perspective, follow five principles.

First, the key principle can be encapsulated as '**Africa leads, African way, African peace; China focus, hot issues focus, multilateral focus**'. This principle places the continent at the centre in the security cooperation between China and Africa, which will contribute to the acceptance and legitimacy of this cooperation. 'Africa leads' stresses the leading role of Africa in its own regional issues; 'African way' stresses Chinese support for 'African Solutions to African Problems' and 'African peace' aims at helping Africa to realize a balance between security and development. The latter principles focus more on implementation. 'China focus' emphasizes the protection of China's overseas interests; 'hot issues focus' highlights the key fields in Sino-Africa cooperation and 'multilateral focus' aims at applying regional and sub-regional platforms, and avoids the non-intervention dilemma in bilateral cooperation.

Secondly, the focus on cooperation should be on early warning. Specifically, this means assisting Africa to build and improve its conflict early warning and response mechanism, especially its capacity in anti-terrorism and peacekeeping; and to help Africa to establish the African Human Security Index system proposed in the First Ten Years Implementation Plan of the Africa Agenda 2063.

Third, partners should necessarily align China-Africa peace and security cooperation with Africa peace and security architecture building, including, for example, to support the building of regional and sub-regional security architecture and their operation; and to support and fund the establishment of an early response system in Africa, to support and fund building a continental peacekeeping force in Africa, to promote the division of labour and cooperation mechanism among African countries in regional and sub-regional institutions.

Fourth, such cooperation should be framed within the broader parameters of the promotion of African development. Development is the first priority and the key to address security problems. Sustainable development will help to improve the balance among development, stability and reformation, providing the basis for 'sustainable transformation' in the longer term.

And fifth, cooperation needs to build up a peaceful environment by supporting and investing in peace and security education. This will help to realize the 'Silence the Guns by 2020' goal of the Africa Agenda 2063 and to build 'a culture of peace' in Africa as proposed by UN 2030 Agenda for Sustainable Development passed in September 2015.

Improving Operational Mechanisms

Beyond the principles discussed above, China's own thinking on African security needs to account for changes in Africa, the policy priorities of African governments and regional organizations as well as attend to areas for bilateral friction that potentially could get in the way of deepening cooperation. These operational mechanisms will ensure that the practical components of cooperation remain on a sound footing as China furthers its engagement in Africa's complex security and development context.

(1) To work at better combining strategies of both parties, China should take into consideration the rising consciousness of strategic planning of Africa in recent years. Rather than unilaterally providing any cooperation initiative, China should combine all relevant development plans together for promoting African development, including, for example, the 'Three Networks (highway, high-speed train and aviation) and Industrialization' initiative of China, the UN 2030 Agenda for sustainable development and the Common Position of Africa on Post-2015 Agenda, and the Africa Agenda 2063 and its First Ten Years Implementation Plan, amongst others.

(2) China should strengthen intellectual support through enhancing the roles of think-tanks, universities from both sides, encouraging them to participate in the building of early warning systems, follow-up and evaluation mechanisms for Sino-Africa security cooperation.

(3) China needs to improve the performance of corporate social responsibility by educating and guiding Chinese entrepreneurs in Africa, improving their consciousness of environment protection, as well as sense of respecting to and integrating in local society.

(4) China should encourage the sharing of experiences by institutions and exchange of views in terms of cross-border security governance, early warning and response mechanism building, social security monitoring, ethnic relations management, etc.

(5) Finally, China ought to gradually promote trilateral cooperation in peace and security field by improving the principles and practices of 'Africa leads, African way, African peace' for guiding trilateral peace

and security cooperation, while still taking full consideration of the sensitivities commensurate with peace and security issues.

If all of these measures are seriously considered and actively integrated into the planning and operational dimensions of China's security cooperation with Africa, the foundations for a mutually supportive form of relations are more likely to be put into place. Linking this cooperation to ongoing international efforts, through peacekeeping and other multilateral initiatives will strengthen the possibility of Chinese-African collaborative efforts, resulting in the growth of a stable development-oriented Africa into the twenty-first century.

CONCLUSION

As this book has demonstrated, China's involvement in the security sphere in Africa is now an established fact. It is a journey that began with China's foray into Africa's independence struggles and, as its economy reached out to engage abroad, is one which is increasingly defined by a common set of concerns. Greater exposure to the conditions on the continent, and in particular, the efforts by Africans to find credible solutions to the problems facing their region, have brought China closer to understanding the complexities which underlie the periodic instability plaguing parts of the continent. Drawing on their own experiences, collaborating with the international community and bringing in new ideas on furthering peace and security represent some of the most notable features China's budding contribution to the debates and practices in this area.

At the same time, there is a need to reflect upon how China and African counterparts are themselves contributing, inadvertently or otherwise, to fomenting the conditions that lead to insecurity. Long-term stability is unlikely to be found in actions that effectively support the unaccountable and corrupt practices of African regimes as much as the recourse by African governments to purely military solutions is unlikely to stem the flow of social violence. In this respect, China's recognized strategic outlook to policy management questions could be well suited to assisting African governments think through sustainable, development-oriented approaches to security issues.

What all of this points to is that the nature of instability and violence in Africa remains a context which will impose its challenges on China, even constraining its involvement in certain regions at times. Platitudes of cooperation and collaboration are, as Deng Xiaoping was wont to say, always in danger of becoming merely 'empty talk'. Chinese and Africans need to be sure that security cooperation retains its focus on practical solutions that respect the needs of participants, especially those victimized by conflict, and actively measure their progress on the basis of these successes.

NOTES

1. 'Open a New Era of China-Africa Win-Win Cooperation and Common Development', Address by Xi Jinping at the opening ceremony of the Johannesburg Summit of The Forum on China-Africa Cooperation, December 4, 2015.
2. *Declaration of the Johannesburg Summit of the Forum on China-Africa Cooperation*, December 25, 2015. http://www.focac.org/eng/ltda/dwjbzjjhys_1/hywj/t1327960.htm, accessed June 11, 2016.
3. ZHANG Chun (2013), *On International Contribution of China-Africa Relationship (ZhongFeiGuanxiGongxianLun)* (Shanghai: Shanghai People's Publishing House), p. 38.
4. ACLED (2016), 'Real-Time Analysis of African Political Violence', *Conflict Trend*, 46, January 2016, p. 2.
5. Scott Straus (2012b), 'Wars Do End! Changing Patterns of Political Violence in Sub-Saharan Africa', *African Affairs*, 111:443.
6. 'The Costs of Corruption to the Mozambican Economy', Policy Brief, Centor de Integridade Publica, No. 24/2016. www.cipmoz.org/images/Documentos/Sem_categoria/Policy_Brief_1_Engl.pdf; '15 Years After the Death of Siba-Siba Macuacua, Still Impunity', *Club of Mozambique*, 15 August 2016. www.clubofmozambique.com/news/15-years-death-siba-siba-macuacua-still-impunity-deutsche-welle/.
7. Devon Curtis (2012), 'The International Peacebuilding Paradox: Power Sharing and Post-Conflict Governance in Burundi', *African Affairs*, 112:446.
8. Armin Rosen (2015), 'This Map Shows What Africa's Deadliest Terror Group May be Planning Next', *Business Insider*, 18 February 2015. http://www.businessinsider.com/boko-haram-in-2015-2015-2.
9. ICC International Maritime Bureau (IBM) (2016), *Piracy and Armed Robbery Against Ships, Report for the Period 1 January–31 December 2015* (London: ICC IBM), January, p. 19.
10. Dirk Steffen (2015), 'Quantifying Piracy Trends in the Gulf of Guinea – Who's Right and Who's Wrong?' *USNI News*, 19 June 2015,.http://news.usni.org/2015/06/19/essay-quantifying-piracy-trends-in-the-gulf-of-guinea-whos-right-and-whos-wrong.
11. Timothy Walker (2016), 'Beyond Piracy: What Next for African Maritime Security?' ISS, 8 February 2016. https://www.issafrica.org/iss-today/beyond-piracy-what-next-for-african-maritime-security.

12. Austin Bay (2016), 'Africa's Third Term Power Grabs: Prelude to War', *Free Republic*, 10 February 2016. http://www.freerepublic.com/focus/f-news/3395435/posts.
13. UNFAO (2016), *2015–2016 El Niño Early Action and Response for Agriculture, Food Security and Nutrition*, Report, Update #9, July 2016, p. 2. http://www.fao.org/3/a-i5855e.pdf.
14. ZHANG Chun (2014), 'Proliferation of Non-Structural Violence and Normalization of African Turbulence (Feijiegou Xing BaoliZhengshengyuFeizhouDongdang de Changtaihua)', *Contemporary World (DangdaiShijie)*, 9, p. 45.
15. Jakkie Cilliers and Steve Hedden (2014), 'Africa's Current and Future Stability', *ISS Paper*, 274, November 2014, p. 4.
16. See, for instance, Chris Alden (2015), 'South African Foreign Policy and the UN Security Council: Assessing Its Impact on the African Peace and Security Architecture', *SAIIA Policy Insights*, 2, June 2015.
17. 'Background Note', Workshop on Agenda 2063 First 10-Year Implementation Plan, Lusaka, Zambia 2–6 March 2015. http://agenda2063.au.int/en/events/workshop-agenda-2063-first-10-year-imple mentation-plan-lusaka-zambia, Annex 3 'Agenda 2063 Financing, Domestic Resource Mobilization and Partnerships'.
18. Xi Jinping (2015), 'Working Together to Write a New Chapter in China-Africa Cooperation', Address by Xi Jinping at the Opening Ceremony of the Johannesburg Summit of the Forum on China-Africa Cooperation, 4 December 2015. http://www.fmprc.gov.cn/mfa_eng/wjdt_665385/zyjh_665391/t1321614.shtml.
19. Xi Jinping (2015), 'China is Here for Peace', Remarks by H.E. Xi Jinping President of the People's Republic of China at the United Nations Peacekeeping Summit, 28 September 2015. http://www.fmprc.gov.cn/mfa_eng/wjdt_665385/zyjh_665391/t1302562.shtml.

Zhang Chun is the Deputy Director of Institute for Foreign Policy Studies, Shanghai Institutes for International Studies (SIIS). His research focuses on China-Africa relations, African peace and security, UN 2030 Agenda for sustainable development, and international relations theory.

Chris Alden holds a Professorship at the Department of International Relations, London School of Economics and Political Science (LSE), has published widely on China-Africa issues and is a research associate of the South African Institute for International Affairs (SAIIA) and Department of Political Sciences, University of Pretoria.

BIBLIOGRAPHY

Aalen, L. 2006. "Ethnic Federalism and Self-Determination for Nationalities in a Semi-Authoritarian State: The Case of Ethiopia," *International Journal of Minorities and Group Rights* 13: 243–261.

Abota, A. 2006. "Ethiopia's Foreign Policy under Emperor Haile Selassie I: An Appraisal" Master's thesis, Addis Ababa University.

Adem, S. 2012. "China in Ethiopia: Diplomacy and Economics of Sino-Optimism," *African Studies Review* 55, no. 1: 143–160.

African Union. 2015. "The People's Republic of China Extends Financial Support to the African Union Mission in Somalia" (retrieved from http://www.peaceau.org/en/article/the-people-s-republic-of-china-extends-financial-support-to-the-african-union-mission-in-somalia).

Ahmed, G. K. 2010. *The Chinese Stance on the Darfur Conflict, South African Institute of International Affairs (SAIIA) Occasional Paper. 67.* Johannesburg: SAIIA.

Akinrrinade, S., and A. Sesay. 1998. *Africa in the Post-Cold War International System.* London: Pinter.

Alden, C., C Zhang, B. Mariani, and D. Large. 2011. "China's Growing Role in African Post-Conflict Reconstruction," *Global Review*, No. 6.

Alden, C. 2015. 'South African Foreign Policy and the UN Security Council: Assessing Its Impact on the African Peace and Security Architecture'. *SAIIA Policy Insights* 2 June: 1–8.

Alden, C., and D. Large. 2011. "China's Exceptionalism and the Challenges of Delivering Difference in Africa," *Journal of Contemporary China* 20, no. 68: 21–38.

Alden, C., and D. Large. 2013. "China's Evolving Policy Towards Peace and Security in Africa: Constructing a New Paradigm for Peace Building?," in

© The Author(s) 2018

C. Alden et al. (eds.), *China and Africa*,

DOI 10.1007/978-3-319-52893-9

Mulugeta Gebrehiwot Berhe and Liu Hongwu eds., *China-Africa Relations: Governance, Peace and Security*. Addis Ababa: Institute for Peace and Security Studies.

Alden, C., and D. Large. 2015. "On Becoming a Norms Maker: Chinese Foreign Policy, Norms Evolution and the Challenges of Security in Africa," *The China Quarterly* 22: 123–142.

AllAfrica. "Africa: China's Growing Role in Africa – Implications for U.S. Policy," http://allafrica.com/stories/201111021230.html?viewall=1   Accessed   1 November 2011

Allo, A. K. 2010. "Ethiopia's Armed Intervention in Somalia: The Legality of Self-Defense in Response to the Threat of Terrorism," *Denver Journal of International Law and Policy* 39.

Armed Conflict and Event Data Project (ACLED). 2016. "Real-Time Analysis of African Political Violence," *Conflict Trend*, No. 46, January. www.acleddata.com/research-and-publications/conflict-trends-reports/

Ayenagbo, K., T. Njobvu, J. V. Soddou, and B. K. Tozoun. 2012. "China's Peacekeeping Operation in Africa: From Unwilling Participation to Responsible Contribution," *African Journal of Political Science and International Relations* 6, no. 2: 22–32.

Ayenagbo, Kossi et al. "China's Peacekeeping Operations in Africa: From Unwilling Participation to Responsible Contribution," *African Journal of Political Science and International Relations* 6, no. 2.

Bay, A. 2016. "Africa's Third Term Power Grabs: Prelude to War," *Free Republic*, 10 February. http://www.freerepublic.com/focus/f-news/3395435/posts.

BBC. 2013. "Mali and Tuareg Rebels Sign Peace Deal" http://www.bbc.com/news/world-africa-22961519. Accessed 17 July 2015.

Benjaminsen, T. A. 2008. "Does Supply-Induced Scarcity Drive Violent Conflicts in the African Sahel?," *Journal of Peace Research* 45, no. 6.

Berhane, D. 2013. "China Provides $1 Billion for Renaissance Dam Transmissions Lines," *Horn Affairs*, April 26, 2013. http://danielberhane.com/2013/04/26/nile-china-finance-billion-dollar-renaissance-dam/.

Bilgin, P., and A. Morton. 2002. "Historicizing the Representations of 'Failed States': Beyond the Cold War Annexation of the Social Sciences?," *Third World Quarterly* 23, no. 1.

Bo, K. 2010. *China's International Petroleum Policy*. Santa Barbara, CA: ABC-CLIO, LLC.

Bøås, M., and L.E. Torheim. 2010. "The Trouble in Mali," 1282; Clionadh Raleigh, "Political Marginalization, Climate Change, and Conflict in African Sahel States," *International Studies Review* 12, no. 1: 73–74.

Bøås, M., and L. E. Torheim. 2013. "The Trouble in Mali- Corruption, Collusion, Resistance," *Third World Quarterly* 34, no. 7: 1279–1292.

Boden, C. 2015. "China in Talks with Djibouti on Establishing Logistics Base," *Associate Press*, (AP) 11/26/2015.

Boukhars, A. 2013. "The Paranoid Neighbor: Algeria and the Conflict in Mali," in F. Wehrey and A. Boukhars eds, *Perilous Desert: Insecurity in the Sahara*. Washington, DC: Carnegie Endowment for International Peace.

Bradbury, R. 2012. "Sudan the Hollow State: What Challenges to Chinese Policy?," *Journal of Politics & International Studies*, no. 8: 362–410.

Brown, K., and C. Zhang. 2009. "China in Africa – Preparing for the Next Forum for China Africa Cooperation," *Chatham House Briefing Note*, June.

Buzan, B., and O. Waever. 2003. *Regions and Power: The Structures of International Security*. Cambridge: Cambridge University Press.

Cabestan, J. P. 2012. "China and Ethiopia: Authoritarian Affinities and Economic Cooperation," *China Perspectives 2012*, no. 4.

Campbell, I. et al. 2012. *China and Conflict-Affected States: Between Principle and Pragmatism*, Saferworld Report, London, January 2012.

Carmody, P. 2008. "Cruciform Sovereignty, Matrix Governance and the Scramble for Africa's Oil: Insights from Chad and Sudan," *Political Geography* 28, no. 6: 353–361.

Centro de Integridade Publica. 2016. 'The Costs of Corruption to the Mozambican Economy', Policy Brief, Centro de Integridade Publica, 24 www.cipmoz.org/images/Documentos/Sem_categoria/Policy_Brief_1_ Engl.pdf; '15 years after the death of Siba-Siba Macuacua, still impunity', *Club of Mozambique*, 15 August 2016. www.clubofmozambique.com/news/15-years-death-siba-siba-macuacua-still-impunity-deutsche-welle/.

China Daily. 2013. "China, AU Pledge to Enhance Friendly Cooperation," http://www.chinadaily.com.cn/china/2013-02/16/content_16225150. htm. Accessed February 16

China Daily. 2015. "China Opens a Permanent Mission to AU" http://www. chinadaily.com.cn/world/2015-05/08/content_20656451.htm

China International Friendship Cities Association. http://www.cifca.org.cn. Accessed 15 February 2015.

China's National Defense. 2009. "China's Participation in UN Peacekeeping Operation (1990–2008)," *China-un.org*. http://www.china-un.org/eng/ zt/wh/t534321.htm. Accessed 17 July 2015.

China's National Defense. 2010. White Paper 2010 (Full Text). http://big5.gov. cn/gate/big5/www.gov.cn/test/2011-03/31/content_1835465.htm. Accessed 17 July 2015.

Cilliers, J., and S. Hedden. 2014. "Africa's Current and Future Stability," *ISS Paper*. 274. November.

Clapham, C. 1996. *Africa and the International System: The Politics of State Survival*. New York: Cambridge University Press.

Cooper, F., and R. Packard. eds. 1998. *International Development and the Social Sciences: Essays on the History and Politics of Knowledge*. California: University of California Press.

Cooper, H. 2007. "Darfur Collides with Olympics, and China Yields," *New York Times*, 13 April. http://www.nytimes.com/2007/04/13/washington/ 13diplo.html?_r=0. Accessed 22 May 2012.

Cooperation (FOCAC) web commentary, 25 March. http://www.focac.org/ eng/jlydh/xzhd/t675242.htm. Accessed 1 February 2014.

Cottey, A., and A. Forster. 2005. *Reshaping Defence Diplomacy: New Roles for Military Cooperation and Assistance*. Oxford: Oxford University Press.

Courtney, R. J. 2011. "A Responsible Power? China and the UN Peacekeeping Regime," *International Peacekeeping* 18, no. 3: 286–297.

Curtis, D. 2012. "The International Peacebuilding Paradox: Power Sharing and Post-Conflict Governance in Burundi," *African Affairs* 112, no. 446.

Dario, C., and R. Fabiani. 2013. "From Disfunctionality to Disaggregation and Back? The Malian Crisis, Local Players and European Interests," *Istituto Affari Internzionali IAI Working Papers*, 13–08 (March).

Davidson, W. 2013. "Egypt, Ethiopia and Sudan Mull New Probe Nile Dam Impact," *Bloomberg News*, October 21.

"Defence Diplomacy," *Policy Papers*, No. 1, Ministry of Defence, UK, 2000. http://www.mod.uk/issues/cooperation/diplomacy.htm/.

De Palva, B. 2011. "France: National Involvement in the Indian Ocean Region," *Future Directions International, Strategic Analysis Paper*, 5 December.

Deng, X. 2011. "Petroleum Cooperation Between China and Sudan," *Sino-Global Energy*, November.

Diarra, S. 2014. "Mali Leans On China As Investments Across Africa Heighten," *Afkinside*r. http://afkinsider.com/75390/mali-leans-on-china-as-invest ments-heighten/#sthash.wXeLmnYt.wReccmNC.dpuf. Accessed 17 July 2015.

Dongyan, Li. 2012. "China's Approach and Prospect of Participation in UN Peacekeeping and Peacebuilding," *Foreign Affairs Review*, No. 3.

Dowd, C., and C. Raleigh. 2013. "The Myth of Global Islamic Terrorism and Local Conflict in Mali and the Sahel," *African Affairs* 12, no. 448: 498–509.

Downs, E. 2008. "China's NOCs: Lessons Learned from Adventures Abroad," in *Fundamentals of the Global Oil and Gas Industry*. London: Petroleum Economist, pp. 27–31.

Duggan, N. 2014a. "The Rise of China Within Global Governance," in B. Dessein ed., *Interpreting China as a Regional and Global Power Nationalism and Historical Consciousness in World Politics*. Basingstoke: Palgrave Macmillan, pp. 91–110.

Duggan, N. 2014b. Sino-EU Security Cooperation in Africa: Case Study of Sino-EU Security Cooperation in Mali and the Gulf of Aden, paper presented at the *44th Annual UACES Conference*, (Cork 1–3 September 2014).

Duggan, N. 2015. "China's Changing Role in Its All-Weather Friendship with Africa," in S. Harnisch, S. Bersick, and J.C. Gottwald eds., *China's International Roles: Challenging or Supporting International Order*. London: Routledge, pp. 207–225.

Eisenman, J., and J. Kurlantzick. 2006. "China's Africa Strategy," *Current History* 105: 691.

Embassy of the Peoples Republic of China in Libya. 2007. "Talking Soft: Common Language Helps Resolve Darfur Issue," 20 September. http://ly.china-embassy.org/eng/zt/xu25/t364648.htm. Accessed 12 May 2012.

European Commission. 2014. European Union, Trade in Goods with Mali. http://trade.ec.europa.eu/doclib/docs/2011/january/tradoc_147319.pdf. Accessed 17 July 2015.

Evans, G., and D. Steinberg. 2007, "China and Darfur: 'Signs of Transition'," *Guardian Unlimited*. http://www.crisisgroup.org/home/index.cfm?id=4891&l=1. Accessed 11 June 2007.

FAO. 2014. *China-Mali South-South Cooperation Project Efficient Agricultural Technologies from China Boost Production in Mali*. Rome: FAO.

Federal Republic of Ethiopia. 2010. "Ministry of Finance and Economic Development," *Growth and Transformation Plan*, Volume I (Addis Ababa).

Felix, B. 2014. Mali Says Signed Accords with China for Projects Worth $11 Billion, *Reuters*. http://www.reuters.com/article/2014/09/15/us-mali-china-idUSKBN0HA1TU20140915. Accessed 17 July 2015.

Flood, D. H. 2013. "A Review of the French-led Military Campaign in Northern Mali," *CTC Sentinel* 6, no. 5.

FOCAC. 2009. Forum on China-Africa Cooperation Sharm El Sheikh Action Plan (2010–2012). http://www.focac.org/eng/dsjbzjhy/hywj/t626387.htm. Accessed 17 July 2015.

FOCAC. 2013. "Conference on 'China-Africa Governance and Development Experience' Held by CCPS," FOCAC Website. http://www.focac.org/chn/xsjl/zflhyjjljh/t1086342.htm. Accessed 9 October 2013.

FOCAC. 2015a. *Declaration of the Johannesburg Summit of the Forum on China-Africa Cooperation*, FOCAC Website, 25 December 2015. http://www.focac.org/eng/ltda/dwjbzjjhys_1/hywj/t1327960.htm. Accessed 26 December 2015.

FOCAC. 2015b. *The Forum on China-Africa Cooperation Johannesburg Action Plan (2016–2018)*, FOCAC Website, 25 December 2015.. http://www.focac.org/eng/ltda/dwjbzjjhys_1/hywj/t1327961.htm. Accessed 28 December 2015.

FOCAC. 2015c. *The Forum on China-Africa Cooperation, Johannesburg Action Plan (2016–2018)* (Combined Draft Version of Africa and China). http://www.dirco.gov.za/docs/2015/focac_action_plan2016_2018.pdf.

Foster, A. 2012. "The Gentle War: Famine Relief, Politics, and Privatization in Ethiopia, 1983–1986," *Diplomatic History* 36, no. 2.

Gebremariam, M. 2005. "Ethio-US Relations," *EthioScope*, January.

Genyi, G. A. 2015. "South Sudan: Resolving Conflicts in Africa – A Test Case for China," *Conflict Studies Quarterly* 13: 17–28.

Gill, B., and C. H. Huang. 2009. "China's Expanding Role in Peacekeeping: Prospects and Policy Implications," *SIPRI Policy Paper*, No. 25, November, p. 26.

Gottwald, J.C., and N. Duggan 2011. "Expectations and Adaptation: China's Foreign Policies in a Changing Global Environment," *International Journal of China Studies* 2, no. 1.

Gottwald, J.C., and N. Duggan 2012. "Diversity, Pragmatism and Convergence: China, the EU and the Issue of Sovereignty," in P. Zhonzgi ed., *Conceptual Gaps in China-EU Relations*. Basingstoke: Palgrave Macmillan.

Grimm, Sven, "The Forum on China-Africa Cooperation – Its Political Role and Functioning," *CCS Policy Briefing*, Centre for Chinese Studies, Stellenbosch, May.

Gueli, R, S. Liebenberg, and E. Van Huyssteen. 2006. *Developmental Peace Missions: Policy Guidelines and Background Reports*. Pretoria: CSIR.

Gueli, R., and S. Liebenberg. 2007. *Developmental Peace Missions: Synergising Peacekeeping and Peace-building in Transition Periods*. Pretoria: ISS. May.

Guo, X. 2010. *On Military Diplomacy and China's Practice*. Beijing: National Defence University Press.

Gutelius, D. 2007. "Islam in Northern Mali and the War on Terror," *Journal of Contemporary African Studies* 25, no. 1: 59–76.

Hackenesch, C. 2011. *Competing for Development? The European Union and China in Ethiopia*. Discussion Paper, Center for Chinese studies, University of Stellenbosch, South Africa, November.

Hang, Z. 2014. "Testing the Limits: China's Expanding Role in the South Sudanese Civil War," *China Brief* 14, no. 19.

Hartnett, D. 2012. China's First Deployment of Combat Forces to a UN Peacekeeping Mission-South Sudan *U.S.-China Economic and Security Review Commission*.

He, W. 2006. "Moving Forward with the Time: The Evolution of China's African Policy", paper presented for Workshop on China-Africa Relations: Engaging the International Discourse Hong Kong University of Science and Technology Center on China's Transnational Relations, November 11–12.

He, W. 2010. "A Chinese Perspective on Africa," Forum on China-Africa.

Healey, S. 2011. "Seeking Peace and Security in the Horn of Africa: The Contribution of Intergovernmental Authority on Development," *International Affairs* 87, no. 1: 105–120.

Herman, F. 2015. "Credibility and Signalling as Strategic Drivers in China's African Security Engagement'," *Chinese Studies* 4: 25–31.

Hille, K. 2013. "China Commits Combat Troops to Mali" http://www.ft.com/cms/s/0/e46f3e42-defe-11e2-881f-00144feab7de.html. Accessed 17 July 2015.

Holslag, J. 2009. "China's Vulnerability in Africa and Options for Security Cooperation with Europe," *Clingendael Asia Forum*, 11 December 2009. http://www.Clingendael.nl/asia/forum.

Holslag, J. 2011. "China and the Coups: Coping with Political Instability in Africa," *African Affairs* 110, no. 440: 367–386.

Holslag, J. "China's Next Security Strategy for Africa," *BICCS Asia Paper* 3, no. 6.

Houser, T. 2008. "The Roots of Chinese Oil Investment Abroad," *Asia Policy* 5: 141–166.

Hu, J. 2012a. "Open Up New Prospects for a New Type of China-Africa Strategic Partnership," Speech at the Opening Ceremony of the Fifth Ministerial Conference of The Forum on China-Africa Cooperation, Beijing, FOCAC website, 19 July. http://www.focac.org/eng/dwjbzjjhys/hyqk/t953115.htm. Accessed 20 July 2012.

Hu, J. 2012b. "President Hu proposes New Measures to Boost China-Africa Ties" http://www.gov.cn/english/2012-07/19/content_2187416.htm.

Huang, C. H. 2007. "US-China Relations and Darfur," *Fordham International Law Journal* 31, no. 4: 827–842.

Hussein, S. 2015. *Terrorism and Counter-Terrorism in Africa Fighting Insurgency from Al Shabaab, Ansar Dine and Boko Haram.* Basingstoke: Palgrave Macmillan.

Intergovernmental Authority on Development. 2011. "Cooperation with China," 21 November 2011. http://igad.int/index.php?option=com_content&view=article&id=370:cooperation-with-china&catid=46:executive-secretary&Itemid=123.

International Criminal Court. 2016. "International Maritime Bureau," *Piracy and Armed Robbery Against Ships, Report for the Period*, 1 January–31 December 2015. London: ICC/IBM, January.

International Crisis Group. 2009. "Growing Roles of China in UN Peacekeeping," *Asia Report*, no. 166, April.

International Crisis Group. 2015. "South Sudan: Keeping Faith with the IGAD Peace Process," *Africa Report* no. 228, July.

Jian, Chen. 2010. "China's Multilateral Diplomacy Facing New Tasks," *Jiefang Daily*, 25 October.

Jiang, A, and J. Zhang. 2013. "Djibouti Welcomes China to Build a Military Base," *Global Times*, 11 March 2013. http://www.chinaafricaproject.com/djibouti-welcomes-china-to-build-a-military-base-translation.

Jiang, H., and J. Luo 2008. "Daerfur Weiji yu Zhongguo zai Feizhou de Guojia Xingxiang Suzao [The Shaping of China's International Image in Africa]," *Zongguo yu Shijie (China and the World)*, pp. 28–42.

Jiang, H., and H. Zhang. 2013. "Managing Security Challenges for Chinese Companies in South Sudan," in *Saferworld, Oil, Security and Community Engagement: A Collection of Essays on China's Growing Role in South Sudan, Saferworld Report*, London: Saferworld, pp. 16–21.

Jiang, W. 2009. "Fueling the Dragon: China's Rise and Its Energy and Resources Extraction in Africa," *The China Quarterly* 199: 585–609.

Jiantao, Ren. 2008. "Strategical Alternatives of Mode of Chinese Democratization," *Academia Bimesteris*, No. 2.

Jok, M. J. 2007. *Sudan: Race, Religion and Violence*. Oxford, UK: Oxfam.

Jundo, J., and D. Frasheri. 2014. "Neo-Colonialism or De-colonialism? China's Economic Engagement in Africa and the Implications for World Order," *African Journal of Political Science and International Relations* 8, no. 7: 185–201.

Kimenyi, M., J.M. Mbaku, and N. Moyo. 2010. "Reconstituting Africa's Failed States: The Case of Somalia," *Social Research* 77: 4.

Kleine-Ahlbrandt, S., and A. Small. 2008. "China's New Dictator Diplomacy," *Foreign Affairs* 38: 38–56.

Lacocq, B. M., G. B. Whitehouse, D. Badi, L. Pelckmans, N. Belalimat, B. Hall, and W. Lacher. 2013. "One Hippopotamus and Eight Blind Analysts: A Multivocal Analysis of the 2012 Political Crisis in the Divided Republic of Mali," *Review of African Political Economy* 40, no. 137: 343–357.

Lanteigne, M. 2014. China's Peacekeeping Policies in Mali: New Security Thinking or Balancing Europe? NFG Working Paper Series, No. 11. NFG Research Group "Asian Perceptions of the EU" Freie Universität Berlin.

Large, D. 2008. "From Non-Interference to Constructive Engagement? China's Evolving Relations with Sudan," in C. Alden, D. Large, and R. Soares De Oliveira eds., *China Returns to Africa: A Rising Power and a Continent Embrace*. London: Hurst Publishers Ltd.

Large, D. 2012. "Between the CPA and Southern Independence: China's Post-Conflict Engagement in Sudan", *SAIIA Occasional Paper*, No. 115.

Lee, J. 2015. "China Comes to Djibouti: Why Washington Should Be Worried," *Foreign Affairs*, April 23.

Lee, M. C., H. Melber, S. Naidu, and I. Taylor. 2007. "China in Africa," *Current African Issues*, No. 33, Uppsala: Nordiska Afrikainstitutet.

Li, A. 2005. "African Studies in China in the Twentieth Century: A Historiographical Survey," *African Studies Review* 48, no. 1: 59–87.

Li, A. 2007. "China-Africa: Policy and Challenges," *China Security* 3, no. 3: 69–93.

Li, A. 2012. "Why the Forum on China-Africa Cooperation-Analyzing China's Strategy in Africa," *Foreign Affairs Review* (Chinese) 29, no. 3.

Li, A. 2013. "Obama's Africa Trip and Implications for China," *The Contemporary World*, No. 10.

Li, X. 2011. "The Partition of Sudan and its Impact on China's Oil Interests," *Contemporary International Relations* 21, no. 6 (online resource).

Li, Y. 2003. "The Present Situation and Prospects of the Sino-Africa Economy and Trade Relationship Development," *Journal of Shanxi Administration School and Shanxi Economic Management School* 17, no. 4.

Liu, G. 2012. "Foreign Assistance and Hijack: Problems and Dilemma of China-Africa Relations," *World Affairs*, No. 4.

Liu, C., and H. Zhang. 2012. "Baohu zai Sudan he Nan Sudan Zhongguo de Haiwei Guojia Liyi [Protecting China's Overseas National Interests in Sudan and South Sudan]," Beihua Daxue Xuebao, (Journal of Beihua University), No. 5.

Lu, S. 2013a. "Some Thoughts on China-Africa New Type of Strategic Partnership," *New Strategy Studies*, No. 1.

Lu, S. 2013b. "Seizing Opportunities and Overcoming Difficulties to Promote the Development of China-Africa Relations," *China International Studies*, No. 2.

Lundestad, G. 1999. *East, West, North, South: Major Developments in International Politics Since 1945.* Oxford: Oxford University Press.

Luo, J. 2013. "Why Sino-African Relationship so Important?" *Study Times*, 1 April.

Madlala-Routledge, N., and S. Liebenberg. 2004. "Developmental Peacekeeping: What are the Advantages for Africa?," *African Security Review* 13, no. 2.

Maliti, T. 2014. "IGAD and Somalia: Now and Then," *Horn of Africa Bulletin* 26, no. 3.

Marchal, R. 2013. "Briefing Military (Mis)Adventures in Mali," *African Affairs* 112, no. 448: 486–497.

Martina, M. 2011. "South Sudan Marks a New Foreign Policy Chapter for China: Official," *Reuters*, 11 February. http://www.reuters.com/article/2014/02/11/us-china-southsudanidUSBREA1A0HO20140211. Accessed 14 March 2014.

Martina, M. 2012. "China's Africa Envoy Says South Sudan Oil May Flow by November," *Reuters*, 15 September. http://www.reuters.com/article/2012/09/15/us-china-southsudan-oilidUSBRE88E03920120915. Accessed 14 April 2013.

Martina, M. 2014. "South Sudan Marks New Foreign Policy Chapter for China: Official", *Reuters*, 11 February. http://www.reuters.com/article/2014/02/11/us-china-southsudanidUSBREA1A0HO20140211. Accessed 14 March 2014.

Martina, M., and D. Brunnstrom. 2015. "China's Xi Says to Commit 8,000 Troops for U.N. Peacekeeping Force," *Reuters*, 28 September 2015. http://news.yahoo.com/chinas-xi-says-commit-8-000-troops-u-160032557.html

Mathews, K. 2013. "China and UN Peacekeeping Operations in Africa," in Gebrehiwot Berhe and Liu Hongwu eds., *China-Africa Relations: Governance, Peace and Security.* Institute for Peace and Security Studies, Addis Ababa University and Zhejiang Normal University.

McGregor, R. 2008. "Chinese Diplomacy 'Hijacked' by Big Companies," *Financial Times*, 16 March. http://www.ft.com/cms/s/0/28b21418-f386-11dc-b6bc0000779fd2ac.html#axzz2VdVRhCdU. Accessed 1 May 2012.

Mesfin, M. 2011. "Ethiopia: Chinese Firm Eyes Gas Export from Calub Through Berbera," *All Africa.com*, 25 July 2011. http://allafrica.com/stories/201107270752.html.

Metafria, G. 2008. *Ethiopia and the United States: History, Diplomacy, and Analysis.* New York: Algora Press.

Ministère de la Dèfense. 2013. Bilan des opèations du 28 janvier. http://www.defense.gouv.fr/operations/actualites/operation-serval-point-de-situation-du-28-janvier-2013. Accessed 17 July 2015.

Ministère de la Dèfense. 2014. Opération Barkhane. http://www.defense.gouv.fr/operations/sahel/dossier-de-presentation-de-l-operation-barkhane/operation-barkhane. Accessed 17 July 2015.

Ministry for Defence. 2014a. China Supports African Rapid Response Forces. http://eng.mod.gov.cn/DefenseNews/2014-12/12/content_4557257.htm. Accessed 17 July 2015.

Ministry for Defence. 2014b. First Chinese Peacekeeping Force in Mali Returns with Great Honor. http://eng.mod.gov.cn/DefenseNews/2014-09/28/content_4540697.htm. Accessed 17 July 2015.

Ministry for Defence. 2015a. Chinese Peacekeeping Troops to Mali Receive UN Peace Medals. http://eng.mod.gov.cn/Peacekeeping/2015-03/26/content_4577156.htm. Accessed 17 July 2015.

Ministry for Defence. 2015b. Chinese Peacekeepers Hit by 31 Rocket Projectiles in Mali. http://eng.mod.gov.cn/DefenseNews/2014-12/12/content_4557336.htm. Accessed 17 July 2015.

Ministry of Commerce. 2002. "Fifty Years of China-Africa Economic and Trade Relations," Ministry of Commerce, 16 July. http://www.mofcom.gov.cn/aarticle/bg/200207/20020700032255.html.

Ministry of Defence. 2011. "Wei Fenghe Meeting with All Participants of Seminar of Presidents of Francophonie-African Military Institutions, May 31, 2011. http://news.mod.gov.cn/diplomacy/2011-05/31/content_4244597.htm.

Ministry of Defence, UK, 2000. *The Strategic Defence Review White Paper* 1998, Ministry of Defence, UK, p. 22. http://www.parliament.uk/Templates/BriefingPapers/Pages/BPPdfDownload.aspx?bp-id=RP98-91.

Ministry of Foreign Affairs, PRC. 2006. *China's African Policy*, January. http://www.fmprc.gov.cn/eng/zxxx/t230615.htm.

Ministry of Foreign Affairs, PRC. 2015a. "Xi Jinping Attends and Addresses UN Leaders' Summit on Peacekeeping," *Ministry of Foreign Affairs of China.* http://www.fmprc.gov.cn/mfa_eng/topics_665678/xjpdmgjxgsfwbcxlhgcl70znxlfh/t1304147.shtml. Accessed 29 September.

Ministry of Foreign Affairs, PRC. 2015b. *Declaration of the Johannesburg Summit of the Forum on China-Africa Cooperation,* 25 December 2015. http://www.focac.org/eng/ltda/dwjbzjjhys_1/hywj/t1327960.htm. Accessed 11 June 2016.

Ministry of Foreign Affairs, PRC. 2016. "Sixth China-African Union Strategic Dialogue Held" http://www.fmprc.gov.cn/mfa_eng/wjbxw/t1265421.shtml.

Moller, L. 2015. "Ethiopia's Great Run: The Growth Acceleration and How to Pace It" working paper, Washington, DC: World Bank Group.

Murithi, T. 2009. "The African Union's Transition from Non-Intervention to Non-Indifference: An Ad Hoc Approach to the Responsibility to Protect?," *IPG* 1.

"National Defence University Comprehensively Facilitate Training Foreign Military," *Jiefanjun Bao*, March 15, 2009.

Niezen, R.W. 1990. "The 'Community of Helpers of the Sunna': Islamic Reform Among the Songhay of Gao (Mali)," *Africa: Journal of the International African Institute* 60, no. 3: 399–424.

Nossiter, A., and P. Tinti. 2013. "Mali Holds Elections After Year of Turmoil" http://www.nytimes.com/2013/07/29/world/africa/mali-holds-elections-after-year-of-turmoil.html?_r=0. Accessed 17 July 2015.

Office of the State Council. 1998. *China's National Defence 1998*, Information Office of the State Council, the People's Republic of China, July 1998. http://www.china.org.cn/e-white/5/index.htm.

Olivier, L. 2008. *Pursuing Human Security in Africa Through Developmental Peace Missions: Ambitious Construct or Feasible Ideal?* Master Thesis, Stellenbosch University.

Oumar, J. 2011. AQIM Launches Indoctrination Campaign along Mali-Mauritania Border," *Magharebia*, 5 August. http://www.magharebia.com/cocoon/awi/xhtml1/. Accessed 17 July 2015.

Pan, L. 2011. "A Historical Survey of China and Africa OAU/AU Relations to 20112, MA Thesis, Addis Ababa University, Addis Ababa, Ethiopia.

Pan, Y. 2012. "Zhongguo de bu Ganshe Waijia: Cong Hanwei Changdao dao Canyu Changdao (China's Non-Interference Diplomacy: From Defensive

Advocacy to Participatory Advocacy) *Shijie Jingji Zhengzhi (World Economics and Politics)*. No. 9: 45–57.

Paris, R. 2004. *War's End: Building Peace After Civil Conflict*: Cambridge University Press.

Park, Y. J. 2009. 'Chinese Migration in Africa' *SAIIA Occasional Paper* Number 24.

Patey, L. A. 2014. *The New Kings of Crude: China, India, and the Global Struggle for Oil in Sudan and South Sudan*. London, UK: Hurst & Company.

People's Daily. 2006. *China's African Policy 2006*. http://en.people.cn/200601/12/eng20060112_234894.html. Accessed 17 July 2015.

People's Daily. 2009. "China's Military Opens First Peacekeeping Training Center Near Beijing," *People's Daily*. http://english.peopledaily.com.cn/90001/90776/90785/6686691.html. Accessed 26 June.

Perlez, J., and C. Buckley. 2015. "China Retools Its Military with a First Overseas Outpost in Djibouti," *New York Times*, 26 November.

Qian, L. 2009. "Review of China's Military Diplomacy in the Past 60 Years," *Qiu Shi Theory*, No.18.

Qian, L. 2012. "Proactively Forging Ahead and Innovating Military Diplomacy," *Qiu Shi Theory* 15.

Qian, Q. ed. 2005. *Dictionary on World's Diplomacy*. Beijing: World Affairs Press.

Ramo, J. C. 2007. "Brand China," *Working Paper*, No. 827, The Foreign Policy Centre, February.

Regler, S. 2013. "The Nexus of Oil Exploration and Civil War: Challenges to the Sino-Africa Cooperation," in B. Gransow ed., *China's South-South Relations*. Berlin: Lit Verlay, pp. 20–36.

Reuters. 2012. "Glitzy New AU Headquarters a Symbol of China-Africa Ties" http://www.reuters.com/article/ozatp-africa-china-idAFJOE80S00K20120129. Accessed 29 January.

Reuters. 2013. "South Sudan Delays Shutdown of Oil Pipelines to Ethiopia," 26 July.

Robinson, S. 2006. "Time is Running Out," *Time*, 10 September. http://www.time.com/time/magazine/article/0,9171,901060918-1533376,00.html. Accessed 21 May 2012.

Rosen, A. 2015. "This Map Shows What Africa's Deadliest Terror Group May be Planning Next," *Business Insider*, 18 February 2015. http://www.businessinsider.com/boko-haram-in-2015-2015-2.

Saferworld. 2011. *China's Growing Role in African Peace and Security*, Saferworld Report, January.

Saferworld. 2012a. *China's Growing Role in African Peace and Security*, Saferworld Report, London, November.

Saferworld. 2012b. *Tackling Insecurity in the Horn of Africa: China's Role*, Saferworld Seminar Report, London, January.

Sanzhuan, G. 2014. "'The Peacekeeping Decision-Making Process and the Modality of Financing in China," in A. De Guttry, E. Sommario, and Z. Lijiang eds., *China's and Italy's Participation in Peacekeeping Operations Existing Models Emerging Challenges*. New York: Lexington Books, pp. 93–116.

Schraeder, P. 1996. *United States Foreign Policy Towards Africa: Incrementalism, Crisis and Change*. Cambridge: Cambridge University Press.

Sesay, A., O. Faseun, and S. Ojo. Eds. 1984. *OAU After Twenty Years*. Boulder, CO: Westview Press.

Shaw, S. 2013. "Fallout in the Sahel: The Geographic Spread of Conflict from Libya to Mali," *Canadian Foreign Policy Journal* 19, no. 2: 199–210.

Shi, Y. 2011. *How the Middle East Uprisings Effect China's Foreign Relations*. Clingendael Asia Forum, The Hague, Netherlands: Clingendael Asia Studies.

Shinn, D 2008. "Military and Security Relations: China, Africa, and the Rest of the World," in Robert I. Rotberg ed., *China into Africa: Trade, Aid and Influence*. Washington, DC: Brookings Institute Press, p. 163.

Shurkin, M. 2014. *France's War in Mali Lessons for an Expeditionary Army.* RAND.

Snow, P. 1988. *The Star Raft China's Encounter with Africa*. London: Weidenfeld and Nicolson.

Soares, B.F. 2005. "Islam in Mali in the Neoliberal Era," *African Affairs* 105, no. 418: 77–95.

Somaliland Press. 2011. "Somaliland, Ethiopia and China to Sign Trilateral Deals," August 14.

Stähle, S. 2008. "China's Shifting Attitude Towards United Nations Peacekeeping Operations", *The China Quarterly*, 195.

Standard Bank. 2011. "China and the US in Africa: Measuring Washington's Response to Beijing's Commercial Advance," *Standard Bank Economic Strategy Paper*, Standard Bank, "Oil Price to Remain at Two-and-a-half-year Peak," Standard Bank Press Release, February 21.

State Council. 2008. *China's National Defense in 2008*, Information Office of the State Council, the People's Republic of China, January 2009. http://english.gov.cn/official/2009-01/20/content_1210227.htm.

State Council. 2011a. *China's National Defense in 2010*, Information Office of the State Council, The People's Republic of China, March 2011. http://english.gov.cn/official/2011-03/31/content_1835499_11.htm.

State Council. 2011b. *China's Peaceful Development*, Information Office of the State Council, the People's Republic of China, September 2011. http://english.gov.cn/official/2011-09/06/content_1941354.htm.

State Council. 2013a. *China-Africa Economic and Trade Cooperation (2013)*, Information Office of the State Council of The People's Republic of China

State Council. 2013b. *The Diversified Employment of China's Armed Forces*, Information Office of the State Council, the People's Republic of China, April 2013. http://eng.mod.gov.cn/Database/WhitePapers/.

Steffen, D. 2015. "Quantifying Piracy Trends in the Gulf of Guinea – Who's Right and Who's Wrong?" *USNI News*, 19 June. http://news.usni.org/2015/06/19/essay-quantifying-piracy-trends-in-the-gulf-of-guinea-whos-right-and-whos-wrong.

Straus, S. 2012. "Wars Do End! Changing Patterns of Political Violence in Sub-Saharan Africa," *African Affairs* 111, no. 443.

Sudan Tribune. 2010. "China Favors Sudan's Unity But Will Respect Referendum Outcome: Envoy", 6 July. http://www.sudantribune.com/China-favors-Sudan-s-unity-but,35591. Accessed 4 March 2013.

Tang, S. 2008. "From Offensive to Defensive Realism: A Social Evolutionary Interpretation of China's Security Strategy," in R. S. Ross and F. Zhu eds., *China's Ascent: Power, Security, and the Future of International Politics*. New York: Cornell University Press, pp. 141–162.

Taylor, F.M. 2011. "'Economic Growth,' Regime Insecurity, and Military Strategy: Explaining the Rise of Noncombat Operations in China," *Asian Security* 7, no. 3: 177–200.

Teitt, S. 2008. "The Responsibility to Protect and China's Peacekeeping Policy," *International Peacekeeping* 18, no. 3: 298–312.

Tekle, A. 1989. "The Determinants of the Foreign Policy of Revolutionary Ethiopia," *Journal of Modern African Studies* 27, no. 3: 479–502.

Tesfaye, A. 2012. "Environmental Security, Regime Building and International Law in the Nile Basin," *Canadian Journal of African Studies* 46, no. 2.

The Guardian. 2010. "China Plays a Strong Hand on Sudan," 17 December. http://www.theguardian.com/world/us-embassy-cables-documents/168423. Accessed 2 March 2014.

United Nations. 2005. *In Larger Freedom: Towards Development, Security and Human Rights for All*, Report of the Secretary-General, United Nations, 21 March 2005. http://www.un.org/largerfreedom/contents.htm. Accessed 20 June.

United Nations. 2010. MONUSCO: United Nations Organization Stabilization Mission in the Democratic Republic of the Congo. http://www.un.org/en/peacekeeping/missions/monusco/background.shtml. Accessed 17 July 2015.

United Nations. 2013a. MINUSMA Mandate. http://www.un.org/en/peacekeeping/missions/minusma/mandate.shtml. Accessed 17 July 2015.

United Nations. 2013b. "UN Security Council Resolution 2100," S/RES/2100, 25 April. http://www.un.org/en/peacekeeping/missions/minusma/documents/mali%20_2100_E_.pdf. Accessed 17 July 2015.

United Nations. 2013c. Background Note United Nations Peacekeeping. http://www.un.org/en/peacekeeping/documents/backgroundnote.pdf.   Accessed 17 July 2015.

United Nations. 2013d. Financing Peacekeeping. http://www.un.org/en/peace keeping/operations/financing.shtml. Accessed 17 July 2015.

United Nations. 2013e. Monthly Summary of Contributions. http://www.un.org/en/peacekeeping/contributors/2013/jan13_1.pdf. Accessed 17 July 2015.

United Nations. 2014. Monthly Summary of Contributions (Police, UN Military Experts on Mission and Troops) as of 31 March 2014" http://www.un.org/en/peacekeeping/contributors/2014/mar14_1.pdf. Accessed 17 July 2015.)

United Nations. 2015a. MINUSMA United Nations Multidimensional Integrated Stabilization Mission in Mali MINUSMA Facts and Figures http://www.un.org/en/peacekeeping/missions/minusma/facts.shtml. Accessed 1 January 2016.

United Nations. 2015b. *Transforming Our World: The 2030 Agenda for Sustainable Development*, UN Document, A/RES/70/1, 21 October.

United Nations. 2016. United Nations Peacekeeping: Contributions by Country. http://www.un.org/en/peacekeeping/resources/statistics/contributors.shtml.

United Nations FAO. 2016. *2015–2016 El Niño Early Action and Response for Agriculture, Food Security and Nutrition*, Report, Update 9 July. http://www.fao.org/3/a-i5855e.pdf.

United Nations General Assembly. 2012. Sixty-Seventh Session Agenda Item 145 (Scale of Assessments for the Apportionment of the Expenses of the United Nations Peacekeeping Operations /Implementation of General Assembly Resolutions 55/235 and 55/236): Report of the Secretary-General," A/67/224/Add.1, 12 December. http://www.un.org/en/ga/search/view_doc.asp?symbol=A/67/224/Add.1. Accessed 17 July 2015.

United Nations General Assembly. 2013. 'Declaration Reaffirms Importance of UN-African Union Partnership, Capping Two-day Event amid Calls for Africans to Take Charge of Peace Efforts," 67 General Assembly, Plenary and Thematic Debate, 74th Meeting, GA/11366, 26 April.

United Nations Security Council. 2006. "Report of the Security Council Mission to the Sudan and Chad, 4–10 June 2006," UN Doc No. S/2006/433, 22 June.

United Nations Security Council. 2008. Security Council Fails to Adopt Sanctions Against Zimbabwe Leadership as Two Permanent Members Cast Negative Votes, 11 July 2008. http://www.un.org/press/en/2008/sc9396.doc.htm. Accessed 17 July 2015.

United Nations Security Council. 2011. "Security Council 6491st Meeting," UN Doc No, S/Res/1970, 26 February.

United Nations Security Council. 2000. Report of the Panel on United Nations Peace Operations, 21 August 2000. http://www.un.org/en/ga/search/view_doc.asp?symbol=A/55/305.

United Nations Security Council. 2012a. "Security Council Calls For Immediate Halt To Fighting Between Sudan, South Sudan," UN Doc No. SC/10632, 2 May.

United Nations Security Council. 2012b. Report of the Secretary-General on the Situation in Mali, S/2012/894, 28 November. http://www.un.org/en/ga/search/view_doc.asp?symbol=S/2012/894. Accessed 17 July 2015.

USAID. 2015. "Agriculture and Food Security" https://www.usaid.gov/et. Accessed 1 December 2015.

Van Hoeymissen, S. 2010 "China's Support to Africa's Regional Security Architecture: Helping Africa to Settle Conflicts and Keep the Peace?," In New Avenues for Sino-African Partnership & Co-operation – China & African Regional Organisations, *The China Monitor*, issue 49:10–14.

Van Hoeymissen, S. 2011a. "China, Sovereignty and the Protection of Civilians in Armed Conflict in Africa: The Emergence of a 'Third Paradigm' of International Intervention?," in Jing Men and Benjamin Barton eds., *China and the European Union in Africa: Partner or Competitor?*. Burlington: Ashgate.

Van Hoeymissen, S. 2011b. "Regional Organizations in China's Security Strategy for Africa: The Sense of Supporting 'African Solutions to African Problems'," *Journal of Current Chinese Affairs*, no. 4: 91–118.

Voice of America. 2014b. "Ethiopia Draws Asian Manufacturing Interests," *Voice of America*, 4 August 2014. http://www.voanews.com/content/ethiopia-drawing-asia-manufacturing-interest/1970953.html.

Walker, T. 2016. "Beyond Piracy: What Next for African Maritime Security?" ISS, 8 February. https://www.issafrica.org/iss-today/beyond-piracy-what-next-for-african-maritime-security.

Walther, O., and D. Christopoulos. 2014. "Islamic Terrorism and the Malian Rebellion," *Terrorism and Political Violence* 0: 1–23.

Wang, G. 2006. *Explanatory Statement on the Vote of the Security Council on Darfur*. New York, 31 August.

Wang, H. 2013. "Finding the Way for Cooperation Between China and America in Africa," *China International Studies*, 2.

Wang, J. 2005. "China's Search for Stability with America," *Foreign Affairs* 84: 5.

Wang, M. 2012a. "Sudan Minzu Guojia Jianshe Shibai de Fenxi [Analysis of the Failure of Sudan's Nation-State Building]," Xiya Feizhou (West Asia and Africa) 1, no. 22: 67–82.

Wang, P. 2014. "China and the Third Pillar," in D. Fiott and J. Koops eds., *The Responsibility to Protect and the Third Pillar Legitimacy and Operationalization*. Basingstoke: Palgrave Macmillan.

Wang, Q. 2013. "China's Military Diplomacy in the Last Decade – Retrospect and Prospect," *Global Review*, 2.

Wang, S. 2008. "Non-Interference and China's African policy: the case of Sudan", report on Symposium on Chinese–Sudanese Relations, London: Centre for Foreign Policy Analysis: 16–17.

Wang, X. 2012b. "Review on China's Engagement in African Peace and Security," China International Studies, No. 32, January/February.

Wang, X. 2014. "Developmental Peace: Understanding China's Africa Policy in Peace and Security," *Global Review*, Spring 2014.

Wang, Y. 2011. *Creative Involvement: A New Direction in China's Diplomacy.* Beijing: Beijing University Press.

Warms, R. L. 1992. "Merchants, Muslims, and Wahhābiyya: The Elaboration of Islamic Identity in Sikasso, Mali," *Canadian Journal of African Studies* 26, no. 3: 495.

Weijian, Li et al., 2010. "Towards a New Decade: A Study on the Sustainability of FOCAC," *West Asia and Africa*, No. 209 September.

Whittle, D. 2015. "Peacekeeping in Conflict: The Intervention Brigade, Monusco, and the Application of International Humanitarian Law to the United Nations Forces," *Georgetown Journal of International Law* 46, no. 4.

Williams, P. 2009. "Africa's Challenges, America's Choice," in Robert R. Tomes, Angela Sapp Mancini, and James T. Kirkhope eds., *Crossroads Africa: Perspectives on U.S.-China-Africa Security Affairs.* Washington, DC: Council for Emerging National Security Affairs.

Williams, P. 2011. *War and Conflict in Africa.* Cambridge: Polity Press.

Wing, S. 2013. "Briefing – Mali: Politics of a Crisis," *African Affairs* 112, no. 248: 476–485.

Workshop on Agenda 2063. 2015. "Background Note," Workshop on Agenda 2063 First 10-Year Implementation Plan, Lusaka, Zambia 2–6 March http://agenda2063.au.int/en/events/workshop-agenda-2063-first-10-year-imple mentation-plan-lusaka-zambia, Annex 3 "Agenda 2063Financing, Domestic Resource Mobilization and Partnerships.

Xi, J. 2013. "Xi Jinping Delivers a Speech at the Julius Nyerere International Convention Center in Tanzania, Stressing China and Africa Will Always Remain Reliable Friends and Faithful Partners," Chinese MOFA, 25 March 2013. http://www.fmprc.gov.cn/eng/topics/xjpcf1/t1025803.shtml.

Xi, J. 2015a. "Working Together to Write a New Chapter In China-Africa Cooperation," Address by Xi Jinping at the Opening Ceremony of the Johannesburg Summit of the Forum on China-Africa Cooperation, 4 December. http://www.fmprc.gov.cn/mfa_eng/wjdt_665385/zyjh_665391/t1321614.shtml.

Xi, J. 2015b. "China is Here for Peace," Remarks by H.E. Xi Jinping President of the People's Republic of China at the United Nations Peacekeeping Summit, 28 September http://www.fmprc.gov.cn/mfa_eng/wjdt_665385/zyjh_665391/t1302562.shtml.

Xi, J. 2015c. "Open a New Era of China-Africa Win-Win Cooperation and Common Development," Address by Xi Jinping at the opening ceremony of the Johannesburg Summit of The Forum on China-Africa Cooperation, 4 December 2015.

Xia, L. 2001. "China: A Responsible Great Power," *Journal of Contemporary China* 10, no. 26: 17–26.

Xiao, T. ed. *Military Diplomacy of PRC*. Beijing: National Defence University Press.

Xiaoguang, Kang. 2002. "Administrative Arrangement Instead of Political Reform Review: On Political Development and Political Stability in Mainland China in 1990s," *Twenty-First Century*, No. 5, August.

Xie, Y. ed. 2009. *Contemporary History of China's Diplomacy, 1949–2009*. Beijing: Chinese Youth Press.

Xinhua. 2009. "Backgrounder: China-Mali Ties in Continuous Development" http://news.xinhuanet.com/english/2009-02/11/content_10802821.htm. Accessed 17 July 2015.

Xinhua. 2012. *Beijing Declaration of the First Forum on China-Africa Local Government Cooperation*, Beijing, 28 August 2012; "Li Keqiang Speech at the Opening Ceremony of the First China-Africa Local Government Forum," http://www.newshome.us/news-2060728-Li-Keqiang-speech-at-the-opening-ceremony-of-the-first-China-Africa-Local-Government-Forum.html. Accessed 27 August 2012.

Xinhua. 2013a. "Sudan Recieves Humanitarian Assistance to Darfur," 5 March. http://english.peopledaily.com.cn/90883/8153201.html. Accessed 12 June 2013.

Xinhua. 2013b. "Turbulent Africa and Virginian for Chinese Migrants," 15 November 2013. http://news.xinhuanet.com/edu/2013-11/15/c_125705827.htm.

Xinhua. 2015a. *China's Second Africa Policy Paper*, 5 December 2015. http://africa.chinadaily.com.cn/2015-12/05/content_22632880.htm. Accessed 6 December.

Xinhua. 2015b. "Interview: Ethiopia Keen to Bolster Cooperation with China in Manufacturing Sector, Ethiopian President Mulatu Teshome," 5 June 2015.

Xiong, W, and J. Zhou. eds. 2000. *Military Encyclopedia*. Beijing: Great Wall Publishing House.

Xu, W. 2010. "Chinese Participation in African Security Cooperation and Its Tendency," *West Asia and Africa*, No. 11.

Xue, L. 2014. *China as a Permanent Member of the United Nations Security Council*: Friedrich-Ebert-Stiftung.

Xun, J. 2013. CEO of the Shandong Huawei Security Group Co., Ltd, China, presentation at the Conference "Managing Security and Risk in China-Africa Relations" on April 25–26, Center for Chinese Studies, Stellenbosch University, South Africa.

Yan, X. 2012. "The Weakening of the Unipolar Configuration," in M Leonard eds, *China 3.0*. London: European Council on Foreign Relations, pp. 112–118.

Yang, M. 2011. "Beihou de Sudan Nanbu Gongtou he Qishi Zhongguo Shiyou Touzi zai Sudan de Shiyou Yinsu [Oil Factors behind Southern Sudan Referendum and Implications to Chinese Oil Investment in Sudan]," *Zhongguo Quanqiu Nengyuan (Sino-Global Energy)*. 16.

Yang, X. 2006. "National Independence and China's Development Path," *Social Science*, No. 3.

Yang, Z. 2012. "Zhongguo yu Nan Sudan Shiyou Hezuo de Jiyu yu Taiozhan [Opportunities and Challenges in Petroleum Cooperation between China and South Sudan]," *Xiya Feizhou (West Asia and Africa)* 3: 90–106.

Yin, H. 2007. *China's Changing Policy on UN Peacekeeping Operations*. Stockholm: Institute for Security and Development Policy.

Yin, H. 2014. "China-EU Cooperation on UN peacekeeping Opportunities and Challenges: A Chinese View," in F. Austermann, A. Vangeli, and W. Xiaoguang eds., *China and Europe in 21st Century Global Politics: Partnership, Competition or Co-Evolution*: Newcastle upon Tyne: Cambridge Scholars Publishing.

Young, J. 1999. "Ethiopia's Western Frontier: Gambella and Benishangul in Transition," *Journal of Modern African Studies* 37, no. 2: 321–346.

Yun, S. 2013. How China Views France's Intervention in Mali: An Analysis Brooking Institution. http://www.brookings.edu/research/opinions/2013/01/23-china-france-intervention-mali-sun. Accessed 17 July 2015.

Zeng, X. 2011. "Sudan Nanbei Fenli Kaoyan Zhongguo Qiye Yingdui Tiaozhan de Nengli [Sudan's North-South Demarcation's Test of the Ability of Chinese Enterprises to Cope with Challenges]," *Guoji Shiyou Jingji (International Petroleum Economics)*, No. 3.

Zha, P. 2005. "China's Changing Attitude to UN Peacekeeping," *International Peacekeeping* 12, no. 1: 87–104.

Zhang, C. 2009. "'Development-Security Nexus': The African Policies of China, EU and USA," *Chinese Journal of European Studies*, no. 3.

Zhang, C. 2010. "Projecting Soft Power through Medical Diplomacy: A Case Study of Chinese Medical Team to Africa," *Contemporary International Relations* (Chinese), No. 3

Zhang, C. 2013a. "China's Engagement in African Post-Conflict Reconstruction: Achievements and Future Developments," in James Shikwati ed., *China-Africa Partnership: The Quest for a Win-Win Relationship.* Nairobi: IREN Kenya.

Zhang, C. 2013b. "Managing China-U.S. Power Transition in a Power Diffusion Era," Conference Proceedings, The International Symposium on The Change of International System and China, 27–28 September, Fudan University, Shanghai.

Zhang, C 2013c. *On International Contribution of China-Africa Relationship (ZhongFeiGuanxiGongxianLun).* Shanghai: Shanghai People's Publishing House.

Zhang, C. 2013d. "The Sino-Africa Relationship: Toward a New Strategic Partnership." Emerging Powers in Africa http://www.lse.ac.uk/IDEAS/pub lications/reports/pdf/SR016/SR-016-Chun.pdf.

Zhang, C. 2014. "Proliferation of Non-Structural Violence and Normalization of African Turbulence (Feijiegou Xing BaoliZhengshengyuFeizhouDongdang de Changtaihua)," *Contemporary World (DangdaiShijie)* 9.

Zhang, W, and Z. Gu. 2013. "China's Law Diplomacy: Theory and Practice," *Global Review*, Summer, pp. 48–50.

Zhao, S. 2014. "A Neo-Colonialist Predator or Development Partner? China's Engagement and Rebalance in Africa," *Journal of Contemporary China* 23, no. 90: 1033–1052.

Zheng, Y. 2006. "De Facto Federalism and Dynamics of Central-Local Relations in China," *Discussion Paper*, No. 8, China Policy Institute, Nottingham University, June.

Zheng, Y. 2007. *De Facto Federalism in China: Reforms and Dynamics of Central-Local Relations.* London: World Scientific.

Zhou, B. 2015 "Birth of Truly Global Chinese Navy," *China Daily*, updated 10 April. http://www.chinadaily.com.cn/opinion/2015-04/10/content_20400202.htm.

Zhu, M. ed. 1999. *An Introduction of Military Thoughts.* Beijing: National Defence University Press.

Zhu, X. 2012. "Sudan Zhanhou Heping Jianshe Jincheng Zhengzi Jihui Lilun de Fenxi [The Analysis of Political Opportunity Theory on the Peace-Building Process of Post-Conflict Sudan]," *Alabo Shijie Yanjiu (Arab World Studies)*, No. 6: pp. 76–88.

Zonglin, Z. 2014. "What Reasons Lie Behind the Decision to Work in a PKO? The Psychosocial Motivations of Chinese Troops and Police Forces," in A. De Guttry, E. Sommario, and L. Zhu eds., *China's and Italy's Participation in Peacekeeping Operations existing Models Emerging Challenges.* New York: Lexington.

中华人民共和国商务部 [Mofcom]. 2002. 马里中国投资开发贸易促进中心 [Mali and China Investment Development and Trade Promotion Center] http://www.mofcom.gov.cn/article/Nocategory/200502/20050200019385.shtml. Accessed 17 July 2015).

中华人民共和国外交部 版权所有 [MFA]. 2015. 马里国家概况 [Mali Country Profiles] http://www.fmprc.gov.cn/mfa_chn/gjhdq_603914/gj_603916/fz_605026/1206_605850/. Accessed 17 July 2015.

张雷 & 马骏 [Zhang, L. and M. Jun]. 2014. 中国为非洲和平安全事务作了哪些贡献? [What where the contribution made by Chinese Security Forces for Africa Peace?] http://top.cntv.cn/2014/05/08/ARTI1399555898101829.shtml. Accessed 17 July 2015.

胡光曲 [Hu, S.].2014. 中国赴马里维和部队开始首次轮换 [Chinese troops began first rotation in Mali] http://www.huaxia.com/thjq/jsxw/dl/2014/09/4074761.html. Accessed 17 July 2015.

INDEX

Printed by Printforce, the Netherlands